OUR SYLVAN HERITAGE

A Guide to the Magnificent Trees
of the South Fraser

To MARG.

BEST WISHES FROM
THE AUTHOR. ENJOY

Susan H. Murray

2004

Fitzhenry & Whiteside

Fitzhenry & Whiteside Limited
195 Allstate Parkway
Markham, Ontario   L3R 4T8

In the United States:
121 Harvard Avenue, Suite 2
Allston, Massachusetts 02134

www.fitzhenry.ca   godwit@fitzhenry.ca

Fitzhenry & Whiteside acknowledges with thanks the Canada Council for the Arts, the Government of Canada through its Book Publishing Industry Development Program, and the Ontario Arts Council for their support of our publishing program.

National Library of Canada Cataloguing in Publication

Murray, Susan Marie, 1953-
         Our sylvan heritage : a guide to the magnificent trees of the South
Fraser / Susan M. Murray.

Includes index.
ISBN 1-55041-781-9

         1. Historic trees—British Columbia—Fraser River Region—Guidebooks.
2. Historic trees--British Columbia—Lower Mainland—Guidebooks.
3. Trees—British Columbia—Fraser River Region—Guidebooks.
4. Trees—British Columbia—Lower Mainland—Guidebooks.   5. Fraser River
Region (B.C.)—Guidebooks. 6. Lower Mainland (B.C.)—Guidebooks. I. Title.

QK203.B7M88 2003   582.16'09711'37   C2003-900587-9

U.S. Publisher Cataloging-in-Publication Data
(Library of Congress Standards)

Murray, Susan M.
    Our sylvan heritage : a guide to the magnificent trees of the South Fraser / Susan M.
Murray.-- 1st ed.
[304] p. : col. ill. , maps ; cm.
Includes index.
Summary: An illustrative guide to the 350 trees of the South Fraser region of British
Columbia, with concise descriptions, native origins, and leaf and flower characteristics.
ISBN 1-55041-781-9 (pbk.)
1. Trees – British Columbia – Identification.   I. Title.
582.16/ 09711 21   QK203.B7.M981 2003

Cover and text design: Darrell McCalla
Printed and bound in Hong Kong

Contents

Acknowledgements

I am indebted to many people who helped locate and evaluate specific trees. The citizens of both Langley and Surrey nominated many of the trees found in this book in their communities, as part of a "Great Tree Hunt" held in recent years. Others include the volunteers past and present of the Fraser Valley Heritage Tree Society, in particular Heather Miller, who accompanied me on tree hunting trips throughout the South Fraser Region.

Thanks to the city and township staffs of the South Fraser Region who devoted time and energy to locate trees for this book:

Tom Farr and Todd Gross, City of Abbotsford Parks and Recreation Department.

Glen Thelin, City of Chilliwack Parks Department.

Nancy McLean, Community Planning and Development, and Frank Van Manen, The Corporation of Delta, Parks and Recreation Department.

Len Walters, Parks and Recreation, Langley City.

Jenny Beran, Planning and Alex Thorburn, Recreation and Cultural Services (Parks) City of Richmond.

Steve Clayton, Owen Croy, Glenn McDonald, Billie-Jo Thiessen and Greg Ward, City of Surrey Parks, Recreation and Culture.

Thanks to the following individuals, Klari and Greg Aitken, Marlene Best, PJ Burns, Alfriede and Jim DeWolf of the "The Glades", Barbara Edwards, Simon Gibson, Ralf Kelman, Michelle Nakano, Norma Senn, Denise Tomyn, and Joe Wiggins who suggested tree locations and individual trees, and to Rob Silins for his technical support.

For the historical notes the following individuals contributed valuable information. Thanks to:

Ron Denman, Chilliwack Museum and Archives.

Kris Foulds, MSA Museum Society, Abbotsford.

Sue Morhun, Community and Heritage Services, the Township of Langley.

Fred and Maureen Pepin, Langley Heritage Society.

Gwen Szychter, Historian, Delta.

Kwantlen University College generously provided a term of educational leave to enable me to begin work on the manuscript.

I am indebted to G.H. Chaster, D.W. Ross and W.H. Warren, authors of *Trees of Greater Victoria*, 1988; Arthur Lee Jacobson, for *Trees of Seattle*, 1989 and Gerald B. Straley, author of *Trees of Vancouver*, 1992 for finding the trees in their communities first.

For assistance in proofreading the initial pages I thank my husband Gerry Lamb and also Jenne Breedon.

A fellow plant lover, Douglas Justice, Associate Director and Curator of Collections at the University of British Columbia Garden and Centre for Plant Research kindly checked for errors in nomenclature. Thanks, Douglas.

A special thank you to Francisca Darts who has inspired me with her lifelong quest to grow and learn about plants. Many of the photographs for this book were taken in the garden she and her husband Edwin created, Darts Hill Garden Park in South Surrey.

To the following groups, organizations and individuals who purchased copies of the book prior to its publication, thank you. This book would not have been published without your financial support.

Beaver Canoe Club.

Central Valley Naturalists.

Chilliwack Horticultural Society.

City of Abbotsford, Parks and Recreation Department.

City of Surrey Parks, Recreation and Culture.

E. H. (Ted) Horsey.

Evergreen Garden Club

Fraser South Rhododendron Society.

Fraser Valley Heritage Tree Society.

Heather Ann Miller.

Kwantlen University College, School of Horticulture.

Kwantlen University College, students, faculty and staff.

Langley Garden Club.

Langley Heritage Society.

Janis Matson.

Murray Nurseries Ltd.

Richmond Garden Club.

Pacific Northwest Chapter International Society of Arboriculture.

Point Grey Senior Secondary Class of 1971.

South Surrey Garden Club.

Finally I am deeply thankful to my friends and family who provided support and encouragement along the way.

Introduction

I magine a Douglas Fir tree so big that it takes four people with arms outstretched to reach around its trunk. When this tree was a teenager, James Kennedy, one of Surrey, British Columbia's first European settlers, had not yet preempted his plot of land on the south bank of the Fraser River. Trees are part of our living heritage; for example, they may have been planted by a community pioneer or in honour of a particular event. *Our Sylvan Heritage* celebrates these magnificent Heritage Trees and locates younger specimens of many other species of trees throughout the South Fraser Region of British Columbia.

As the Fraser Valley became more urban, trees that once provided shade, food, wildlife habitat, or were historic landmark trees, were removed to make way for new subdivisions. As the character of the land changed, the issue of quality of life became important to many residents. Today small pockets of old growth timber, second growth trees and imported or exotic deciduous and coniferous trees contribute to the arboreal richness of the region. Trees are an essential part of the fabric of our communities and to many people integral to their quality of life.

This book includes the majority of native and exotic trees found in the South Fraser Region, including a few very rare trees found only in gardens such as Darts Hill Garden Park in Surrey or Minter Gardens in Rosedale. There are concise descriptions of over three hundred and fifty different kinds of trees, including their native origins and the leaf and flower characteristics of many species. Key ways to identify each type of tree are an important part of the species descriptions. Tree entries are listed alphabetically first by scientific name in the A–Z Tree Listing section of the book. Scientific names and spelling are largely based on the taxonomic work presented by Arthur Lee Jacobson in *North American Landscape Trees* 1996. Douglas Justice, associate director of the University of British Columbia Botanical Garden and Centre for Horticulture provided an update on scientific nomenclature just prior to press time. One or more common names are given with each description and cross-referenced in the index. The common name listed first is the name used in the South Fraser Region, while other common names listed may be found in various sources such as nursery catalogues or other reference materials. Major synonyms of the preferred scientific name are listed beneath the most current name when appropriate. The abbreviation Syn. appears before these older names.

A concise description of the leaves, buds, flowers, fruit, bark, or branching pattern of the trees is given when they are of ornamental significance or used to identify the tree in one or more seasons. Some flowers or fruits are not ornamental or are insignificant in size and are not described because the focus of this book is on readily available characteristics, which may be used to identify the trees in the field. The mature height or spread when given in the description of the tree is the size that the tree may reasonably expect to grow in the South Fraser Region. When this height is not reliably known, then the mature height the tree grows in its native range is given.

The geographical scope of the book embraces nine communities; the cities of Abbotsford, Chilliwack, Langley, Richmond, Surrey, and White Rock, also the Township of Langley, the Corporation of Delta and the village of Rosedale. These communities lie south of the Fraser River in the Fraser Valley and west of Hope, British Columbia. 700 locations are listed where individual or groups of trees can easily be viewed. Visitors to the South Fraser Region, as well as residents who wish to know more about the trees in their area, will find the book very useful in locating good places to view outstanding trees, large and small, in each community.

Whenever possible, those trees chosen for inclusion (all else being equal), are mature rather than young, large rather than small, and in good condition with growth typical of the species. Open grown trees on public rather than private lands have been favoured for inclusion in the book. In a number of cases young trees along streets and in parks have been listed when mature specimens are not readily found in the South Fraser Region. This is particularly true when the tree is a newer cultivar of a more familiar species. Sometimes a less than perfect example or younger tree may be listed because it is found on a site where there are a number of other trees that can be viewed. Trees surveyed on private property can easily be seen from the sidewalk or street. The Garry Oaks on Sumas Mountain and the giant Douglas Fir and Western Red Cedar trees located in the Elk Creek Rainforest in Chilliwack are two exceptions. These groups of trees are included because of their uniqueness in the South Fraser Region.

The Diameter at Breast Height (DBH) in centimetres is sometimes listed for a specific tree when the tree is of remarkable size for its species. This measurement was taken at the standard height of 1.4 metres from ground level. Occasionally the estimated height in metres or the circumference in metres of a specific tree is also given.

One important way that this guide differs from others is the inclusion of over one hundred historical footnotes or thumbnail sketches of the pioneers and early settlers of the South Fraser Region. These footnotes may describe who planted the trees, or when or why they were planted. Sometimes a discussion of the architectural style of the home or date that the home was built is given as well since this often provides a rough planting date and historical context for the trees on the property. A number of the trees in the book have been designated heritage in their respective communities. This is noted after the tree's address in the book with an asterisk (*).

Tools used to survey the trees for the book.

Douglas and Carl Lamb measuring a *Picea sitchensis*, Sitka Spruce in Tynehead Regional Park in Surrey

Trees were surveyed for this book through 1996–2002. The trees in Surrey were among the first to be inventoried. In 1996, to increase public awareness of the value of trees in their community, the staff and management of the Parks and Recreation Commission of the City of Surrey, in partnership with the Surrey Heritage Advisory Commission to city council, BC Hydro and Power Authority, and the Fraser Valley Heritage Tree Society, initiated a "Great Tree Hunt." Later the British Columbia Heritage Trust became one of the sponsors of the project. An evaluation format was developed, and then the Parks and Recreation Commission of the city of Surrey produced a "Great Tree Hunt" Brochure. Sixty thousand copies were printed and thousands distributed to public schools and recreation facilities. Members of the public submitted nominations of the outstanding trees in their neighbourhood. Many of the trees nominated were submitted by families, who expressed a deep personal attachment and concern for "their" trees, and included letters and pictures to emphasize the importance of protection for these trees. The Parks and Recreation Commission organized evaluation days that took members of the Fraser Valley Heritage Tree Society out into the community to evaluate the trees nominated by the public. Each tree, of the hundreds of trees nominated, was evaluated and entered into a computer database.

An integral part of the evaluation process was the establishment of a tree subcommittee of the Heritage Advisory Commission to the City council of Surrey. This group met with staff from the Parks and Recreation Commission, and the Fraser Valley Heritage Tree Society to review the recommended trees. The Heritage Advisory Commission designated as Heritage Trees, or as a Heritage Tree group, one hundred and eight trees. These recommendations were carried forward by this group to the city of Surrey's Council, which approved the placement of the trees in Schedule B of the city's Tree Preservation By-law as Significant Trees. This is a huge step forward in tree preservation because it offers bylaw protection to each Heritage Tree or Heritage Tree Group. Trees listed as Significant Trees in Schedule B have been marked with an asterisk (*) in the A–Z Tree Listings.

Many of the Heritage Trees in the City of Surrey have been commemorated by the placement of a rock at their base with a bronze plate. The first plaquing ceremony of a Heritage Tree was held at Sullivan Park in Surrey on April 19, 1997 with His Honour the Mayor Doug McCallum presiding. He unveiled a plaque celebrating a magnificent Butternut, *Juglans cinerea*. This was a significant milestone in the city of Surrey's care for its urban forest and natural heritage. On May 15, 1997 a huge and very rare hybrid walnut, *Juglans cinerea* x *Juglans sieboldiana* var. *cordiformis* was plaqued in Dartshill Garden Park in South Surrey, BC. The work begun in this bold project continues in the city of Surrey and formed the basis for this book. Each year new trees are added to the list of Heritage Trees in Surrey.

The trees in the Township and the city of Langley were surveyed in 1999 to 2002. The writer inventoried the trees in the communities of Abbotsford, Chilliwack, Delta, Richmond, Rosedale and White Rock in the fall of 2001 and spring of 2002. At the present time none of these communities provide significant bylaw protection to their Heritage Trees.

The trees of the nine communities of the South Fraser Region were inventoried in a number of ways. Some were identified during windshield surveys, others in field surveys or noted from community tree planting data, Heritage Tree lists, garden or park plans and inventories.

Several of the field surveys were adventures in their own right. Finding the elusive native *Quercus garryana*, or Garry Oak population on the south slope of Sumas Mountain in Abbotsford required sleuthing skills on behalf of the author. A party of naturalists and City of Abbotsford employees and friends were dispatched, with great enthusiasm to locate this rare group of trees. First the private landowner who graciously allowed the group to tramp across his property was consulted; he recommended looking at the closest oak tree by the access road. This tree was quickly but unhappily identified as an English Oak, *Quercus robur* by the long stalks attached to the acorns. The next tree identified as a Garry Oak by the landowner proved to be a second English Oak. Where were the Garry Oaks? A single leaf was fetched from amid the blackberry tangle. It was Garry Oak, the species easily identified by the brown woolly underside of the leathery leaf, but where were the trees? Tramping a little further, and looking up high on the rocky southern slope a tiny forest of Garry Oak trees was visible, thrusting knarled and twisted limbs out from under the shade of the old growth Douglas Fir. At last the rare and elusive Garry Oak!

The author takes all responsibility for any mis-identifications in this book.

Where to Find the Trees

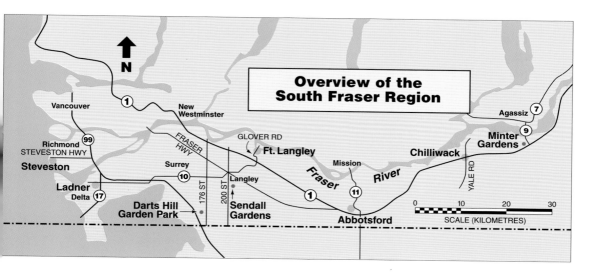

The best places to find good specimens of trees are easily accessible. School grounds, cemeteries and cenotaphs, golf courses, parks, municipal buildings such as hospitals, and municipal halls, street boulevards, medians, and the front gardens of private residences all offer opportunities for viewing trees. Here is a listing by community of some of the better places to view individual specimens, groups of trees or unusual and rare trees. A number of good quality specimens can be viewed at each location.

1. Abbotsford

Civic Centre
32315 South Fraser Way, Abbotsford

The Civic Centre, Clearbrook Public Library, Justice Centre, School District Administrative Offices and Provincial Courthouse building have been well landscaped and a number of trees are easily viewed. The white blossoms of the semi-circular planting of dozens of *Prunus* x *yedoensis* 'Akebono', Daybreak Cherry south of the City Hall are outstanding in the spring. A large *Platanus* x *hispanica*, London Plane grows as a regal lawn specimen on the south side of the Hall. A small *Tilia* x *euchlora*, Crimean Linden graces the parking lot of the Provincial Courthouse. Several groups of *Nyssa sylvatica*, Black Gum, grace the southern lawn area of Clearbrook Library, two *Parrotia persica*, Persian Ironwood, frame either side of the entrance to the Library while a row of *Zelkova serrata*, Chinese Zelkova marks the west side of the building. A perfectly formed *Rhus typhina*, Staghorn Sumac grows by itself on the west side of the Police Station.

Dunach Elementary School and Dunach Park
30357 Downes Rd, Abbotsford

Dunach Elementary School is a heritage school with an extensive history spanning one hundred years. Many of the nearby original residents came from Scotland so a Scottish name, Dunach, which means a fortified place was selected for the school. The school was built in 1898 at the present location, when the first one-room school on the south side of Downes Road burned down sometime between 1892 and 1898. Over the years the school's name changed many times as it became a Matsqui high school and back again to an elementary school. Eventually the original name was reinstated. The school grounds on the east contain a good assortment of trees with the largest Red Oak in the South Fraser Valley among them. The trees were probably planted around 1900.

The Matsqui Municipal Hall, which officially opened on July 1, 1899 with a Dominion Day Celebration, was located on what is now Dunach Park. Dunach Park, which is to the north of the elementary school, is well treed with a number of large specimens such as *Fagus sylvatica*, European Beech, large Scotch Elms, *Ulmus glabra*, Sitka Spruce, *Picea sitchensis* and Bigleaf Maples, *Acer macrophyllum*.

Hogan Family Nature Park
2860 block Debruyne Road off Bradner Road, Abbotsford

The Hogan family donated this 5.3-hectare park to the people of Abbotsford in the early 1990's. The Salmon River, which has its outlet into the Fraser River in Fort Langley, flows through the park. Salmon spawn here, as it is the headwaters of the Salmon River. This section of the river can dry up completely some years. The park features a circular nature trail. The native trees, *Thuja plicata*, Western Red Cedar, *Tsuga heterophylla*, Western Hemlock and deciduous species such as *Betula papyrifera*, Paper Birch and *Acer macrophyllum*, Bigleaf Maple are very large and imposing. One Black Cottonwood, *Populus balsamifera* ssp. *trichocarpa*, a few minutes walk from the small parking lot, is adjacent to the bridge crossing the river and has a large trunk diameter of 164 cm.

Hougen Park
South off Highway 1 on Cole Road, Abbotsford

The Sumas River bounds Hougen Park on the west. In the winter months the park can be inundated by floodwaters, which cover the access road and reach the toe of the slope.
The park was developed from trees donated by a local resident, Chris Beck. The large Paper Birch, *Betula papyrifera*, is one of the few original native trees of the twenty or so different tree species found in the park. Most of the remaining species are introduced and exotic species. The last planting in the park took place in 1972 at the south end of the park. Some of the larger trees were moved in the early 1970's from the Tourist Information booth, which was originally beside Highway 1. A dappled shade is cast on picnickers in the summer by a row of very large weeping willows, *Salix* x *sepulchralis* var. *chrysocoma*, which line the banks of the Sumas River. Four perfectly shaped *Æsculus* x *carnea* 'Briotii', Ruby Horse Chestnut bloom prolifically in late May and into June. The yellow foliage of *Thuja plicata* 'Zebrina', Variegated Western Red Cedar brightens the dreary grey days of late winter in Hougen Park.

Jubilee Park
McCallum Road south of Essendene, Abbotsford
See the map of Abbotsford city centre.

Jubilee Park was developed and named in honour of the Diamond Jubilee of the Confederation of Canada on July 1, 1927. Originally owned by the Jubilee Recreation Association, the property was purchased by the village of Abbotsford in 1934 and used as a public sports park for many years. Some of the older trees are remnants of a row of memorial trees planted along the western boundary of the park for soldiers who did not return from World War I. The original western park boundary extended into what today is the centre of McCallum Road. When the road was widened in the late 1940's and early 1950's, the trees were moved inside the new park boundary. Some trees survived the move some did not.

Jubilee Park is home to twenty different species of trees, some very rare in the South Fraser Region. Each season brings different interest to this small urban park. When in bloom in the late spring, a large *Magnolia tripetala*, Umbrella Tree, on the south side of the MSA Library, perfumes the entire park. The dark young leaves of Purple Leaf Birch, *Betula pendula* 'Nigra' unfold in the early spring near the centre of the park. Two mature *Tilia* 'Petiolaris', Pendent Silver Lime trees, adjacent to McCallum Road offer their intoxicating scented flowers in late June and into July. Two large *Fraxinus excelsior* f. *diversifolia*, Singleleaf Ash, rare in the South Fraser Region, are planted next to an ordinary European Ash just to the west of the Tennis Court. The branches of the two *Sorbus aria*, Whitebeam, growing in the centre of the park are heavily laden with bright red fruit in October.

Trethewey House Heritage Site and Mill Lake
2313 Ware Street, Abbotsford
See the map of Abbotsford city centre.

Trethewey House was designated as a heritage site in 1983 and is now managed by the MSA Museum Society. The Abbotsford Lumber Company built the bungalow in 1920 for the timber baron Joseph Ogle Trethewey. It was constructed in the Arts and Crafts architectural style. The house has been restored to resemble the 1925 era. Trethewey House is representative of two of

Abbotsford's earliest industries; logging and brick manufacturing. J.O. Trethewey and his brothers, owners of the Abbotsford Lumber Company, purchased the sawmill on the adjacent Mill Lake in 1902. Trethewey House itself was constructed of the best fir lumber milled by the company. Chimney and fireplace bricks were made from clay mined on Sumas Mountain and fired at Clayburn Village. Abbotsford Lumber Company became the largest employer in Abbotsford and the third largest forestry employer in British Columbia at that time. The Great Depression and the reduction of easily accessible timber caused the mill to close in the mid-1930's.

Pseudotsuga menziesii, Douglas Fir, Trethewey House Heritage Site, Abbotsford

The four large Douglas Firs, *Pseudotsuga menziesii,* at Trethewey House Heritage Site are typical of what you might have seen in the area at the time the mill was flourishing. The gardens adjacent to the house are landscaped sensitively, reflecting the early period, with a *Magnolia stellata,* Star Magnolia, *Pinus sylvestris,* Scots Pine, *Betula papyrifera,* Paper Birch, *Sorbus aucuparia,* European Mountain Ash, *Gleditsia triacanthos* f. *inermis,* Thornless Honey Locust, *Cornus* 'Eddie's White Wonder', Eddie's White Wonder Dogwood. The second resident family, the Des Mazes, planted the large Butternut to the south of the house.

A number of good specimens are located in John Mahoney Park adjacent to the house and part of the Mill Lake circular park. These trees include several well shaped *Acer macrophyllum,* Bigleaf Maple, *Picea orientalis,* Oriental Spruce, and English Walnut, *Juglans regia.*

2. Chilliwack

CFB (Canadian Forces Base) Chilliwack
SW corner of Vedder Road and Keith Wilson Road,
Vedder Crossing, Chilliwack

December 7, 1941 the Japanese bombed Pearl Harbor. A strong military presence was needed on the west coast of Canada to combat the threat of war in North America. On April 24, 1942, 1200 soldiers arrived via train to Chilliwack, and marched south to the newly created military post named Camp Chilliwack in Vedder Crossing on the banks of the Chilliwack River. This first group, which took a muddy hog farm and orchard and created a new training camp for the Royal Canadian Engineers was the first of thousands of soldiers posted to CFB Chilliwack, until the permanent closure of the base in 1996. CFB Chilliwack was the site of the Canadian Forces School of Military Engineering and Officer Candidate School and provided the administration for other military bases in British Columbia. Dozens of permanent buildings and other facilities were constructed at the 255-hectare base during the fifty-four year tenure of the military. Today other organizations are renovating the buildings originally established by the military. The Royal Canadian Mounted Police (RCMP) purchased fifteen hectares of the site for use as their Pacific Region Training Academy. During the opening ceremonies for the academy in November of 2001, the former base commander presented a large heavy shillelagh or walking stick to mark the passing of command from the Canadian military to the RCMP. The Chilliwack School District is making use of some of the facilities. The long-term use of the remaining CFB lands is under debate.

An extensive collection of trees was planted along the streets and around the buildings on the base. At forty to fifty years in age, many of the trees are a good size and are generally open grown, with large wide spreading crowns. A few have been topped sometime in the past, but overall the collection is in excellent condition and well worth a visit.

The street names of CFB Chilliwack commemorate the battles and campaigns of World War I, II and the Korean War. Amiens, Arnhem Road, Arras, Caen Road, Calais Crescent, Cambrai, Dieppe, Korea Road, Normandy Drive, Scheldt, Sicily, Vimy Avenue, and Ypres, are all reminders of Canadian military history. A beautiful *Tilia cordata* grows on the west side of Calais Crescent at the intersection of Calais Crescent and Arnhem Road, (both WW II). On the southwest side of Calais Crescent at Caen Road (WW II), a large *Æsculus hippocastanum*, Horse Chestnut, and two good-sized *Acer pseudoplatanus*, Sycamore Maple reside. Three magnificent *Platanus* x *hispanica*, London Plane trees, two huge *Acer saccharinum*, Silver Maple and three good-sized, European Ash, can be found on the west side of Vimy Avenue (WW I) near the parade ground. Two well-grown *Chamæcyparis lawsoniana* 'Stewartii', Golden Lawson's Cypress, grace the northwest corner of Sicily Road and Normandy Drive (both WW II). A tall *Chamæcyparis lawsoniana* 'Glauca', Blue Lawson's Cypress is located on Hong Kong Road (WW II). Colonel J.E. (Jack) Crosman, base commander from 1977 to 1980 called CFB Chilliwack "our little botanical garden" in an interview in 1991.[1]

Coqualeetza, Stó:lo Centre
7201 Vedder Road, Sardis, Chilliwack

Today, Coqualeetza is the administrative centre for the Stó:lo Nation. The site has a rich history. Luckakuck Creek and the nearby Chilliwack River were a traditional First Nations fishery. Stó:lo oral history tells of Coqualeetza as a site fundamental to the origin of the sockeye salmon.

In more recent times, a small Methodist school for First Nations children was built on the site in 1889, but subsequently burned down in 1891. By 1894 a much larger school, the second Residential Indian school in British Columbia was built there. Thomas Hooper, the same Vancouver architect who later designed Chilliwack's City Hall, planned it. This red-bricked school was demolished to make way for an even larger building. In 1935 a tuberculosis treatment centre was added to the facility. The Federal Government, in 1941, bought the Methodist school, turning it into a hospital, which was in use until 1969.

It is hard to date the trees at Coqualeetza, but there are a number of very large specimens that were likely planted in the 1930's and 1940's and perhaps earlier. An *Abies concolor* on the west side of the building is the largest Silver Fir found in the South Fraser Region. Unfortunately, the *Ulmus americana*, American Elm and the two *Ulmus glabra*, Scotch Elm, that line the driveway facing Vedder Road were topped at some distant time, but are still very large and impressive trees in full leaf. The garden area in front of the building also contains good-sized *Acer pseudoplatanus*, Sycamore Maple, *Platanus* x *hispanica*, London Plane, *Quercus robur*, English Oak and a *Picea pungens*, Colorado Blue Spruce among others.

Gwynne-Vaughan Park
Hope River Road, Fairfield Island, Chilliwack

The centrepiece of Gwynne-Vaughan Park is the garden, which surrounds the home originally built in 1896, and purchased in 1902 by David Edward Gwynne-Vaughan. Mr. Gwynn-Vaughan was described as a "gentleman farmer." His passion as gardener is evident all around the 2.8-hectare site. His daughter, Mrs. Adelaid Bateman, who lived in the house until her death, willed the property to the District of Chilliwack in 1993. Rarities abound in this turn of the 19th century heritage garden, restored through volunteer effort. A rare Fantail Willow, *Salix udensis* 'Sekka', grows happily to the north of the house, while the largest *Thujopsis dolobrata*, Hiba Arborvitae, found in the South Fraser Region grows to the west and a large *Hamamelis virginiana*, Common Witchhazel, grows on the east side of the house. The site also contains a lovely large Corkscrew Hazel, *Corylus avellana* 'Contorta' with its curly twisted limbs, a large *Acer pseudoplatanus*, Sycamore Maple, and a *Juglans regia*, English Walnut. The branches of a huge *Magnolia* x *soulangiana*, Saucer Magnolia arch over the driveway.

Yarrow Central Park
Southeast corner of Kehler Street and Yarrow Central Road, Chilliwack

This small park contains a collection of trees planted in the late 1940's. Four *Acer pseudoplatanus* f. *variegata*, Variegated Sycamore Maple, grow along Yarrow Central Road. A bright *Chamæcyparis lawsoniana* 'Stewartii' graces the park. The golden colour of the foliage of this conifer is well contrasted by the purplish red foliage of the *Acer platanoides* 'Crimson King', Crimson King Maple, nearby. The delicately divided leaves of a European Cutleaf Birch, *Betula pendula* 'Laciniata', soften the silhouette of this mature tree at the south end of Yarrow Central Park.

3. Delta

**Jubilee Farm, later the Augustinian Monastery of B.C.
3900 Arthur Drive, Ladner, Delta.**
See the map of the village of Ladner.

The original residence was constructed in 1893 for Thomas and
Annie McNeely as the main house for their large Jubilee Farm.
The land was the site in the 1880's of Mainland Nursery, also
owned by McNeely and Ernest Hutcherson. Fruits and vegetables were the main crop of the nursery. Thomas McNeely died in
1900 and Mrs. McNeely left most of her estate to the Catholic
Church when she died in 1929. Archival photos show a well-developed landscape prior to 1929 so the mature trees on site
could be well over a century old.

The Catholic diocese maintained the property as a clerical
seminary for a time but eventually
sold it to the Our Mother of
Consolation Monastery, and it
became the third Augustinian
monastery to be established in
Canada. The Our Mother of
Consolation Monastery took over
the property in 1943. The original
plan for the monastery was to provide retreats, to become a centre for
pilgrimages and celebrations. In
addition to the regular parish work,
a grammar school was opened in
1944. The Sacred Heart Elementary
School, and a new Sacred Heart
parish church to the north of the
monastery site continue the work
begun by the brothers. The original
monastery property in Ladner covered a total of 21.3 hectares. The main buildings of the
monastery have a park-like landscape and at one time there was
an extensive garden. The brothers of the monastery supported
the members of the Order and guests very successfully through
astute management of the farmlands, especially with the cash
crops grown in the greenhouse.

Acer platanoides 'Schwedleri', Jubilee Farm,
later the Augustinian Monastery of B.C., Delta

Now the land and buildings at the rear of the property are slated for redevelopment. The magnificent trees that surround the main building will be preserved. In this group of very large trees are several massive *Chamæcyparis pisifera* 'Squarrosa', Moss Sawara Cypress, several large *Acer pseudoplatanus*, Sycamore Maple, one of which is variegated. The Variegated Sycamore Maple is the largest in the South Fraser Region, with a height of twenty-three metres and a crown spread of twenty-four metres. A very rare twenty-five metre high *Acer cappadocicum*, Coliseum Maple, is the largest of its species in the South Fraser Region. Several *Castanea dentata*, American Chestnut are happily growing on the south side of the house.

Delta Nature Reserve, North Delta
Access from Nordel Court

The Delta Nature Reserve covers an area sixty hectares in size. It lies in the northeastern corner of Burns Bog. The Nature Reserve, which is the only portion of Burns Bog that is protected, is less than two percent of the total area of the bog itself. Burns Bog is distinguished as the largest undeveloped urban landmass on the continent. It was originally over four thousand hectares in size. Today the bog has been reduced to 3200 hectares today due to the encroachment of urban development. Burns Bog is a superlative example of an estuarine-raised (dome-shaped) peat bog. It is 4.5 metres above sea level at its highest point in the centre and about 1.8 metres above sea level at its perimeter. Burns Bog is so large it can easily be seen from space. Burns Bog is the largest raised bog on the west coast of the Americas. Amazing but true, Burns Bog is three times as effective as a tropical rain forest in storing carbon dioxide.

Thousands of years ago, when the ice age ended, plants well adapted to the tundra colonized this area of North America. As the climate changed, these species relocated to the colder mountaintops, but some, such as Labrador Tea and Bog Laurel, were able to thrive in the acidic nutrient deficient growing conditions of the bog. *Pinus contorta* var. *contorta*, Shore Pine, commonly found in Burns Bog, is quite tolerant of poor and wet soils. Other trees, which can be viewed there, are a grove of *Thuja plicata*, Western Red Cedar, *Betula pendula*, European White Birch and *Betula papyrifera*, Paper Birch. Burns Bog is highly deserving of preservation and protection from further encroachment. As an ecosystem, it has both regional and global significance. Some of British Columbia's rarest species are found there.

Access Delta Nature Reserve by heading north to Nordel Way from Highway 91. Turn right at the second set of traffic lights to Nordel Court and travel on to the Great Pacific Forum at 10388 Nordel Court. Park in the southeast corner of the lot and proceed to the red brick walkway. Continue on the path under the Nordel Way overpass. The gravel access road, which carries on into the start of the boardwalks and trails of the Delta Nature Reserve, is directly ahead.

Memorial Park and Arthur Drive, Ladner, Delta
See the map of the village of Ladner.

Ladner or Ladner's Landing, as it was originally called, offers an interesting walking tour of very large and stately trees associated with the history of the community. Several trees in Memorial Park, a massive American Elm, *Ulmus americana,* and a remnant Holly and Pear orchard to the west of the library are associated with William Ladner and later his son Paul. One of the largest American Elms, *Ulmus americana,* found in the South Fraser Region, graces the boulevard east of the library. An example of a "Royal Oak" English Oak, *Quercus robur,* planted in honour of the Coronation of King George VI and Queen Elizabeth in 1937 is located at the southeast corner of the Memorial Park, adjacent to the secondary school. The tree is plaqued in memory of Mrs. Sauderberg but it was originally planted, as were the English Oaks that line the northern edge of the park, as part of the fervor associated with that Royal event. An excellent grove of mature Horse Chestnut trees, *Æsculus hippocastanum,* designated as Heritage Trees by City Council shades the western limit of the park.

To the west of Memorial Park along Arthur Drive a number of excellent trees can be viewed in the landscapes of the lovely Heritage homes built in the 1920's. Arthur Drive was the address to have in Ladner at that time. Good examples of *Fagus sylvatica,* European Beech, *Catalpa speciosa,* Western Catalpa, and very fine *Pinus nigra,* Black Pine create a verdant corridor leading south to the outskirts of the village to Kirkland House and the handsome *Acer pseudoplatanus,* Sycamore Maple, growing there.

4. Langley

Fort Langley
See the map of the village of Fort Langley.

Historic Fort Langley is the birthplace of British Columbia. It is a compact and friendly village boasting a number of excellent tourist facilities such as good restaurants, several museums, quaint and colourful craft shops and artists' studios. Fort Langley National Historic Site is a great place to begin a tour of the village. The Fort Langley National Historic Site provides an interactive experience of the sounds, sights and everyday life of an 1850's Hudson Bay Trading Post. The village of Fort Langley has a number of very significant Heritage Trees such as the *Acer macrophyllum*, Bigleaf Maples, planted to commemorate the fallen soldiers of World War I. A huge *Fagus sylvatica* Atropurpurea Group, Copper Beech on Copper Beech Street was planted in 1881 by James Houston, the discoverer of gold in British

Prunus 'Shirotae', Fort Langley Community Hall, Langley

Columbia. Mature oaks, Douglas Fir, Horse Chestnuts and other trees are found along the streets and ways of the village, including one of the largest Bigleaf Maple, *Acer macrophyllum* recorded in British Columbia.

Kwantlen University College, Langley campus
20901 Langley Bypass

Construction of the Langley campus of Kwantlen University College was completed in 1993. One of the major tenants on campus is the School of Horticulture. Landscape Architect Cornelia Oberlander designed the landscape of the campus, creating the core planting of an arboretum as directed by the author, a consultant on the project. Larger tree specimens such as *Fagus sylvatica*, European Beech, were moved from the City of Langley's original nursery on the north side of the Langley Bypass and planted onto the grounds. Younger specimens were purchased and planted in 1993 by a landscape contractor. In the ensuing years, the students of the Horticulture programs at

Quercus palustris, Kwantlen University College, Langley

Kwantlen, under the direction of faculty, have planted many new trees on campus and added substantially to the collection. To date there are over one hundred and fifty tree species represented. While the bulk of trees are still relatively young, this is a good spot to view a number of maple species and their cultivars and several rare trees such as x *Chitalpa tashkentensis* and *Quercus phellos,* Willow Oak.

Portage Park
52 St and 204 Ave, Langley City

Early travellers began their portage from the Nicomekl River to the Salmon River, and then on to Fort Langley and the Fraser River from this park. Sir James Macmillan and his party passed this way on the 14th of December 1824. It was the first appearance of the white man in the area. A beautifully carved wooden canoe portaged by two paddlers, dedicated August 25, 2000 at Langley City Hall, marks the route Macmillan would have taken from Portage Park to the Salmon River. Several trees of note in Portage Park are a mature *Acer ginnala*, Amur maple, large Sitka Spruce, *Picea sitchensis* and a row of *Fagus sylvatica* 'Dawyck', Dawyck Beech. A massive Sitka Spruce growing in the flood plain of the Nicomekl River, to the south of the park, was already one hundred years old when Macmillan's party portaged past in 1824.

Sendall Gardens
5549- 204th Street, Langley City
See the overview map of the South Fraser Region
to locate the garden.

This 1.6-hectare property had been a private home and garden for several generations before the City of Langley Parks and Recreation Department acquired it in the mid-1970's. At that time the garden was derelict, and from 1975 to 1985 the Parks department foreman Bill Heubener, who lived in the residence on site, undertook what he called a "labour of love" in transforming the grounds into a multi-roomed garden. The garden was again renovated in 1998 with major improvements made to the retaining walls and pathway system.

The front garden was originally a flat expanse with few interesting plants. Heubener created various levels with soil excavated from other city projects and planted a wide range of trees and shrubs. Today the garden is a treasure trove of trees and shrubs. Notable is the planting of three *Calocedrus decurrens*, Incense Cedar on the west side of the path, the *Sequoiadenron giganteum* 'Pendulum', Weeping Giant Sequoia that drapes itself over the rockwork of the small fountain. A very large *Acer pseudoplatanus* Atropurpureum Group, Purple Sycamore Maple grows adjacent to the house and a two *Ginkgo biloba*, Maidenhair Trees and a *Magnolia grandiflora*, Evergreen Magnolia are behind the house. The garden to the south of the residence has been left as a natural wooded ravine, with two ponds for waterfowl.

Williams Park
6600 Block 238 St, Salmon River Uplands, Langley

Williams Park was originally cleared around 1889. "If one of the trees was too big, you used to take an auger and bore a slanting hole down. Then you'd put a stick in that and get down on your knees and bore a draft hole until you could touch that with a stick. Then you'd get a fire going with vine maple or hardwood, you'd put the coals in the hole and blow and start a draft, and burn the trees down, those big ones. Most of the other ones, they'd just saw or chop them down. You never done it when it was too dry because you had to watch it or a fire would start. But you'd go out there at night and see three or four great trees, all like torches; it was a wonderful sight. That stuff is worth hundreds of dollars today, but it wasn't worth anything then."[2] Pioneer Charles Williams and his family cleared the land of the giant Western Red Cedar, *Thuja plicata*, Douglas Fir, *Pseudotsuga menziesii*, and Bigleaf Maples, *Acer macrophyllum* that had thrived there for five hundred years.

The property was sold several times before Dr. and Mrs. D.H. Williams, (no relation to the pioneer named Williams) purchased the 13-hectare site for three hundred and fifty dollars an acre in 1954. Over a twelve-year period Dr. and Mrs. Williams and their sons, Don and Paul planted a wide range of trees and shrubs, which have grown to a good size today.

Don Williams recalled a hurricane in 1958 that toppled hundreds of cottonwoods in the park. The landscape was littered with trees knocked over at their roots like giant pick-up sticks. Months of work, often standing ten metres above the ground on top of six layers of deadfall was needed to clear away the fallen trees.

A large Duchess apple tree, *Malus* 'Duchess', is a living reminder of the life of the early settlers in the area. Bears were particularly fond of the dry tart flesh of the apples of this tree, which bears fruit in alternate years. A lovely English Walnut tree, *Juglans nigra*, which was 15 cm in diameter when the Williams purchased the property in 1954, is also a remnant of earlier times. Don Williams recounted how his mother would pickle the walnuts by harvesting the nuts long before they were ripe, and plunging them in a brine. The nuts could be preserved for years this way, and the soft blackened walnut would be eaten shell and all as a savoury dish with meat such as lamb.

The Williams in honour of various family members planted many of the exotic and native trees that now grace the park. A *Quercus coccinea*, Scarlet Oak was purchased in 1955-56 by Paul Williams as a birthday gift for his mother, while the beautiful *Liquidambar styraciflua*, American Sweetgum was planted at the same time to mark the wedding anniversary of his parents. Both these trees were purchased from Murray Nurseries Ltd. in Vancouver, the author's family business. A *Liriodendron tulipifera*, Tuilp Tree and a number of the English, Red and Pin Oaks were planted to mark family birthdays or anniversaries. Often the trees in the park were propagated from collected seed, or by cuttings made by Paul Williams and nurtured in a little nursery on the property and then later planted out. The collection of crabapples was grown from seedlings gathered as fruit in the fall of 1960-61 at the University of Wisconsin Arboretum. The *Chamæcyparis lawsoniana*, Lawson's Cypress to the west of the picnic shelter was grown from cuttings collected from the University of British Columbia campus.

The Township of Langley bought the property in 1966 as part of a 1967 Centennial project and it is a popular park for walkers and picnickers.

5. Richmond

Burkeville
Residential area immediately to the east of the Vancouver International Airport

Burkeville is a tiny community on Sea Island, surrounded on its west and south extremities by the runways and service buildings of the Vancouver International Airport. Russ Baker Way borders Burkeville on the north, and Miller Road is the southern limit of the community. Constructed from 1941-1944, Burkeville was designed and built under the Dominion Government's Wartime Housing Plan to alleviate the housing shortage caused by the new aircraft industry and air force station at the airport. Three hundred and twenty-eight homes were built for the employees and families of Boeing Aircraft Company and other local aviation companies. Stanley Burke, the president of Boeing Aircraft of Canada, Ltd. provided the name for the small community. The original bungalows fell into one of three designs, had one of four roof colours and one of three wall colours. The streets, with names like Catalina, Douglas, Handley, Anson, Hudson, Wellington, Stirling and Lancaster commemorate the aircraft used in the Second World War. Boeing is the name of the main street of Burkeville.

The first residents moved into Burkeville in January 1944. At the outset, these homes were viewed as temporary housing stock and were to be dismantled after World War II. Burkeville was financed and built by the Federal Government, which originally expropriated the land in order to have control over the area for the protection of the servicemen and wartime industries. In 1947, the government allowed the sale of the homes to private individuals. The community of Burkeville has continued as a relatively isolated and close-knit community in Richmond. Over the decades several large schemes to expand the airport or the road system through the community have caused significant alarm. Burkeville has survived the encroachment of development for six decades through the determination of its residents to protect Burkeville's unique community flavour.

Burkeville is a delightful place to stroll the quiet curving streets and admire the mature landscape. Handley Avenue is lined with a lovely double aisle of American Elms. Siberian Elms grace Catalina Crescent while a double row of London Plane trees, *Platanus* x *hispanica,* arches over Hudson. The south end of Lancaster contains a row of magnificent *Catalpa speciosa.* Burkeville Community Park is well endowed with many very large and well-grown trees such as *Fraxinus ornus, Platanus* x *hispanica, Quercus rubra* and *Catalpa speciosa.*

Fantasy Garden World
10800 No. 5 Road, Richmond

Fantasy Garden World, originally called Bota Gardens was built in 1980 by John Massot as a Botanical display garden. Bill and Lillian Vander Zalm, Mr. Vander Zalm a former premier of British Columbia, bought the garden in 1984. A succession of owners including Mr. Vander Zalm have added a number of tourist features to the 4.9-hectare garden. Currently the garden is owned by offshore interests and is languishing. The garden is open during the spring, summer and early fall. There is an admission fee.

Landscape Architect Raoul Robillard designed the ponds and waterways of Bota Gardens. The garden took a year and a half to construct. The placing of the hundreds of rhododendrons was simplicity itself. John Massot gathered rhododendrons of mixed mature heights and colours, in full bloom and placed them on large flat nursery trailers. He hand placed each cultivar with a complementary colour companion according to the actual blossom colour to achieve a dazzling display of blooms.

As with every nursery grower, John Massot, originally of Massot Nurseries Ltd, had an interesting story to tell of his family's origin in the nursery business. His grandfather, a wheat farmer in France, planted a hectare of poplars from cuttings. The poplar rooted, grew well and sold quickly. The family progressed from growing poplars to fruit trees to evergreens to a wide range of nursery stock. John Massot emigrated from France to Canada in 1953.

The tree collection at Fantasy Garden World is maturing well, unfortunately the seasonal displays of bulbs and annuals are skimpy and in places there are more blackberries than plantings. The eighty different species of trees are worth the trip though, including some uncommon trees such as *Acer cappadocicum* 'Aureum', Golden Coliseum Maple, *Catalpa bignonioides, Cryptomeria japonica* 'Cristata', Cockscomb Cypress,

Cunninghamia lanceolata, Davidia involucrata, Fraxinus excelsior 'Pendula', *Fraxinus excelsior* 'Jaspidea', Yellow Ash, *Pinus densiflora* 'Umbraculifera', *Salix babylonica* var. *pekinensis* 'Tortuosa' and *Taxodium distichum*. The *Sequiadendron giganteum* 'Pendulum' at the entrance is a magnificent weeping tree that is the largest one found in the South Fraser Region.

Millennium Botanical Garden and Arboretum, North McLennan Community Park.
Garden City and Alberta Rd, Richmond

North McLennan Park is a large 8.5-hectare site that is currently under development as the "jewel in the necklace" of Richmond parks. Much of the park is still in a native state with *Betula pendula*, European White Birch and *Pinus contorta* var. *contorta,* Shore Pine growing in boggy areas. Located in the northwest corner of the North McLennan Community Park, adjacent to Garden City Road, the Millennium Botanical Garden and Arboretum officially opened on October 28, 2001. The Millennium Botanical Garden and Arboretum showcases the trees of the Pacific Rim. The Arboretum's tree list is quite extensive and informative signage has been place throughout. Many common native trees of the South Fraser Region such as *Acer circinatum*, Vine Maple, *Chamæcyparis nootkatensis,* Nootka Cypress and *Quercus garryana,* Garry Oak, have been planted to represent North America and the eastern side of the Pacific Ocean. *Araucaria araucana*, Monkey Puzzle and *Nothofagus antarctica,* Antarctic Beech hail from South America. The countries and islands found on the western side of the Pacific Ocean or in the Western Pacific Rim, are represented by a number of Maple species such as *Acer capillipes*, Red Snakebark Maple, several magnolias such as *Magnolia denudata,* Yulan Magnolia from China and other trees such as *Quercus acutissima,* Saw-toothed Oak, from Korea, Japan and China. There is a small parking lot on Alberta Road; a pathway leads from the parking area to the Arboretum.

Richmond Nature Park
11851 Westminster Highway, Richmond

Located in the Fraser River estuary, this 40.5-hectare nature park is a sphagnum-moss bog where cranberry and blueberry shrubs, salal, and other bog plants thrive. The park is crisscrossed by many self-guiding trails. The trees worth viewing on this site are the *Pinus strobus*, Eastern White Pine and the *Pinus sylvestris*, Scots Pine in the parking lot. *Betula papyrifera*, Paper Birch, *Betula pendula*, European White Birch grow throughout the site as does small *Tsuga heterophylla*, Western Hemlock and *Pinus contorta* var. *contorta*, Shore Pine.

Steveston Park, Martial Arts Centre
4111 Moncton Street, Steveston, Richmond
See the map of the village of Steveston.

The Martial Arts Centre is located in Steveston Park, along with the Steveston Community Centre and the Steveston Japanese Canadian Cultural Centre. The Martial Arts Centre was constructed in 1971 as a Centennial Project and officially opened on March 18, 1972. The centre is a lovely example of traditional Japanese architectural design sympathetically adapted to our coastal landscape. The Martial Arts Centre is internationally recognized as a training facility for Kendo and Judo. It is unique in that it is the only dojo house outside Japan.

The garden, designed by Landscape Architect Raoul Robillard, contains several interesting trees such as a large *Sophora japonica*, Japanese Pagoda Tree, *Aralia elata*, Japanese Angelica Tree, a *Cercidiphyllum japonicum*, Katsura Tree, all native to Japan. The courtyard between the Martial Arts Centre and the Japanese Canadian Cultural Centre has a number of well-grown *Acer palmatum*, Japanese Maple.

Steveston Park is a wonderful place to view good-sized trees. There is a row of very large *Populus alba*, White Poplar, west of the Fenton street entrance to the park, and several very old but declining *Picea sitchensis*, Sitka Spruce and *Acer rubrum*, Red Maple, north of the Japanese Canadian Cultural Centre. The row of unusual *Sorbus* x *thuringiaca* 'Fastigiata', Oakleaf Mountain Ash, behind the Centre, has such a perfect tight pyramidal form it looks as if it has been precision sheared.

6. Rosedale

Minter Gardens
52892 Bunker Road, Rosedale
See the overview map of the South Fraser Region to locate the garden.

Brian and Faye Minter first saw the site of the future Minter Gardens on Christmas Day in 1977 while on a family drive. At that moment in time a dream was born, to create one of the most beautiful gardens in the world on that hilly site of natural beauty lying in the shadow of Mount Cheam. Minter Gardens is set in natural woodland on six hectares of rolling land. Architect Peter Thornton used the undulating natural topography to great effect, to create a series of pathways that slope gently enough to allow wheelchair access and at the same time incorporate into the lay-out the existing *Thuja plicata*, Western Red Cedar, trees which grow in the garden in abundance. Some of these trees are easily thirty metres tall. Thornton also designed the rustic building complex at the entrance to the garden to reflect the simple farm architecture of the surrounding community. Stonemason Kevan Maxwell created a very fine series of dry stonewalls from rock on the site. The site, which had no existing streams or pools, was drilled to locate an underground lake, which now supplies water to the burbling rills, rivulets and ponds in the garden. Topsoil stripped from the parking area created the flowerbeds. The garden was opened in 1980 after one year of construction. The topography made possible ten individual garden rooms in both formal and informal styles. The garden rooms include a Rhododendron Garden, Hillside Garden, Rose Garden, Formal Garden, a maze and others. The

Taxus baccata 'Fastigiata', Minter Gardens, Rosedale

garden contains a large collection of sixty different species of trees. There are a number of unusual maple species including, *Acer japonicum* 'Aconitifolium', Fullmoon Maple, *Acer cappadocicum*, Cappadocicum Maple, *Acer negundo* 'Variegatum', and three different Japanese Maple, *Acer palmatum* 'Butterfly',

'Shishigashira' and 'Linearilobum'. The Rhododendron Garden contains a lovely collection of Magnolias, in particular a beautiful *Magnolia dawsoniana*, Dawson Magnolia. To the west of the Formal Garden, several *Robinia pseudoacacia* 'Frisia' are growing well on the slope. A stately *Fagus sylvatica* 'Pendula' punctuates the north end of the Meadow Garden. The south patio of the Trillium Restaurant is accented by a lovely *Cornus florida* 'Rainbow', Rainbow Dogwood.

7. Surrey

Darts Hill Garden Park
1660 - 168 St, South Surrey
See the overview map of the South Fraser Region
to locate the garden.

The creators of Darts Hill Garden Park, Edwin and Francisca Darts were originally from two different spheres; Edwin was born in Vancouver in 1903 and Francisca in The Hague, Netherlands in 1916. They purchased their 3-hectare property in Surrey in 1943 to grow fruit trees. The land was overgrown bush, regrowth from the logging of the forest giants in the late 1890's. Edwin cleared the remaining stumps by dynamiting them. Next, the young couple hand cleared the site with the most basic of tools; axes, two-handed saws and shovels. In those early days little was mechanized, in fact the site did not even have water or electricity. As their first interest was fruit production, an orchard of apple, pear, apricot and nut trees such as Walnut and Filbert was planted in the developing garden. The magnificent centrepieces of the garden, growing just below the house, are now two Hybrid Walnut trees, *Juglans cinerea* x *Juglans ailanthifolia* var. *cordiformis*, and remnants of this nut-growing period. While exhibiting their nuts and fruit at the Agricultural exhibition at the Pacific National Exhibition in Vancouver a display sponsored by the Alpine Garden Club of British Columbia ignited their enthusiasm for all things horticultural. Francisca joined the Royal Horticultural Society and over the ensuing years obtained a wide variety of unusual seeds from that source, which were propagated and planted throughout the garden.

The Darts donated their garden to the City of Surrey in 1994. The City purchased an adjoining 8.9 hectares of undeveloped land to create a larger park site. The work begun by the Darts fifty-five years ago is a rich collection today of trees, shrubs and perennial plants. The Rhododendron and Magnolia collection is simply outstanding. Edwin Darts favorite Rhododendron was *R.*

Larix kaempferi, Darts Hill Garden Park, Surrey

lacteum hybrid, a vibrant yellow blooming shrub now planted by the west gate of the garden. The garden logo is a stylized Magnolia flower, emphasizing Mrs. Darts enthusiasm for this beautiful genus of plants. Over two hundred and forty different species of trees can be found in Darts Hill Garden Park. The goal of the city of Surrey, in accordance to Mrs. Dart's wishes, is to continue her lifelong work and to create a horticultural centre for the preservation, enhancement and development of plants.

At the 2002 convocation of Kwantlen University College, Francisca Darts was awarded an honorary Doctor of Laws Degree, a tribute to her lifetime of exploration and learning in horticulture. In her address to the graduates she said, "I did not have the opportunity to attend university or high school when I was young because at that time in Northern Manitoba, where I lived, there were no high schools and therefore my high school education had to be obtained at home; and to attend university was out of the question…To have a particular interest in a particular subject is a gift to be followed and explored… I was fortunate in having a husband who encouraged my horticultural adventures; he always said when I was in doubt, 'You can do it, go ahead'. I pass that on to you along with my personal advice to have faith in yourself. I urge you to never stop learning: it is necessary and exciting." [3]

Darts Hill Garden Park was designated a Heritage Tree Site in 1997. The park contains many exceptionally fine specimens, many of the trees are the largest found in the South Fraser Region, including several *Abies pinsapo* 'Glauca', Spanish Fir, three *Calocedrus decurrens*, Incense Cedar, a large *Corylus avellana* 'Contorta', Corkscrew Hazel, *Castanea sativa*, Sweet Chestnut, *Morus alba*, White Mulberry, *Magnolia macrophylla*, Bigleaf Magnolia, *Mespilus germanica*, Medlar, *Nothofagus antarctica*, Antarctic Beech, *Parrotia persica*, Persian Ironwood, *Paulownia tomentosa*, Empress Tree, *Picea orientalis*, Oriental Spruce, *Thujopsis dolobrata* 'Variegata', Variegated Hiba Arborvitae, *Umbellularia californica*, California Bay Tree, *Cunninghamia lanceolata*, China Fir, and a *Sequioadendron giganteum* 'Pendulum', Weeping Giant Sequoia.

Although not currently open to the public, the garden is available for group tours and in the future it will be accessible to everyone. To visit the gardens as a group, contact Surrey Parks, Recreation and Culture at (604) 501-5100.

Green Timbers Park and Urban Forest
9800- 140 St, Whalley, Surrey

Green Timbers Park and Urban Forest has four distinct areas that are of interest to the visitor, the nature trails, which make up three-quarters of the forested park, and the Ministry of Forest site in the northwest corner of the park, which contains the Inaugural Planting, the Sixtieth Year Commemorative Planting, and the Arboretum.

As early as 1860, attempts were made to designate Green Timbers as parkland. In the 1920's the giant trees on both sides of the Pacific Highway had become famous, attracting tourists from as far south as San Diego. Fred Baker, a Surrey homesteader and his son Harry drove their Model T pick-up down the dirt road into Surrey Municipal Hall in Cloverdale to protest the logging of the last remaining virgin stand of timber adjacent to Pacific Highway. This 1928 journey along with his neighbours was to no avail. Unfortunately, conservation of resources was not fashionable at the time.

Harry Baker was just a teenager in 1928 when an enormous Douglas Fir was cut down just south of Green Timbers. He counted five hundred and fifty growth rings on the felled Douglas Fir stump.

The Abbotsford Lumber Company had left a stand of trees, sixty-one metres wide, on either side of the Pacific Highway (now called the Fraser Highway) from Hjorth Road to Fleetwood with the idea of having the Provincial Government create a permanent park along the highway. Victoria ignored the

public request to set aside the last old growth fir stands on the
Pacific Highway for a park. The Lumber Company advertised in

Acer campestre, Green Timbers Arboretum,
Surrey

the newspapers, warning people
that they would regret the destruc-
tion of the ancient trees. Nobody
responded. "Farewell," eulogized
the *Columbian,* " there it stood, a
magnificent specimen of Douglas
Fir, towering above a desolate sea
of stumps. This one bit of highway
was unique to the traveler.
Especially on a hot summer day it
was with a keen sense of pleasure
that one entered its shade and
breathed in the invigorating
atmosphere… But regret in vain;
Green Timbers is gone." [4] The last
stand of virgin timber in Surrey
was cut in July of 1930. Approximately four billion board feet of
timber was harvested in the
municipality of Surrey from 1880-1930.

A promise was made to protestors like Fred Baker that the
forest would be replanted and then preserved in perpetuity. To
this end, in 1929 the new B.C. Forest Service located at the corner of Townline Road (96 Avenue) and Pacific Highway began
to prepare the ground for a "Production Forest nursery" to be
established there. On March 15,1930 an "Inaugural Plantation"
was put into the ground by 26 selected foresters, politicians,
newspaper reporters, farmers and businessmen. MLA John
Walter Berry planted the first tree. A speech was made in the
Chinook language remarking on the importance of the establishment of the new forest. It marked the beginning of reforestation
in British Columbia. Green Timbers Nursery was established in
1930, and the parcel of land around it was subdivided into one
hundred and five plots of two hectares each for planting in1931;
347,000 trees including a Garry Oak Plantation were planted
over the next seven years.

The Inaugural Plantation was forgotten until records of its
existence were discovered in the Provincial Archives recently. Of

the one hundred and twenty-one seedlings which were planted that day, twenty-seven have survived. Of these, the original planters set thirteen out in 1930. The remaining fourteen, which were planted as spares, have been assigned to individuals whose trees did not thrive. All of the trees in the Inaugural Plantation were Douglas Fir with the exception of three Lawson's Cypress. Restoration of this grove, which marked the true beginning of reforestation in British Columbia, is in progress.

In 1996 Green Timbers was dedicated by Referendum as an Urban Forest.

On the Sixtieth Anniversary of the Inaugural Planting on March 15, 1990 a commemorative planting was made as a replica of the first one. Descendants of the original planters were on hand to plant new seedlings. To the west of the Inaugural Plantation, Premier Bill Van Der Zalm planted the province of British Columbia's two billionth forest tree seedling in 1989. An additional twenty forest trees seedlings were planted in 2000 to mark the Millennium year. The Green Timbers Heritage Society began the restoration of this plantation and also the Arboretum in 1998. In June 1989, then President of the B.C. Forest History Association, Bill Young, wrote in the *Forestry Chronicle*: "Green Timbers is the site of B.C.'s first forest plantation" and "should be dedicated as a British Columbia Heritage Forest".

The Arboretum, planted in 1930, contains one hundred and twenty-five native and nonnative species of trees. Some are very rare and not found anywhere else in the South Fraser Region. The Arboretum was neglected for many years, but recently the Green Timbers Heritage Society has begun the work of restoring the area. The trees have been identified, labelled, and restorative pruning begun.

An enjoyable and informative one-hour walk can be taken through Green Timbers Park. Begin at the parking lot on 100 Avenue east of 144 Street. The Salal Trail runs along the eastern part of the park and can be accessed from the parking lot. On the trail there are huge fir stumps and the bed of the logging railway, evidence of past activity. The Trillium Trail is north of 100 Avenue; several of the oldest Douglas Firs in Green Timbers Park are growing there.

Mound Farm Park
5202- 168 Street, Cloverdale, Surrey

Mound Farm Park has been in private hands until it was recently acquired by the City of Surrey as a new park. Mound Farm Park is currently under development and it is not open to the public. A trail system, winding its way through the magnificent stand of native trees, is under construction. What make Mound Farm Park outstanding are the large native conifers, a few that were not logged in Surrey's early history and are of very great size today.

Peace Arch Park
King George Highway and 0 Avenue, South Surrey

Almost five hectares of land in Canada along the USA and Canada border were dedicated in 1886 for the benefit of the public as an international park. This land grant, the first parkland grant in Surrey, is known today as Peace Arch Park. A similar parcel of land was dedicated on the American side of the border for the purpose of a park. The familiar landmark, the Peace Arch, was constructed in 1920. British Columbia Premier John Oliver and Senator J.H. King of Washington State officially dedicated the park on September 6, 1921 with a crowd of ten thousand in attendance. This commemorated one hundred years of peace between Canada and the United States. On the American side of the arch the following is inscribed, "Children of A Common Mother"

Fagus sylvatica, Peace Arch Park, Surrey

and on the Canadian side "Brethren Dwelling Together in Peace and Unity". A piece of the sailing ship the *Mayflower* (1620) is embedded in the walls of the arch. There is also a piece of the first steamship on the Pacific Ocean, the SS *Beaver* (1835).

Peace Arch Park is home to an excellent collection of mature trees likely planted in the 1920's when the park was constructed. Eight have been designated as Heritage Trees by the city of Surrey. Massive European Beech, *Fagus sylvatica* ring the hillside surrounding the Peace Arch itself. These trees are some of the largest beech found in the South Fraser Region. Several stately conifers such as *Pinus monticola*, Western White Pine, *Larix decidua*, European Larch, *Cedrus atlantica*, Atlas Cedar, *Chamæcyparis lawsoniana*, Lawson's Cypress and a *Ginkgo biloba*, Maidenhair tree are perfectly formed open grown lawn specimens. Two maples of good size and form designated as Heritage Trees are an *Acer palmatum* Atropurpureum Group, Red Japanese Maple and an *Acer platanoides* 'Crimson King', Crimson King Maple growing on the west side of the park.

Redwood Park
Entrance at 17900 20th Avenue, South Surrey

Redwood Park comes by its name honestly. It contains the largest stand of Giant Sequoia or Sierra Redwood trees, *Sequoiadendron giganteum* north of the forty-ninth parallel. The dozens of tightly grown Sierra Redwoods are but one species of an extensive botanical garden created by two very unusual twin brothers, David and Peter Brown.

When the David Brown family arrived in Surrey to homestead in 1878, the land was thickly forested. The roads were rough trails or surveyor's cut lines. To reach their new sixty-five hectares homestead from Ferndale, Washington, Mr. and Mrs. Brown, with their seven children, including twins David and Peter moved all their belongings north on a stone boat drawn by a pair of oxen. Mr. Brown Sr. had to build a bridge over the Campbell River and clear an eight hundred-metre trail through the sixty metre high Douglas Firs before he could bring the family onto the property. The nearest store at that time was far off in the city of New Westminster.

Illness set the twins David and Peter apart at an early age, when scarlet fever struck them deaf. They became proficient lip readers, and had the unnerving habit, when talking to each other, of moving their lips but issuing no sounds, though they spoke aloud to others. On their twenty-first birthday in 1893, the brothers inherited thirty-two hectares of recently logged south facing property from their father. Originally the twins were to plant and manage a small fruit and nut farm. Shortly after inheriting the property, the twins took a train trip to Santa Clara in Northern California to visit a cousin. There they were overwhelmed with the splendour of the giant Sierra Redwoods and arrived home with their pockets full of seeds. They planted the seeds and began to lay out the property as an orchard as originally planned, planting walnuts and also dozens of conifers from all over the continent. The twins began a worldwide search for seeds and tree species suitable for planting on their property. A magnificent English Walnut is a remnant of their nut orchard and is growing to the south of the Tree House. Eventually, the twin brothers became recluses, living in their house in the forest. They continued to plant new tree species and maintain their garden for over fifty years.

The city of Surrey opened Redwood Park in 1960. The park contains hundreds of specimens, with over thirty different tree species. In some parts of the park exotic trees such as *Castanea sativa*, Sweet Chestnut and *Quercus robur*, English Oak, that were originally planted by the Brown brothers have naturalized.

Nine trees at Redwood Park have been declared Significant Trees under the City of Surrey Tree Preservation By-law. These trees were selected because of the large size or rarity within the community. These are *Calocedrus decurrens*, Incense Cedar, *Castanea sativa*, Sweet Chestnut, *Chamæcyparis lawsoniana* 'Stewartii', Golden Lawson's Cypress, *Juglans regia*, English Walnut, *Metasequoia glyptostoboides*, Dawn Redwood, *Quercus rubra*, Red Oak, *Sequiadendron giganteum*, Giant Sequoia, *Thujopsis dolobrata*, Hiba Arborvitae and *Ulmus glabra* 'Lutescens', Golden Elm. These trees were plaqued in 1998 by the Fraser Valley Heritage Tree Society to acknowledge them.

Municipal Hall Complex
14245- 56 Avenue, Newton, Surrey

The Municipal Hall complex has forty different tree species growing in the landscape around the dozen or so buildings that make up the complex. Opened in the fall of 1962, the Surrey Municipal Hall has been very well landscaped, with the plantings updated and refurbished over the years by the Parks and Recreation department. Two very lovely *Chamæcyparis nootkatensis* 'Pendula Group', Weeping Nootka Cypress, stand on the east side of the building, while on the west side, a group of *Picea omorika*, Serbian Spruce, frames the side entrance. Two very fine mature *Acer palmatum* 'Sazanami' grace the southeast corner of the building. The tiny leaves of this cultivar are among the smallest of all the Japanese Maples. The feathery leaves of an *Albizia julibrissin*, Silk Tree, cast a filtered shade under the deeper shade of the mature Douglas Fir trees on the east side of the Municipal Hall. A number of elegant trees such as the white flowered Japanese Snowbell, *Styrax japonicus* and *Davidia involucrata*, Dove Tree, are growing around the shore of the pond.

Prunus 'Shirotae', Municipal Hall Complex, Surrey

A number of other public buildings and the landscapes around them can be viewed at the Municipal Hall Complex. Trees worthy of note are the grove of the *Cercidiphyllum japonicum*, Japanese Katsura, at the front entrance to the Provincial Courthouse. There is an *Arbutus menziesii*, Arbutus, on the south side and a mature *Abies grandis* on the east side of this building. The building housing the offices of the Fraser Health Region has a lovely *Acer cappadocicum*, Coliseum Maple, on the east side, while a *Magnolia* x *soulangiana* 'Lennei', Lenné Magnolia is growing at the northwest corner of the building. The entrance to the Royal Canadian Mounted Police (RCMP) building is graced by an espaliered *Cedrus atlantica* 'Glauca Pendula', Weeping Blue Atlas Cedar that has been trained and presses tightly against the concrete wall surface.

The Glades
561- 172nd Street, Surrey

In 1956 when Murray Stephen, a Fellow of the Royal Horticultural Society of London, and his wife, Lydia, bought the South Surrey property now known as the "The Glades", it was a thicket of native cedar, hemlock, alder and well-clothed in blackberry, horsetail and ferns. They worked long hours to create the two-hectare garden. Rhododendrons and azaleas were their main interests, and they imported seeds from all over the world. An overstory of exotic trees was also planted on the site. It was

Mr. Stephen's dream come true. As a child in England, he wandered one day into the garden of a stately home. From that moment on he planned to someday create a beautiful garden where any who wished might stroll.

After Murray Stephen's death in 1970, Lydia remarried. With her new partner, Bruce Hill, she continued to maintain "The Glades", opening the garden each May to visitors. Eventually, old age and poor heath forced them to close the garden to the public.

After Bruce died in 1993 and Lydia in 1994 the garden was acquired by its present owners, Jim and Elfriede De Wolf. The De Wolf's have revitalized the garden by embarking on an extensive program of clearing, pruning, transplanting, thinning, planting new materials, cataloging the huge collections of rhododendrons, trees and other shrubs. The garden is once again open to the public in May. It houses an extensive collection of fine trees in addition to the rhododendrons that entice so many viewers to the garden.

Forest Walk, The Glades, Surrey

The garden contains approximately seventy-six different tree species. Ten of these trees are listed as Significant Trees under the City of Surrey Tree Preservation Bylaw. These ten trees were selected for their large size or rarity. They are *Davidia involucrata*, Dove Tree, *Liriodendron tulipifera*, Tulip Tree, *Magnolia kobus*, Kobus Magnolia, *Magnolia wilsonii*, Wilson's Magnolia, *Metasequoia glyptostroboides*, Dawn Redwood, *Pinus strobus*, Eastern White Pine, *Quercus canariensis*, Mirbeck's Oak, *Thuja plicata*, Western Red Cedar and *Umbellularia californica*, California Bay. In January 1998, the Fraser Valley Heritage Tree Society placed a plaque at the entrance to the garden recognizing the Heritage Trees of "The Glades".

[1] Denman, R.W.R. *50 Years of Military Presence in the Fraser Valley Camp Chilliwack 1942-1992.* p. 41.

[2] Orchard, Imbert. *Pioneer Childhood in the Lower Fraser Valley.* p. 6.

[3] Darts, F. Convocation address, May 24, 2002.

[4] Cherrington, from "Green Timbers", *The British Columbian,* Treleaven, Vol.II, p. 63, p. 296.

A

When we plant trees, we are doing what we can to make our planet a more wholesome and happier dwelling place for those who come after us, if not for ourselves.

Oliver Wendell Holmes, (1809–1894), American physician, poet and humorist

Abies pinsapo 'Glauca', cones

Abies amabilis

Pacific Silver Fir or Amabilis Fir

This tall conical fir, native to the middle to high elevations of the Coast Mountains, is not commonly grown in the Fraser South Region. Its shiny bright green needles are held in a flattened spray, with a third set of shorter needles, which point forward, on top of the branchlet. This uppermost series of needles often completely hides the twig. The underside of the notched tipped blunt needles is banded with silvery stomata, giving rise to the tree's common name, Silver Fir. Like the more common Grand Fir, the foliage has a lovely spicy smell. The stubby buds are resinous and purplish brown in colour. The large barrel-shaped cones are deep purplish in colour as well. Pacific Silver Fir grows forty metres high with a broadly pyramidal form.

Where to see the trees:

Abbotsford

818 Mckenzie Rd, a great conical specimen.

Chilliwack

Yarrow Community Park, north end of Community St, Yarrow. There are a number of young trees at the rear of the park.

Please note: any tree marked with an asterisk(*) has been designated a community heritage tree.

White Fir or Colorado Fir

Abies concolor, Stó:lo Centre, Sardis   *Abies concolor* 'Candicans', foliage

White Fir is a beautiful fir native to the mountains of southern Colorado. It reaches a mature height of fifteen metres with a conical shape. White Fir is not commonly found in the South Fraser Region. The soft flexible needles, which curve outwards and upward on the branchlet, are the longest of any of the firs grown here. The species name 'Concolor' refers to the uniform needle colour, which is pale bluish green on both sides. Young trees are stiff and symmetrical, with branches radiating out and upward.

Where to see the trees:

Chilliwack

10005 Kenswood Dr, Little Mountain.

The Waverly, 8445 Young St.

Stó:lo Centre, 7201 Vedder Rd, Sardis, a magnificent tree, fourteen metres tall, on the west side of the main building.

Langley

Aldergrove United Church, northwest corner of 272 St and 26 Ave, Aldergrove, eight good-sized specimens.

Kwantlen University College, 20901 Langley Bypass, Langley City. There are two trees to the east of the front entrance turnaround circle on the main campus.

Did You Know?

The members of the genus *Abies*, the true Firs, can be easily distinguished from other conifer genera. The cones of *Abies* are held upright on the branches of the tree. The cones break apart on the tree rather than falling intact to the ground like the cones of other conifers. The needles when pulled or fallen from the branchlets leave a shallow circular depression or pit in the stem. The buds of *Abies* are blunt, rounded and often stubby. The bark of young trees is characteristically greyish and smooth with resin blisters or bubbles. One way to remember the difference between *Abies* and *Picea*, or Spruce, a conifer often confused with *Abies*, is the following. *Abies* have pits (referring to the shallow depression) and *Picea* have pegs. *Picea*, or Spruce needles leave a short, stiff peg on the stem when they fall from a branchlet as part of the petiole of the needle remains behind.

Abies grandis
Grand Fir

Where to see the trees:

Abbotsford

34751 Marshall Rd, a lovely tree.

Hazelwood Cemetery, 34000 block Hazelwood. The tree has a measured height of forty-four metres and a DBH of 121 cm and is a perfect open-grown specimen that dominates the cemetery.

Musselwhite Cemetery, SE corner of Old Yale Rd and Marshall Rd, at the southeast end of the cemetery.

Chilliwack

Edwards Street Park, corner of Princess Ave and Edwards St.

Gwynne-Vaughan Park, northwest corner of Williams Rd and Hope River Rd, Fairfield Island, throughout the back pasture with one *Abies concolor*.

Townsend Park, southwest corner of Ashwell Rd and Hodgins Ave, three young trees south of the outfield of baseball diamond 4.

Yarrow Community Park, north end of Community St, Yarrow, a number of young trees at the rear of the park.

Delta

4385 Arthur Dr, Ladner.

Langley

City Park, 207 St and 48 Ave, Langley City.

SW corner of 232 St and Fraser Highway, Southeast Langley.

5183- 240 Ave, Salmon River Uplands.

Williams Park, 6600 block 238 St, Salmon River Uplands.

Lindell Beach

2045 Lindell Ave.

Richmond

3051 Garry St, Steveston.

Surrey

Provincial Courthouse, 14340- 57 Ave, Newton, east side of the building, southeast corner of the parking lot.

Abies grandis, Hazelwood Cemetery, Abbotsford

Abies grandis, foliage

At eighty metres in height, Grand Fir is the largest and the fastest growing of the firs native to southwestern British Columbia. It typically grows at low to middle elevations on a range of sites from river flats to fairly dry slopes. It is easily identified because the long dark green needles lie flat in two ranks on either side of the branchlets. Both the upper and lower sides of the branchlet are visible because of the flat comb-like arrangement of the needles. The underside of the needles is characterized by two distinct horizontal rows of white stomata. When crushed, the foliage has the spicy smell of citrus. The bark is greyish-brown, smooth with resinous blisters. Mature trees often have a dome-shaped top. At one time Grand Fir was common but now large specimens are often remnants left in the landscape after urban development. It is not commonly grown as a landscape tree in the South Fraser Region.

Abies nordmanniana, Darts Hill
Garden Park, Surrey

Abies nordmanniana, foliage

This large stately fir, reaching eighteen metres at maturity, is native to the Caucasus area east of the Black Sea. It grows in its native range at altitudes of two thousand metres. The lustrous, almost black green needles point upward and forward and densely cover the branchlets. The underside of the needles is lined with white stomata. When crushed the needles smell of citrus. The buds are not or only slightly covered in resin. Nordmann Fir is rare in the South Fraser Region.

Where to see the trees:

Surrey

Darts Hill Garden Park, 1660- 168 St, South Surrey*, Garden Bed 30. This forty-year-old tree is twenty metres high with a DBH of 35 cm.

Abies pinsapo

Spanish Fir, Bottlebrush Fir or Hedgehog Fir

Native to Spain and occurring at altitudes of 1,500 metres there, Spanish Fir is a delightful addition to the landscape. It may reach thirty-five metres high in its native range. The needles, which radiate around the branchlet, are stubby and stiff like a bottlebrush, but do not pierce the hand when touched. The needles are typically olive green to pale blue and covered in a glaucous bloom. There is considerable variation in foliage colour much like the variability of the colour of *Picea pungens*, Colorado Blue Spruce seedlings. The Spanish Fir forms with

Where to see the trees:

Abbotsford

30195 Huntingdon Rd, two large trees on either side of the driveway.

Delta

4563- 46A St, Ladner, a large well-formed specimen with a 60 cm DBH.

Abies pinsapo

Spanish Fir, Bottlebrush Fir or
Hedgehog Fir

darker blue colour may be selected seedlings, or grafted and should be more properly called *Abies pinsapo* 'Glauca'. The rounded buds of the Spanish Fir tree are very resinous.

Abies pinsapo 'Glauca'

Silver Spanish Fir

Abies pinsapo 'Glauca', foliage

Abies pinsapo 'Glauca', Darts Hill Garden Park, Surrey

Where to see the trees:

Surrey

Darts Hill Garden Park, 1660- 168 St, South Surrey*, Garden Bed 29. This lovely forty-year-old tree is fifteen metres high with a DBH of 40 cm. A second large specimen can be found in Garden Bed 25.

The foliage of this cultivar is very glaucous blue in comparison to the species.

Noble Fir is native to the Cascade Mountains and the coastal mountains of Washington, Oregon and Northern California. In its native habitat Noble Fir grows to thirty metres tall. The bluish four-sided needles are twisted upward and clothe the top of the branchlets thickly. The lower surface of the branchlet is exposed due to the upswept needle pattern. The green cones, which when mature turn purplish brown, are very large, at least 10 cm wide and 20 cm long. Yellow bract tips come out of the cone scales and curve down, giving the cone a shaggy appearance.

Where to see the trees:
Surrey
Green Timbers Arboretum, 9800- 140 St, Whalley, a number of very large trees.

Acer campestre
Hedge Maple or Field Maple

Acer campestre, foliage

Hedge Maple is native to Europe and North Africa, where it grows ten to fifteen metres high with a round form. It is commonly grown all over North America, but is surprisingly uncommon in the South Fraser Region. The palm-sized leaves are three- to five-lobed. The lobes are very blunt, which distinguishes it from many other maples grown locally. The stem, when broken, bleeds a white milky sap. The dark green leaves remain on the tree late into the fall, and colour a golden yellow. The seed wings of the Hedge Maple's samara spread at 180-degree angles to one another.

Where to see the trees:
Delta
Jubilee Farm, later the Augustinian Monastery of British Columbia, 3900 Arthur Dr, Ladner. There is a large somewhat misshapen tree, due to the shading from taller neighbouring trees, on the south side of the building and a smaller shrubby tree to the north of the building.

Surrey
Green Timbers Arboretum, 9800- 140 St, Whalley, growing on the north side of the cooling and sorting shed.

Acer campestre 'Evelyn'
Queen Elizabeth ® Hedge Maple

Where to see the trees:

Langley

Fraser Hwy from 206 St to 207 St on both sides of the Fraser Hwy, Langley City.

Surrey

14510- 84 Ave, Fleetwood.

13931- 88 Ave, Whalley.

Queen Elizabeth® Maple is a medium-sized tree with an upright growth habit in youth. As the tree ages it becomes rounded with a flat top. The leaves are larger and darker green than Hedge Maple, *Acer campestre*. The branches are produced at a 45-degree angle to the trunk.

Acer capillipes
Red Snakebark Maple or Red Stripebark Maple

Acer capillipes, bark

Native to Japan, this small to medium-sized tree grows to thirteen metres high with an irregular round form. It is noted for its pale green and white vertical-striped bark. The toothed leaves are thin and soft, usually three-lobed, sometimes unlobed or five-lobed. They turn an outstanding red or orange-red in the fall. The leaf size and shape are very like *Acer rufinerve*, but *Acer capillipes* does not display the short bristly tufts of red hair on the veins on the bottom of the leaves. The samara, which hang in long chains are held at 120- 180 degrees from each other. The samara also has tufts of red hair. Red Snakebark Maple is an uncommon tree in the South Fraser Region.

Where to see the trees:

Richmond

Millennium Botanical Garden and Arboretum, N McLennan Community Park, Granville Ave and Garden City Rd.

Surrey

The Glades, 561- 172 St, South Surrey, on the north side of Garyland trail by a cedar log.

Cappadocicum Maple or Coliseum Maple

Acer cappadocicum, foliage.

Cappadocicum Maple is a large dome-shaped tree reaching twenty metres in height. It is native to the Caucasus, from the Himalayas to western China. The thin leaves are hand-sized, untoothed with five to seven lobes. The underside is tufted with hair on the leaf axils. The unfolding leaves in the spring are coppery while the summer colour is bright green. In the fall, the leaves turn a lovely clear yellow. When cut, the leaf stem exudes a white milky sap. The seed wings are held at 120-180 degrees from each other. Cappadocicum Maple is a very rare tree in the South Fraser Region.

Where to see the trees:

Delta

Jubilee Farm, later the Augustinian Monastery of British Columbia, 3900 Arthur Dr, Ladner, a massive specimen, approximately twenty-five metres high, with a DBH of 120 cm.

Rosedale

Minter Gardens, 52892 Bunker Rd, left of the main path, just beyond the footbridge.

Surrey

Green Timbers Arboretum, 9800- 140 St, Whalley, an open grown tree on the northwest side of the arboretum.

Fraser Health Region office, 14265- 56 Ave, Newton, a large tree on the east side of the building.

Acer cappadocicum 'Aureum'

Golden Cappadocicum Maple or Golden Coliseum Maple

The young leaves in the spring unfold reddish, turn yellow, and then as they mature, turn green and back to yellow again in the fall. Golden Cappadocicum Maple is very rare in the South Fraser Region.

Where to see the trees:

Richmond

Fantasy Garden World, 10800 No 5 Rd, in the southeast corner of the garden.

Acer circinatum
Vine Maple

Where to see the trees:

Richmond

Fantasy Garden World, 10800 No 5 Rd.

Millennium Botanical Garden and Arboretum, N McLennan Community Park, Granville Ave and Garden City Rd.

Steveston Park, 4111 Moncton St, Steveston.

Rosedale

Minter Gardens, 52892 Bunker Rd, just to the west of where the main garden path begins its one-way loop around the garden.

Surrey

City Hall, 14245- 56 Ave, Newton, west side of the building.

Crescent Park, 128 St and Crescent Road, South Surrey.

Darts Hill Garden Park, 1660- 168 St, South Surrey, Garden Bed 1.

Elgin Heritage Park, a lovely grove west of the Historic Stewart Farm located at 13723 Crescent Road, South Surrey.

The Glades, 561- 172 St, South Surrey, Azalea walk near the totem, pond side.

Acer circinatum, fall colour

Vine Maple is a small usually multi-stemmed tree, reaching ten metres in height with a vase to round shape. It is native to southwestern British Columbia and south into Washington and Oregon. It grows naturally along the edges of forests, streams and lakesides. The yellowish green leaves are almost circular in shape, with seven to nine lobes. The leaves of the Vine Maple are among the first trees to turn colour in the South Fraser Region. Often they begin to turn bright red and orange by the middle of August. The young twigs and youngest of the multiple trunks are often bright green or reddish green in colour. The wings of the green samara are held almost at a 180-degree angle to one another. The flower, while small, is quite colourful for a maple. The dark red and white flowers are clustered at the end of the shoots. Vine Maple is a very common tree in the parks and natural areas of the South Fraser Region.

Did You Know?

The common name for Vine Maple may have arisen since explorers portaging their boats up river found its flexible sprawling stems a nuisance. The tree often sends out branches, which become almost horizontal. These branches take root where they make contact with the earth. Colonies of these trees made portaging difficult, as climbing around and through the slippery limbs was almost impossible, hence the name Vine Maple.

Acer cratægifolium
Hawthorn Leaf Maple

Acer cratægifolium, fall colour, Darts Hill Garden Park, Surrey

Acer cratægifolium, foliage.

Hawthorn Leaf Maple is a native of Japan; it is rarely found in the South Fraser Region. Hawthorn Leaf Maple reaches a mature height of nine metres with an upright oval form. The small dark leaves are slightly three-lobed and have tiny rusty hairs on the underside. The trunk is weakly striped green and white. The fall colour is very variable ranging from yellow to red to dark purple.

Where to see the trees:
Surrey
Darts Hill Garden Park, 1660- 168 St, South Surrey, Garden Beds 8 and 29.

Acer davidii
Père David's Maple

Acer davidii, Darts Hill Garden Park, Surrey

Acer davidii, foliage

Père David's Maple is indigenous to China. It is a small to medium-sized tree, growing fifteen metres tall with an upright oval shape.

Acer davidii
Père David's Maple

Where to see the trees:

Richmond

Millennium Botanical Garden and Arboretum, N McLennan Community Park, Granville Ave and Garden City Rd.

Surrey

Darts Hill Garden Park, 1660- 168 St, South Surrey, Garden Beds 1 and 23.

The bark is very beautifully vertically striped white and green. The leaves are hand-sized, toothed but unlobed. If lobes are present, they are two tiny ones at the leaf base. The samara, which ripen in the late summer and fall, hang in long clusters. Père David's Maple is not common in the South Fraser Region.

Acer davidii 'Serpentine'
Serpentine Maple

Acer davidii 'Serpentine', fall colour

Where to see the trees:

Langley

Ground Effects Wholesale Nursery Ltd, 6123- 216 St, Milner, a small tree on the south side of the entry drive.

Rosedale

Minter Gardens, 52892 Bunker Rd, at the southern end of the Lake Garden.

The Serpentine Maple is a relatively recent introduction to our landscape, available locally since 1990. It has very attractive white-striped purple or brown branches. The lobed leaves are hand-sized with red stems.

Acer x *freemanii* 'Armstrong' Syn. *A. rubrum* 'Armstrong'
Armstrong Maple

Armstrong Maple is a hybrid between *Acer rubrum* and *Acer sacharrinum*. It combines the best features of each of its parents, the brilliant orange-red fall colour of the Red Maple and the drought tolerance of the Silver Maple.

Acer x *freemanii* 'Armstrong'
Syn. *A. rubrum* 'Armstrong'

Armstrong Maple

Acer x *freemanii* 'Armstrong',
City Park, Langley

Acer x *freemanii* 'Armstrong', foliage

Armstrong Maple grows fifteen metres in height. The leaves of Armstrong Maple resemble the Silver Maple parent more than the Red Maple, with its silver undersides, five-lobed leaf shape and long leaf stems. The silhouette of this fast-growing tree make it easy to identify as it maintains a very tight columnar form, gradually spreading out at maturity.

Where to see the trees:

Abbotsford

City Hall, 32315 South Fraser Way, southwest corner of the parking lot near Justice Way.

Delta

Police Station, 4455 Clarence Taylor Cr, Ladner. There are several good-sized trees on the east side of the building directly across the street.

Langley

Kwantlen University College, 20901 Langley Bypass, Langley City, two specimens at the east exit to the main campus.

City Park, 207 St and 48 Ave, Langley City. There are two specimens of good size on the east side of the park opposite 5004 and 5014- 207 St.

Richmond

5000 block Gilley Rd, Hamilton area, a row of street trees.

Acer x *freemanii* 'Morgan'

Morgan Maple

Morgan Maple will eventually develop a rounded oval shape at maturity. With its spectacular orange-red leaves it is superlative for fall interest. This very fast-growing tree, which grows to fifteen metres, has large and deeply lobed leaves.

Where to see the trees:

Chilliwack

Chilliwack Public Library, 45860- 1 Ave, one tree on the southwest corner of the building.

Salish Park, 45860- 1 Ave, a row along the parking lot.

Wells Landing Park, off Coach Lamp Dr, Sardis.

Acer x *freemanii* Scarlet Sentinel™
Syn. *Acer rubrum* 'Scarsen'

Scarlet Sentinel™ Maple

Where to see the trees:
Abbotsford
Median planting on McClure Rd from Clearbrook Rd to Gladwin Rd.

Chilliwack
Family Place, 45845 Wellington Ave.

South Sumas Rd on the north to south side from Tyson Rd to Wiltshire Rd, Sardis.

The large dark green foliage of this strongly upright rather narrow tree, which grows fifteen metres tall, makes it an excellent tree for streetscapes. In the fall, the five-lobed leaves, which closely resemble Silver Maple, turn yellow-orange to orange-red in colour.

Acer glabrum
Douglas Maple or
Rocky Mountain Maple

Where to see the trees:
Richmond
Millennium Botanical Garden and Arboretum, N McLennan Community Park, Granville Ave and Garden City Rd.

Small, growing to ten metres tall, and often shrubby, the Douglas Maple is native to the coastal and interior regions of British Columbia. Its palm-sized leaves are three- to five-lobed and coarsely toothed. The fall colour is a bright orange to red. The two large wings of the samara are held in a "V" shape or almost parallel. Douglas Maple is often found growing on drier more open sites than its cousin Vine Maple. It is drought tolerant, and with its small size and neat habit would make a suitable choice for a dry-land landscape. This tree is not common in the planted landscape, but is found on the rocky slopes of the mountains surrounding the Fraser Valley.

Acer griseum
Paperbark Maple

This elegant small to medium-sized maple, which reaches ten to fifteen metres in height, is native to China. Paperbark Maple is distinctive for several reasons. The beautiful reddish tan coloured bark peels away in curly threads and papery swatches. The foliage is also unusual for

Acer griseum, Kwantlen University College, Langley

Acer griseum, bark

Acer griseum, leaves.

a maple in that it is trifoliate; the leaf is divided into three blunt-toothed leaflets. The leaves are a soft blue-green on top and a paler grey-green on the bottom. The leaflets turn a rich orange-red in the late fall. The wings of the samara are held in a wide V-shape.

Did You Know?

The species name griseum is Latinized from the French word for the colour grey, "gris", which refers to the greyish-whitish underside of the tri-foliate leaf.

Where to see the trees:

Abbotsford

5471 Mt Lehman Rd.

Chilliwack

University College of the Fraser Valley, 45600 Airport Rd, northeast corner of Building C, Health Sciences.

Langley

Kwantlen University College, 20901 Langley Bypass, Langley City, three small specimens planted in 1995 at the entrance to the Field Lab.

Hazelgrove Farm, 8651 Glover Rd, Ft Langley.

Richmond

Millenium Botanical Garden and Arboretum, N McLennan Community Park, Granville Ave and Garden City Rd.

Fantasy Garden World, 10800 No 5 Rd.

Rosedale

Minter Gardens, 52892 Bunker Rd, north end of the Playground area.

Surrey

The Glades, 561- 172 St, South Surrey, Garyland at the log.

Darts Hill Garden Park, 1660- 168 St, South Surrey, Garden Bed 14.

Acer japonicum

Full Moon Maple or Downy Japanese Maple

Acer japonicum, foliage

Acer japonicum, emerging leaves and flowers

Where to see the trees:

Langley

Canada Trust, 19653 Willowbrook Dr, Willoughby.

Surrey

Darts Hill Garden Park, 1660- 168 St, South Surrey, Garden Bed 26.

Full Moon Maple, native to Japan, is a small attractive tree much like its very common cousin *Acer palmatum*. In comparison, Full Moon Maple is very rare in the South Fraser Region. It can be differentiated from *Acer palmatum* by its downy leaf stalk, larger and nine- to eleven-lobed rounded leaf. The fall colour of this maple is red or sometimes yellow. The wings of the samara are held nearly horizontal to one another or in a very wide "V" shape, looking like the propeller of an airplane. Full Moon Maple reaches nine metres at maturity with a round shape.

Acer japonicum 'Aconitifolium'

Fernleaf (Full Moon) Maple or Cutleaf (Full Moon) Maple

Acer japonicum 'Acontifolium', foliage

Acer japonicum 'Acontifolium', fall colour.

Acer japonicum 'Aconitifolium'
Fernleaf (Full Moon) Maple or Cutleaf (Full Moon) Maple

Growing three metres tall, Fernleaf Maple is more commonly planted than the species, *Acer japonicum*, which is mentioned above. This Maple lives up to its name; each of its large leaf lobes are dissected and sharply toothed, looking like the divided fronds of a fern. The overall appearance is delightful, particularly in the fall when the leaves turn crimson red.

Where to see the trees:
Langley

Kwantlen University College, 20901 Langley Bypass, Langley City, one small specimen planted in 1996 at the east side of the base of the Highway 10 overpass to the Field Lab.

Surrey

Darts Hill Garden Park, 1660- 168 St, South Surrey, Garden Bed 10.

Rosedale

Minter Gardens, 52892 Bunker Rd, directly to the west of the pond in the Lake Garden.

Acer macrophyllum
Bigleaf Maple

Acer macrophyllum, early spring, Redwood Park, Surrey

Acer macrophyllum, trunk

Huge dinner plate-sized leaves characterize this maple, which has the largest leaves of any native Canadian tree and the largest maple leaf in the world. Bigleaf Maple is native to southwestern British Columbia and south of the border, always growing within 320 kilometres of

Acer macrophyllum
Bigleaf Maple

Where to see the trees:
Abbotsford

33882 Elm St, a huge open-grown tree.

Hogan Family Nature Park, 2860 block Debruyne Rd, several very big trees in the park, one of the larger trees with a DBH of 122 cm.

Upper Sumas Elementary School, 36321 Vye Rd, a large tree with a DBH of 120 cm to the southwest of the school.

Dunach Park, NW corner of Mt Lehman Rd and Downes Rd, several large trees with a DBH of 120 cm.

John Mahoney Park, the entrance at the north end of Adanac St, three good-sized trees.

McMillan Elementary School, 2310 McMillan Rd.

Chilliwack

On Camp River Rd from Chapman Rd to Gill Rd, East Chilliwack, a farm row of huge Bigleaf Maples, some 100 cm and more in diameter.

Chilliwack Cemeteries, 10010 Hillcrest Dr, Little Mountain, a picturesque tree sited on a knoll with Mt Cheam in the background.

Canadian Forces Base, Keith Wilson Rd and Vedder Rd, Vedder Crossing, on the north side of Calais Cr at Scheldt Rd.

48685 McConnell Rd, East Chilliwack, the fifth largest Bigleaf Maple in British Columbia with a circumference of 8.99 m and a height of 26.8 metres and a DBH of 200 cm, a second tree on the property is almost as large.

Delta

Jubilee Farm, later the Augustinian Monastery of British Columbia, 3900 Arthur Dr, Ladner, a massive specimen.

Sunbury Park, Centre St and Dunlop Rd, North Delta, several good-sized trees to the north of the baseball diamond on the slope down to the historic fishing village of Annieville.

the coast. The gigantic dark green leaves are five- to seven-lobed and turn a clear yellow to mustard colour in the fall. When cut, the leaf stalk exudes a white milky sap. The small yellow flowers are quite showy, appearing in early spring, at the same time as the leaves are unfurling. They hang in long cylindrical clusters from the branchlets. The huge samaras are hairy and drift down from their lofty perches, twirling like tops in September and October. Bigleaf Maple is a very common tree in all of the communities of the South Fraser Region. It grows to thirty metres in height with a round to upright oval form.

Did You Know?

When Great Britain declared war on Germany on August 4, 1914, bringing Canada into the First World War, the population of Langley Township was just a few thousand. During the summer of 1914, a group of men, known as the Langley Volunteers, drilled both on foot (in the hall at Murray's Corners) and on horseback. Grocer Arthur Johnston, Municipal Administrator Archie Payne, and Doctor Benjamin Butler Marr were prominent among the organizers. Dr. Marr was the first Langley man to offer his services officially and was enlisted in August of 1914. By September the Langley Volunteers were gazetted as "C" Squadron, 31 BC Horse (Mounted Rifles). While overseas in a hospital in France, Marr and Payne made a pact that if they returned to Langley, they would attempt to have Langley's streets renamed in honour of those who had died on active service. Both men did return, and Marr in particular, set about creating a series of memorials to the fallen. These included two cenotaphs, one in Murrayville Cemetery and one in Fort Langley Cemetery; the renaming of many local

Acer macrophyllum, Cenotaph in the Murrayville Cemetery, Langley.

roads, and the planting of a series of commemorative trees. As many as thirty-five trees were planted during the early 1920's throughout Langley Township in honour of Langley's war dead. These trees, planted at intersections were primarily Bigleaf Maple. Very few of these trees survive today. Trees which survive and which may with some certainty be identified with a particular soldier are listed adjacent with the soldier's name in brackets. A small triangular white fence originally enclosed each tree. One of the three posts supporting the fence was taller than the others, and a crosspiece affixed to it bore the surname of the individual commemorated. Two hundred and eighty men and boys from the Langley area enlisted or were drafted into the Canadian forces during the years 1914 to 1918. Of these, approximately one in ten did not return home.

In an interview, Alf Trattle, son of Alfred William Trattle, who died in the first World War at Vimy Ridge, said, "My father died when I was around five. My younger brother never got a chance to know him, so this tree has been nice for the family. Our family knew the Marrs quite well," Trattle continued, adding that Dr. Marr delivered him as a baby. "That was how it was then, neighbours knew each other and helped each other. You see Dr. Marr planted those trees for my dad and the other men. He wanted to honour those men and he did".[1]

Where to see the trees:

Langley

8820 Nash St, Fort Langley, this is one of the largest Bigleaf Maples in British Columbia with a circumference of 7.5 metres and a DBH of 240 cm. It is easily viewed in the front garden.

Traffic Island, Glover Rd at 96 Ave, Ft Langley (A.W. Wilson, planted in 1923).

SW corner of Trattle St and 96 Ave, Ft Langley (Alfred William Trattle, died in 1917 at Vimy Ridge, tree planted in 1923).

SW corner of Wright St and 96 Ave, Ft Langley (Jessie Wright, tree planted in 1923).

SE corner of Glover Rd and 216 St, Milner (Art Johnston).

23245- 40 Ave, Southeast Langley.

Richmond

2100 Stirling Ave, Burkeville, a well-shaped tree.

18960 River Rd, East Richmond, a large tree with a DBH of 160 cm.

Millennium Botanical Garden and Arboretum, N McLennan Community Park, Granville Ave and Garden City Rd.

Surrey

Hazelmere Cemetery, 19184- 16 Ave, South Surrey

Redwood Park, 17900- 20 Ave, South Surrey.

1 Tamminga, M. "Uprooting History", *The Langley Times*, Sunday, January 6, 2002, page 11.

Acer negundo

Box Elder, Manitoba Maple, or Ash-leaved Maple

Acer negundo, foliage

Box Elder is native to southern Ontario and Manitoba, where it grows twenty metres tall with an upright oval form. With its three to seven pale green leaflets, it is the only native Canadian maple with compound leaves. The fall colour is often a good yellow. The tree is dioecious, meaning that there are male and female trees. The winged samara, produced only by the female tree, is an excellent winter identifier as the long chains of nearly parallel wings hang in the tree for many months. Box Elder is rarely cultivated in the South Fraser Region.

Where to see the trees:

Langley

6690- 216 St, Milner, a row of four trees.

7296 Telegraph Trail, Northeast Langley, a row of four mature male trees.

Richmond

Fantasy Garden World, 10800 No 5 Rd.

Burkeville Park, 1031 Lancaster Cr, Burkeville, a number of large trees in this small park.

1051 Wellington Cr, Burkeville.

Acer negundo 'Variegatum'

Variegated Box Elder

Acer negundo 'Variegatum', toppled over in 2001

Acer negundo 'Variegatum', foliage and developing samara

Acer negundo 'Variegatum'
Variegated Box Elder

Variegated Box Elder is relatively common in the South Fraser Region. It grows fifteen metres tall with a round shape. Variegated Box Elder is a female clone with leaflets that are edged creamy-white, or entirely white in colour. Occasionally individual branches will revert back to the green type and must be pruned out to maintain the appearance of the tree. The samara are also variegated, the seed green and the wing white. In the dormant period, Variegated Box Elder has a very shaggy, unkempt appearance.

Where to see the trees:

Langley
4986- 203 St, Langley City.

Rosedale
Minter Gardens, 52892 Bunker Rd.

Surrey
City Hall, 14245- 56 Ave, Newton, between the Provincial Courthouse and the City Hall.

Acer palmatum
Japanese Maple

Acer palmatum, Williams Park, Langley

Japanese Maple, native to southwest China, Korea and Japan, is very commonly planted in all the communities of the South Fraser Region. It is usually a small multi-trunked tree with slender green or red branches and stems. The leaves are variable in size but usually have five to seven palmate midgreen lobes and turn brilliant flame-like colours in the fall. It is a very delicate and airy tree, often used as a focal plant in the landscape. Reaching six to eight metres tall at maturity, Japanese Maple has a horizontal oval form.

Where to see the trees:
Abbotsford
33511 Rainbow Ave, a huge specimen.

2324 Lobban Ave, two splendid trees.

34665 Mila St.

Dunach Elementary School, 30357 Downes Rd, two large trees along the east fence line.

Abbotsford City Hall, 32315 South Fraser Way, a group on the north side of the building.

Provincial Courthouse, 32202 South Fraser Way, on the south side of the building.

Chilliwack
Municipal Hall, 8550 Young Rd.

46399 Chilliwack Central Rd.

10040 Timberline Pl.

Salish Park, 45860- 1 Ave.

Skelton Park, opposite Chilliwack Municipal Hall at 8550 Young Rd.

NW corner of Spadina Ave and Corbould St.

45655 Kipp Ave.

Acer palmatum
Japanese Maple

Acer palmatum, fall colour

Where to see the trees:

Delta

Ladner Community Centre, 4734- 51 St, Ladner.

Langley

Michaud Heritage House, 5202- 204 St, Langley City, a lovely mature specimen.

Sendall Gardens, 20166- 50 Ave, Langley City, several wonderful specimens to the south of the house and at the northwest side of the parking lot.

Telegraph Trail, Northeast Langley.

Williams Park, 6600 block 238 St, Salmon River Uplands.

Richmond

2040 Stirling Ave, Burkeville.

Millennium Botanical Garden and Arboretum, N McLennan Community Park, Granville Ave and Garden City Rd.

Fantasy Garden World, 10800 No 5 Rd.

Steveston Park, 4111 Moncton St, Steveston. A number of trees in the park and a row of trees planted under the larger Variegated Maples adjacent to Moncton Street, south of the children's playground.

Rosedale

Minter Gardens, 52892 Bunker Rd, several good-sized specimens, a well formed one north of the maze.

Acer palmatum Atropurpureum Group

Acer palmatum Atropurpureum Group, 96 Avenue, Fort Langley

This group name applies to any seedling or cultivar with reddish or purplish foliage. Many Redleaf Japanese Maple cultivars are listed in nursery catalogues and commonly found in landscapes throughout the South Fraser Region. Commonly growing 8–10 metres in height, Redleaf Japanese Maple has a horizontal oval form.

Did You Know?

The huge Redleaf Japanese Maple at 23137- 96 Ave, Ft Langley, with a DBH of 45 cm is likely a remnant of the elaborately landscaped grounds of the estate home constructed by architect Charles Edward Hope in 1909 and called "Illahie" or in Salish "My Home." The main house burned down in 1929 but the carriage house of the two-hectare estate is just a stone's throw away from the Redleaf Japanese Maple at 23155- 96 Ave.

Where to see the trees:

Abbotsford
MSA General Hospital, 2179 McCallum Rd, at the Emergency entrance, a very lovely mature tree.

Delta
Delta Arts Centre, 11489- 84 Ave.

Langley
23137- 96 Ave, Ft Langley.

Dr. Marr residence, 9090 Glover Rd, Ft Langley.

Sendall Gardens, 20166- 50 Ave, Langley City, a wonderful specimen at the entry to the garden on the southeast side of the parking lot.

Richmond
Fantasy Garden World, 10800 No 5 Rd.

Steveston Park, 4111 Moncton St, Steveston, in the interior courtyard of the Japanese Canadian Cultural Centre.

Surrey
Peace Arch Park, King George Hwy and 0 Ave, South Surrey*.

Acer palmatum 'Butterfly'

Butterfly Japanese Maple

Butterfly Japanese Maple grows 3.5–4.5 metres tall with a vase form. The deeply divided small leaves of this unusual cultivar are mostly grey-green, edged with creamy white and when young, have a pink tinge to them. The branch-

Acer palmatum 'Butterfly'
Butterfly Japanese Maple

Where to see the trees:
Rosedale

Minter Gardens, 52892 Bunker Rd, several reasonable sized specimens in the garden, one at the west side of the entrance to the Chinese Penjing Garden.

Surrey

Darts Hill Garden Park, 1660- 168 St, South Surrey, Garden Bed 15a

Acer palmatum 'Butterfly', variegated foliage

lets are purple and held stiffly upright. The leaves are tinted with magenta in the fall. The overall effect is very showy.

Acer palmatum Dissectum Atropurpureum Group

Red Laceleaf Maple or Red Threadleaf Maple

This group name applies to any seedling or cultivar with reddish, purplish or bronze-coloured leaves that has finely dissected foliage. Many Red Laceleaf Maple cultivars are listed in nursery catalogues and commonly grown in landscapes throughout the South Fraser Region. Red Laceleaf Maple has weeping branches with an umbrella shape. It is a small tree growing three metres or less in height.

Where to see the trees:
Delta

Southwest corner of Arthur Dr and 47 Ave, Ladner.

Langley

Canada Trust, 19653 Willowbrook Dr, Willoughby.

Kwantlen University College, 20901 Langley Bypass, Langley City.

Richmond

Steveston Park, 4111 Moncton St, Steveston.

Acer palmatum Dissectum Atropurpureum Group, Kwantlen University College

Acer palmatum 'Linearilobum'

**Strapleaf Maple or
Fingerleaf Maple**

Acer palmatum 'Villa Toranto', a linearilobum Maple cultivar.

This group name applies to *Acer palmatum* cutivars that have very narrow, widely spaced, strap-like leaf lobes. The leaves are almost divided or dissected to the base of the leaf. This group is not as common as Redleaf Japanese Maples or Laceleaf Japanese Maples and usually grows less than three metres tall.

Where to see the trees:
Rosedale
Minter Gardens, 52892 Bunker Rd, north end of the Meadow Garden.

Acer palmatum 'Sango Kaku'

Coralbark Maple

Acer palmatum 'Sango Kaku'.

Coralbark Maple is grown almost exclusively for the outstanding display of red colour on the young stems. This tree makes a good winter foil for the occasional snowfall in the South Fraser Region. Reaching a mature height of six metres, Coralbark Maple has a vase shape in youth. The leaves are small and light green throughout the growing season, turning yellow in the fall.

Where to see the trees:
Surrey
City Hall, 14245- 56 Ave, Newton, on the east face of the retaining wall to the south of the east parking lot.

Darts Hill Garden Park, 1660- 168 St, South Surrey, Garden Bed 33.

The Glades, 561- 172 St, South Surrey, on the south side of the driveway.

Acer palmatum 'Sazanami'

Sazanami Maple

Where to see the trees:

Surrey

City Hall, 14245- 56 Ave, Newton, two very fine mature trees near the south-east corner of the building.

Acer palmatum 'Sazanami', City Hall, Surrey

Sazanami Maple is noted for its very tiny green leaves, among the smallest of all the Japanese Maples. The fall colour is an outstanding golden yellow that warms a cold October day. Sazanami Maple grows five to nine metres tall with a round form.

Acer palmatum 'Shishigashira'

Crested Maple or Lion's Mane Maple

Where to see the trees:

Abbotsford

2001 Marshall Rd, two small trees on either side of the front entry to the building.

Chilliwack

6025 Glenmore Dr, Sardis, a young tree.

Richmond

Fantasy Garden World, 10800 No 5 Rd.

Rosedale

Minter Gardens, 52892 Bunker Rd, near the Floral Ladies.

Surrey

Darts Hill Garden Park, 1660- 168 St, South Surrey, Garden Bed 19.

The Glades, 561- 172 St, South Surrey, at the lattice fence.

Acer palmatum 'Shishigashira', foliage

With its tightly held small leaves, Crested Maple presents an unusual appearance. The dark green seven-lobed leaves are wrinkled and compactly held on short upright branchlets. From a distance, the tree has a ropelike look. Crested Maple grows three to four metres tall with a distinct vase shape.

Moosewood, Striped Maple or Stripebark Maple

Native to the northeast United States and southeastern Canada, Moosewood is a small to medium round tree, reaching a mature height of ten metres. The light green leaves have three forward-pointing lobes and a doubly serrated margin. The flowers and fruit are produced in pendulous clusters. The wings of the samara are held at 90 degrees to one another. The stems and bark are the most outstanding features of this maple. Immature stems are greenish or red-brown while older stems and bark are bright green and strongly striped with white vertical lines. The greenish white stripes eventually turn grey and darken in colour.

Acer pensylvanicum, bark

Where to see the trees:

Surrey

Darts Hill Garden Park, 1660- 168 St, South Surrey, Garden Bed C4.

Acer platanoides

Norway Maple

Acer platanoides, Fort Langley Community Hall, Langley

Acer platanoides, flowers

A European native, Norway Maple is one of the most common cultivated trees in the South Fraser Region. It is a tall robust tree reaching eighteen to twenty-one metres with a round form. Each of the large hand-sized leaves is five-lobed with finely pointed sharp tips.

Acer platanoides

Norway Maple

Where to see the trees:

Abbotsford

Eldridge Rd, west of North Parallel Rd, a farm row of trees on the north side of Eldridge Rd.

Hougen Park, south off Highway 1 on Cole Rd.

Upper Sumas Elementary School, 36321 Vye Rd, three large trees on the east side of the school.

Chilliwack

Canadian Forces Base, Keith Wilson Rd and Vedder Rd, Vedder Crossing, south of the RCMP Complex on Calais Cr.

Delta

Hospital, 5800 Mountain View Blvd, Ladner, east side of the parking lot.

Langley

20300 block 53 Ave, Langley City.

Dr. Marr residence, 9090 Glover Rd, Ft Langley.

Fort Langley National Historic Site, 23433 Mavis St, Ft Langley.

Fort Langley Community Hall, 9167 Glover Rd, Ft Langley.

Richmond

Southarm Park, Garden City Rd and Williams Rd.

The leaves, midgreen to dark green in the growing season, turn butter yellow in the fall. When cut, the stems exude a white milky sap. The small yellowish green flowers are somewhat showy, appearing in mid to late March, as the young leaves are unfurling. The large plump dormant bud is characteristically a greenish maroon to purple in colour. The large winged samaras are held almost horizontally to one another and sometimes persist on the tree into the winter months.

Did You Know?

Doctor Benjamin Butler Marr (1882- 1939) planted the Norway Maples at his home at 9090 Glover Road in Fort Langley in the early 1920's. He called the trees "Oregon Maples." Dr. Marr was the first medical practitioner in the Langley area. He kept a large stable of fine horses and gave each one a good workout with daily long-distance gallops as he made his house calls. He was a fine rider but was injured on his wedding day in 1913 when he was racing to the church with his best man. A trace broke causing the wheels of the buggy they were riding in to jam. The buggy flipped over, throwing Dr. Marr's friend clear. Marr was dragged by the horses and suffered a broken collarbone and three cracked ribs. To the consternation of his young seventeen-year-old bride, Isabel Drew, the daughter of the local blacksmith, he arrived at the church bloodied and bruised but on time. Following the wedding ceremony the wedding party, accompanied by most of the town, travelled by charter boat to New Westminster. Marr briefly checked into the Royal Columbian Hospital prior to departing on his honeymoon to Alaska. Dr Marr was one of the individuals responsible for the commemorative tree-planting program throughout Langley Township in honour of the World War I dead.

When Dr. Marr bought his first car in 1919 after the First World War, he was shown how to drive and reverse the car by the garage owner. Dr. Marr backed out of the garage, across Yale Road and into the ditch, shouting, "Whoa, Whoa."

Acer platanoides
Norway Maple

The Fort Langley Community Improvement Society planted the Norway Maple trees on the lawn of the Fort Langley Community Hall in 1931. According to tradition, the trees on the north side of the hall were planted by the men of the community while those trees on the south were planted by the women of the community. Though not First World War commemorative trees, these trees are historically significant, providing an early example of the sort of community spirit that can still be found in communities throughout the Fraser Valley today. The economic and social conditions in the "Dirty Thirties" inspired many community groups to band together; the result was the construction of a number of these early halls, which stand as a testament to each community and their gritty determination to survive. The Fort Langley Community Hall, constructed by volunteer labour in an uplifting Classical Revival Architectural style is a very impressive landmark, framed beautifully by the two rows of Norway Maples. It was designated a Municipal Heritage Site in 1979. The Norway Maples were topped or beheaded about twenty years ago. They have received restorative pruning and appear ready to grow an additional seventy years.

Acer platanoides, Marr House, Langley.

"Whosoever beheads a tree shall himself likewise be beheaded."

A law of Otto the Great of Germany (912- 973AD)

Acer platanoides 'Columnare'
Columnar Maple

Columnar Maple, as the name suggests, is a Norway Maple cultivar with very dense columnar growth with branches that spread out at a 60-90-degree angle from the parent stem. The dark green leaves are often smaller than the species. Columnar Maple reaches a height of eighteen metres at maturity.

Where to see the trees:

Chilliwack

South Sumas Rd on the north to south side from Tyson Rd to Wiltshire Rd, Sardis.

University College of the Fraser Valley, 45600 Airport Rd, east of Building G, Childcare Centre.

Langley

Douglas Cr, Langley City, a street tree planting.

Surrey

13966- 29 Ave, South Surrey.

2873- 139A St, South Surrey.

Acer platanoides 'Crimson King'
Crimson King Maple

Where to see the trees:

Abbotsford

5500 block Bradner Rd, on the east side of the road.

5486 Riverside Rd, Matsqui Prairie, two trees.

McKee Blvd, a street tree planting.

Chilliwack

Fairfield Island Park, 46000 Clare Ave, Fairfield Island.

Portage Park, Portage Av and Woodbine St.

Stó:lo Centre, 7201 Vedder Rd, Sardis.

Yarrow Central Park, southeast corner of Kehler St and Yarrow Central Rd, several large specimens.

Reimer's Nursery Ltd, 4586 No 3 Rd, Yarrow.

Delta

4411- 50 St, Ladner.

Langley

20300 block 53 Ave, Langley City.

Belmont Dairy Farms, 21151 Old Yale Rd, Murrayville.

Langley Lawn Cemetery, 4393- 208 St, Southwest Langley. This splendid tree dominates the skyline of the cemetery.

Richmond

Fantasy Garden World, 10800 No 5 Rd.

Surrey

Darts Hill Garden Park, 1660- 168 St, South Surrey, Garden Bed 8.

Peace Arch Park, King George Hwy and 0 Ave, South Surrey*.

The Glades, 561- 172 St, South Surrey.

Acer platanoides 'Crimson King', Lawn Cemetery, Langley

Crimson King Maple is the most commonly planted purple-leafed form of Norway Maple in the South Fraser Region. The dark purple leaf colour persists throughout the growing season. The maroon-yellow flowers are particularly attractive against the unfolding new leaves. The fall colour of the leaves is a lovely maroon to reddish bronze. Crimson King does not grow as large as the species, reaching fifteen metres in height with a round form.

Did You Know?

Nick Reimer planted the lovely row of Crimson King Maple trees on the south property line of his Yarrow nursery in 1955-56.
• The Berry Family planted the large Crimson King Maple at Belmont Dairy Farms in Langley in 1921.
• Murray Stephen planted the large Crimson King Maple in The Glades on March 15, 1956, marking the beginning of the development of this superb Rhododendron garden.

Crimson Sentry Maple

Where to see the trees:

Chilliwack

Fairfield Island Park, 46000 Clare Ave, Fairfield Island.

Langley

Kwantlen University College, 20901 Langley Bypass, Langley City, two small specimens at the west entry to the main campus on Glover Road.

Surrey

2026- 160 St, South Surrey.

2082- 136A St, South Surrey.

Acer platanoides 'Crimson Sentry', foliage.

Crimson Sentry Maple, which originated as a bud sport of Crimson King Maple, is much smaller, more compact and dense than its parent. Crimson Sentry Maple reaches 7.5- 8 metres in height with an upright oval shape. The foliage is similar, deep purple in the growing season, turning to maroon to reddish brown in the fall.

Did You Know?

Chilliwack parks horticulturalists, Bruce Broughton, Dick Hayward, Kevin Maxwell and Al Nichol designed and planted the front entrance and parking area of Fairfield Island Park in 1977 with Crimson Sentry Maples.

Deborah Maple

Deborah Maple is a colourful selection of Norway Maple. It has a vigorous growth habit, growing fourteen metres in height with a round shape. The leaves in the spring are orange-red, turning green and red. The fall colour is a good yellow-orange.

Did You Know?

Deborah Maple was selected from an *Acer platanoides* 'Schwedleri' seedling by John Mathies, a Chilliwack nursery grower and introduced into the nursery trade in 1975- 76 by his company, Cannor Nurseries Ltd. of Chilliwack. Deborah Maple is named after his eldest daughter.

Where to see the trees:

Chilliwack

South Sumas Rd on the north to south side from Tyson Rd to Wiltshire Rd, Sardis.

Dover Place Cul-de-sac, Sardis.

Surrey

11091- 163A St, Guildford, a street tree planting.

11102- 163A St, Guildford, a street tree planting.

3637- 156A St, South Surrey.

3662- 156A St, South Surrey.

Acer platanoides 'Drummondii'

Harlequin Maple or Silver Variegated Maple

Harlequin Maple has striking bright green leaves edged with creamy-white. It grows ten metres tall with an upright oval form.

Where to see the trees:

Chilliwack

The Waverly, 8445 Young St.

Townsend Park, southwest corner of Wolfe Rd and Ashwell St, at the west end of the park.

Sardis Senior Secondary School, 45460 Stevenson Rd, Sardis, on the south side of the Chilliwack Track.

Surrey

15522- 19 Ave, South Surrey.

9036- 144A St, Whalley.

Acer platanoides 'Emerald Queen'

Emerald Queen Maple

Emerald Queen Maple is a very fast growing oval-shaped tree. It reaches a mature height of fifteen metres. The leathery leaves emerge a reddish-purple in colour and mature to a deep glossy green. The fall colour is a beautiful clear yellow.

Where to see the trees:

Chilliwack

10495 Reeves Rd, East Chilliwack, a farm entry row of good-sized trees.

Little Mountain Elementary School, 9900 Carlton St, Hope River Trail Extension.

University College of the Fraser Valley, 45600 Airport Rd, Chilliwack, an entry row of trees at the Meadowbrook Drive entrance.

South Sumas Rd on the north to south side from Tyson Rd to Wiltshire Rd, Sardis.

Acer platanoides 'Globosum'
Globe Norway Maple

Acer platanoides 'Globosum', Boundary Bay Road, Delta.

Acer platanoides 'Globosum', foliage.

Globe Norway Maple is a small top-grafted tree with a dense round crown, shaped like a pom-pom. It grows 4.5 metres tall with a dense, tight habit, creating a very formal appearance. The foliage of Globe Norway Maple emerges reddish-green, ages to medium green, and turns yellow in the fall.

Where to see the trees:

Delta

NE boulevard 3 Ave and Boundary Bay Rd, Boundary Bay.

Surrey

14559- 82 Ave, Fleetwood, a street tree planting.

16281- 110A Ave, Fleetwood, a street tree planting.

68th Ave, between 127th St and 128th St, Newton, a street tree planting.

Acer platanoides 'Royal Red'
Royal Red Maple

With its deep purple leaves and maroon to reddish-bronze fall colour, Royal Red Maple is similar to Crimson King Maple. It may be a hardier selection than Crimson King Maple. Eventually Royal Red Maple becomes a rounded medium-sized tree reaching twelve metres in height.

Where to see the trees:

Chilliwack

5450- 5575 Cedar Creek Rd, Promontory Heights, a street tree planting.

Little Mountain Elementary School, 9900 Carleton St.

Fairfield Island Park, 46000 Clare Ave, Fairfield Island, by the bleachers on the soccer fields.

Did You Know?

The row of trees planted along the edge of Little Mountain Elementary School in Chilliwack was planted in 1998 to 1999. Each division of students, grades one to six in the school, were allotted a tree and assisted with the planting of their tree.

Acer platanoides 'Royal Red'
Royal Red Maple

On South Sumas Rd from Silverthorne east, Sardis.

Sardis Park, Britton Ave parking lot, Sardis.

Sardis Senior Secondary School, 45460 Stevenson Rd, Sardis, on the south side of Chilliwack Track.

Skelton Park, opposite Chilliwack Municipal Hall at 8550 Young Rd.

Townsend Park, SW corner of Ashwell Rd and Hodgins Ave, a mixed planting of Royal Red Maple and Linden on the north side of the field and two trees in the playground area.

Surrey

2067- 138A St, South Surrey.

2115- 138A St, South Surrey.

15455- 19 Ave, South Surrey.

Acer platanoides 'Schwedleri'
Schwedler Norway Maple

Acer platanoides 'Schwedleri', foliage, Jubilee Farm, later the Augustinian Monastery of British Columbia

Acer platanoides 'Schwedleri', foliage

Schwedler Norway Maple grows eighteen metres tall with a round to upright oval shape. The leaves of this older form of Norway Maple begin purplish red in the spring and turn green with purple venation during the growing season. Fall colour is purple, orange and red.

Where to see the trees:
Abbotsford

Hougen Park, south off Highway 1 on Cole Rd.

Delta

Jubilee Farm, later the Augustinian Monastery of British Columbia, 3900 Arthur Dr, Ladner. There is a very tall tree with a substantial height of twenty-four metres, which provides a stunning backdrop for the religious shrine in the northwest corner of the property.

Acer pseudoplatanus
Sycamore Maple or Planetree Maple

Acer pseudoplatanus, flowers

Acer pseudoplatanus, 154 Street, Cloverdale, Surrey

Sycamore Maple is very commonly found in the South Fraser Region. It reaches a mature height of eighteen metres with a round form. The dark green leaves of this maple are hand-sized, thick, often with a wrinkled texture. The three-lobed to five-lobed leaves are light green or greenish white in colour on the underside. Nondescript mustard-yellow fall colour is the norm. The yellowish flowers are produced in May on pendulous cone-shaped inflorescences. The dormant buds are bright green unlike the similar but purple-coloured buds of Norway Maple. The bark on mature trees is orangish brown. The bark flakes and peels in a similar manner to *Platanus* x *hispanica*, London Plane or Sycamore, hence the common name, Sycamore Maple. The samaras are held almost parallel to each other.

Did You Know?

Hawthorne Grove, owned by William and Edna Kirkland, was built in 1911. It became a centre of community social life in Ladner. The newly organized Lawn and Bowling Club used the lawns of Hawthorne Grove for their games and practices in 1917.
• James Brunton, senior, constructed the cute California-bungalow-style house at 4644- 51 St, Ladner in 1925 for Alex Scott. In the 1920's, Alex Scott

Where to see the trees:
Abbotsford

Hougen Park, south off Highway 1 on Cole Rd.

38819 Vye Rd, a splendid tree on the north side of the road.

Chilliwack

Gwynne Vaughan Park, Williams Rd and Hope River Rd, Fairfield Island.

Stó:lo Centre, 7201 Vedder Rd, Sardis.

47813 McGuire Rd, Sardis, a magnificent old farm row of several different species of trees on the south side of the road including two huge Sycamore Maples.

Canadian Forces Base, Keith Wilson Rd and Vedder Rd, Vedder Crossing, two trees southwest on Calais Cr at Caen Rd.

Delta

Jubilee Farm, later the Augustinian Monastery of British Columbia, 3900 Arthur Dr, Ladner, two massive specimens, one with a DBH of 115 cm.

Hawthorne Grove, The Kirkland Residence, 4026 (4140) Arthur Dr, Ladner.

Scott House, 4644- 51 St, Ladner.

Langley

Murrayville Cemetery, 21405- 44 Ave, Murrayville.

Trinity Western University, 7600 Glover Rd, Willoughby.

Acer pseudoplatanus

Sycamore Maple or Planetree Maple

Richmond
London Heritage Farm, 6511 Dyke Rd, Steveston.

NE corner of Finn Rd and No 4 Rd, a very attractive row planting.

12004 No 2 Rd, Steveston, a row of three very good specimens.

Surrey
18537- 54 Ave, Cloverdale.

was a grocer in Ladner and later became the owner of the local pool hall.

• London Heritage Farm is a 1.9-hectare site overlooking the south arm of the Fraser River. The London brothers built the farmhouse in the 1880's. The house has been fully restored and furnished to recreate early farm life in Richmond. It is open to the public. An attractive traditional herb and flower garden, a rose arbour and fruit trees and a fruit garden can be found on the east side of the house. When the London farm was in production, potatoes were its main crop. The Sycamore Maples, which border Dyke Road, are approximately 70 cm diameter at breast height; they were likely planted in the early 1950's.

Acer pseudoplatanus Atropurpureum Group

Purple Sycamore Maple

Acer pseudoplatanus Atropurpureum Group, Wright Street, Fort Langley

Acer pseudoplatanus Atropurpureum Group, foliage and developing samara

Where to see the trees:

Abbotsford
Hougen Park, south off Highway 1 on Cole Rd.

Delta
4529 Arthur Dr, Ladner.

Delta Secondary School, 4615- 51 St, Ladner, row of trees on the south side of the school.

Ladner Community Centre, 4734- 51 St, Ladner, a large, well-shaped tree with a height of eighteen metres and a DBH of 65 cm.

This name is applicable to any seedling of Sycamore Maple with deep purple to pinkish purple colouring on the bottom of the leaf. As the leaves of Purple Sycamore Maple unfurl in the spring, they are usually a greenish bronze. It grows eighteen metres in height with a round form.

Acer pseudoplatanus
Atropurpureum Group

Purple Sycamore Maple

Did You Know?

Hassall House, situated between the railway tracks and the Fraser River, was purchased from the Soldier's Settlement Board. Jack Hassall, born in Birmingham, England in 1886, brought his wife, Christina, to the Glen Valley in 1918. Jack Hassall was a soldier in both the Boer War and World War I. Mr. and Mrs. Hassall were not the original owners of the house, which was built in 1917, but purchased it before it was finished. Just to the north of the house, at the north foot of 272 Street, which was called Jackman Road originally, passengers and freight were put ashore by the riverboat *Skeena*.

Where to see the trees:

Langley

9147 Wright St, Ft Langley.

Sendall Gardens, 20166- 50 Ave, Langley City.

Milner Education Centre, 6656 Glover Rd, Milner.

27090- 88 Ave, Northeast Langley.

Glen Valley Regional Park, Two-Bit Bar, 272 St and River Rd, Northeast Langley, three trees planted to the northeast of the Hassall House.

Surrey

The Glades, 561- 172 St, South Surrey.

Acer pseudoplatanus
Variegatum Group

Variegated Sycamore Maple

Acer pseudoplatanus Variegatum Group, Trattle Street, Fort Langley

The group name *variegatum* applies to any Sycamore Maple seedling with white or yellow variegated foliage. Variegated Sycamore Maple is rare in the South Fraser Region. It grows to twenty metres with a round shape.

Where to see the trees:

Abbotsford

38213 Vye Rd, three stunning trees on the north side of the road.

Chilliwack

Yarrow Central Park, southeast corner of Kehler St and Yarrow Central Rd. There are four large specimens here, several are beautifully open-grown trees with full crowns that were likely planted in the late 1940's.

Delta

Jubilee Farm, later the Augustinian Monastery of British Columbia, 3900 Arthur Dr, Ladner. This tree, a massive specimen with a DBH of 150 cm, is the largest Variegated Sycamore in the South Fraser Region.

Langley

8862 Trattle St, Ft Langley, a lovely well-formed tree.

Acer pseudoplatanus
Variegatum Group

Variegated Sycamore Maple

Where to see the trees:

Richmond

Steveston Park, 4111 Moncton St, Steveston. There is a row of good-sized trees bordering Moncton Street south of the children's playground and a second row is located on the north side of the park, west of the Fentiman Place entrance.

Acer rubrum

Red Maple, Scarlet Maple or Swamp Maple

Where to see the trees:

Abbotsford

Hougen Park, south off Highway 1 on Cole Rd.

Median planting on Old Yale Rd from Blue Jay St to Townline Rd.

Chilliwack

Happy Wilkinson Park.

Canadian Forces Base, Keith Wilson Rd and Vedder Rd, Vedder Crossing, on the west side of Calais Cr at Arnhem Rd.

Delta

11688- 82 Ave, North Delta, a very large tree.

Langley

20300 block 53 Ave, Langley City.

9206 Wright St, Ft Langley.

Aldergrove Lake Regional Park, 272 St and 8 Ave, Southeast Langley, a row of trees adjacent to the parking lot for the Blacktail Group Picnic area.

Trinity Western University, 7600 Glover Rd, Willoughby, two large trees southeast of the Reimer Student Centre.

Richmond

Steveston Park, 4111 Moncton St, Steveston.

Fantasy Garden World, 10800 No 5 Rd.

Surrey

Darts Hill Garden Park, 1660- 168 St, South Surrey, Garden Bed 1.

The Glades, 561- 172 St, South Surrey.

Acer rubrum, Trinity Western University, Langley

Red Maple and its many cultivars are commonly planted in the South Fraser Region. Red Maple reaches a mature height of eighteen to twenty-five metres with an upright oval form. A native of eastern and central Canada, Red Maple has red buds, red flowers, red seeds and often colours a brilliant scarlet in the fall. The three-lobed to five-lobed leaves are thin, fluttering readily in the breeze, showing the silvery underside. The tiny spider-like burgundy flowers are produced in dense clusters or knobbles in early spring, before the leaves emerge. They are showy in numbers. The samara mature in mid-summer and the wings are held at a 60-degree angle to one another.

Acer rubrum 'Bowhall'
Bowhall Maple

Bowhall Maple has an upright narrow form in youth, becoming pyramidal to columnar as it ages. It reaches a mature height of twelve metres. Fall colour is reddish orange.

Where to see the trees:
Abbotsford
Delair Park, Delair and Old Yale Rds.

Median planting on McClure Rd from Trethewey St to Gladwin Rd.

Langley
Kwantlen University College, 20901 Langley Bypass, Langley City, a row of trees planted in 1993 on the circular boulevard west of Kwantlen Way.

Surrey
7493- 151A St, Newton, a street planting.

7498- 151A St, Newton.

Acer rubrum 'Bowhall', fall colour, Kwantlen University College, Langley

Acer rubrum Karpick®
Karpick® Maple

This seedless cultivar is narrow as a young tree, maturing to an oval shape. The midgreen foliage of Karpick® Maple turns yellow to orange in the fall. The strong form and bright red twigs help identify it in the winter months. It grows twelve metres tall.

Where to see the trees:
Abbotsford
Median planting on Old Yale Rd to McClure Rd from Crossley Drive to Clearbrook Road, in front of Ellwood Park.

Acer rubrum Northwood®
Northwood® Maple

Northwood® Maple has medium to dark green foliage which turns crimson-red to orange in the fall. At maturity the tree has a round to upright oval shape. It is a male cultivar. The branches arise at a 45-degree angle to the main trunk. Northwood® Maple was selected from native seedlings collected near Floodwood, Minnesota, so it is one of the hardiest of the Red Maple cultivars. It grows to twelve metres tall with an upright oval form.

Where to see the trees:
Chilliwack
Fairfield Island Park, 46000 Clare Ave, Fairfield Island, at the northwest corner of the park.

Acer rubrum Red Sunset®
Syn. *A. rubrum* 'Franksred'

Red Sunset® Maple

Where to see the trees:

Abbotsford

Clearbrook Public Library, 32320 Dahlstrom Ave, at the southeast corner of the parking lot, several young trees.

Chilliwack

Townsend Park, Ashwell Rd and Hodgins Ave, a row of trees on the north side of the park.

Twin Rinks Ice Arena, 5745 Tyson Rd, Sardis, a street tree planting alternating with Autumn Purple Ash.

North side of Bole Ave between College St and Young Rd.

Langley

4915- 205A St, Langley City, just to the east entrance of City Park, 207 St and 48 Ave, Langley City.

Kwantlen University College, 20901 Langley Bypass, Langley City, a double avenue of trees planted in 1993 to the east of Kwantlen Way.

On 212 St from 88 Ave to Walnut Grove Dr, Walnut Grove, a lovely street planting.

Richmond

McLean Park, 2500 McLean Ave, Hamilton area, a large grove of young trees planted in 1998- 2000.

Rosedale

Minter Gardens, 52892 Bunker Rd, a medium-sized tree growing to the north of the Floral Peacock.

Surrey

12981- 17A Ave, South Surrey.

1650- 136 St, South Surrey.

South Surrey Arena, 2199- 148 St, South Surrey.

Acer rubrum Red Sunset®, flowers

Acer rubrum Red Sunset®, fall colour

Red Sunset® Maple is the most commonly planted Red Maple cultivar in the South Fraser Region. The glossy deep green foliage turns a flame orange-red to red. At maturity Red Sunset® Maple has a broad, upright oval shape and reaches fifteen metres in height.

Did You Know?

The song "Red Sails in the Sunset" provided the inspiration for Red Sunset® Maple's name.

Redvein Maple or Grey-budded Snakebark Maple

Acer rufinerve, foliage and samara

The leaves of Redvein Maple are predominately three-lobed with two much smaller lobes, close to the base of the leaf. The bristly rust-red hairs on the veins of the underside of the leaf and the seeds are easily seen using a hand lens. The yellow flowers are produced in long, hanging chains followed by chains of very small samara. Fall colour is yellow. Young twigs of the Redvein Maple are grey and downy. The buds are grey and very plump, like the breast of a pigeon. The young bark of this Snakebark Maple is green with white stripes and when mature turns grey brown. Reaching a mature height of nine to ten metres and an upright oval form, *Acer rufinerve*, is rare in the South Fraser Region. It is a native of Japan.

Where to see the trees:

Chilliwack

The Waverly, 8445 Young St. There are two trees, one on the lawn adjacent to the parking lot, and the second one on the side of the building adjacent to Young Street.

Langley

5662- 5670- 208 St, Langley City.

Surrey

South Surrey Arena, 2199- 148 St, South Surrey, a good-sized tree on the west side of the arena.

Acer saccharinum
Silver Maple

Acer saccharinum, Gilmore Crescent, Richmond.

Acer saccharinum, bark.

Where to see the trees:

Chilliwack

43238 Yale Rd West, Greendale.

41995 Yale Rd West, Greendale.

Chilliwack Golf and Country Club, 41894 Yale Rd West, Greendale, to the west of the clubhouse.

Canadian Forces Base, Keith Wilson Rd and Vedder Rd, Vedder Crossing. On the northwest side of Calais Cr, there are two trees on the east side of the tennis courts on Sicily Rd at Normandy Dr.

Langley

Houston Residence, 26104 Fraser Hwy, Aldergrove.

7092 Glover Rd, Milner.

Norman Residence, 4681- 240 St, Salmon River Uplands.

Langley Community Music School, 4899-207 St, Southwest Langley, a very large tree immediately to the south of the building.

Richmond

Richmond District Incentive School, southwest corner of Steveston Hwy and Shell Rd, a planting of four large trees.

10291 Gilmore Cr, a magnificent large tree.

Silver Maple is native to the southeastern region of Ontario, Quebec and into New Brunswick. It is a very tall, fast-growing tree, reaching thirty-five metres at maturity. The foliage is five-lobed, and deeply incised to more than halfway to the centre of each leaf. The lobes are slim-waisted. The underside of the leaf is very white or silver. The fall colour is commonly pale yellow to orange and sometimes red. The samaras, which are held at a 90 degree angle to one another, ripen in late spring and are shed at once. Silver Maple is a common tree in the South Fraser Region.

Did You Know?

The Houston Residence on Fraser Highway, designed by an Aldergrove architect, Mr. Dodd, in the Spanish Colonial Revival style, was built in the 1920's for Mr. and Mrs. James Houston. One room in the house has a very high ceiling, built to accommodate Mrs. Houston's piano classes. A mature Horse Chestnut and a Copper Beech tree are planted next to the Silver Maple.

• When the Norman Residence on 240 Street in Langley was deeded to Mrs. Melvina Lucinda Norman in 1891, the land was heavily treed. Prior to construction the original forest was cleared and new trees were planted later. The mature Silver Maple tree and the two Sugar Maples adjacent, placed by Mr. and Mrs. Benjamin Norman, frame the elegant Craftsman-style home they built in 1910. The architecture of the house is a lovely example of the style prevalent in the Edwardian era. Mr. Norman, an architect originally from Quebec, died in 1916 in a fall from the roof of the house.

• General Currie School in Richmond, built in 1919, is named after General Sir Arthur Currie, who was born in Ontario in 1875, and taught school in Sidney and Victoria. General Currie was a distinguished soldier in the First World War. With the rank of lieutenant general, Currie became the first Canadian commander, from 1917, of Canada's overseas forces. He went on to become the Vice-Chancellor of McGill University. The very attractive building is the only school in Richmond still in its original state and location. The architectural style, as designed by architect Joseph H. Bowman, is Tudor with Craftsman influences.

Where to see the trees:

Richmond

General Currie School, 8220 General Currie Rd, three large trees, two on the north side and one on the south side of the General Currie School Heritage Site.

Southarm Park, Garden City Rd and Williams Rd.

Rosedale

Minter Gardens, 52892 Bunker Rd, a small tree to the southeast of the footbridge, overhanging the pathway.

Surrey

Darts Hill Garden Park, 1660- 168 St, South Surrey, Garden Bed 8.

Green Timbers Arboretum, 9800- 140 St, Whalley.

Redwood Park, 17900- 20 Ave, South Surrey, near the playground.

The Glades, 561- 172 St, South Surrey, behind the totem pole.

Acer saccharum

Sugar Maple

Sugar Maple is native to Eastern Canada where it grows twenty-five metres high with an upright oval shape. Its yellowish green leaves are usually five-lobed. The end lobe is quite square in appearance. Fall colour is a butter yellow, occasionally orange with reds. The samaras mature in the fall. The seed wings are somewhat horseshoe-shaped and held almost parallel to one another. Sugar Maple is a rare tree in the South Fraser Region.

Acer saccharum, fall colour

Acer saccharum
Sugar Maple

Where to see the trees:
Abbotsford
3320 Bradner Rd, a farm row of stately trees.

Langley
Norman Residence, 4681- 240 St, Salmon River Uplands, two mature trees.

5404- 216 St, Milner.

Acer saccharum, 216 Street in Milner, Langley

Did You Know?

Canada's arboreal emblem is the generic maple, usually represented by the Sugar Maple. The maple leaf has been a symbol of Canada since the 1700's. It has been depicted on Canadian coins since 1876. The Maple leaves depicted on the one-cent coin are botanically incorrect as the leaf arrangement shown is an alternate one. Maples have an opposite leaf arrangement. Since the proclamation in 1965 of Canada's new flag, the maple leaf has become Canada's preeminent symbol. Sugar Maple or *Acer saccharum* is stylized on our national flag.

- Jonathan Culbert originally planted the Sugar Maple located in front of the Blair farm on 216 Street in Langley in the 1890's. Culbert, visiting Ontario, returned home to Langley with several Sugar Maple seedlings, which he planted on the family farm. All of the original seedlings died except this mature tree. This tree in turn produced seedlings, which have grown to significant size alongside the original tree.

Acer saccharum 'Commemoration'
Commemoration Sugar Maple

Acer saccharum 'Commemoration', fall colour

Where to see the trees:
Langley
Kwantlen University College, 20901 Langley Bypass, Langley City. Planted in 1993, these trees form a street planting on the circular boulevard at the east entrance to the campus.

The dark glossy foliage of this cultivar is heavily textured. The fall colour is butter yellow-orange red. At maturity, Commemoration Sugar Maple will have an oval to rounded shape.

Acer saccharum Green Mountain®
Green Mountain® Sugar Maple

Acer saccharum Green Mountain®, foliage

The foliage of Green Mountain® Sugar Maple is hairy on the underside. The upper surface of the leaves is dark, thick and covered with a waxy bloom. The fall colour is yellow to orange. It grows fourteen metres high with a broadly oval shape.

Where to see the trees:
Langley
Kwantlen University College, 20901 Langley Bypass, Langley City, three trees planted in 1993 at the east end of the easternmost building on the main campus.

Acer shirasawanum 'Aureum'
Syn. *Acer japonicum* 'Aureum'
Golden Fullmoon Maple

Acer shirasawanum 'Aureum', foliage

Golden Fullmoon Maple, native to Japan, is a small tree to 4.5-6 metres tall. The golden yellow leaves are eleven- to thirteen-lobed. The tree is best grown in partial or light shade as the foliage has a tendency to scorch in the full sun. Golden Fullmoon Maple is a rare tree in the South Fraser Region.

Where to see the trees:
Langley
Kwantlen University College, 20901 Langley Bypass, Langley City, a small tree planted in the Gazebo Garden at the Field Lab.

Rosedale
Minter Gardens, 52892 Bunker Rd, a small tree in the Hillside/Alpine Garden.

Surrey
Darts Hill Garden Park, 1660- 168 St, South Surrey, Garden Bed 28.

Acer tataricum ssp. *ginnala*
Syn. *Acer ginnala*

Amur Maple or Siberian Maple

Where to see the trees:

Delta

9190 Ladner Trunk Rd.

Langley

Portage Park, 52 St and 204 Ave, Langley City, in the southwest corner of the park.

Northeast corner of Glover Rd and Highway 10, Langley City.

Poppy Estate Public Golf Course, 3834-248 St, Aldergrove. There is a row of ten trees to the south of the pro shop.

Richmond

Millennium Botanical Garden and Arboretum, N McLennan Community Park, Granville Ave and Garden City Rd.

Fantasy Garden World, 10800 No 5 Rd.

Surrey

Darts Hill Garden Park, 1660- 168 St, South Surrey, Garden Bed 26.

Acer tataricum ssp. *ginnala*, foliage

Another Maple from China, Eastern Siberia, Korea and Japan, Amur Maple is a small tree. The leaves, though three-lobed, do not look at all like a maple leaf. The middle lobe of the dark green leaf is much longer than the other two lobes. The fall colour is often scarlet. The samaras persist late into the fall and the seed wings are held almost parallel to one another. Amur Maple is not very common in the South Fraser Region. It grows to 4.5 metres high with a horizontal oval shape.

Acer Pacific Sunset®
Syn. *Acer* x *truncatum* x *A. platanoides* 'Warren Red'

Pacific Sunset® Maple

Where to see the trees:

Chilliwack

Chilliwack Golf and Country Club, 41894 Yale Rd West, Greendale, an entry row of trees planted at an off-set to one another.

5601- 5722 Thornhill St, Promontory Heights.

Promontory Park West, Teskey Rd, Promontory Heights.

Promontory Rd, Promontory Heights.

Surrey

16512- 109A Ave, Fleetwood, a street planting.

Pacific Sunset® Maple is a hybrid cross between *Acer* x *truncatum* and *A. platanoides.* When mature, Pacific Sunset® Maple has an upright oval form with a height of nine to ten metres. The leaves are very glossy dark green, turning yellow-orange to bright red in the fall.

Æsculus x *carnea* 'Briotii', Langley Secondary School, Langley

Æsculus x *carnea* 'Briotii', flowers

Ruby Horse Chestnut is a lovely medium-sized tree to ten metres high with a round form. The foliage is dark green and slightly wrinkled in comparison to the more common Horse Chestnut. The leaves are also compound, with mostly five but sometimes seven leaflets. The trumpet-shaped flowers are spectacular in May. Dark red, they are held upright in large cone-shaped inflorescences. The dormant buds are slightly sticky and the green and brown freckled nut husks are slightly prickly which easily distinguishes them from common Horse Chestnut. Ruby Horse Chestnut trees are somewhat rare in the South Fraser Region.

Where to see the trees:

Abbotsford

Hougen Park, south off Highway 1 on Cole Rd. There are four of these lovely trees in the park.

Chilliwack

4464 Community St, Yarrow.

Fairfield Island Park, entry off Clare Ave, Fairfield Island, south of baseball diamond D.

University College of the Fraser Valley, 45600 Airport Rd, a young tree east of Building G, Childcare Centre.

Delta

5438- 44 Ave, Ladner.

John Oliver Municipal Park, 11600 block Ladner Trunk Rd.

Langley

236- 264 St, Southeast Langley. These two trees in the front garden are the largest Ruby Horse Chestnuts in the South Fraser Region.

Langley Secondary School, 21405- 56 Ave, Milner, a row of trees on the south side of the school.

21100 block 48 Ave, a row of street trees, whose touching crowns completely cover the road below.

Sendall Gardens, 20166- 50 Ave, Langley City.

Surrey

City Hall, 14245- 56 Ave, Newton, a row of five trees south of the building in the lawn adjacent to Highway 10.

Green Timbers Arboretum, 9800- 140 St, Whalley, in the northwest corner of the arboretum.

Æsculus hippocastanum
Common Horse Chestnut

Æsculus hippocastanum, South Delta Recreation Centre, Delta

Æsculus hippocastanum, flowers

Where to see the trees:

Abbotsford

Hougen Park, south off Highway 1 on Cole Rd.

Chilliwack

Canadian Forces Base, Keith Wilson Rd and Vedder Rd, Vedder Crossing. There are a number of Common Horse Chestnuts on the base. A large tree is growing south of RCMP Complex on Calais Cr, another on the northeast corner of Calais Cr and Caen Rd.

Stö:lo Centre, 7201 Vedder Rd, Sardis.

Delta

South Delta Recreation Centre, 1720- 56 St, Tsawwassen.

4555 Arthur Dr, Ladner.

Memorial Park, 47 Ave and Delta St, Ladner*.

South side of Ladner Trunk Rd between 72 Ave and 80 Ave, a farm row of good-sized trees.

Langley

Belmont Dairy Farms, 21151 Old Yale Rd, Murrayville.

Houston Residence, 26104 Fraser Hwy, Aldergrove, Langley.

9000 Glover Rd, Ft Langley.

Common Horse Chestnut is one of the most commonly planted deciduous trees in the South Fraser Region. It forms a statuesque upright oval-to-round-shaped tree of twenty to twenty-two metres in height at maturity. The very large, medium green leaves usually have seven leaflets. The showy trumpet flowers are produced in May in long, upright cone-shaped inflorescences. Each floret is white with a dab of yellow at its throat, which matures to red. The nut husks, which enclose one or two beautiful mahogany-coloured nuts, are very spiny. In winter this tree is easy to identify because the large dormant dark brown buds are sticky to the touch.

Did You Know?

The lovely grove of twelve Horse Chestnut trees in Memorial Park in Delta are approximately eighteen metres high. The largest tree has a DBH of 80 cm. Delta Council designated the trees as Heritage Trees on March 25, 1997.* The property the trees reside on was part of the original farmstead of Ladner's namesake, William H. Ladner. Later the land became Paul Ladner's farm. 1.6 hectares of land was bought from him in 1919, to build a park

Common Horse Chestnut

and athletic field. It was named Memorial Park to honour the fallen soldiers of World War One. A cenotaph, dedicated May 22, 1921, is placed at the south end of Delta Street in the park.

• John "Jack" W. Berry, a prominent citizen of the area, built the farmstead on Old Yale Road in Langley in 1901-1902. The farmhouse was constructed of timber cleared from the land. The site contains a number of very large and mature trees including the Horse Chestnut. This working dairy farm is still owned by the Berry Family.

• There are eighteen Horse Chestnuts in the boulevard planting at 9000 Glover Road in Fort Langley on the east side of the cemetery and another six stand opposite, on the east side of the road, between Francis Avenue and the north end of Doctor Marr's Fort Langley office and house. They are thought to have been planted as saplings in the early 1920's by the Fort Langley Community Improvement Society, and may have been the offspring of the three massive chestnuts that once stood in front of the Wilkie house. A triangular fence once surrounded each chestnut, but there were no crosses, as, contrary to popular belief, the trees were planted strictly for the purposes of street beautification as opposed to commemoration of the WW I war dead. Their planting may have been the result of the spread to Fort Langley of some of the urban design principles known to residents such as developer/realtor Charles Edward Hope, who had homes in both Fort Langley and Vancouver at the time of the planting of the Common Horse Chestnuts.

• Goldwin Herschel Harris owned the farmhouse built in 1912 at 11620 No. 4 Rd, Richmond. Harris settled in Richmond in 1894. He married Agnes Isabella Kidd, in 1904. Agnes Isabella was the oldest daughter of Thomas Kidd, a very prominent pioneer and landowner in the South Arm area of Richmond. Goldie Harris was at first Thomas Kidd's employee, but it is likely that the 40-hectare farm and farmhouse was given to the newlyweds as a gift. The house is architecturally Edwardian in style with Craftsman influences. Goldie Harris died in 1947. Thomas Kidd later lived in the house and carried on writing the stories of Richmond's pioneers here until his death.

Æsculus hippocastanum, Glover Road, Fort Langley

Where to see the trees:

Richmond

Goldie Harris House, 11620 No. 4 Rd, a mature specimen growing along the edge of the ditch.

NW corner Minoru Blvd and Granville Ave, a double row of large trees at the entry to Minoru Park.

11751 Bird Rd.

Surrey

Cloverdale Elementary School, No 10 Hwy and 178 St, Cloverdale, a row of fifteen trees.

White Rock

White Rock Elementary School, 1273 Fir St, on the west side of the school.

Æsculus pavia

Red Buckeye, Red Flowering Buckeye or Fire-cracker Plant

Where to see the trees:

Surrey

Darts Hill Garden Park, 1660- 168 St, South Surrey, Garden Bed C1.

Native from Virginia to Florida, Louisiana and Texas, Red Buckeye is a small tree reaching a height of six metres. The palmately compound leaves stay dark green well into the fall but seldom turn colour. Showy red tubular flowers are produced in upright panicles in May. Smooth-skinned green nut husks litter the ground under the tree in the autumn.

Æsculus turbinata

Japanese Horse Chestnut

Æsculus turbinata, bark

Similar to, but more elegant, *Æsculus turbinata* has larger and hairier leaflets than Common Horse Chestnut. The leaves have five to seven leaflets, with downy orange tufts on the veins beneath. The fall colour is a wonderful orange, with tints of red, yellow and even blue. The flower is borne on an upright panicle several weeks after the bloom of Common Horse Chestnut. The nut husks are egg-shaped, rough and lack spines. The tree listed below was the only specimen found in the South Fraser Region.

Where to see the trees:

Abbotsford

2770 Mount View St, a wonderful old tree with a DBH of 133 cm.

Ailanthus altissima, Hudson's Bay Avenue, Fort Langley

Ailanthus altissima, foliage and fruit

Tree of Heaven, a native of China, reaches twelve to eighteen metres in height. It has a very tropical appearance. The huge pinnately compound leaves are very large, up to one metre long on young trees. The leaflets have one to three teeth on both sides near the base of each leaflet. Tree of Heaven is dioecious, which means that there are both male and female trees. The female produces large masses of single-winged seeds, which ripen in August and September. Tree of Heaven seeds are red tinged, offering a good contrast to the bright, glossy green leaves. The seeds remain on the tree for months. The grey bark has a snake bark look to it with its slender, twisted vertical creases. It is not a very common tree in the South Fraser Region.

Where to see the trees:

Abbotsford
32189 Huntingdon Rd.

2168 Lobban Rd, two very large specimens.

Chilliwack
45296 Watson Rd, Sardis, three good-sized trees.

Delta
8508 Terrace Dr, North Delta, several small trees on the south side of the property.

Langley
8890 Hudson Bay St, Ft Langley.

Richmond
Steveston Park, 4111 Moncton St, Steveston, east side of the entrance to the Martial Arts Centre.

White Rock
15100 block Marine Drive, the residence east of the beach access walkway, two large trees, and the largest one on the west side of the lot.

Albizia julibrissin
Silk Tree or Mimosa

Where to see the trees:
Chilliwack
The Waverly, 8445 Young St.

Delta
Leisure Centre, 4600 Clarence Taylor Cr, Ladner, three young trees on the south side of the centre.

Langley
City Hall, 20399 Douglas Cr, a very small tree.

Richmond
Millennium Botanical Garden and Arboretum, N McLennan Community Park, Granville Ave and Garden City Rd.

Surrey
City Hall, 14245- 56 Ave, Newton, between the Provincial Courthouse and the Municipal Hall.

Darts Hill Garden Park, 1660- 168 St, South Surrey, Garden Bed 5.

White Rock
NW corner of Columbia Ave and Centre St.

The signature of the Silk Tree is its wide-spreading vase shape, which eventually matures to a flat top. The leaves are doubly pinnately compound. Each leaflet is tiny in the extreme, creating a very delicate and airy effect. The leaves of this native of western Asia partially close on dull dark days, and fully close at night. The leaves often fall green making the fall colour nondescript. The flowers produced in August and early September are soft confections of long pink stamens looking like an old-fashioned barber's brush. The fragrance of the flowers is delightful. The seedpod is unusual as each seed is clasped tightly like a plastic-bubble strip of vitamins, each seed a discrete bump.

Did You Know?
This lovely tree planted at the front entrance of The Waverly, an Extended Care facility in Chilliwack by Bruce Broughton ten to twelve years ago, is now seven to eight metres high. It is the largest *Albizia* found by the author in the South Fraser Region.

Albizia julibrissin var. *rosea*
Hardy Silk Tree or Hardy Mimosa Tree

Albizia julibrissin var. *rosea,* flowers, Darts Hill Garden Park

Where to see the trees:
Surrey
Darts Hill Garden Park, 1660- 168 St, South Surrey, Garden Bed 11.

The Glades, 561- 172 St, South Surrey, south side of the house.

The flowers of this tree are a deeper pink than the species. It is also supposed to be hardier.

Aralia elata, Kwantlen University College   *Aralia elata*, fruit

Wicked prickles on stiffly upright thick stems mark the ungainly winter look of Japanese Aralia. In leaf, the huge bipinnately compound leaves that can easily reach a metre in length soften its appearance. The small flowers, produced in late July to August, are frothy masses of white held in huge clusters. The small black fleshy fruit, which resembles birdshot, ripens in November. Japanese Aralia readily forms impenetrable thickets unless volunteers are pruned out. This large shrub or small tree reaches six to nine metres in height. It is not often grown in the South Fraser Region.

Aralia elata 'Variegata'
Variegated Japanese Aralia or Japanese Angelica Tree

The very rare Variegated Japanese Aralia is characterized by the creamy white margins of its leaflets.

Where to see the trees:

Rosedale

Minter Gardens, 52892 Bunker Rd, growing on the east side of the entrance to the Chinese Penjing Garden.

Where to see the trees:

Abbotsford

2795 Mount View Ave, two wonderful old trees.

Chilliwack

Meadowlands Golf and Country Club, 47831 Yale Rd East, a large tree forming a thicket behind the oil tank on the west side of the clubhouse.

Delta

Pioneer Library, 4683- 51 St, Ladner, a good specimen on the east side of the library.

Langley

Sendall Gardens, Langley City, south of the duck pond.

Kwantlen University College, 20901 Langley Bypass, Langley City

Richmond

Steveston Park, 4111 Moncton St, Steveston, west side of the entrance to the Martial Arts Centre.

Surrey

9062- 144 St, Fleetwood, three trees.

Darts Hill Garden Park, 1660- 168 St, South Surrey, Garden Bed 30.

Araucaria araucana
Monkey Puzzle

Araucaria araucana, D.A. McKee House, (Delta Lodge), Delta, a female tree

Araucaria araucana, female cones

Did You Know?

McKee House in Delta, completed in 1906 for David Alexander McKee, was constructed in a Tudor Revival Architectural style. David McKee originally purchased the property from William Ladner in 1904. David and his wife Margaret named the property "Westholme."

Native to southern Chile and southwestern Argentina, the Monkey Puzzle tree is commonly planted in the South Fraser Region. Its distinctive foliage and shape are hard to mistake. The dark evergreen leaves are thick, stiff and very spiny-pointed. Monkey Puzzle is dioecious, meaning there are male and female trees. The male tree produces a cucumber-shaped pollen cone. The female produces a huge dessert plate-sized cone that takes two years to mature. As a young tree, Monkey Puzzle has a stiff, strongly pyramidal shape. As the tree matures it becomes more round-headed in appearance and may reach a height of twenty metres.

Where to see the trees:

Abbotsford

32641 Bevan Ave.

John Mahoney Park, off Ware St, a small tree by the bridge of the Mill Lake boardwalk

Jubilee Park, McCallum Rd south of Essendene.

Chilliwack

Camp River Community Hall, Camp River Rd, East Chilliwack. The tree is located on the farm to the east of the hall.

Woodbine St and Yale Rd East, south side of Yale Rd East.

45577 Spruce Dr, Sardis, a female tree with its branches right down to the ground.

Meadowlands Golf and Country Club, 47831 Yale Rd East, a large tree in the parking lot.

Delta

D.A. McKee House, (Delta Lodge), 4501 Arthur Dr, Ladner. It is a female tree and a perfect mature specimen with a DBH of 60 cm and a height of eighteen metres.

4585 Arthur Dr, Ladner, an exceptional specimen.

4640- 62 St, Ladner, a beautiful specimen.

5215 Ferry Rd, Ladner, a magnificent tree.

11755- 72 Ave, North Delta, a well-shaped female tree.

Langley

20712 Douglas Cres, Langley City, a good-sized female tree.

22979- 88 Ave, Ft Langley.

Richmond

8760 Steveston Hwy.

Millennium Botanical Garden and Arboretum, N McLennan Community Park, Granville. Ave and Garden City Rd.

Rosedale

Minter Gardens, 52892 Bunker Rd, north of the Trillium Restaurant.

Surrey

Meridian Golf Centre, 1054-168 St, South Surrey.

100 metres south of 152 St and King George Hwy, South Surrey.

Darts Hill Garden Park, 1660-168 St, South Surrey, Garden Bed 26.

Arbutus, Canada's only native broadleaf tree is also one of the most picturesque. It is native to the hot, dry, rocky bluffs of the Strait of Georgia and south in maritime Washington and Oregon, where it grows into twisted and crooked shapes. It is almost always found within eight kilometres of the sea. Its most ornamental characteristic, when it can be found growing in gardens, is the reddish bark that peels and flakes into papery-thin rolls to reveal a pale green or orange underneath. On some trees the trunk has the appearance of terracotta-coloured marble. The leaves are dark green and leathery. In the fall, old leaves turn rusty-red and fall from the tree, papering the ground underfoot with crunchy dried leaves. The small urn-shaped white flowers are borne in late May to June in cone-shaped clusters, often at the top of the tree. The fruit, which ripens in late October, is first a showy bright orange turning to red. Birds favour the berries. Arbutus reaches a mature height of twenty metres.

Arbutus menziesii, branching pattern

Where to see the trees:

Abbotsford

John Mahoney Park, off Ware St, a small tree to the east of the bridge of the Mill Lake boardwalk.

Chilliwack

45330 Bernard Ave, this tree is growing at the far eastern end of the range normally expected for the species.

Delta

White Birch Manor, 11905- 80 Ave, North Delta, a lovely symmetrical crown and perfect foliage, a very large tree.

5617- 120 St, west end of Panorama Ridge.

Richmond

Millennium Botanical Garden and Arboretum, N McLennan Community Park, Granville Ave and Garden City Rd.

Surrey

12101 Sullivan St, Crescent Beach, Surrey.

Darts Hill Garden Park, 1660- 168 St, South Surrey, Garden Bed 26.

Provincial Courthouse, 14340-57 Ave, Newton, south of the building.

B

So plant as though you will live forever:
so labour as though you will die tomorrow.

Mark Twain, (1835–1910), American humorist and author

Betula albo-sinensis var. *septentrionalis,* emerging leaves and catkins in early spring

Betula albo-sinensis var. *septentrionalis*

Chinese Paper Birch, Chinese Red Birch or Northern Chinese Red-barked Birch

Chinese Paper Birch is very rarely grown in the South Fraser Region. When it is grown, it is primarily for the fabulous copper to orange to pink-coloured peeling bark. When the tissue-thin bark peels away, a white glaucous bloom is revealed. The yellow-green leaves turn a moderately attractive yellow in the fall. The chartreuse catkins, which are produced in profusion on mature trees, are very showy in March to April. Chinese Paper Birch grows eighteen metres tall with a round form.

Where to see the trees:

Langley
Kwantlen University College, 20901 Langley Bypass, Langley City, Gazebo Garden at the Field Lab.

Richmond
Millennium Botanical Garden and Arboretum, N McLennan Community Park, Granville Ave and Garden City Rd.

Betula albo-sinensis var. *septentrionalis,* Queen Elizabeth Park, Vancouver

Betula albo-sinensis var. *septentrionalis,* bark

Betula alleghaniensis
Syn. *Betula lutea*

Yellow Birch, Gold Birch, Curly Birch or Hard Birch

Betula alleghaniensis, bark

Betula alleghaniensis, fall colour

Yellow Birch is native to southern Ontario, Quebec and the Maritimes. It reaches a mature height of twenty-five metres. The warm bright yellow fall colour of Yellow Birch is unparalleled, except by a closely related species, *Betula lenta.* The dull, dark green oval leaves are set off by the superb exfoliating cinnamon brown bark of the trunk. Young bark peels horizontally into short, curling tissue-thin strips. The yellowish twigs, when broken, smell and taste of wintergreen. Yellow Birch is rarely grown in the South Fraser Region.

Where to see the trees:

Langley

Kwantlen University College, 20901 Langley Bypass, Langley City, north side of the entry to the Field Lab.

Did You Know?

Yellow Birch or *Betula alleghaniensis* is the arboreal emblem of the province of Quebec. This provincial tree was adopted in December of 1993.

Betula lenta

Sweet Birch, Cherry Birch or Black Birch

Where to see the trees:

Abbotsford

SW corner of Alta Ave and Ware St.

Langley

Kwantlen University College, 20901 Langley Bypass, Langley City, north side of the entry to the Field Lab.

4188- 240 St, Salmon River Uplands, planted in 1976.

Betula lenta, Salmon River Uplands, Langley

Betula lenta
Sweet Birch, Cherry Birch or Black Birch

Vibrant yellow fall colour sets this little-grown birch apart from any other in the South Fraser Region. The leaves and catkins are similar to Yellow Birch. The bark on young trees is similar to cherry bark; it is dark-coloured and heavily textured with horizontal lenticels. Like Yellow Birch, the reddish brown twigs, when broken, smell and taste of wintergreen. *Betula lenta* is a native of the northeastern United States and is rarely grown in the South Fraser Region. It reaches a mature height of twenty metres with a round shape.

Betula papyrifera
Paper Birch or Canoe Birch

Betula papyrifera, branching pattern, Mckenzie Road, Abbotsford.

Betula papyrifera, Municipal Hall, Langley

Paper or Canoe Birch is native to most of Canada. Commonly found in parks and natural settings throughout the South Fraser Region, it has a tall, loosely upright oval shape. Paper Birch reaches a mature height of twenty-five metres. The key identifying feature is the creamy white, peeling, papery-thin bark found on older trees. A reddish orange inner bark appears once the outer white layer has peeled away. Sometimes young trees at the forest edge are confused with Bitter Cherry, since in youth the bark of Paper Birch can be very dark.

Watch for the horizontal raised lines of lenticels on the bark. The triangular midgreen leaves are larger than European White Birch, and turn a clear yellow in the fall.

Where to see the trees:

Abbotsford

Hogan Family Nature Park, 2860 block Debruyne Rd, several very big trees in the park, one of the larger trees with a DBH of 62 cm.

Hougen Park, south off Highway 1 on Cole Rd.

South Poplar Elementary School, southwest corner of Huntingdon Rd and Gladwin Rd, several large open-grown trees on the east and south side of the school.

818 Mckenzie Rd, a pictur-esque specimen.

Trethewey House (M.S.A. Museum), 2313 Ware St, north side of the house.

SW corner of Clarke Dr and McDougall Ave.

Chilliwack

Stó:lo Centre, 7201 Vedder Rd, Sardis.

East bank of the Sumas River, south of the CNR tracks, east of the confluence of the Fraser River.

Delta

Delta Nature Reserve, parking lot to access trails located at 10388 Nordel Crt, North Delta.

Langley

City Park, 207 St and 48 Ave, Langley City, a grove of trees south of Al Anderson Memorial Pool.

Municipal Hall, 4914- 221 St, Murrayville.

8975 Royal St, Ft Langley, a huge specimen.

Navy League of Canada, 4315-272 St, a row of large trees along 272 Ave.

Richmond

King George Park, a grove of large trees on the east side of Cambie Rd and Thorpe Rd, East Richmond.

McLean Park, 2500 McLean Ave, Hamilton area.

Millennium Botanical Garden and Arboretum, N McLennan Community Park, Granville Ave and Garden City Rd.

Richmond Nature Park, 11851 Westminster Hwy.

Rosedale

Minter Gardens, 52892 Bunker Rd, several good-sized trees in the lawn area to the west of the Formal Garden.

Surrey

The Glades, 561- 172 St, South Surrey, at the east end of the ridge.

White Rock

The Water Tower, SW corner of Merklin St and North Bluff Rd.

Did You Know?

Paper Birch or *Betula papyrifera* is the arboreal emblem of the province of Saskatchewan. This provincial tree was adopted in June of 1988.

• The Paper Birch growing at the east end of the native grove area near the mouth of the Sumas River is the second largest one recorded in British Columbia. It measures 5.1 metres in circumference with a height and crown width of 16. 76 metres.

• The Water Tower is a promi-nent White Rock landmark. It is an actual working well site. The well draws water from an aquifer 155 metres below the ground. The large reservoir was constructed in 1962 and is thir-ty-one metres tall. It is made of steel and concrete, which was continuously poured so that the structure has no joints in the concrete. It holds 1,672,928 litres of water.

Betula pendula

European White Birch, White Birch or Silver Birch

Where to see the trees:

Abbotsford

2262 Bevan Ave, two trees.

Hougen Park, south off Highway 1 on Cole Rd.

Chilliwack

Fairfield Island Park, 46000 Clare Ave, Fairfield Island.

Chilliwack Golf and Country Club, 41894 Yale Rd West, Greendale.

Stö:lo Centre, 7201 Vedder Rd, Sardis.

46105 Roy Ave, Sardis.

Delta

Sacred Heart Elementary School, 3900 Arthur Dr, Ladner.

Hazelhurst, Benson/Williamson Residence, 5820 River Road, Crescent Area.

Delta Nature Reserve, parking lot to access trails located at 10388 Nordel Court, North Delta.

Richmond

Richmond Nature Park, 11851Westminster Hwy, Richmond, the park has many of these trees.

Southarm Park, Garden City Rd and Williams Rd.

Surrey

City Hall, 14245- 56 Ave, Newton, south-west corner of the building.

Darts Hill Garden Park, 1660- 168 St, South Surrey, Garden Bed 22.

Surrey Big Bend Regional Park, north foot of 104 St, Guildford.

Rosedale

Minter Gardens, 52892 Bunker Rd, several groups, one to the north of the Floral Flag.

Betula pendula, Darts Hill Garden Park, Surrey

Betula pendula, foliage

European White Birch is very common in the South Fraser Region. It is a native to Europe, including Great Britain and Asia Minor. The dark green leaves of this birch are triangular and turn a mediocre yellow in the fall. The bark, which peels away, is not as ornamental as the Paper Birch. As the tree ages the bark at the base of the trunk becomes darkly ridged and furrowed. European White Birch often has a pendulous habit, which creates its distinctive winter silhouette. It grows twelve to eighteen metres tall. The brittle branches and smaller twigs make this Birch a nuisance to clean up after strong fall and winter winds. It is also susceptible to bronze bark borer, an insect that cause the tops of the trees to die back.

The triangular leaves of Cutleaf Weeping Birch are incised at the margins, with each indentation regularly spaced around the edge. All parts of the tree weep, giving the tree a pendulous outline. Cutleaf Weeping Birch is commonly found in the South Fraser Region.

Where to see the trees:

Chilliwack

South median of Edson Dr at South Sumas Rd, Sardis, a row of eight large and well-shaped trees.

Happy Wilkinson Park.

Sardis Senior Secondary School, 45460 Stevenson Rd, Sardis, three good-sized trees.

Stö:lo Centre, 7201 Vedder Rd, Sardis.

Yarrow Central Park, Southeast corner of Kehler St and Yarrow Central Rd.

Betula pendula 'Purpurea'
Purpleleaf Birch

Betula pendula 'Purpurea', Royal Roads University, Victoria

Betula pendula 'Purpurea', foliage

Purpleleaf Birch is not commonly grown here. Its lovely dark reddish purple leaves unfold in the spring, maturing to a dark bronze-green. The orange, copper and bronze fall colour is unusual for a European White Birch. Purpleleaf Birch grows ten metres tall.

Where to see the trees:

Abbotsford

Jubilee Park, McCallum Rd south of Essendene, in the centre of the park.

Chilliwack

Townsend Park, Ashwell Rd and Hodgins Ave, three trees on the east side of the concessions building.

Betula pendula 'Youngii'
Young's Weeping Birch

Betula pendula 'Youngii', branching pattern, Second Avenue, Chilliwack

Betula pendula 'Youngii', foliage

Betula pendula 'Youngii', Langley Secondary School, Langley

The bold umbrella shape of the crown of this small tree makes it easy to identify at all times of the year. The slim branchlets arch up slightly, then cascade to the ground, creating a curtain of foliage. Young's Weeping Birch is top-grafted, usually at two metres in height or occasionally higher, onto a straight trunk.

Where to see the trees:
Abbotsford
Abbotsford City Hall, 32315 South Fraser Way, on the southwest corner of the building.

Jubilee Park, McCallum Rd south of Essendene, a group of trees on the south side of the park.

Chilliwack
46010 Second Ave, a gorgeous tree of great size.

Langley
Langley Secondary School, 21405- 56 Ave, Milner, a row of four good-sized specimens.

Richmond
Fantasy Garden World, 10800 No 5 Rd.

Steveston Park, 4111 Moncton St, Steveston.

Rosedale
Minter Gardens, 52892 Bunker Rd, several good-sized specimens throughout the garden.

Betula utilis var. *jacquemontii*
Jacquemont Birch, White-barked Himalayan Birch or Kashmir Birch

Betula utilis var. *jacquemontii*, Darts Hill Garden Park, Surrey

Betula utilis var. *jacquemontii*, bark

Spectacular creamy white paper-thin bark graces the trunk of Jacquemont Birch. Often grown as a multi-stem tree, it is the finest of the white-barked birches for the South Fraser Region. Large specimens are not common here as it has only been available locally since the early 1980's. A native of the northwest Himalayas, southwest and central Nepal, the Jacquemont Birch has medium green teardrop-shaped leaves that turn yellow in the fall. In its native range it reaches a mature height of eighteen to twenty metres.

Where to see the trees:

Abbotsford
Abbotsford City Hall, 32315 South Fraser Way, a group on the north side of the building.

Chilliwack
Fairfield Island Park, 46000 Clare Ave, Fairfield Island, a group of small multi-stemmed trees by the pond.

45567 Worthington Place, Sardis, a large well-grown tree.

Langley
Kwantlen University College, 20901 Langley Bypass, Langley City, Gazebo Garden at the Field Lab.

Richmond
City Hall, 6911 No 3 Rd, a large grove of multi-stem trees on the west and south side of the building.

9000 block Alberta Rd, a young street planting.

Accent Inn, 10551 St Edwards St, Bridgeport.

Surrey
Darts Hill Garden Park, 1660- 168 St, South Surrey, Garden Bed 23.

South Surrey Arena, 2199- 148 St, South Surrey, three young trees on the south side of the arena.

C

I like trees because they seem more resigned to the way
they have to live than other things do.[1]

Willa Silbert Cather, (1873–1947), American novelist and poet

Calocedrus decurrens, Sendall Gardens, Langley

Calocedrus decurrens, foliage and open cones

Calocedrus decurrens
Incense Cedar

Incense Cedar is so called because the foliage has a strong incense-like smell when crushed. It is a native evergreen of the western United States from Oregon to Nevada and into California. The emerald green scale-like foliage remains brightly coloured throughout the year, but is most noticeable in the dark gloom of winter. The small brown cones, which resemble a duck's bill, ripen in October. The reddish brown bark is fibrous and often furrowed. Incense Cedar is not very common in the South Fraser Region. Incense Cedar grows fifteen metres tall.

Where to see the trees:
Delta
Municipal Hall, 4500 Clarence Taylor Cr, Ladner, a small specimen on the south side of the pond.

4501 Arthur Dr, Ladner, five trees in a row along Arthur Drive.

Langley
Sendall Gardens, 20166- 50 Ave, Langley City.

23787- 59 Ave, Salmon River Uplands.

Richmond
Millennium Botanical Garden and Arboretum, N McLennan Community Park, Granville Ave and Garden City Rd.

Rosedale
Minter Gardens, 52892 Bunker Rd, north of the Maze.

Surrey
Darts Hill Garden Park, 1660- 168 St, South Surrey*, Garden Bed 26.

Green Timbers Arboretum, 9800- 140 St, Whalley.

Redwood Park, 17900- 20 Ave, South Surrey*, south of the Tree House.

1 O Pioneers!, 1913, pt.II, ch.8.

European Hornbeam or Common Hornbeame

Carpinus betulus, foliage and developing fruit

European Hornbeam, native to Asia Minor and Europe, is a medium-sized deciduous tree, growing fifteen metres tall. The medium green foliage has a corrugated look to it due to the strong leaf venation. The fall colour is an unremarkable yellow. To identify European Hornbeam look for the distinctive fruit. This curious structure is a pendulous chain of tiny nuts, each nut held on a long green wing or bract, which is at the centre of two shorter bracts. In September to October, the chain of fruit matures to a tan colour. The sinuous grey bark is smooth. European Hornbeam is not commonly grown in the South Fraser Region.

Where to see the trees:

Chilliwack

Park, SE corner of Manuel Rd and Vedder Rd, Sardis, a very large specimen.

Yarrow Community Park, north end of Community St, Yarrow.

Langley

Kwantlen University College, 20901 Langley Bypass, Langley City, one tree on the main campus.

Carpinus betulus 'Fastigiata'
Pyramidal European Hornbeam

While the species is not often grown, Pyramidal European Hornbeam is very common along boulevards, in streetscapes and parks. Only pyramidal when very young, this tree becomes a dense upright oval shape. It reaches a mature height of fifteen metres.

Carpinus betulus 'Fastigiata'
Pyramidal European Hornbeam

Carpinus betulus 'Fastigiata', City Park, Langley City

Carpinus betulus 'Fastigiata', foliage

Where to see the trees:

Chilliwack

General Hospital, 45600 Menholm Rd, a row on the north and east sides of the hospital.

Salish Park, 45860- 1 Ave.

Delta

Health Centre, 4470 Clarence Taylor Cr, Ladner.

Langley

City Park, 207 St and 48 Ave, Langley City, a large specimen on the west side of the parking lot.

Sendall Gardens, 20166- 50 Ave, Langley City.

McMillan Place, 20303- 53 Ave, Langley City.

Surrey

68th Ave, between 127th St and 128th St, Newton, a street tree planting.

Carpinus betulus 'Frans Fontaine'
Frans Fontaine European Hornbeam

Where to see the trees:

Richmond

No 5 Rd from Cambie Rd south to the Highway 99 overpass, a street planting on both sides of the street, planted in 1997.

Frans Fontaine European Hornbeam is a recent introduction to the South Fraser Region. It has a very tight, strongly upright habit. The new branches grow in toward the centre of the tree, creating a tidy, compact outline.

Carya ovata

Shagbark Hickory or Little Shellbark Hickory

Reaching a height of eighteen to twenty-four metres, Shagbark Hickory produces a straight slender trunk. It is native to the southern Great Lakes Region of Ontario. It is found in southern Quebec, to Minnesota, and south to Georgia and Texas. The large yellow-green compound leaves usually have five leaflets but occasionally can have seven. The nut, contained in a thick woody husk, is sweet and edible. When the nut is ripe the husk splits along its seams to the base. The bark of this tree is its chief identifying feature. On mature trees, the bark hangs untidily in long vertical plates. The lower ends, or both ends of the bark plates, hang freely and curve upward. Shagbark Hickory is rare in the South Fraser Region.

Where to see the trees:

Chilliwack

47835 Camp River Rd, East Chilliwack, a huge tree.

Castanea dentata

American Chestnut, American Sweet Chestnut or Chestnut

American Chestnut is the only *Castanea* endemic to Canada. It is found in the southern Great Lakes Region of Ontario. Chestnut blight has all but decimated the thriving mature forests of this tree in the eastern United States and Canada where it was once a common deciduous tree reaching lofty heights of thirty-five metres and more. The long, tapering, glossy green leaves of American Chestnut turn yellow in the fall. The leaf margins are very sharp-pointed, and bristle tipped. The upper and lower surfaces of the leaf lack hairs when mature. Brown edible nuts are produced in a spiny brown husk called a burr that splits into sections when ripe. The sweet nuts are small and hazelnut like. To distinguish between this species and the Chinese Chestnut check

Where to see the trees:

Abbotsford

2350 Midas St, a young tree.

Second Christian Reformed Church of Abbotsford, 34631 Old Clayburn Rd, a huge tree on the east side of the parking lot.

Chilliwack

9675 Young Rd North, two good-sized trees.

47835 Camp River Rd, East Chilliwack.

46283 Prairie Central Rd, Sardis, a well-shaped young tree.

Delta

11922 Woodhurst Dr, west end of Panorama Ridge, a young tree.

Augustinian Monastery, 3900 Arthur Dr, Ladner, a massive specimen with a DBH of 105cm.

Castanea dentata

American Chestnut, American Sweet Chestnut or Chestnut

Langley

Immanuel Lutheran Church, northeast corner of 272 St and 32 Ave, Aldergrove. There are two very large trees on the north side of the parking lot.

5094- 232 St, Salmon River Uplands.

2784- 264 St, Southeast Langley, a large open-grown tree.

the twigs and buds. The chestnut-coloured twigs and buds are hairless while those of the Chinese Chestnut are very hairy. The bark of mature trees has wide, flat-topped ridges.

Castanea mollissima

Chinese Chestnut

Where to see the trees:

Surrey

Redwood Park, 17900- 20 Ave, South Surrey, east of the Tree House, many in the wooded area southwest from the Redwood plantation and a number of very large mature trees have naturalized on the west boundary of the park.

Chinese Chestnut is a medium-growing tree reaching eighteen metres at maturity. Like the American Chestnut, the leaves are long and coarsely toothed, each tooth tipped with a sharp bristle. The undersides of the dark green leaves are usually hairy, at the very least pubescent on the veins. The dormant buds and twigs are also pubescent, the twigs with long spreading hairs. The spiny husks or burrs contain two to three dark brown edible nuts. The husk breaks open in October, releasing the nuts.

Castanea sativa

Sweet, Italian, Spanish or European Chestnut

Where to see the trees:

Surrey

Darts Hill Garden Park, 1660- 168 St, South Surrey*, Garden Bed 22.

Redwood Park, 17900- 20 Ave, South Surrey, in the open area west of the parking lot.

Castanea sativa, foliage and mature burrs

Native to southern Europe, North Africa, and Asia Minor, Sweet Chestnut is commonly grown in Europe for its edible nuts. It reaches forty metres in height in its native range. The dark green leaves are long, sharply pointed and covered with pubescence when young. The leaves turn yellow then brown in October. Some trees produce large, plump, round nuts (up to 3 cm in diameter) within the prickly green husks or burrs. Other trees produce three to four flat nuts, which are not worth harvesting for food. A key identifying feature is the dark brown stringy bark, which is strongly ridged, the ridges often spiraling around the trunk.

Castanea sativa
Sweet, Italian, Spanish or European Chestnut

Catalpa bignonioides
Southern Catalpa, Common Catalpa Eastern Catalpa, Indian Cigar or Bean Tree

Catalpa bignonioides, Van Dusen Botanical Garden, Vancouver, fall colour

Southern Catalpa is native to the southeastern United States. It is smaller than the more commonly grown *Catalpa speciosa*, reaching ten to twelve metres in height with a strongly rounded outline. The large, heart-shaped, pale green leaves are pubescent beneath, and more triangular pointed at the tip than Western Catalpa. White showy flowers are produced in loose upright panicles in late July to August; making it one of last the deciduous trees to bloom locally. Each flower is banded with two yellowish ridges, which fade to red-orange; purple-brown spots decorate the tube and lower lobe of the flower. The seed-pod (less than one cm wide) is much thinner walled than *Catalpa speciosa*. Hanging from the tree like brown slender beans in October, they persist for some time. Southern Catalpa is uncommon in the Fraser South Region.

Where to see the trees:
Abbotsford
33881 Elm St, a huge open-grown tree with a DBH of 80 cm.

The Gardens, 34909 Old Yale Rd, several trees mixed in with a larger planting of Western Catalpa.

Langley
24355- 48 Ave, Salmon River Uplands, first tree on the west side of the entry driveway.

Richmond
Fantasy Garden World, 10800 No 5 Rd.

Surrey
Darts Hill Garden Park, 1660- 168 St, South Surrey, Garden Bed 11.

Catalpa speciosa

Western Catalpa, Northern Catalpa or Hardy Catalpa

Where to see the trees:

Abbotsford

33639 George Ave, Matsqui Prairie village, three large trees.

32084 Harris Rd, a large farm tree.

Jubilee Park, McCallum Rd south of Essendene, at the northern edge of the park.

The Gardens, 34909 Old Yale Rd, twelve trees mixed in with several Southern Catalpa.

Chilliwack

NE corner of Second Av and Nowell St.

Fairfield Island Park, 46000 Clare Ave, Fairfield Island.

Sardis Elementary School, 45775 Manuel Rd, Sardis, southwest corner of the school grounds, a row of trees.

Sardis Park, Sardis, a row of eight large trees at the west entrance to the park on School Lane.

Canadian Forces Base, Keith Wilson Rd and Vedder Rd, Vedder Crossing, a median planting on the Boulevard, north of Keith Wilson Rd.

Delta

Ottewell House, 4605 Arthur Dr, Ladner.

Beach Grove Golf Club, 5946- 12 Ave, Tsawwassen, a lovely specimen in the northeast corner of the parking lot.

Delta Secondary School, 4615- 51 St, Ladner, a row of four approximately fifteen metres high and with a DBH of 60 cm on the north side of the parking lot.

4260 River Road West Rd, Ladner.

Langley

Kwantlen University College, 20901 Langley Bypass, Langley City, two medium-sized specimens in the Gazebo Garden at the Field Lab.

3700 block 272 St, Southeast Langley, a large tree.

2414- 264 St, Southeast Langley.

Catalpa speciosa, developing seedpod

Catalpa speciosa, flowers

Western Catalpa is a very large deciduous tree, reaching a mature height of thirty metres. The upright oval winter silhouette differentiates this species from Southern Catalpa. Native to southern Illinois and Indiana to Tennessee and Arkansas, the exceptionally large, heart-shaped, midgreen leaves of Western Catalpa stand out boldly in the landscape. The tips of the leaves are narrowly pointed as compared to the blunt tips of *Catalpa bignonioides*. Fall colour of this commonly grown tree is often yellow-green to yellow. Large showy flowers are produced in late June to early July in the South Fraser Region. They are white, with yellow blotches and with a bit of purple speckling the throat of

Western Catalpa, Northern Catalpa or Hardy Catalpa

each blossom. Stout green bean-like seedpods up to 50 cm long hang from the tree in autumn, often remaining in place well into December.

Did You Know?

The three large Catalpa trees planted on George Avenue in Matsqui Village, Abbotsford, were likely planted in 1929 as part of the planting of the school grounds adjacent to the trees. The trees were donated by Colony Farm at Essondale, and were planted according to a Department of Education Plan.

• The three-story Craftsman-style Ottewell House on Arthur Drive in Ladner was built in 1915. Frederick Ottewell, who first arrived in Delta in 1912, was one of Delta's first veterinarians. He operated his animal practice out of the family home on Arthur Drive. Later the front room on the main floor of the house was Egidius Wientjes' barbershop. Wientjes cut and clipped hair for twenty years here before his retirement. Bernice Williston and her husband Douglas bought the Ottewell house in 1965. Mrs. Williston, a retired florist, is credited with the landscaping of the property so perhaps she planted the Western Catalpa.

Where to see the trees:

Richmond

Burkeville Park, 1031 Lancaster Cr, Burkeville, a number of very fine trees in this small park.

260- 540 Lancaster Cr, Burkeville, a row of splendid trees.

151, 191 and 231 Catalina Cr, Burkeville, a row of lovely trees.

SE corner of Sanders Rd and Garden City Rd.

Surrey

The Peninsula, 2500- 152 St, South Surrey, an excellent tree at the entry to the condominium complex.

On 32 Ave to the east of 172 St, a row of young trees along 32 Avenue.

Cedrus deodara, Cenotaph, Abbotsford

Cedrus deodara

Deodar Cedar or Himalayan Cedar

Cedrus deodara, foliage

Cedrus deodara
Deodar Cedar or Himalayan Cedar

Where to see the trees:

Abbotsford

Cenotaph, southeast corner of Laurel and Montrose Ave, three large trees handsomely frame the cenotaph.

Jubilee Park, McCallum Rd south of Essendene.

The Gardens, 34909 Old Yale Rd.

Chilliwack

Salish Park, 45860- 1 Ave.

Delta

11948 McKee Dr, west end of Panorama Ridge, a large tree.

Richmond

Steveston Park, 4111 Moncton St, Steveston, southwest of the Martial Arts Centre.

Fantasy Garden World, 10800 No 5 Rd.

Southarm Park, Garden City Rd and Williams Rd.

Surrey

Darts Hill Garden Park, 1660- 168 St, South Surrey, Garden Bed 18.

One of the most graceful of all the large conifers grown in the South Fraser Region, Deodar Cedar is native to the Western Himalayas from Afghanistan to western Nepal. It reaches a mature height of thirty-five metres. Glaucous blue green needles are produced singly on the current year's growth of the tree, but older branches are densely clothed with short spur branchlets that present the long flexible needles in tufts or whorls. Deodar Cedar is very drooping and graceful, the small branches are very pendulous, even the topmost leader bends down. Large resin-flecked green cones grow on the tops of the branches and are barrel-shaped. When mature, which takes several years, the cones turn brown and woody.

Cedrus deodara 'Aurea'
Golden Deodar Cedar or Golden Himalayan Cedar

Cedrus deodara 'Aurea', Steveston Park, Richmond

Cedrus deodara 'Aurea', foliage

Cedrus deodara 'Aurea'
Golden Deodar Cedar or Golden Himalayan Cedar

In comparison to Deodar Cedar, the Golden Deodar Cedar reaches a significantly smaller mature size of fifteen metres. The needles, which are golden yellow in the spring, turn a yellowish green in the fall. Needles exposed to the sun on the southern side of the tree or on the outermost needles, usually exhibit stronger golden colour than foliage shaded in the centre of the tree or on its north side. Golden Deodar Cedar is somewhat common in the South Fraser Region.

Where to see the trees:
Chilliwack

Skelton Park, opposite Chilliwack Municipal Hall at 8550 Young Rd.

Fairfield Island Park, 46000 Clare Ave, Fairfield Island, east side of the soccer fields, in the knoll area.

Richmond

Steveston Park, 4111 Moncton St, Steveston, two groups of several well-formed trees on the west and east sides of the Martial Arts Centre.

Cedrus atlantica
Atlas Cedar

Atlas Cedar is native to the Atlas and Riff Mountains of Algeria and Morocco. It reaches a mature height of fifty metres. A subspecies of Cedar of Lebanon, Atlas Cedar differs in that it has a taller crown and the branchlets are less congested within the crown. The dark green or bluish needles, which are held in whorls, are often shorter than Cedar of Lebanon. In the South Fraser Region, Atlas Cedar, particularly Blue Atlas Cedar, is very common while Cedar of Lebanon is not often grown. The branches of Atlas Cedar ascend, while the branches of Cedar of Lebanon are held in a horizontal plane. The branches of Deodar Cedar, which is also commonly grown, strongly weep or droop at the tips. The upright barrel-shaped cones of Atlas Cedar are smaller (6–10 cm high) versus the 8–12 cm high cones of the Cedar of Lebanon.

Where to see the trees:
Surrey

Darts Hill Garden Park, 1660- 168 St, South Surrey, Garden Bed 17.

Peace Arch Park, King George Hwy and 0 Ave, South Surrey.

Cedrus atlantica 'Glauca'

Blue Atlas Cedar or Silver Atlas Cedar

Cedrus atlantica 'Glauca', Lord Byng Elementary School, Richmond

Where to see the trees:

Abbotsford

Northwest corner of Old Yale Rd and McMillan Rd.

Chilliwack

East side of Sheffield Way and Silver Ave, Sardis.

Salish Park, 45860- 1 Ave.

46349 Hope River Rd, Fairfield Island.

Sardis Park, School Lane and Manuel Rd, Sardis.

Townsend Park, Ashwell Rd and Hodgins Ave, three trees on the west side of the concessions building.

University College of the Fraser Valley, 45600 Airport Rd.

Delta

Leisure Centre, 4600 Clarence Taylor Cr, Ladner, south side of the centre in the Rotary Park Planting.

Richmond

Lord Byng Elementary School, 3711 Georgia St, Steveston.

Fantasy Garden World, 10800 No 5 Rd.

North end of the junction of Steveston Hwy and Coppersmith Way.

Surrey

Darts Hill Garden Park, 1660- 168 St, South Surrey*, Garden Bed 11.

The Glades, 561- 172 St, South Surrey, on the west ridge, up from the tool shed.

In youth it is a pyramidal-shaped tree, maturing to a flat-topped crown with wide-spreading branches. The needles are steel blue, with a glaucous bloom. Blue Atlas Cedar is very commonly grown in the South Fraser Region.

Did You Know?

The two huge Blue Atlas Cedar trees on the west side of the new Lord Byng Elementary School building in Richmond were likely planted in 1930 or earlier, when a fourteen-room school was built there with financial contribution from the Japanese community. Steveston's first one-room school was built in 1897 on the site and a succession of schools has been built there subsequently. Steveston Public School was renamed Lord Byng School in honour of the Governor General of Canada in 1922.

• The two Blue Atlas Cedars frame the tiny Hide Hyodo Shimizu Heritage Garden. The garden is based upon a Traditional Garden in Kyoto, Japan. Its creation commemorates the work in the Japanese-Canadian community of Hide Shimizu, a teacher at Lord Byng School from 1926 to 1946. Fifteen rocks have been seated in flat concrete planes in this diminutive garden. As you stroll through, some of the rocks are out of sight in the lee of larger rocks. The plaque dedicated in 1997 reads, "Not all things are visible to the eye, but are known only to the heart."

Cedrus atlantica 'Glauca Pendula'
Blue Weeping Atlas Cedar

Cedrus atlantica 'Glauca Pendula', foliage

Cedrus atlantica 'Glauca Pendula', Arthur Drive, Delta

Blue Weeping Atlas Cedar is distinguished by its artistic habit. It is often trained to cascade over retaining walls, or is espaliered against flat surfaces. The architectural outline of the tree, with its long arching branches complete with drooping tips, creates a strong accent in the landscape.

Where to see the trees:

Delta
4211 Arthur Dr, Ladner.

Richmond
Fantasy Garden World, 10800 No 5 Rd.

Langley
Campus Crusade for Christ, 20385- 64 Ave, Willoughby, two on either side of the sign.

Surrey
RCMP Detachment, 14355- 57 Ave, Newton, an espaliered specimen on the south wall of the building.

South Surrey Arena, 2199- 148 St, South Surrey, a young tree on the south side of the building.

Cedrus brevifolia
Cyprus Cedar or Cyprian Cedar

Native to the mountains of Cyprus, the Cyprian Cedar is rare in the South Fraser Region. It has very short, dark grey-green needles that grow to 2 cm long but usually less than 1.2 cm long. The leader of the tree in youth arches downward. The branches of the tree are often short and held in strong horizontal planes. It reaches a mature height of twenty-five metres.

Where to see the trees:

Chilliwack
Salish Park, 45860- 1 Ave, two good-sized-trees on the south side of the main pond.

Fairfield Island Park, 46000 Clare Ave, Fairfield Island, on the east side of the soccer fields.

Cedrus libani
Cedar of Lebanon or Lebanon Cedar

Cedrus libani, Chaumont, France

Where to see the trees:

Richmond

4340 River Rd, a very young tree.

Surrey

Darts Hill Garden Park, 1660- 168 St, South Surrey, Garden Bed 11.

Rarely grown in the South Fraser Region in comparison to the Atlas Cedar or Deodar Cedar, the Cedar of Lebanon is an impressive tree at maturity, reaching a grand height of forty-five metres. It grows into a majestic conifer with a flat-topped crown, stiff, strongly tiered horizontal branches and a large buttressed trunk. The short, 1–3 cm long needles are stiff and dull dark green. The purple-brown, barrel-shaped cones take two years to mature.

Cercidiphyllum japonicum
Katsura Tree

Cercidiphyllum japonicum, Provincial Courthouse, Surrey

Native to Japan and Western China, the Katsura Tree is a wonderful medium-sized tree reaching a mature height of eighteen metres. Grown primarily for its foliage, the heart-shaped leaves emerge a shimmering coppery red colour in the early spring, age to chartreuse then to blue-green in the summer and turn a range of vibrant fall colours, from buttery yellow to oranges and reds with hints of purple in early October. Sometimes all these fall colours are seen on the same tree at the same time. The tree is often multi-stemmed or is branched low on the trunk. A neat, upright pyramidal habit

Cercidiphyllum japonicum, fall colour

marks the winter silhouette of the Katsura Tree, particularly in youth. The sharp-pointed bright red dormant buds resemble the claws of a lobster. Katsura Tree is quite common in the South Fraser Region.

Where to see the trees:

Abbotsford

34560 Merlin Dr, a lovely large specimen with a DBH of 40 cm.

City Police Department, 2838 Justice Way, southwest corner of the parking lot.

5680 Riverside Rd, Matsqui Prairie village.

Chilliwack

Municipal Hall, 8550 Young Rd.

Delta

Municipal Hall, 4500 Clarence Taylor Cr, Ladner, a small tree on the north side of the pond.

North Delta Recreation Centre, 11415- 84 Ave, a row of trees at the entry to the centre.

Langley

5500 block 203 Ave, Langley City, three trees.

Sendall Gardens, 20166- 50 Ave, Langley City, a large tree southeast of the duck pond.

Kwantlen University College, 20901 Langley Bypass, Langley City, a young specimen in the Gazebo Garden at the Field Lab.

200 St at 44 Ave, centre median, Langley City, two trees.

4526 Southridge Cr, Murrayville. This is the largest Katsura Tree found in the South Fraser Region.

Richmond

Fantasy Garden World, 10800 No 5 Rd.

McLean Park, 2500 McLean Ave, Hamilton area.

Steveston Park, 4111 Moncton St, Steveston.

Rosedale

Minter Gardens, 52892 Bunker Rd, a lovely specimen on the west side of the Arbor Garden.

Surrey

14593- 81A Ave, Fleetwood.

16345- 110 Ave, Guildford.

Darts Hill Garden Park, 1660- 168 St, South Surrey, Garden Bed 11.

Provincial Courthouse, 14340- 57 Ave, Newton, a fine grouping at the west entrance.

Redwood Park, 17900- 20 Ave, South Surrey, in the open area west of the parking lot.

South Surrey Arena, 2199- 148 St, South Surrey.

Cercidiphyllum japonicum 'Morioka Weeping'

Weeping Katsura

Cercidiphyllum japonicum 'Morioka Weeping', fall colour,
Darts Hill Garden Park, Surrey

Cercidiphyllum japonicum 'Morioka
Weeping', foliage

Where to see the trees:

Rosedale

Minter Gardens, 52892 Bunker Rd, west
of the Hillside/Alpine Garden.

Surrey

Darts Hill Garden Park, 1660- 168 St,
South Surrey, north end of the Magnolia
Walk.

Weeping Katsura is a small umbrella-shaped
tree, reaching a mature height of six to seven
metres. With its lovely blue-green foliage and
delicate pendulous branching habit, it is one of
the best weeping trees found in the South
Fraser Region, but, at present, is uncommon.

Cercidiphyllum magnificum
Syn. *Cercidiphyllum japonicum* var. *magnificum*

Mountain Katsura

Cercidiphyllum magnificum, unfolding leaves in the early spring

Cercidiphyllum magnificum, Darts Hill
Garden Park, Surrey

Native to the mountains of Japan, the Mountain Katsura has puckered, dark blue-green
leaves, which are larger than the Katsura Tree.

Mountain Katsura

In wintertime the twigs produce large peg-like spurs, which bear the dormant buds, quite unlike the Katsura tree with its straight or short-spurred branchlets bearing the claw-like buds. Mountain Katsura reaches a mature height of twelve to thirteen metres. Mountain Katsura is very rare in the South Fraser Region.

Where to see the trees:

Surrey
Darts Hill Garden Park, 1660- 168 St, South Surrey, Garden Bed 3.

Cercis canadensis

Eastern Redbud

Cercis canadensis, foliage

Cercis canadensis, flowers

Native to the central and eastern United States, southern Ontario and parts of northern Mexico, Eastern Redbud is a small twiggy tree, reaching a height of six to seven metres in the South Fraser Region. The dark green to blue-green, thin heart-shaped leaves emerge a reddish purple colour in the spring. They often colour bright yellow in the fall. The pink to reddish pea-like flowers are produced in clusters. The flowers arise on very short stalks along the main stems and branches of the tree before or at the time the leaves unfurl in early spring. The floral effect can be quite good but it is not reliable in our mild coastal climate. For consistent flowering, the buds require a chilling

Where to see the trees:

Delta
Municipal Hall, 4500 Clarence Taylor Cr, Ladner, front entry of the Municipal Hall.

Langley
Kwantlen University College, 20901 Langley Bypass, Langley City, a small tree growing at the east entrance of the campus, on the north side of the detention pond.

Surrey
Green Timbers Arboretum, 9800- 140 St, Whalley, to the south of the Heritage buildings.

Cercis canadensis
Eastern Redbud

period similar to what they might receive in their native habitat. The fruit is a flat pea-like pod, which persists over the winter months. In the dormant season, the zigzagging branching pattern of the tree helps to identify the Eastern Redbud. Dormant buds are red and poke out of the bark tissues like little pimples. Eastern Redbud is relatively common in the South Fraser Region.

Cercis canadensis 'Forest Pansy'
Forest Pansy Redbud

Where to see the trees:
Chilliwack

Exhibition Park, near the main door to the Curling Club.

Municipal Hall, 8550 Young Rd.

Langley

Kwantlen University College, 20901 Langley Bypass, Langley City, Gazebo Garden at the Field Lab.

Surrey

Darts Hill Garden Park, 1660- 168 St, South Surrey, Garden Bed 28.

South Surrey Arena, 2199- 148 St, South Surrey, two good-sized trees on the west side of the arena.

Cercis canadensis 'Forest Pansy', fall colour

The new growth of Forest Pansy Redbud is a saturated deep purple colour. The strong purple colour is held well into the summer, but as temperatures increase it may soften into purple-green. Fall colour ranges through red, green and orange on the same plant. Young stems are also red-purple colour.

Chamæcyparis lawsoniana
Lawson's Cypress, Port Orford Cedar or Oregon Cedar

Chamæcyparis lawsoniana, Peace Arch Park, Surrey

Chamæcyparis lawsoniana, bark

Lawson's Cypress is a tall majestic conifer reaching a height of thirty metres. Native to southwest Oregon and to northwest California, it has seen reductions in its numbers here due to *Phytopthora* root rot. This root disease has caused the decline of Lawson's Cypress in the South Fraser Region for several decades. At one time, Lawson's Cypress was very common in the South Fraser Region, at least in one or another of its many forms or cultivars. The green scale-like foliage of Lawson's Cypress looks very similar to the leaves of Western Red Cedar, *Thuja plicata*, but there are several differences. The foliage of Lawson's Cypress has a faint sour smell when crushed and the tiny leaves have white lines beneath. The leaves of Western Red Cedar are bright green, unlined underneath and smell fresh and sweet. The pea-sized cones of Lawson's Cypress, particularly when immature and tightly closed, resemble a miniature soccer ball, while the cones of Western Red Cedar are cigar-shaped when green. The overlapping cone scales of Western Red Cedar, when woody and mature, resemble the opening petals of a tulip flower.

Where to see the trees:

Abbotsford

2283 Lobban Ave.

Dunach Park, NW corner of Mt Lehman Rd and Downes Rd, a large multi-trunked tree with very green foliage.

Matsqui, Sumas, Abbotsford Centennial Library, 33660 South Fraser Way, on the northwest side of the entrance.

Chilliwack

44555 Vedder Mountain Rd, Yarrow.

Stö:lo Centre, 7201 Vedder Rd, Sardis.

Surrey

Green Timbers Arboretum, 9800- 140 St, Whalley.

School District No 36, Administrative Offices, 14225- 56 Ave, Newton, on the west side of the building.

Peace Arch Park, King George Hwy and 0 Ave, South Surrey.

Redwood Park, 17900- 20 Ave, South Surrey, southeast from the Tree House.

Chamæcyparis lawsoniana
'Erecta Virdis'

Green Column Cypress or Green Pyramid Cypress

Chamæcyparis lawsoniana 'Erecta Viridis', Boundary Bay Cemetery, Delta

The strong symmetrical shape of Green Column Cypress creates a very stately silhouette in the landscape. Its dark, emerald green foliage is held in tight vertical sprays, adding to the precise appearance of the tree. Very few cones are produced by this Lawson's Cypress cultivar. It is relatively common in the South Fraser Region.

Where to see the trees:

Abbotsford

Dunach Elementary School, 30357 Downes Rd, a large tree along the east fence line.

2575 Campbell Ave.

Chilliwack

7295 Chilliwack River Rd, Sardis.

Delta

Boundary Bay Cemetery, 56 St and 8 Ave, Tsawwassen, a very fine specimen that dominates the view.

Langley

5505- 248 St, Salmon River Uplands, two large trees on the south property line.

John Cornock Residence, 8140- 272 St, Northeast Langley. An impressive tree frames the lovely farmhouse with many other mature trees on the property, such as a large Elm and a Linden.

Surrey

1109- 168 St, South Surrey.

Redwood Park, 17900- 20 Ave, South Surrey, southeast from the Tree House.

9132- 120th Street, Whalley, two lovely trees.

Did You Know?

John Cornock, born in Erin, Ontario in 1853, his wife Eliza, and their four children lived in a log cabin for fifteen years until their large two-story farmhouse in Glen Valley in Northeast Langley was built in 1905.

Chamæcyparis lawsoniana
Glauca Group
Blue Lawson's Cypress

Chamæcyparis lawsoniana 'Glauca Group', foliage and cones

Blue Lawson's Cypress is very common in the South Fraser Region. It reaches a height of twenty-five metres, with a strongly pyramidal shape. The foliage is deep grey-blue in colour.

Where to see the trees:
Abbotsford

33970 Victory Blvd.

Hougen Park, south off Highway 1 on Cole Rd.

Chilliwack

Canadian Forces Base, Keith Wilson Rd and Vedder Rd, Vedder Crossing, south side of Hong Kong Rd.

Langley

Compost Demonstration Garden, 4885-221 St, Murrayville.

NW corner of Hitchingpost Cr and Saddle-horn Cr, Salmon River Uplands, a very large tree.

Newlands Golf and Country Club, 21045-48 Ave.

Chamæcyparis lawsoniana 'Stewartii'
Stewart's Golden Lawson Cypress,
Wintergold Cypress or Sunshine Tree

Stewart's Golden Lawson Cypress is the most common golden yellow cultivar found in the South Fraser Region. It grows into a large symmetrical cone shape, twenty to twenty-four metres high. The foliage is slightly pendulous at the tips, giving the tree a very soft and graceful appearance.

Where to see the trees:
Chilliwack

Canadian Forces Base, Keith Wilson Rd and Vedder Rd, Vedder Crossing, southeast corner of the parade ground at Vimy Ave, two trees on the northwest corner of Sicily Rd and Normandy Dr.

Sardis Park, School Lane and Manuel Rd, Sardis.

Yarrow Central Park, southeast corner of Kehler St and Yarrow Central Rd, a mature specimen in the centre of the park.

Surrey

1109- 168 St, South Surrey.

Redwood Park, 17900- 20 Ave, South Surrey*.

Chamæcyparis lawsoniana 'Stewartii', Salmon River Uplands, Langley

Chamæcyparis lawsoniana 'Stewartii'

Stewart's Golden Lawson Cypress, Wintergold Cypress or Sunshine Tree

Where to see the trees:

Langley

19700 block 48 Ave, Langley City.

Fort Langley National Historic Site, 23433 Mavis St, Ft Langley.

7296 Telegraph Trail, Northeast Langley.

5670- 246 St, Salmon River Uplands, Langley.

22075- 16 Ave, Southeast Langley, an open-grown specimen that dominates the front garden.

Chamæcyparis lawsoniana 'Wisselii'

Wissel's Lawson Cypress

Chamæcyparis lawsoniana 'Wisselii', foliage and pollen cones

Chamæcyparis lawsoniana 'Wisselii', Aberdeen Cemetery, Abbotsford

Where to see the trees:

Abbotsford

Aberdeen Cemetery, 29200 Fraser Highway, a gorgeous tree.

Chilliwack

45750 Wellington Ave, a magnificent tree.

47435 Swallow Cr, Little Mountain, a young specimen.

Reaching a mature height of fifteen metres, Wissel's Lawson Cypress has very distinctive foliage. The dark bluish green leaves are produced in dense tufts that form larger twisted and thickened sprays that sweep upward on the branches. In the spring, the male pollen-bearing flowers are very showy.

Chamæcyparis nootkatensis, Kwantlen University College

Chamæcyparis nootkatensis, foliage and pollen cones

Nootka Cypress is a primarily coastal evergreen, growing to a height of twenty to forty metres. It grows from southern Alaska to northwest California, but at higher elevations in southern latitudes. The leaves of Nootka Cypress are blue-green or grey-green, sharp to the touch and smell catty when crushed. The cones are the size of a nickel, round, ripening purple and finally turning brown. The tree has a pyramidal shape with upward swooping branch tips. Flattened sprays of leaves droop vertically from the branchlets. The shaggy mature bark is silver-grey, peeling away in short vertical strips. Examples of the species are not commonly grown in the South Fraser Region.

Where to see the trees:

Chilliwack

Canadian Forces Base, Keith Wilson Rd and Vedder Rd, Vedder Crossing, west side of Calais Cr at Arnhem Rd.

Langley

Kwantlen University College, 20901 Langley Bypass, Langley City, a single specimen to the west of the Daycare building.

Richmond

Millennium Botanical Garden and Arboretum, N McLennan Community Park, Granville Ave and Garden City Rd.

Surrey

Darts Hill Garden Park, 1660- 168 St, South Surrey, Garden Bed 1.

Green Timbers Arboretum, 9800- 140 St, Whalley, along the north roadway of the arboretum.

Did You Know?

Nootka Cypress is the namesake for Cypress Provincial Park on the North Shore Mountains. A giant, 290 cm diameter at breast height, approximately 1200-year old Nootka Cypress tree is growing on the west side of the main road, just south of the access road to the cross-country ski area parking lot. The elevation here is approximately 900 metres above sea level. To access a grove of massive Nootka Cypress, from the Cypress Bowl downhill parking lot follow the trail behind the snowboard rental hut and strike east. Cross a deep gully and carry on until the trail splits, the left fork travels through several groves of huge trees. Ten minutes of walking brings you to a magnificent Nootka Cypress with a DBH of over 300 cm, fifty metres to the right of the trail where it intersects with the old Mount Strachan trail.

Chamæcyparis nootkatensis
Pendula Group
Weeping Nootka Cypress

Where to see the trees:

Chilliwack

Yarrow Central Park, southeast corner of Kehler St and Yarrow Central Rd.

Chilliwack Municipal Airport, 46244 Chilliwack Airport Rd, two good-sized trees.

47455 Swallow Cr, Little Mountain, a very attractive grouping of trees on a slope.

Delta

4493 Arthur Dr, Ladner.

Langley

Christian Life Assembly, 21277-56 Ave, Milner, a beautiful grove of trees at the front entry to the church.

6010- 237 A Street, Salmon River Uplands.

Richmond

Fantasy Garden World, 10800 No 5 Rd, this tree is the largest one in the South Fraser Region.

Rosedale

Minter Gardens, 52892 Bunker Rd, southern end of the Lake Garden.

Surrey

City Hall, 14245- 56 Ave, Newton, two good specimens on the southeast corner of the building.

The Glades, 561- 172 St, South Surrey, Azalea walk at Murray Lane west.

Chamæcyparis nootkatensis Pendula Group, a grove of trees at the Christian Life Assembly, Langley

Chamæcyparis nootkatensis Pendula Group, cones and foliage

Weeping Nootka Cypress makes a graceful slender tree, growing twenty metres high. The top of the tree, main branch tips and all the lateral branches weep. The sprays of leaves hang limply, like washing on a line. The tree is more often yellow-green in colour than the species, *Chamæcyparis nootkatensis*, which is green to blue-green in colour. Weeping Nootka Cypress trees, especially young specimens, are common in the South Fraser Region.

Chamæcyparis obtusa 'Gracilis'
Dwarf Hinoki Cypress

Chamæcyparis obtusa 'Gracilis',
Skelton Park, Chilliwack

Chamæcyparis obtusa 'Gracilis', foliage

Dwarf Hinoki Cypress, which is native to Japan, can be easily identified by the blunt leaf scales and when these are overturned, there is a conspicuous whitish "X" mark on the underside. The foliage of Hinoki Cypress is very sweet smelling when crushed. An elegant conifer eventually reaching a height of seven to ten metres with great age, Dwarf Hinoki Cypress is very slow growing. The emerald-green foliage grows in tufted and cupped sprays that sweep and twist upwards. Trees seldom produce cones. Dwarf Hinoki Cypress is very common in the South Fraser Region.

Where to see the trees:
Abbotsford
The Gardens, 34909 Old Yale Rd.

Chilliwack
Municipal Hall, 8550 Young Rd.

Skelton Park, opposite Chilliwack Municipal Hall at 8550 Young Rd.

Richmond
Fantasy Garden World, 10800 No 5 Rd.

Chamæcyparis pisifera 'Boulevard'
Syn. *Chamæcyparis pisifera* 'Cyanoviridis'
Boulevard Moss Cypress

Chamæcyparis pisifera 'Boulevard', foliage

Chamæcyparis pisifera 'Boulevard'
Syn. *Chamæcyparis pisifera* 'Cyanoviridis'

Boulevard Moss Cypress

Where to see the trees:

Langley

Sendall Gardens, 20166- 50 Ave, Langley City, at the east side of the entrance to the parking lot.

Surrey

Darts Hill Garden Park, 1660- 168 St, South Surrey, Garden Bed 24a.

The foliage of this commonly grown conifer is needle-like, light blue-green in the growing season. The dense foliage ages to a grey-blue in the winter months. Boulevard Moss Cypress is a small conifer, broadly pyramidal in form, reaching a mature height of six metres. It has a soft fluffy billowy appearance from a distance.

Chamæcyparis pisifera f. *plumosa*
Plume Sawara Cypress

Chamæcyparis pisifera f. *plumosa*, foliage

Chamæcyparis pisifera f. *plumosa*, Murrayville Cemetery, Langley

Where to see the trees:

Abbotsford

Jubilee Park, McCallum Rd south of Essendene, five trees on the north side of the park immediately behind the MSA Centennial Library.

Langley

Murrayville Cemetery, 21405- 44 Ave, Murrayville.

Originally from Japan, Plume Sawara Cypress is commonly found in the South Fraser Region. The green foliage is feathery and very softly textured, but is still somewhat prickly to the touch. A dense, pyramidal tree, it reaches a mature height of twelve to fifteen metres. The woody brown cones of Sawara Cypress are small and rounded, growing to .5 cm across.

Chamæcyparis pisifera 'Plumosa Aurea',
Trinity Western University, Langley

Chamæcyparis pisifera 'Plumosa Aurea'
Gold Plume Cypress

Where to see the trees:
Abbotsford,
Hazelwood Cemetery, 34000 block Hazelwood Ave, a row at the northeast end of the grounds.

Chilliwack
Stö:lo Centre, 7201 Vedder Rd, Sardis.

Delta
North Delta Recreation Centre, 11415- 84 Ave.

Langley
Trinity Western University, 7600 Glover Rd, Willoughby, two trees to the west of Robson Hall.

Richmond
Fantasy Garden World, 10800 No 5 Rd.

Surrey
Darts Hill Garden Park, 1660- 168 St, South Surrey, Garden Bed 24a.

Very common in the South Fraser Region, Gold Plume Cypress is similar to forma *plumosa* above but the young foliage is bright yellow, maturing to brown-yellow in the winter months. Gold Plume Cypress reaches a mature size of six to nine metres.

Chamæcyparis pisifera 'Squarrosa'
Moss Sawara Cypress, Moss Cypress or Brown Junk Tree

Common in the South Fraser Region, Moss Cypress is the largest of the Sawara Cypresses, growing ten to twelve metres tall. The feathery, pale blue-grey foliage appears soft and billowy but is prickly to the touch. It rarely produces cones.

Where to see the trees:
Abbotsford
Dunach Elementary School, 30357 Downes Rd, a large tree along the east fence line.

33481 Nelson Ave, an open-branched mature tree with sculptural appeal.

Chilliwack
General Hospital, 45600 Menholm Rd.

Portage Park, Portage Av and Woodbine St.

Chamæcyparis pisifera 'Squarrosa',
Boundary Bay Cemetery, Delta

Chamæcyparis pisifera 'Squarrosa'

Moss Sawara Cypress, Moss Cypress or Brown Junk Tree

Chamæcyparis pisifera 'Squarrosa', foliage

Where to see the trees:

Delta

Augustinian Monastery, 3900 Arthur Dr, Ladner, two massive specimens, one with a DBH of 140 cm and a height of nineteen metres is the largest Moss Sawara Cypress in the South Fraser Region. The bark of these two trees is very attractive.

Boundary Bay Cemetery, 56 St and 8 Ave, Tsawwassen, several very fine specimens.

Langley

Trinity Western University, 7600 Glover Rd, Willoughby, one tree west of McMillan Hall.

Surrey

Darts Hill Garden Park, 1660- 168 St, South Surrey, Garden Bed 2.

x *Chitalpa tashkentensis* 'Pink Dawn'

Pink Dawn Chitalpa

x *Chitalpa tashkentensis* 'Pink Dawn', flowers

Where to see the trees:

Langley

Kwantlen University College, 20901 Langley Bypass, Langley City, at the entry to the Field Lab underneath the European Beech tree.

Surrey

Darts Hill Garden Park, 1660- 168 St, South Surrey, Garden Bed 27.

Very rare in the South Fraser Region, Pink Dawn Chitalpa is a bigeneric hybrid. Its parents are *Catalpa bignonioides* a medium-sized deciduous tree and *Chilopsis linearis*, a large evergreen shrub native to the southwestern United States and Mexico. Pink Dawn Chitalpa is a small deciduous tree, growing six to ten metres tall, with pale green, long lance-shaped leaves. The trumpet-shaped dark pink flowers are showy and are produced in late June to early July.

Cladrastis kentuckea
Syn. *Cladrastis lutea*
Yellowwood or Yellow Ash

Cladrastis kentuckea, pinnately compound leaf

Cladrastis kentuckea, fall colour

Yellowwood is native to North Carolina, Tennessee and Kentucky. It reaches a mature height of fifteen metres. The pinnately compound leaves unfold a soft yellow-green, are bright green in the summer and turn a rich golden yellow in the fall. Each leaf is thickened at the base, completely enclosing the developing dormant bud. The white fragrant flowers are pea-shaped, produced in long pendulous panicles in June. The fruit is a pea-like brown pod. Yellowwood comes by its common name because the heartwood is bright yellow. The outer bark is very like the smooth grey bark of European Beech.

Where to see the trees:
Surrey
Darts Hill Garden Park, 1660- 168 St, South Surrey, Garden Beds C1 and 40.

Cornus controversa

Giant Dogwood, Great Dogwood or Table Dogwood

Where to see the trees:

Surrey

Darts Hill Garden Park, 1660- 168 St, South Surrey, Garden Bed 4.

Cornus controversa, flat flower heads

Native from the Himalayas to China, Korea, Japan, Taiwan and Vietnam, Giant Dogwood, may reach a mature height and spread of ten metres. It has a very strongly layered branching habit. The flat flower heads appear in June on the tops of the branches, each one with many tiny white star-shaped blossoms. Giant Dogwood is one of the very few dogwoods that has its leaves held alternately; most dogwoods have an opposite leaf arrangement. The fruit is a blue-black pea-sized berry, ripening in October. Giant Dogwood is rare in the South Fraser Region.

Cornus controversa 'Variegata'

Variegated Giant Dogwood or Wedding Cake Tree

Where to see the trees:

Surrey

Darts Hill Garden Park, 1660- 168 St, South Surrey, Garden Bed 37.

Cornus contoversa 'Variegata', flowering heads and variegated foliage

Cornus controversa 'Variegata'
Variegated Giant Dogwood or Wedding Cake Tree

A highly picturesque tree, Variegated Giant Dogwood typically reaches a mature height and spread of three to four metres. The strongly layered branching habit with the large flat heads in June of small white star-shaped blossoms give rise to its common name of Wedding Cake Tree. This dogwood is one of the very few dogwoods that has its leaves held in an alternate arrangement; most dogwood have an opposite leaf arrangement. Each unequally sided and curled leaf is edged in creamy white. Variegated Giant Dogwood is rare in the South Fraser Region.

Cornus 'Eddie's White Wonder'
Eddie's White Wonder Dogwood

Cornus 'Eddie's White Wonder', Salmon River Uplands, Langley

Cornus 'Eddie's White Wonder', fall colour

Eddie's White Wonder Dogwood originated locally. Henry M. Eddie, a Fraser Valley nursery grower hybridized the plant from British Columbia's native dogwood, *Cornus nuttallii* and the smaller dogwood native to Eastern Canada, *Cornus florida* in the late 1930's. Eddie's White Wonder Dogwood carries characteristics of both parents. It has the strongly pyramidal form and four large creamy bracts of our coastal native, but a smaller overall size and the floriferousness of its Eastern parent. Eddie's

Where to see the trees:
Abbotsford

32141 Dahlstrom Ave.

33451 Rainbow Ave, a huge specimen.

2050 Guilford St.

35045 Marshall Rd, a lovely tree.

2687 McCallum Rd, a good-looking tree.

School District No 34 Administrative Offices, 2790 Tims St, two good-sized trees.

Trethewey House (M.S.A. Museum), 2313 Ware St, west side of the garage.

33551 Holland Ave.

Cornus 'Eddie's White Wonder'

Eddie's White Wonder Dogwood

Where to see the trees:

Chilliwack

Municipal Hall, 8550 Young Rd, a row of trees on the east side of city hall in the staff parking lot.

Canadian Forces Base, Keith Wilson Rd and Vedder Rd, Vedder Crossing, many young trees.

42150 Yarrow Central Rd, Yarrow.

Delta

All Saints' Anglican Church, 4755 Arthur Drive, Ladner, five young trees on the south side of the church.

Langley

Sendall Gardens, 20166- 50 Ave, Langley City.

The Redwoods Golf Course, 22011- 88 Ave, Northwest Langley, a young planting of trees on the berm along the street.

20611- 44 Ave, Murrayville.

4702- 238 St, Salmon River Uplands.

White Wonder blooms in May and may also rebloom in late August and September with a second flush of flowers. The fall colour is often orange-red. With *Cornus* Eddie's White Wonder, the tight, button-like pale green cluster of true flowers is not enclosed by the floral bracts over the winter. *Cornus nuttallii* has similar naked true flowers, but in the winter or early spring the cluster is much larger, looser and darker green. Eddie's White Wonder Dogwood is commonly planted in the South Fraser Region.

Richmond

Fantasy Garden World, 10800 No 5 Rd.

Surrey

City Hall, 14245- 56 Ave, Newton, a number of small trees in the west parking lot.

Darts Hill Garden Park, 1660- 168 St, South Surrey, Garden Bed 23.

Provincial Courthouse, 14340- 57 Ave, Newton, several young trees on the north side of the parking lot.

Cornus florida

Eastern Flowering Dogwood or Flowering Dogwood

Cornus florida, floral bracts

Cornus florida, fall colour, Salmon River Uplands

Flowering Dogwood is a small tree reaching a mature height of six to eight metres. The horizontal purplish green to greyish branches swoop

Eastern Flowering Dogwood or Flowering Dogwood

upwards at the tips giving the tree an open airy appearance. The winter silhouette is greatly enhanced by the plump floral buds at the end of each stem. The medium to dark green leaves turn an outstanding red-orange to purple-red in the fall. The flower is smaller than our native dogwood, *Cornus nuttallii*, but it is produced in great abundance in May. Four white bracts subtend the clusters of tiny yellow-green flowers; it is these bracts that are more often thought of as the flower petals. Each bract has a purple edged bit cut out of the tip. The showy clusters of fruit are bright red, each one lozenge shaped, ripening in October. The mature bark of Eastern Flowering Dogwood is broken into blocky plates reminiscent of an alligator's back. *Cornus florida* is not as common in the South Fraser Region as the pink flowering types.

Where to see the trees:
Abbotford

33480 Nelson Ave.

33590 Harris Rd, Matsqui village.

Langley

23823- 58A Avenue, Salmon River Uplands.

Surrey

SW corner of Northern Cr and 168 St.

Cornus florida 'Rainbow'
Rainbow Flowering Dogwood

Cornus florida 'Rainbow', fall colour

Rainbow Flowering Dogwood is not as floriferous as some other cultivars, but when it does bloom the floral bracts are white. The tree is noted for its variegated foliage; the leaves are brightly yellow- and green-banded in the summer and turn carmine red with purple overtones in the autumn.

Where to see the trees:
Langley

23862- 58A Avenue, Salmon River Uplands.

Rosedale

Minter Gardens, 52892 Bunker Rd, on the south side of the Trillium Restaurant.

Cornus florida f. *rubra*

Pink Flowering Dogwood, Pink Dogwood or Red Dogwood

Cornus florida f. *rubra*, in bloom, Darts Hill Garden Park, Surrey

Where to see the trees:

Abbotsford

2360 Guilford Dr, a good-sized young tree.

2150 Mirus Dr.

Jubilee Park, McCallum Rd south of Essendene.

Chilliwack

45573 Princess Ave, a good-sized tree.

Family Place, 45845 Wellington Ave.

University College of the Fraser Valley, 45600 Airport Rd.

Delta

5125- 45 Ave, Ladner.

Langley

NW corner of 36 Ave and 200 St, Brookswood.

4501 Southridge Cr, Murrayville.

Richmond

Fantasy Garden World, 10800 No 5 Rd.

Surrey

City Hall, 14245- 56 Ave, Newton, between the Provincial Courthouse and the Municipal Hall.

City Hall, 14245- 56 Ave, Newton, west side of the building.

Darts Hill Garden Park, 1660- 168 St, South Surrey, Garden Bed 25.

Fraser Health Region office, 14265- 56 Ave, Newton, two attractive specimens on the west side of the building.

Cornus florida f. *rubra*, floral bracts

Pink Flowering Dogwood is a small but elegant tree, reaching a mature height and spread of six metres. The branches are purplish, often with a whitish bloom on the youngest stems. Like the species, the upward swooping branch tips are helpful in identifying the tree in winter. The floral bracts are often a delicate pink, but can be pinkish-red. The purple-green leaves have a strong wavy edge and the leaves may appear cupped. Fruit is seldom produced on this very commonly grown form of Eastern Dogwood.

Kousa Dogwood or Chinese Dogwood

Cornus kousa, Salmon River Uplands, Langley

Cornus kousa, fruit

Native to China, Korea, and Japan, Kousa Dogwood reaches a mature height of six metres. Vase-shaped in youth, it ages into a rounded tree with strongly tiered branches. The floral bracts are four in number, very sharply pointed and creamy white. They age to a soft pink. Appearing in June, several weeks later than our native dogwood, the spectacular blooms last for weeks. As they develop, they look like tiny stars, creating an arboreal Milky Way of blooms. The wavy blue-green leaves turn deep orange-red to scarlet in the fall. The fruit, which looks like half of a raspberry, is very ornamental, ripening in September to October.

Where to see the trees:

Chilliwack

Municipal Hall, 8550 Young Rd.

University College of the Fraser Valley, 45600 Airport Rd, south side of Building D, Multi-purpose Complex.

Chilliwack Cemeteries, 10010 Hillcrest Dr, Little Mountain, a double row of trees planted in large containers.

Delta

Hospital, 5800 Mountain View Blvd, Ladner, a lovely large specimen at the entrance to Admitting.

North Delta Recreation Centre, 11415-84 Ave, Delta.

Langley

NW corner of 237A St and 58 Ave, Salmon River Uplands.

Rosedale

Minter Gardens, 52892 Bunker Rd, a group of large specimens in the north-ernmost bed of the Meadow Garden.

Surrey

City Hall, 14245- 56 Ave, Newton, west side of the building, on the south side of the pond.

Darts Hill Garden Park, 1660- 168 St, South Surrey, Magnolia Walk and Pasture, Garden Beds 4 and 22.

The Glades, 561- 172 St, South Surrey, Azalea walk past the lookout, south.

Cornus kousa 'Satomi'

Satomi Chinese Dogwood or Pink Chinese Dogwood

Where to see the trees:

Chilliwack

City Hall, 8550 Young Rd, one tree near the rear entrance.

Langley

Kwantlen University College, 20901 Langley Bypass, Langley City, at the northwest base of the Highway overpass.

Surrey

18653- 53 Ave, Cloverdale.

10919- 129 St, Whalley.

Darts Hill Garden Park, 1660- 168 St, South Surrey, Magnolia Walk and Pasture, Garden Bed 34.

Cornus kousa 'Satomi', floral bracts

Satomi Chinese Dogwood originated in Japan, and is relatively common in the South Fraser Region. The flowers are very pleasing as they develop, as they resemble tiny blushing pink stars. When mature, the large, long-lasting floral bracts are a deep pink.

Cornus mas

Cornelian Cherry, Long Cherry tree or Dogwood Cherry

Where to see the trees:

Langley

Kwantlen University College, 20901 Langley Bypass, Langley City, several young trees along the east perimeter of the turf demonstration area at the Field Lab.

Rosedale

Minter Gardens, 52892 Bunker Rd, two specimens on the east side of the Arbor Garden.

Surrey

Darts Hill Garden Park, 1660- 168 St, South Surrey, Garden Bed 10.

Cornus mas, foliage

Not commonly grown in the South Fraser Region, Cornelian Cherry is often a large multi-stemmed shrub or small tree reaching five metres in height. Its thin, bright yellow floral parts look like long-legged spiders perched on the stems when the tree is blooming in February. The leaves are strongly veined, which is typical of most members of the dogwood genus.

Cornelian Cherry, Long Cherry Tree or Dogwood Cherry

The leaves turn purple-red in the fall. The cherry red fruit is fleshy and oblong-shaped (like an elongated cherry) and is produced in August and September.

Cornus nuttallii

Pacific Dogwood or Western (White) Dogwood

Cornus nuttallii, 96 Avenue, Fort Langley   *Cornus nuttallii*, floral bracts

Pacific Dogwood is the province of British Columbia's floral emblem. It is native to the south coastal region, and south to Oregon and Northern California. Pacific Dogwood reaches a mature height of fifteen metres. While it has a strong pyramidal shape, the tree is most noted for its extravagant display in April to May of four (six) white floral bracts, which surround the tiny true flowers. Each large inflorescence is showy and long lasting. In some years, Pacific Dogwood will bloom again lightly in the fall. The foliage is midgreen and slightly wavy along the edge. The leaves are strongly veined, the veins curve parallel to the leaf margin. The leaves turn good orange, red and yellow in the fall. The tightly clustered fruit, which is crimson red, is produced in September to October and is sought after by birds. Pacific Dogwood is common in the South Fraser Region.

Where to see the trees:

Abbotsford

MSA General Hospital, 2179 McCallum Rd, in the west parking lot near the southwest corner of the main building, a very large good-looking tree.

Chilliwack

General Hospital, 45600 Menholm Rd.

5660 Extrom Rd, Ryder Lake.

Canadian Forces Base, Keith Wilson Rd and Vedder Rd, Vedder Crossing, a tree on the southwest corner of Calais Cr at Caen Rd.

Langley

23048- 96 Ave, Ft Langley.

Murrayville Cemetery, 21405- 44 Ave, Murrayville, a row of very fine mature trees planted on the east side of the cemetery between the grand old Red Oaks.

5798- 246 St, Salmon River Uplands.

Cornus nuttallii
Pacific Dogwood or Western (White) Dogwood

Where to see the trees:

Richmond

Steveston Hwy and No 6 Rd, a street tree planting on both sides of the street.

Millennium Botanical Garden and Arboretum, N McLennan Community Park, Granville Ave and Garden City Rd.

Surrey

Darts Hill Garden Park, 1660- 168 St, South Surrey, Garden Bed 8.

Green Timbers Arboretum, 9800- 140 St, Whalley, at the northwest roadway entrance to the arboretum on the east side.

The Glades, 561- 172 St, South Surrey.

2339- 168 St, South Surrey.

NW corner of 100 Ave and 141 Street, Whalley.

Cornus nuttallii 'Colrigo Giant'
Colrigo Giant Dogwood

Cornus nuttallii 'Colrigo Giant', floral bracts

Where to see the trees:

Surrey

Darts Hill Garden Park, 1660- 168 St, South Surrey, north side of the main entry walkway.

Colrigo Giant Dogwood is a superior selection to the species, with very large inflorescences up to 18 cm across. The heavily textured leaves are larger too, and colour well in the fall. The cultivar name arises from the first letters of the name "Columbia River Gorge", where the original tree was found growing in 1949.

Did You Know?

The City of Surrey and the Fraser Valley Heritage Tree Society planted the *Cornus nuttallii* 'Colrigo Giant', on March 11, 2000 in Darts Hill Garden Park. The bronze plaque set on the granite boulder at the base of the tree says, "In recognition of Susan M. Murray for her contribution to tree preservation."

Corylus avellana
Common Hazelnut, Common Filbert, European Hazel or Filbert

Corylus avellana, foliage

Corylus avellana, Sendall Gardens, Langley

Native to Europe, Western Asia and North Africa, Common Hazelnut is often grown as a very large thicket-producing shrub but it can be trained into a small tree growing to eight metres tall. The thin, dark green leaves are almost round and covered with a soft hair on both surfaces. The fall leaf colour is warm golden yellow. In the early winter, the dangling yellow male catkins easily identify Common Hazelnut. The tan-coloured young stems are patterned with horizontal lenticels, much like cherry bark. The developing hazelnuts are partially enclosed in green papery nut husk. In October and November, the tasty dark brown hazelnuts are harvested in local Fraser Valley nut orchards for the Christmas market. Hazelnuts are commonly grown as a nut-producing tree throughout the South Fraser Region. It has naturalized in some areas, becoming an important food source for squirrels and birds such as Stellar Blue Jays and crows.

Where to see the trees:
Abbotsford
3065 Clearbrook Rd, a row of trees remnant from an early orchard.

Chilliwack
41995 Yale Rd West, Greendale.

Langley
Sendall Gardens, 20166- 50 Ave, Langley City.

Hazelgrove Farm, 8651 Glover Rd, Ft Langley.

Surrey
Darts Hill Garden Park, 1660- 168 St, South Surrey, Garden Bed 25 and a delightful allée of mature trees to the west of the Magnolia Walk.

Elgin Heritage Park, a lovely grove west of the Historic Stewart Farm located at 13723 Crescent Road, South Surrey.

Corylus avellana 'Contorta'

Corkscrew Hazel, Harry Lauder's Walking Stick, Contorted Hazel or Curly Hazel

Corylus avellana 'Contorta', Darts Hill Garden Park, Surrey

Corylus avellana 'Contorta', foliage and catkins

Corkscrew Hazel, as the name suggests, has spirally twisted stems, catkins and leaves. In the dormant season, the tree is very picturesque, but in the summer the leaves are thickly produced and obscure its most desirable trait. Relatively common, Corkscrew Hazel seldom produces nuts in the South Fraser Region.

Where to see the trees:

Abbotsford

34154 Larch St.

Chilliwack

Gwynne Vaughan Park, Williams Rd and Hope River Rd, Fairfield Island.

Salish Park, 45860- 1 Ave, at the edge of the pond.

Canadian Forces Base, Keith Wilson Rd and Vedder Rd, Vedder Crossing, on Dundern Ave, an odd specimen growing on a single stem and grafted at 1.4 meters in height.

University College of the Fraser Valley, 45600 Airport Rd, Building B, Agriculture and west side of Building C, Health Sciences.

Langley

21691- 44A Ave, Murrayville.

Sendall Gardens, 20166- 50 Ave, Langley City.

Richmond

Fantasy Garden World, 10800 No 5 Rd, a very large tree.

Surrey

Darts Hill Garden Park, 1660- 168 St, South Surrey*, Garden Bed 25. This tree is one of the largest Corkscrew Hazelnuts in the South Fraser Region.

The Glades, 561- 172 St, South Surrey, on the East Ridge near the house.

Purple Filbert or Purple Giant Filbert

Purple Filbert is somewhat rare in the South Fraser Region. The dark purple leaves, which age to dark purple-green by late summer, are very handsome. Dormant buds, male catkins, nut husks and immature nuts are also purple. The nut husk grows twice the length of each nut, widening at the tip, covering the nut like a sock.

Where to see the trees:

Richmond

Fantasy Garden World, 10800 No 5 Rd.

Langley

Sendall Gardens, 20166- 50 Ave, Langley City.

4800 block 208 St, Langley City.

Surrey

City Hall, 14245- 56, Newton, to the east of the pond garden.

Corylus maxima 'Purpurea', foliage

English Hawthorn, English Woodland or English Midland Hawthorn

Cratægus lævigata 'Plena', the flowers of this cultivar are double white, fading to pink

Cratægus lævigata 'Plena', fruit

Cratægus lævigata
Syn. *Cratægus oxyacantha*

English Hawthorn, English Woodland or English Midland Hawthorn

Where to see the trees:

Langley

City Park, 207 St and 48 Ave, Langley City, on the northeast corner of the park behind the baseball backstop. This tree is *Cratægus lævigata* 'Plena', a double-flowered variety which produces lovely white flowers which age to pale pink.

Very commonly found in the South Fraser Region, English Hawthorn is a small, messy, deciduous tree growing to six to eight metres tall. It is armed with stout thorns, though it is less thorny than the Common Hawthorn, with which it is often confused. The leaves of English Hawthorn are three- to five-lobed and turn yellow-orange in the fall. The flowers are white. They are produced in mid to late May in flat clusters. The fruit is scarlet red and ripens in September and October. The fruit has two or three seeds.

Cratægus x *lavalleei*

Lavalle Hawthorn

Where to see the trees:

Langley

Douglas Park, 20550 Douglas Cr, Langley City, wonderful mature specimen at the northeast corner of the park.

Boulevard planting between 207 and 208 St on 90A Ave, Walnut Grove.

Williams Park, 6600 block 238 St, Salmon River Uplands.

Richmond

Fantasy Garden World, 10800 No 5 Rd.

Garry Point Park, west end of Moncton St, Steveston, a group of young trees at the east side of the parking lot.

Surrey

9133- 138A St, Whalley.

9148- 138A St, Whalley.

Cratægus x *lavalleei,* in bloom, Douglas Park, Langley

A wide-spreading oval at maturity, Lavalle Hawthorn grows to six metres high by eight metres wide. Its lustrous dark green leaves persist until Christmas, after turning a lovely orange-red, sometimes with purplish tints. The flowers are produced in flat-topped clusters in late May to June; each small bloom has five white petals. The haws, or fruit, resemble tiny apples. They ripen to orange or scarlet in November, and are held on the tree well into winter or until the birds devour them. Lavalle Hawthorn has few thorns in comparison to most hawthorns, but each thorn is a sizable one.

Common Hawthorn, English Hawthorn, May Tree or Singleseed Hawthorn

Cratægus monogyna, fruit

Naturalized throughout the South Fraser Region, Common Hawthorn has five- to seven-lobed leaves. Often the tree defoliates in August due to fungal disease problems. The white flowers are produced in early to mid May. The scarlet fruit contains only one seed. It ripens in September to October and like the fruit of all *Cratægus*, birds especially favour them. *Cratægus* bark separates into small rectangular plates and is an easy way to identify this genus in the winter. Common Hawthorn grows six to eight metres tall.

Where to see the trees:

Abbotsford
Jubilee Park, McCallum Rd south of Essendene, on the west boundary of the park.

Chilliwack
Portage Park, Portage Ave and Woodbine St.

Delta
Memorial Park, 47 Ave and Delta St, Ladner, Park, a large specimen on the north side of the park near the corner of Delta St and 47 Ave.

Langley
Portage Park, 52 St and 204 Ave, Langley City, at the south end of the park.

224 St to 228 St on 40 Ave, Southeast Langley, a hedgerow on both sides of the road.

Richmond
Millennium Botanical Garden and Arboretum, N McLennan Community Park, Granville Ave and Garden City Rd.

Surrey
Meridian Golf Centre, 1054- 168 St, South Surrey, south of the entry gate.

Cratægus persimilis 'Prunifolia'
Syn. *Cratægus* x *prunifolia*

Plumleaf Hawthorn, Broadleaf Cockspur Hawthorn

The leaves of this hawthorn resemble a plum; they are oval-shaped, leathery dark green and turn an outstanding crimson fall colour. The white flowers bloom in late May to early June. The large plump haws are produced in pendulous clusters, each haw hanging from a long stem. They ripen in late October to November, and fall then, as do the leaves. Each of the haws has two to three seeds in it.

Where to see the trees:

Chilliwack
Canadian Forces Base, Keith Wilson Rd and Vedder Rd, Vedder Crossing, on Dundern Ave.

Cryptomeria japonica

Japanese Cedar or Japanese Redwood

Where to see the trees:

Langley

Newlands Golf Course, 21025- 48th Ave, Murrayville, at the east end of the parking lot.

Richmond

Fantasy Garden World, 10800 No 5 Rd.

4460 Moncton St, Steveston, a good-sized tree.

Surrey

Darts Hill Garden Park, 1660- 168 St, South Surrey, Garden Bed 4a.

Redwood Park, 17900- 20 Ave, South Surrey, east of the Tree House.

Cryptomeria japonica, cones and foliage

Native to China and Japan, Japanese Cedar is a large evergreen conifer, reaching a mature height of thirty metres. It maintains a very strong pyramidal form throughout its life. The blue-green needle-like leaves are prickly and point toward the branch tip, like a braided rope. They become bronze coloured over the winter but green again in the spring. The cones are produced on the very tips of the branchlets. When mature, the dark brown cones are the size of a penny and almost perfectly round. When the cones are still young and green, the pointed scaly exterior resembles a medieval mace. Japanese Cedar bark is reddish brown and like our native Western Red Cedar, it peels away in long strips. As the tree ages, the trunk of Japanese Cedar develops a thick buttress, with sinuous vertical thickenings.

Cryptomeria japonica 'Cristata'
Cockscomb Japanese Cedar

Cryptomeria japonica 'Cristata', Darts Hill Garden Park, Surrey

Cryptomeria japonica 'Cristata', branch fasciation

This bizarre cultivar is of note because the tips of some of the branches exhibit fasciation, where individual branchlets are fused together, creating a mass of joined tissue. The coarse-textured fleshy branch ends resemble the comb of a rooster. Cristata means crested in Latin. Cockscomb Japanese Cedar is rare in the South Fraser Region.

Where to see the trees:

Langley
Sendall Gardens, 20166- 50 Ave, Langley City.

Richmond
Fantasy Garden World, 10800 No 5 Rd.

Surrey
Darts Hill Garden Park, 1660- 168 St, South Surrey, Garden Beds 7 and 8.

Cryptomeria japonica 'Elegans'
Plume Cryptomeria or Plume Cedar

A colourful cultivar, Plume Cryptomeria's evergreen foliage ages to bronze-green then turns plum purple in the fall. The soft fluffy and needle-like foliage is not prickly like the species.

Where to see the trees:

Chilliwack
Salish Park, 45860- 1 Ave.

Langley
5084- 238 St, Salmon River Uplands.

9299- 213 St, Walnut Grove.

Cryptomeria japonica 'Elegans', foliage

Cryptomeria japonica 'Sekkan Sugi'

Sekkan Sugi Japanese Cedar or Golden Cryptomeria

Where to see the trees:

Chilliwack

Gwynne Vaughan Park, Williams Rd and Hope River Rd, Fairfield Island, a young tree.

Skelton Park, opposite Chilliwack Municipal Hall at 8550 Young Rd.

Canadian Forces Base, Keith Wilson Rd and Vedder Rd, Vedder Crossing, a large tree on Normandy Dr, in the garden of the residence.

Surrey

Darts Hill Garden Park, 1660- 168 St, South Surrey*, Garden Bed 15a.

Cryptomeria japonica 'Sekkan Sugi', golden tipped foliage

Rare in the South Fraser Region, Sekkan Sugi Japanese Cryptomeria reaches a mature height of seven metres with lovely conical form. The foliage is edged bright golden yellow.

Cunninghamia lanceolata

China Fir or Chinese Fir

Cunninghamia lanceolata, Darts Hill Garden Park, Surrey

China Fir is an unusual but very messy conifer since entire branches turn brown and are shed by the tree. Often clusters of mature cones, each the size of a one-dollar coin, fall to the ground attached to the branches. The ripe woody cones resemble the rosette of a rose flower. The dark green to bluish green needles of China Fir are wide, and exceedingly sharp. The tree often looks ratty, as the leaves persist on the branches for several years, dead and brown, before they are shed. China Fir may grow to a height of thirty or more metres, but the relatively young specimens growing in the South Fraser Region are much smaller in size.

Where to see the trees:

Chilliwack

Canadian Forces Base, Keith Wilson Rd and Vedder Rd, Vedder Crossing, northeast corner of Calais Cr and Caen Rd.

46740 Yale Rd East, an exceptionally green tree, more typical of the wild form found growing in China.

Richmond

Millennium Botanical Garden and Arboretum, N McLennan Community Park, Granville Ave and Garden City Rd.

Fantasy Garden World, 10800 No 5 Rd.

Cunninghamia lanceolata 'Glauca'
Blue China Fir

Cunninghamia lanceolata 'Glauca', needles and developing cones.

The needles of this cultivar are conspicuous steel blue, with a whitish bloom.

Where to see the trees:
Surrey

Darts Hill Garden Park, 1660- 168 St, South Surrey*, Garden Beds 5 and 32.

Cupressus cashmeriana
Bhutan Weeping Cypress or Kashmir Cypress

Cupressus cashmeriana, Darts Hill Garden Park

Cupressus cashmeriana, foliage

Strongly conical in form, the Bhutan Weeping Cypress has pendulous branches clothed in feathery, silvery blue-green foliage. It is a native conifer of Bhutan, Sikkim and Northern Assam. The reddish-brown bark peels away vertically. It is rarely grown and not reliably hardy in the South Fraser Region.

Where to see the trees:
Surrey

Darts Hill Garden Park, 1660- 168 St, South Surrey, Garden Bed 31.

D

To plant a pine, one need be neither God nor poet,
one need only to own a shovel.

John Muir, (1838–1914), American naturalist and founder of the Sierra Club

Davidia involucrata, fall colour

Davidia involucrata, showy white bracts

Davidia involucrata

Dove Tree, Handkerchief Tree or Kleenex Tree

Native to western China, the Dove Tree is unfortunately not commonly grown in the South Fraser Region. It is a medium-sized tree, pyramidal in youth, reaching a height of twelve to fifteen metres. Its heart-shaped, mid-green leaves have a strongly toothed margin and turn yellow in the fall, infrequently orange and scarlet. The true flower is a small brush-like affair subtended by two very showy white bracts. Each large floral bract flops down like a limp tissue, fluttering in the slightest breath of wind. They are unequal in size, the larger bract may be 20 cm long. Blooming time is late May to June. The green fruit resembles a small hard pear; it ripens to a russet colour late in the fall and hangs from a long stalk well into the winter. The orange to brown bark of mature trees adds winter colour and pattern, as it resembles scaly jigsaw pieces flaking from the trunk.

Where to see the trees:

Chilliwack

47565 Hope River Road, Fairfield Island, on the east side of the driveway.

Fairfield Island Park, 46000 Clare Ave, Fairfield Island.

Langley

Kwantlen University College, 20901 Langley Bypass, Langley City, on the northeast of the Highway overpass in the berm planting.

Richmond

Millennium Botanical Garden and Arboretum, N McLennan Community Park, Granville Ave and Garden City Rd.

Fantasy Garden World, 10800 No 5 Rd.

Rosedale

Minter Gardens, 52892 Bunker Rd, south end of the Lake Garden.

Dove Tree, Handkerchief Tree or Kleenex Tree

Where to see the trees:

Surrey

City Hall, 14245- 56 Ave, Newton, south side of the pond.

Darts Hill Garden Park, 1660- 168 St, South Surrey, Garden Beds C1 and 16.

The Glades, 561- 172 St, South Surrey, at the east end of Garyland Trail.

Diospyros virginiana

Persimmon, Sugar Plum Tree or Winter Plum

Diospyros virginiana, bark   *Diospyros virginiana,* foliage

Persimmon is very rare in the South Fraser Region. Native to the eastern and southeastern United States, it reaches twenty metres in height at maturity. The dark green lustrous leaves turn yellow-green to yellow in the fall. The tree is dioecious; the urn-shaped flowers are white, blooming in May to June. The fruit, when produced, is the size of a two-dollar coin. It is fleshy and edible after receiving several frosts in September or October. The fruit is light orange with a reddish flush, covered in a waxy bloom and attractively subtended by four persistent calyx lobes, which gives it the appearance of a dainty collar frill. The dark grey-black bark is deeply fissured and cut into smaller blocks.

Where to see the trees:

Surrey

Darts Hill Garden Park, 1660- 168 St, South Surrey, Garden Bed 2a.

Did You Know?

The Persimmon or Sugar Plum Tree figures prominently in the children's Christmas poem "Twas the night before Christmas".

E

The problem with city trees is that we take them for granted.
We tend to notice them only when they're gone.

Rowan Rowntree

Eleagnus angustifolia, pea-sized fruit

Eleagnus angustifolia
Russian Olive, Oleaster or Silver Berry

Russian Olive, native to west-central Asia, is a small to medium-sized deciduous tree reaching seven to ten metres high. The winter silhouette of Russian Olive is twiggy and irregular, as the branches grow higgledy-piggledy. In spring and summer it is clothed in willowy silver-grey foliage. The tree is a good colour contrast to the predominantly green landscape since its leaves are dull green and scaly on the top surface and silvery-scaly below. The cream-coloured flowers, borne in May are sweetly scented, small and trumpet shaped. Like the pea-sized yellow fruit, which ripens in September to October, the flowers are hidden from view by the foliage. Sometimes the young silvery stems may be thorny. Fibrous and shredding into thin narrow pieces, the mature bark is reddish brown. Russian Olive is not often found in the South Fraser Region.

Eleagnus angustifolia, Morton Arboretum, Lisle, Illinois

Where to see the trees:
Abbotsford
Matsqui Recreation Centre, 3106 Clearbrook Rd, a good-sized tree on the west side of the building.

Chilliwack
Parkholm Lodge, 9090 Newman Rd, a large tree on the south side of the garden.

Embothrium coccineum
Chilean Firebush
or Chilean Flameflower

Embothrium coccineum, flowers

Native to Chile and Argentina, Chilean Firebush is rarely grown since it is not reliably hardy in the South Fraser Region. The mostly evergreen leaves are nondescript, the branching habit of this small tree scraggly and open. The flowers, which are the Chilean Firebush's claim to fame are long narrow trumpets, vivid scarlet in colour and highly attractive to humming-birds. The flowers are produced in the thousands in May and are followed by unusual long beak-like woody fruits, which split and release their seeds.

Where to see the trees:

Surrey
The Glades, 561- 172 St, South Surrey, west ridge midway down the south side.

Eucryphia glutinosa
Hardy Eucryphia

Eucryphia glutinosa, flowers

Hardy Eucryphia is a rare deciduous or semi-evergreen shrub or small tree reaching a height of three to six metres. The dark green lance-

Where to see the trees:

Surrey
Darts Hill Garden Park, 1660- 168 St, South Surrey, Garden Bed 19.

Eucryphia glutinosa
Hardy Eucryphia

shaped leaflets are usually produced in fives or sometimes threes. The scented flowers are the diameter of a two-dollar coin, with four milky white petals and a luxurious puff of orange-tipped stamens in August to September. Fall colour is crimson.

Euonymus europaeus
Common Spindle Tree or European Spindle Tree

Euonymus europaeus, pink fruit capsule with orange seeds

Where to see the trees:

Abbotsford

33083 Bevan Ave, southeast side of Mill Park.

Chilliwack

Sardis Park, Sardis, two very large and artfully pruned specimens at the west entrance gate to the park on School Lane.

Richmond

Fantasy Garden World, 10800 No 5 Rd.

Surrey

The Glades, 561- 172 St, South Surrey, west ridge, centre and pond.

A small tree reaching a typical height of three to four metres, Common Spindle Tree is somewhat common in the South Fraser Region. The irregular, sprawling habit and green four-angled stems are good winter identifying characteristics. The leaves are dull dark green in the summer, turning crimson in the fall. The flower is insignificant but the fruit is a delicate, dull reddish pink four-parted capsule, that when it opens in October to November, reveals brilliant orange seeds hanging by slender threads.

F

Trees, by virtue of their universal presence, majestic yet human in scale, bridging the gap between earth and air, are the rightful symbols of all which humankind aspires to in its relationship with the planet.

Oscar Beck, painter, work titled "Beeches", Acrylic on paper

Fagus sylvatica, Peace Arch Park, Surrey

Fagus sylvatica
European Beech

European Beech is a very commonly planted tree, along with its many cultivars, in the South Fraser Region. Left to grow unimpeded, it becomes one of the stateliest of all the deciduous trees. Often growing wider than tall, European Beech trees may reach twenty to thirty metres high. The spreading scaffold branches grow to immense size, as does the main trunk. The leaves are elliptical in shape, with a gently waving edge, mid to dark green turning golden copper in the fall. On some trees the foliage browns and persists on the tree well into winter. The dormant buds are long, narrow and sharply pointed, sufficiently sharp to break the skin. The flowers are of little consequence but the fruit is produced in a prickly woody husk, which splits open revealing the triangular chestnut-brown nuts. Beechnuts are highly favoured by wildlife. The bark is smooth and grey, and as the tree ages it becomes more wrinkled and lumpy, resembling an elephant's leg.

Where to see the trees:
Abbotsford
Dunach Park, NW corner of Mt Lehman Rd and Downes Rd.

Chilliwack
Stö:lo Centre, 7201 Vedder Rd, Sardis.

University College of the Fraser Valley, 45600 Airport Rd.

Langley
21166 Old Yale Rd, Murrayville.

Richmond
Fantasy Garden World, 10800 No 5 Rd.

Rosedale
Minter Gardens, 52892 Bunker Rd, a grove of trees at the entry to the Rose Garden.

Surrey
12691- 14 Avenue, South Surrey*.

Green Timbers Arboretum, 9800- 140 St, Whalley, south of the uncovered bunker.

Peace Arch Park, King George Hwy and 0 Ave, South Surrey*, six trees, the largest with a DBH of 130 cm.

The Glades, 561- 172 St, South Surrey, behind Semiahmoo's Tribute.

Did You Know?
The original house on Old Yale Road in Murrayville in Langley was built in 1887. The European Beech was planted soon after by the Berry Family.

Fagus sylvatica Atropurpurea Group
Syn. *Fagus sylvatica* 'Atropunicea' or 'Atropurpurea'

Copper Beech or Purple Beech

Where to see the trees:

Abbotsford

MSA General Hospital, 2179 McCallum Rd, on the north side of the Emergency entrance, a huge tree with a DBH of 110 cm.

2715 Mount View Ave, a lovely large tree.

33947 Victory Blvd.

Jubilee Park, McCallum Rd south of Essendene, on the west side of the park.

Aberdeen Cemetery, 29200 Fraser Highway, a large open-grown tree.

Chilliwack

9049 School St.

9750 Gillanders Rd, a stunning tree with a splendid view of Mt Cheam in the background.

Chilliwack Museum, 45820 Spadina Ave, two well-pruned trees at the front entry.

45723 Kipp Ave, two huge trees, the largest in Chilliwack, one with a DBH of 150 cm.

Fairfield Island Park, 46000 Clare Ave, Fairfield Island, a row of beeches that were originally a nursery row on the west perimeter of the park.

47465 Fairfield Rd, Fairfield Island, three massive trees.

Chilliwack Cemeteries, 10010 Hillcrest Dr, Little Mountain.

6800 Chilliwack River Rd, Sardis.

Foothills Farm, 7450 Upper Prairie Rd, Sardis.

8395 Chilliwack Mountain Rd.

46618 Prairie Central Rd, Sardis.

Canadian Forces Base, Keith Wilson Rd and Vedder Rd, Vedder Crossing on Normandy Dr, in the garden of the residence.

Leghorn Ranch, 6530 Chilliwack River Rd, Vedder Crossing.

6674 Chilliwack River Rd, Vedder Crossing.

Fagus sylvatica Atropurpurea Group, Kipp Avenue, Chilliwack

More common in the South Fraser Region than the green species of European Beech, and reaching an equal stature at maturity, Copper Beech is a magnificent deciduous tree. The emerging leaves are shimmering copper-red, turn purple, age to purple green and fade to bronze-green with tints of purple by the end of the growing season. The fall colour is often a rich golden yellow to yellow-copper.

Did You Know?

The two beautiful Copper Beech trees, which artfully frame the main entrance of the Chilliwack Museum, were planted around 1915. The Museum building was Chilliwack's original City Hall, constructed in 1911 to 1912 to a design by Vancouver architect Thomas Hooper. It was designed in a Classical Revival style, and meant to face the Five Corners intersection. The citizens of Chilliwack, imbued with youthful optimism, felt that the building of a Hall was justified due to the burgeoning growth in their city's population; 3,690 people in 1901 to 9,172 in 1911, a whopping forty percent increase. Sixty-nine years later, growth again caused a move, when the city of Chilliwack amalgamated with the Township of Chilliwack to form the District of Chilliwack. A new larger City Hall was needed to accommodate a much larger municipal staff. The site of the

Fagus sylvatica Atropurpurea Group
Syn. *Fagus sylvatica* 'Atropunicea' or 'Atropurpurea'

Copper Beech or Purple Beech

Fagus sylvatica Atropurpurea Group, Chilliwack Museum

Old City Hall, now the Chilliwack Museum, was designated a National Historic Site in 1987.

• The Houston Residence, designed by an Aldergrove architect by the name of Mr. Dodd in the Spanish Colonial Revival style was built in the 1920's for Mr. and Mrs. James Houston. One room in the house has a very high ceiling, built to accommodate Mrs. Houston's piano classes. A mature Horse Chestnut and a Silver Maple are planted next to the Copper beech tree.

• The statuesque Copper Beech on Glover Road is a prominent landmark at the southern approach to Fort Langley. It was likely planted when the house was built, circa 1912.

• James Houston, one Fort Langley's most colorful early settlers, planted the Copper Beech on Copperbeech Avenue in Fort Langley in the 1880's. Houston, originally from Dunfermline, Scotland, from a wealthy family of ship owners, ran away to seek his fortune. He was shipwrecked off the coast of New Zealand and taken prisoner by Maori tribesmen. He escaped by swimming out to sea to a passing ship. Houston carried on to South America, where pirates and political shenanigans caused him difficulty. He was again shipwrecked, this time off the coast of Mexico.

Eventually, Houston made his way to the Pacific Northwest as an officer on a ship in 1856. Upon hearing of the discovery of gold on the Columbia River, he deserted his post. He and a partner were prospecting along the Pend Oreille River, when Indians killed his partner and left

Where to see the trees:

Delta

Jubilee Farm, later the Augustinian Monastery of B.C., 3900 Arthur Dr, Ladner.

Kerr Residence, 3621 Arthur Drive, Ladner.

4618 Arthur Dr, Ladner, an imposing open grown tree with a diameter at breast height of 115 cm.

Langley

Houston Residence, 26104 Fraser Hwy, Aldergrove.

8903 Glover Rd, Ft Langley.

9147 Gay St, but growing on Copperbeech Ave, east of Wright St, Ft Langley. The branches of this magnificent tree, with a DBH of 140 cm, sweep to the ground. It is one of largest Copper Beeches in the South Fraser Region.

2231- 264 St, Southeast Langley.

Richmond

5771 Moncton St, Steveston.

No 6 Rd, 100 yards south of River Rd on the west side of No 6 Rd.

Surrey

The Glades, 561- 172 St, South Surrey, across from Semiahmoo's Tribute.

Fagus sylvatica Atropurpurea Group
Syn. *Fagus sylvatica* 'Atropunicea' or 'Atropurpurea'

Copper Beech or Purple Beech

Fagus sylvatica Atropurpurea Group,
Copper Beech Avenue, Fort Langley

Houston with a couple of arrows in his back. Searching for more peaceful territory he headed north into the Okanagan Valley. Within a few miles of the border disaster struck again. A second group of Indians robbed him of all his possessions. Crossing the border he headed for Fort Kamloops and arrived in a sorry state. In the spring of 1857, Houston began prospecting for gold in the creeks near the fort. There, on Tranquille Creek, he made the first gold discoveries in British Columbia. By 1858, while most of the population stampeded north with gold rush fever, Houston was carving a farm out of the virgin timber on the east side of the Salmon River, near the Hudson's Bay Company farm in Fort Langley. In 1872 he was one of the landowners who signed the petition to incorporate the rural district into a municipality. In fact, Chilliwack and Langley were the first two rural districts in B.C. to incorporate under the newly legislated Municipality Act of 1872. Houston became a councillor of the new municipality.

Fagus sylvatica 'Dawyck'
Dawyck Beech or Columnar Beech

Fagus sylvatica 'Dawyck', Darts Hill
Garden Park, Surrey

Dawyck Beech is a narrowly conical tree, reaching a mature size of fifteen metres high or more by three to four metres wide. There are also golden and purple foliage versions of this fastigiate tree.

Where to see the trees:
Abbotsford
Clearbrook Public Library, 32320 Dahlstrom Ave, a number of young specimens on the north and west side of the building.

Chilliwack
Salish Park, 45860- 1 Ave.

Townsend Park, SW corner of Ashwell Rd and Hodgins Ave, in the parking lot.

Fagus sylvatica 'Dawyck'
Dawyck Beech or Columnar Beech

Delta

Police Station, 4455 Clarence Taylor Cr, Ladner, east side of the building.

North Delta Recreation Centre, 11415- 84 Ave.

Langley

Portage Park, 52 St and 204 Ave, Langley City, a row of good-sized trees along the southern edge of the park.

NE corner of 54 St and 204 Ave, Langley City, a row of three on the boulevard.

SW corner of Park Ave and Douglas Cr, Langley City, a street tree planting.

Richmond

Francis Rd from Gilbert Rd to No 2 Rd, a street tree planting.

Surrey

Darts Hill Garden Park, 1660- 168 St, South Surrey, Garden Bed 16.

Fagus sylvatica 'Dawyck', Langley City

Fagus sylvatica 'Dawyck Gold'
Gold Dawyck Beech or Gold Columnar Beech

Gold Dawyck Beech is a narrowly conical tree, reaching a mature size of fifteen metres high or more by three to four metres wide. The leaves of this fastigiate cultivar are golden as they emerge in the spring and age to a brilliant green in the summer. The leaves of Gold Dawyck Beech will not sunburn.

Where to see the trees:

Chilliwack

Yale Rd East at Nowell-Auld Phillips.

Surrey

8346- 134A St, Newton, a street planting.

Fagus sylvatica 'Dawyck Purple'
Purple Dawyck Beech or Purple Columnar Beech

Purple Dawyck Beech is a narrowly conical tree, reaching a mature size of fifteen metres high or more by three to four metres wide. The leaves of this fastigiate cultivar are purple as they emerge in the spring and age to a brilliant green in the summer.

Where to see the trees:

Surrey

8347- 134A St, Newton.

7080- 129A St, Whalley.

Fagus sylvatica var. *heterophylla* 'Aspleniifolia'
Fern-Leaf Beech

Fagus sylvatica var. *heterophylla* 'Aspleniifolia', City Park, Langley City

The leaves of Fern-Leaf Beech are narrow and deeply cut. The lustrous dark green leaves turn lovely burnt umber in the fall.

Where to see the trees:

Langley

City Park, 207 St and 48 Ave, Langley City.

9062 Church, Ft Langley.

Rosedale

Minter Gardens, 52892 Bunker Rd, southern end of the Lake Garden.

Surrey

Darts Hill Garden Park, 1660- 168 St, South Surrey, Garden Bed 5.

Fagus sylvatica var. *heterophylla* f. *laciniata*
Cutleaf Beech

Did You Know?

R.H. Brock built this beautifully sited farmhouse at 46040 Higginson Road in Sardis in 1904. James A. Higginson, for whom the road is named, attended Guelph Agricultural College in 1900. In 1905, he married Jessie De Wolf, the daughter of a pioneer Fairfield Island farmer. For many years, the Higginsons operated a dairy farm at Kinkora, which means "haunt of the Fairies" in Gaelic.

- The craftsman-style bungalow at 7447 Vedder Road, was built as a retirement home in 1911 for Chilliwack's first historian, Horatio Webb. Mr. Webb, who arrived in Chilliwack in 1870, was the Deputy Sheriff, tax assessor and collector for the municipality of Chilliwack.

Fagus sylvatica var. *heterophylla* f. *laciniata*, Kinkora, Chilliwack

The Cutleaf Beech is similar to Fern-Leaf Beech but does not have as elegant an appearance. The leaves of this cultivar are obviously toothed, with sinuses reaching one third of the way to the midrib of the leaf but the leaves are not nearly as finely nor as deeply cut as the Fern-Leaf Beech. Fern-Leaf Beech may have leaves so dissected that the parts are strap-like.

Where to see the trees:

Abbotsford

2224 Guilford St.

Chilliwack

Kinkora, 46040 Higginson Rd, Sardis, two immense trees with their branches sweeping to the ground. A lovely wetland in behind offers a spectacular setting for these majestic trees.

Webb Heritage House, 7447 Vedder Rd, Sardis. This tree was recently over-pruned.

6674 Chilliwack River Rd, Vedder Crossing.

Reimer's Nursery Ltd, 4586 No 3 Rd, Yarrow.

Fagus sylvatica 'Pendula'

Weeping Beech

Two forms of Weeping Beech are commonly found in the South Fraser Region. Strongly pendulous branches and dark green leaves are characteristic of both forms. The mushroom form grows with a wide-spreading crown with several upright-weeping leaders. The overall effect is rather like a circus tent. The second form is more fountain-like, growing tall and narrow with a dominant central leader, its arching pendulous branches cascading down like rills of water.

Fagus sylvatica 'Pendula', Minter Gardens, Rosedale

Where to see the trees:

Abbotsford

3854 Clayburn Rd, a large tree with a mushroom shape, overhanging a wall.

Chilliwack

5640 Vedder Rd, Vedder Crossing.

Rosedale

Minter Gardens, 52892 Bunker Rd, a very fine specimen with a fountain form located on the northeast side of the Meadow Garden at a pathway intersection.

Surrey

City Hall, 14245- 56 Ave, Newton, northwest end of the pond, fountain form.

South Surrey Arena, 2199- 148 St, South Surrey, several young trees with fountain form on the north and southeast sides of the arena.

Fagus sylvatica 'Purple Fountain'
Purple Fountain Beech

Fagus sylvatica 'Purple Fountain', foliage and nut husk

Fagus sylvatica 'Purple Fountain', Kwantlen Unversity College, Langley

Where to see the trees:

Langley

Kwantlen University College, 20901 Langley Bypass, Langley City, on the northeast of the Highway overpass in the berm planting.

Surrey

Darts Hill Garden Park, 1660- 168 St, South Surrey, Garden Bed 2.

Purple Fountain Beech is a very narrow weeping tree forming one central leader from which the pendulous branchlets hang gracefully. The deep purple foliage ages to a slightly lighter colour in late summer.

Fagus sylvatica 'Rohan Obelisk'
Syn. *Fagus sylvatica* 'Obelisk'
Red Obelisk Beech

A relatively new cultivar, not yet common in the South Fraser Region, Red Obelisk Beech has strongly upright branches with a tight pyramidal shape and purple leaves in the growing season. Fall colour of Red Obelisk Beech is reddish-purple.

Where to see the trees:
Chilliwack

Fairfield Island Park, 46000 Clare Ave, Fairfield Island, north of baseball outfield, between baseball diamonds A and C.

Townsend Park, SW corner of Ashwell Rd and Hodgins Ave, on the east side of the parking lot

Twin Rinks Ice Arena, 5745 Tyson Rd, Sardis, four young trees in the parking lot.

Fagus sylvatica 'Tricolor'
Tricolor Beech

Rarely grown in the South Fraser Region, Tricolor Beech prefers a shady site to preserve its unusual leaf colouration. Each purple-green leaf has a pink margin as it unfolds, which turns to white with age. At less than eight to ten metres tall, Tricolor Beech reaches a much smaller mature size than the species.

Where to see the trees:
Langley
24355- 48 Ave, Salmon River Uplands, midway on the east side of the entry drive.

Rosedale
Minter Gardens, 52892 Bunker Rd, at the playground area.

Fagus sylvatica 'Tricolor', fall colour

Fraxinus americana Autumn Applause®
Autumn Applause® Ash

The green compound leaves of Autumn Applause® Ash, grow 20–25 cm long, each with usually seven, but sometimes five or nine long-stalked plump leaflets. The fall colour is an outstanding deep maroon. The tree, with its compact oval shape, is smaller than the species, reaching a mature height of twelve to fourteen metres. This male cultivar is seedless. Autumn Applause® Ash is usually found as a young tree in the South Fraser Region, but as these trees age the bark characteristics of the species will become evident. The bark on mature trees is ash grey to grey-brown, and strongly furrowed in a netted pattern.

Where to see the trees:
Abbotsford
Median planting on Old Yale Rd to McClure Rd from Crossley Drive to Clearbrook Rd, in front of Ellwood Park.

City Police Department, 2838 Justice Way, southeast corner of the parking lot.

Chilliwack
Barber Park, at Barber Dr and Henley Ave, three trees at the north end of the park.

On Victoria Ave, between College St and Young Rd, on the south side of Victoria Ave.

Surrey
16588- 110 Ave, Guildford.

16470- 108 Ave, Guildford.

Fraxinus americana Autumn Purple™

Autumn Purple™ Ash

Fraxinus americana Autumn Purple™, foliage

Fraxinus americana Autumn Purple™, fall colour

Where to see the trees:

Chilliwack

On the south side of Bole Ave between College St and Young Rd including the Farmer's Market parking lot, Chilliwack.

Municipal Hall, 8550 Young Rd, southeast corner of the building.

Townsend Park, SW corner of Ashwell Rd and Hodgins Ave, at the concession building.

Twin Rinks Ice Arena, 5745 Tyson Rd, Sardis, a street tree planting alternating with Red Sunset® Maple.

Langley

Cul-de- sac at 207 St and 93 Ave, Walnut Grove.

20353- 64 Ave, Willoughby.

Surrey

5783- 126 St, Newton.

12623- 56A Ave, Newton.

The deep green compound leaves of Autumn Purple™ Ash, grow 20–25 cm long, each with usually seven, but sometimes five or nine long, glossy stalked plump leaflets. The fall colour varies from yellow-orange to orange-red to purple. The tree, with its roundish form, is smaller than the species, reaching a mature height of fourteen metres. This male cultivar is seedless. Autumn Purple™ Ash is usually found as a young tree in the South Fraser Region, but as these trees age the bark characteristics of the species will become evident. The bark on mature trees is ash grey to grey-brown, and strongly furrowed in a netted pattern.

Fraxinus angustifolia 'Raywood'
Syn. *Fraxinus oxycarpa* 'Raywood'

Raywood Ash or Claret Ash

Fraxinus angustifolia 'Raywood', foliage

Fraxinus angustifolia 'Raywood', in the fall, Robert Tait Elementary School, Richmond

Raywood Ash is a small ash tree, reaching a mature height of twelve to fifteen metres. It is a very finely textured tree, with pinnately compound leaves, each one with seven or nine leaflets. The dark green, stalkless, lustrous leaflets are very narrow, less than a pencil thickness in diameter, with very sharply toothed margins. The fall colour is among the showiest in the South Fraser Region; the base of the leaflets turns golden yellow while the tips are deep wine purple, and eventually the whole leaflet turns rich purple. Very few seeds are produced by this cultivar.

Where to see the trees:

Chilliwack

Townsend Park, southwest corner of Ashwell Rd and Hodgins Ave, a mixed planting with Patmore Ash running north to south between fields A and B.

Townsend Park, Ashwell Rd and Hodgins Ave, a row of trees west of the football field.

46634- 46734 and 46743- 46775 Braeside Ave, Promontory Heights.

Promontory Park West, Teskey Rd, Promontory Heights.

University College of the Fraser Valley, 45600 Airport Rd, Airport Road entrance boulevard and spotted around the campus.

Richmond

Robert Tait Elementary School, 10071 Finlayson Dr, a row of trees on the west side of the school.

Surrey

14279- 18A Ave, South Surrey.

1972- 143A St, South Surrey.

Fraxinus excelsior

European Ash or English Ash

Native to Europe and southwest Asia, European Ash is very commonly found in the South Fraser Region. It can reach great size as shown by the mature trees on McGuire Road in Chilliwack, which are close to thirty metres in height. The stalkless pinnately compound leaves (nine to eleven leaflets) are a dull green, and often drop green or an insipid yellow-green in the fall. The lower branches are upswept, while the dormant buds are stubby, hairy and black. The single-winged samara, which resembles a beaver's tail in outline, ripens brown in pendulous clusters in October.

Where to see the trees:

Abbotsford

Hougen Park, south off Highway 1 on Cole Rd.

Jubilee Park, McCallum Rd south of Essendene, two large trees west of the tennis court.

Chilliwack

Municipal Hall, 8550 Young Rd.

Fairfield Island Park, 46000 Clare Ave, Fairfield Island.

47813 McGuire Rd, Sardis, a splendid old farm row of several different species of trees on the south side of the road including three European Ash, the easternmost one with a massive girth of 190 cm.

Canadian Forces Base, Keith Wilson Rd and Vedder Rd, Vedder Crossing, a very large tree on the south side of Calais Cr opposite Building No 114, also a grove of seven trees on the northwest side of Calais.

Yarrow Community Park, north end of Community St, Yarrow.

Delta

John Oliver Municipal Park, 11600 block Ladner Trunk Rd, a large tree with a DBH of 52 cm.

Langley

Derby Reach Regional Park, 2200 Block Allard Cr, Northwest Langley, a grove of young trees at the entry kiosk.

Richmond

Pumphouse Pub and Grill, 6031 Blundell Rd, several very large trees, the tree on the east margin of the parking lot is excellent.

Steveston Park, 4111 Moncton St, Steveston.

Surrey

Darts Hill Garden Park, 1660-168 St, South Surrey, Garden Bed 1.

Redwood Park, 17900- 20 Ave, South Surrey, many trees naturalized in the wooded area north of the open play area and south of the washrooms.

Singleleaf Ash or One-leaved Ash

Fraxinus excelsior f. *diversifolia*, Jubilee Park, Abbotsford

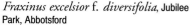

Fraxinus excelsior f. *diversifolia*, bark

Rare in the South Fraser Region, Singleleaf Ash is unusual in that only the toothed terminal leaflet is formed, or occasionally there are two or three toothed leaflets. Generally, it has a single leaf, which colours yellow-green in the fall. This form is seed producing, which distinguishes it from *Fraxinus excelsior* 'Hessei', which is also a Singleleaf Ash, but is seedless.

Where to see the trees:

Abbotsford

Jubilee Park, McCallum Rd south of Essendene, two large trees west of the tennis court.

Golden Ash, Golden Twigged Ash or Striped Bark Ash

Rare in the South Fraser Region, Golden Ash is a large-growing tree with lovely golden-green foliage with nine to eleven leaflets that turn green in the summer and a bright sunshine yellow in the fall. The golden twigs that may be striped, and black dormant buds are quite showy in the winter.

Where to see the trees:

Richmond

Fantasy Garden World, 10800 No 5 Rd.

Fraxinus excelsior 'Pendula'
Weeping Ash or Weeping European Ash

Where to see the trees:

Richmond

Fantasy Garden World, 10800 No 5 Rd, several very pleasing trees in the garden by the pond.

Weeping Ash has strongly pendulous branches and an umbrella form that weeps to the ground. Weeping Ash, with its coarse-textured appearance in the winter, is rarely found in the South Fraser Region. Its mature height depends on the height of the original graft union.

Fraxinus excelsior 'Westhof's Glorie'
Westhof's Glorie Ash

Fraxinus excelsior 'Westhof's Glorie', buds and flowers

Where to see the trees:

Chilliwack

University College of the Fraser Valley, 45600 Airport Rd, a row of trees adjacent to the turnaround east of Building D, Theatre.

Westhof's Glorie Ash has a very dense regular habit with upright-growing green branches, which creates an oval form. The leaflets emerge late as a deep brown colour and age to a bluish green. They are held on the tree well into November. Westhof's Glorie Ash is nearly seedless. It is rare in the South Fraser Region.

Fraxinus nigra 'Fall Gold'
Fall Gold Black Ash or Fall Gold Swamp Ash

Where to see the trees:

Langley

Kwantlen University College, 20901 Langley Bypass, Langley City, on the north edge of the pond on the Main campus.

Fall Gold Black Ash, a selection made at the Morden Research station in Morden, Manitoba, is superior to the species, reaching a mature height of twelve metres and a spread of eight metres. Typical of ash trees, the foliage is pinnately compound with seven to eleven dark,

Fall Gold Black Ash
or Fall Gold Swamp Ash

green-toothed leaflets. All but the terminal leaflets are stalkless. The golden fall colour of the leaves is held into early October. The large terminal bud is very dark brown to almost black, resembling a pointed ski toque. Fall Gold Black Ash is seedless.

Fraxinus ornus

Flowering Ash or Manna Ash

Fraxinus ornus, in flower

Fraxinus ornus, flower

Native to southern Europe and southwest Asia, the dense, round-headed form of Flowering Ash reaches twelve to fifteen metres at maturity. The midgreen pinnately compound leaflets are usually seven in number and colour plum and red purple in the fall. The creamy white flowers of Flowering Ash are highly ornamental, appearing in late May. Fluffy cone-shaped plumes decorate the tree. The individual florets are tiny and slightly scented. The floral effect is long lasting, followed by clutches of drooping single-winged samara that are persistent. The plump terminal buds are fuzzy and grey-brown in colour. A cut stem exudes a sweet sap or "manna", which was used in its native range for its medicinal properties. Flowering Ash is relatively common in the South Fraser Region.

Where to see the trees:

Chilliwack

Yarrow Community Park, north end of Community St, Yarrow.

Langley

Sendall Gardens, Langley City.

Williams Park, 6600 block 238 St, Salmon River Uplands.

Richmond

Burkeville Park, 1031 Lancaster Cr, Burkeville, a good-sized tree opposite 1160 Lancaster Cr.

Surrey

Redwood Park, 17900- 20 Ave, South Surrey, three trees at the entrance to the park.

Fraxinus ornus 'Arie Peters'
Arie Peters Flowering Ash

Where to see the trees:

Chilliwack

5497- 5608 Alpine Cr, north of Teskey Way, Promontory Heights.

Surrey

8182- 145 St, Fleetwood.

8203- 145 St, Fleetwood.

Arie Peters Flowering Ash differs from the species in that it has more vertical branches creating an upright oval crown. The narrow leaflets are dark green and pointed. The blooming time of this selection is very long indeed, with the peak bloom in late May to June and recurrent blooming until September. Seeds are similar to the species. Arie Peters Flowering Ash is a recent introduction to the South Fraser Valley.

Fraxinus ornus 'Victoria'
Victoria Flowering Ash

Fraxinus ornus 'Victoria', in flower

Fraxinus ornus 'Victoria', in flower, Fort Langley National Historic Site, Langley

Where to see the trees:

Langley

Fort Langley National Historic Site, 23433 Mavis St, Ft Langley.

Victoria Flowering Ash is named after the city of Victoria on Vancouver Island. It is a very densely branched, top-grafted selection that matures into a small round-headed tree about ten metres high. The large, dark, green leaflets, seven in number, stay green well into November. The grey dormant buds are also larger than the species. Victoria Flowering Ash is seedless.

Fraxinus pennsylvanica, Douglas Park, Langley City

Fraxinus pennsylvanica, bark

Where to see the trees:
Abbotsford

South Poplar Elementary School, south-west corner of Huntingdon Rd and Gladwin Rd, a large open grown tree on the east fence line of the school.

2783 McCallum Rd, a massive mature tree.

Chilliwack

Canadian Forces Base, Keith Wilson Rd and Vedder Rd, Vedder Crossing, three large trees on the east side of the tennis courts on Sicily Rd at Normandy Dr.

Chilliwack Municipal Hall, 8550 Young Rd, a large tree at the front parking lot.

University College of the Fraser Valley, 45600 Airport Rd, around Building E, Student Services.

Delta

Delta Secondary School, 4615- 51 St, Ladner, several trees approximately four-teen metres tall and with a DBH of 40 – 45 cm on the east and west sides of the school.

Langley

Douglas Park, 20550 Douglas Cr, Langley City.

21857- 64 Ave, Milner.

Richmond

Stevston Park, 4111 Moncton St, Steveston, three good-sized trees east of the children's playground.

Southarm Park, Garden City Rd and Williams Rd.

Green Ash is a commonly found species in the South Fraser Region. Native to Saskatchewan, Manitoba, southern Ontario, Quebec and the Maritimes, it grows into a medium-sized tree of fifteen to eighteen metres high at maturity. The twiggy, upright oval habit has branches that swoop up at the ends in a "U" shape. The foliage has five to nine leaflets. The buds are tan to rusty brown, and woolly. The fruit is produced in pendulous clutches of dozens of beaver tail-shaped single-winged samara. The branchlets of Green Ash lack hairs while those individuals also identified as *Fraxinus pennsylvanica* but with hairy branchlets are Red Ash. In horticulture, the Green Ash group predominates. Green Ash is often the first tree in the South Fraser Region to turn a rich yellow in the fall, and one of the first to defoliate, the leaves dropping by mid October. The distinctive bark is greyish brown, and ridged in a flat diamond pattern.

Fraxinus pennsylvanica 'Bergeson'
Bergeson Ash or Bergeson Green Ash

Where to see the trees:
Chilliwack
5401- 5428 Highroad Cr, Promontory Heights.

Promontory Park West, Teskey Rd, Promontory Heights.

Wells Landing Park, Glenroy Dr, Vedder Crossing.

Surrey
3628- 156A St, South Surrey.

3673- 156A St, South Surrey.

Growing fifteen metres tall, Bergeson Ash has an upright oval form. The slender leaflets are shiny and turn yellow in the fall. The bark of this selection is bronze coloured. Bergeson Ash is seedless.

Fraxinus pennsylvanica 'Johnson'
Leprechaun™ Ash or Leprechaun™ Green Ash

Where to see the trees:
Surrey
16839- 83A Ave, Fleetwood.

16861- 83A Ave, Fleetwood.

Introduced in the early 1990's, Leprechaun™ Ash is true to its trademarked name. It is a very dwarf and tight, top-grafted form of Green Ash. With a strong round shape, the tree matures at five to six metres high by the same distance wide. The foliage is half the size of ordinary Green Ash trees. Leprechaun™ Ash is rare in the South Fraser Region.

Fraxinus pennsylvanica 'Marshall (Seedless)'
Marshall Ash or Marshall Green Ash

Where to see the trees:
Richmond
Park Operations entrance, 5599 Lynas Lane.

The leaves of Marshall Ash are lustrous dark green, and turn sunshine yellow in the fall. It grows fifteen metres high with a somewhat irregular oval form. It is seedless. Marshall Ash is commonly found in the South Fraser Region.

Patmore Ash or
Patmore Green Ash

Fraxinus pennsylvanica 'Patmore', foliage

Fraxinus pennsylvanica 'Patmore', fall colour

Patmore Ash reaches a height of fourteen metres. Its symmetrical upright branches create a more uniform oval-shaped crown than that of the Marshall Ash. Dark green lustrous leaves have five- to seven-toothed leaflets. The leaves colour yellow in the fall. Patmore Ash is seedless.

Where to see the trees:

Chilliwack

Townsend Park, SW corner of Ashwell Rd and Hodgins Ave, a mixed planting with Raywood Ash running north to south between fields A and B.

Promontory Road between Teskey Rd and Pumphouse, Promontory Heights.

Wells Landing Park, Glenmore Dr, Vedder Crossing.

Langley

Kwantlen University College, 20901 Langley Bypass, Langley City, growing on the north edge of the pond on the main campus.

Surrey

14412- 18A Ave, South Surrey.

1629- 142 St, South Surrey.

G

He who plants a tree plants a hope.

Lucy Larcom, (1824–1893)

Ginkgo biloba, in spring, Peace Arch Park, Surrey

Ginkgo biloba, fall colour

Ginkgo biloba
Maidenhair Tree

Native to eastern China, Maidenhair Tree reaches a massive size to thirty metres high and with an equal spread. It is extremely long-lived, with specimens recorded at one thousand years of age in its native range. It is somewhat

Where to see the trees:

Abbotsford

Clearbrook Public Library, 32320 Dahlstrom Ave, a young specimen on the northeast corner of the building.

2211 Mountain Dr, a young tree.

Chilliwack

45573 Princess Ave, a good-sized tree.

University College of the Fraser Valley, 45600 Airport Rd, between parking lots 5 and 6, west of Cherry Ford, a second tree near the old main ditch.

7018 Eden Dr, Sardis, a tree with very good form.

46583 Prairie Central Rd, Sardis.

Delta

298- 67A St, Boundary Bay.

Leisure Centre, 4600 Clarence Taylor Cr, Ladner, two small trees on the east side of the building.

Langley

Sendall Gardens, 20166- 50 Ave, Langley City, to the south of the residence.

Richmond

3011 Broadway St, Steveston, a young but attractive tree.

Millennium Botanical Garden and Arboretum, N McLennan Community Park, Granville Ave and Garden City Rd.

Fantasy Garden World, 10800 No 5 Rd.

Rosedale

Minter Gardens, 52892 Bunker Rd, south margin of the pond in the Lake Garden.

Ginkgo biloba
Maidenhair Tree

common in the South Fraser Region, but the trees are small and young. The form of the tree is awkwardly pyramidal in youth with sparse and irregular branching. The dull green fan-shaped leaves, often with a ruffled edge, are very different from any other deciduous tree. Sometimes the leaves are partially split in half. The leaves are produced in clusters on short spur branches and turn a rich golden yellow in the fall. The maidenhair tree is dioecious. Male trees, which are usually named cultivars such as *Ginkgo biloba* 'Autumn Gold', are commonly planted since the plum-like orangey-coloured fruit produced by the female tree smells of rotten eggs when ripe in the fall.

Where to see the trees:

Surrey

Darts Hill Garden Park, 1660- 168 St, South Surrey, Garden Bed 2.

Green Timbers Arboretum, 9800- 140 St, Whalley, south of the cooling and sorting shed.

Peace Arch Park, King George Hwy and 0 Ave, South Surrey*.

The Glades, 561- 172 St, South Surrey, Garyland trail, east end and driveway south.

Gleditsia triacanthos
Honeylocust

A lofty, tall tree to forty-five metres tall, and native to southern Ontario and the central and eastern United States, Honeylocust is relatively rare in the South Fraser Region in comparison to the much more common thornless form. Honeylocust is easily identified in the dormant season by the zigzagging fine-textured branch-lets and the wicked finger-length thorns that are branched and densely clothe the trunk. The dormant buds are clustered at each change of direction or node, making the stem knobby like knuckles. The foliage is very delicate, with fine, pinnately or even bi-pinnately compound light green leaves. The scented flowers are pro-duced in long pendulous clusters. Individual florets are pea-like, creamy-white and appear in late May to June. The seedpods are like large, flat, broad-bean pods. Dark brown and woody when ripe in October, they become spirally twisted, often persisting on the tree until well after Christmas.

Where to see the trees:

Langley

Sendall Gardens, 20166- 50 Ave, Langley City.

Gleditsia triacanthos f. *inermis*
Thornless Honeylocust

Where to see the trees:

Abbotsford

Trethewey House (M.S.A. Museum), 2313 Ware St, two small specimens south of the house.

Provincial Courthouse, 32202 South Fraser Way, on the south side of the building.

Chilliwack

Happy Wilkinson Park.

North side of Hope River Rd and Merritt Dr.

Townsend Park, Ashwell Rd and Hodgins Ave, a row of trees on the west side of the concessions building.

SW corner of Panorama Dr and Patterson Rd, a good-sized tree.

Langley

On Glover Rd from 88 Ave to St Andrews St, Fort Langley, a double row of young street trees.

5014- 207 St, Langley City.

Williams Park, 6600 block 238 St, Salmon River Uplands.

Richmond

School Board Office, 7811 Granville Ave.

Southarm Park, Garden City Rd and Williams Rd.

Surrey

17677- 57 Ave, Cloverdale, two medium-sized trees.

White Rock

The Promenade parallel to Marine Drive, a shapely row of young trees.

Gleditsia triacanthos f. *inermis,* bi-pinntately compound leaves

Thornless Honeylocust is very common in the South Fraser Region. It is a splendid tall tree native to southern Ontario and the central and eastern United States. Thornless Honeylocust is easily identified in the dormant season by the zigzagging fine-textured branchlets. The dormant buds are clustered at each change of direction or node, making the stem knobby like knuckles. The foliage is very delicate, with fine, pinnately or even bi-pinnately compound light green leaves. The scented flowers are produced in long pendulous clusters. Individual florets are pea-like, creamy-white and appear in late May to June. The seedpods are like large, flat, broad-bean pods. Dark brown and woody when ripe in October, they become spirally twisted, often persisting on the tree until well after Christmas.

Shademaster® Honeylocust

Where to see the trees:

Chilliwack

Townsend Park, southwest corner of Ashwell Rd and Hodgins Ave, six trees on the slope between soccer pitch C and D, by the bleacher and spectator areas.

Surrey

2068- 180 St, South Surrey.

2085- 180 St, South Surrey.

Gleditsia triacanthos Shademaster®, foliage

Shademaster® Honeylocust is a strong-growing vigorous cultivar to fourteen metres high with ascending branches which spread outward at maturity creating an irregularly vase-shaped crown. The foliage, which is dark green, turns yellow in the fall and remains on the tree later than most. Shademaster® Honeylocust rarely produces fruit.

Gleditsia triacanthos 'Skycole'

Skyline® Honeylocust

Reaching a mature height of fourteen metres, Skyline® Honeylocust has a strongly pyramidal outline with a dominant central leader. The branches reach upward at steep angles of 60-90 degrees. The leaflets in spring have a bronze-red tint and age to dark green, turning golden yellow in the fall.

Where to see the trees:

Chilliwack

Fairfield Island Park, 46000 Clare Ave, Fairfield Island, a row of trees planted on the south side of the soccer fields and in-between the soccer fields.

Little Mountain Elementary School, 9900 Carleton St, Little Mountain, three trees along the Hope River Trail Extension.

Townsend Park, southwest corner of Ashwell Rd and Hodgins Ave, at the concession area and eight trees planted between the soccer fields, interplanted with Royal Red Maple.

Surrey

14648- 17 Ave, South Surrey.

14736- 17 Ave, South Surrey.

Gleditsia triacanthos 'Suncole'
Sunburst® Honeylocust

Where to see the trees:
Chilliwack
Townsend Park, southwest corner of Ashwell Rd and Hodgins Ave, six trees at the west end of the park near the large conifer planting.

Langley
Kwantlen University College, 20901 Langley Bypass, Langley City, a young tree along the south perimeter of the golf course a the field lab.

Rosedale
Minter Gardens, 52892 Bunker Rd, growing on the slope of the zigzag trail in the Rhododendron Garden.

Surrey
8480- 156B St, Fleetwood.

8481- 156B St, Fleetwood.

8467- 15A St, South Surrey.

Gleditsia triacanthos 'Suncole', foliage

Common in the South Fraser Region, the foliage of Sunburst® Honeylocust emerges a sunshine yellow and ages to a bright green except for the newest growth. The fall colour is a bright yellow. The sprawling, irregular habit, with branches poking out higgledy-piggledy, is characteristic of this tree. Sunburst® Honeylocust is both thornless and seedless.

Gymnocladus dioica
Kentucky Coffeetree
or Kentucky Mahogany

Gymnocladus dioica, bark and compound leaves

Where to see the trees:
Surrey
Darts Hill Garden Park, 1660- 168 St, South Surrey, Garden Bed C1.

Rare in the South Fraser Region, Kentucky Coffeetree grows naturally as far north as southern Ontario but is more common in the central and eastern United States. It reaches a

Gymnocladus dioica, Morton Arboretum, Lisle, Illinois

Gymnocladus dioica, foliage

mature height of eighteen to twenty metres. It has gargantuan, up to one metre long, bipinnately compound leaves. The leaves emerge late in the spring a pinkish to purplish colour, age to dark bluish green and may turn yellow in the fall. The highly scented flowers are produced in a large cone-shaped inflorescence in late May to early June. This tree is unlikely to produce its bean-like pods in the South Fraser Region since it is primarily dioecious and both a male and female tree is needed for pollination. The winter silhouette is open and sparse, as Kentucky Coffeetree tends to produce few large branches.

H

Today I have grown taller from walking with the trees.

Karle Wilson Baker

Halesia monticola, flowers

Halesia monticola, bark

Halesia monticola
Syn. *Halesia carolina* var. *monticola*
Mountain Silverbell

Reaching a mature height of eighteen to twenty-four metres in its native range of West Virginia, Ohio, to Florida and eastern Oklahoma, Mountain Silverbell is very rare in the South Fraser Region. The 10–12 cm long leaves are elliptical in shape and turn yellow in the fall. The flower is delightful. It is white, and hangs in clusters from short stems in May. The fruit, which ripens into a four-winged silvery seed, is also ornamental and quite persistent.

Where to see the trees:
Surrey
Darts Hill Garden Park, 1660- 168 St, South Surrey, Garden Beds C3 and 16.

Chinese Witchhazel

Hamamelis mollis, foliage

Hamamelis mollis, flowers

Where to see the trees:

Abbotsford

Clearbrook Public Library, 32320 Dahlstrom Ave, several young trees at the south entrance.

Delta

Municipal Hall, 4500 Clarence Taylor Cr, Ladner, a row of six young trees in the centre median.

Langley

Kwantlen University College, 20901 Langley Bypass, Langley City, a planting of several specimens in the berm to the south of the shop building on the main campus. There is a small tree at the north end of the Highway overpass.

Richmond

Millennium Botanical Garden and Arboretum, N McLennan Community Park, Granville Ave and Garden City Rd.

Surrey

Darts Hill Garden Park, 1660- 168 St, South Surrey, Garden Beds 7 and 25.

Commonly grown in the South Fraser Region, Chinese Witchhazel is one of the earliest to bloom and most reliable of our small flowering trees. Its spidery four-petalled yellow blooms are borne in profusion and are often evident by late December. They hold well into mid February and look stunning when graced with a dusting of snow. The spicy scent of the flowers is sweetly pervasive. The large leaves are hand-sized with a wavy edge and the top and bottom surfaces are fuzzy. Medium dull green in the growing season, they often colour yellow and sometimes red in the fall. The fruit is a hard, two-sided fuzzy capsule that clings tightly to the stem in clusters. It ripens in September to October. The tan-coloured young branches are warty in appearance.

Hamamelis virginiana
Common Witchhazel

Where to see the trees:

Chilliwack

Gwynne Vaughan Park, Williams Rd and Hope River Rd, Fairfield Island, a very large tree.

Richmond

Fantasy Garden World, 10800 No 5 Rd.

Hamamelis virginiana, foliage

Hamamelis virginiana, fall colour

Native to southern Ontario, southern Quebec and the Maritimes, Common Witchhazel is not commonly grown in the South Fraser Region. When found, it is usually a multi-trunked, small tree to five to six metres high. The dark green leaves lack hairs on the top and bottom surfaces with the exception of the lower leaf veins. They have an irregular wavy edge and turn yellow in the fall. The fragrant flower is similar in appearance to the Chinese Witchhazel but it is produced in late September to early November when the leaves are falling. The spider-like petals are yellow, twisted and quite showy. The fruit is a woody two-valve fuzzy pod, which ripens the following autumn.

I

A tree symbolizes life, which can only flourish on Earth
if all the people of the world decide to defend it.

Ola'h Gyorgy

Ilex aquifolium, evergreen leaves and berries

Ilex aquifolium
English Holly

English Holly is ubiquitous in the South Fraser Region. Its brilliant red fruit and prickly, glossy, evergreen leaves are often used at Christmas time as decorations in wreaths and door swags. Native to Europe, North Africa and southwestern Asia, English Holly reaches treelike portions of fifteen to eighteen metres in height if left to grow undisturbed. It has naturalized in many parks and wild areas because birds easily disperse it. The white four-petalled male or female flowers are largely insignificant. Because English Holly is dioecious only the female trees are berry producing.

Where to see the trees:

Abbotsford
Jubilee Park, McCallum Rd south of Essendene.

Chilliwack
Gwynne Vaughan Park, Williams Rd and Hope River Rd, Fairfield Island.

Stö:lo Centre, 7201 Vedder Rd, Sardis

Delta
Pioneer Library, 4683- 51 St, Ladner, a grove of trees on the west side of the library.

Langley
Fort Langley Cemetery, 23105 St Andrews St, Fort Langley

Surrey
City Hall, 14245- 56

Did You Know?

The orchard of Common Pear and English Holly trees is growing on land originally owned by William H. Ladner, the founder of the community, which now bears his name. Paul Ladner, his son, planted the orchard surrounding the farmhouse, which burned down in 1980, almost a century after its construction. Paul Ladner sold sprigs of bright red-berried English Holly at Christmas time locally and to Eastern Canada and beyond. His widow, Winifred, continued to market cut Holly branches after his death in 1944.

J

He that plants trees loves others beside himself.[1]

Thomas Fuller, (1654–1734)

Juglans cinerea, foliage and catkins in spring

Juglans cinerea, branching pattern, Williams Park, Langley

Juglans cinerea
Butternut or White Walnut

Native to southern Ontario, southern Quebec and New Brunswick, Butternut is often a low-branching medium-sized tree reaching a height of eighteen metres and a spread of fifteen metres. The large, dark yellow-green pinnately compound leaves have eleven to nineteen almost stalkless fuzzy leaflets. The leaf stalk and twigs are also densely hairy. The fall colour is yellow to yellow-brown. The butter-tasting nuts are enclosed in egg-shaped and sized husks. The bright green husks are very sticky and hairy and fall to the ground in September. Butternut is easily distinguishable in the winter because the flat vertical ridges of the bark are white-grey. The ridges zigzag together in a close-netted pattern. Another aid to winter identification is the large leaf scar immediately below the fuzzy dormant bud. The leaf traces

Where to see the trees:
Abbotsford

Abbotsford News, 34375 Cyril St.

Trethewey House (M.S.A. Museum), 2313 Ware St, a large tree southeast of the house.

North side of Wells Rd, east of Powerhouse Rd, a farm row of good-sized trees.

29400 River Road, specimen planted around 1946.

29292 River Road.

27790 River Road.

Chilliwack

Paisley House, 45632 Wellington Ave.

51665 Yale Rd East, Rosedale.

7032 Chilliwack River Rd, Sardis.

---

[1] Thomas Fuller, Gnomonologia (1732).

appear as dark dots resembling the face of a monkey. Atop the monkey's head is a fuzzy cap. Butternut is relatively common in the South Fraser Region.

Did You Know?

Louis William Paisley, a realtor and Reeve of the Township of Chilliwack, built Paisley House in 1895. The architectural style resembles the Queen Anne style. Isaac Kipp, another well-known community pioneer, retired to Paisley House after purchasing it in 1899. A 1915 photo of the Kipps' Fiftieth Wedding Anniversary depicts the Butternut as a sapling.
• The two mature butternut trees on the south side of 96 Avenue in Walnut Grove, Langley, were most likely planted as part of a farm perimeter in 1912. These trees are the namesake trees for the community of Walnut Grove.
• The butternut tree in Sullivan Park is adjacent to the Peace Grove. The Sullivan Park Peace Grove is a planting of trees representing the provinces and territories and was dedicated to international peace in 1992, the year of Canada's 125 birthday.

Where to see the trees:

Langley

8997 Nash St, Ft Langley.

SE corner of Mavis St and King St, Ft Langley.

Derby Reach Regional Park, Allard Cr, Northwest Langley, a lovely open-grown specimen 200 metres east of the easternmost end of the campground.

1215- 264 St, Southeast Langley.

21100 96 Ave, Walnut Grove.

Williams Park, 6600 Block, 238 St, Salmon River Uplands.

Surrey

6091- 181 A St, Cloverdale*.

Sullivan Park, 15300- 62A Ave, Newton* a majestic mature tree.

Juglans cinerea x *J. ailanthifolia* var. *cordiformis,* Darts Hill Garden Park, Surrey

Juglans cinerea x
Juglans ailanthifolia var. *cordiformis*
Canadian/ Japanese Walnut hybrid

Juglans cinerea x *J. ailanthifolia* var. *cordiformis,* Darts Hill Garden Park, Surrey.

Juglans cinerea x
Juglans ailanthifolia var. *cordiformis*
Canadian/ Japanese Walnut hybrid

Where to see the trees:

Surrey

Darts Hill Garden Park, 1660 - 168 St, South Surrey*, Garden Bed 24b. This magnificent tree is the focal point of the garden. A second tree to the west, both trees planted by Mrs. Darts at the same time is significantly smaller than the tree at the foot of the stairs.

This hybrid Walnut is extremely rare in the South Fraser Region. It exhibits characteristics of both parents. The catkins of this hybrid Walnut are typical of Walnuts in general and droop from the branches in great quantity in late May. They resemble long, fuzzy green caterpillars.

Juglans nigra
Black Walnut

Juglans nigra, fall colour

Juglans nigra, Locks Pharmacy, Main Street, Chilliwack

Black Walnut is relatively common in the South Fraser Region. Native to the warmest parts of southern Ontario and south into the United States, Black Walnut may grow twenty-seven metres high, but here it is more likely to grow fourteen to fifteen metres high with a wide-open spreading crown to eighteen metres across. The pinnately compound leaves have fifteen to twenty-three yellow-green leaflets that turn golden in the fall. The leaflets are long and narrowly pointed. The leaves smell acrid and sweet when crushed. The fruit is a nut contained in a round, pale green golf-ball-sized husk. The husk surface is pimpled and doesn't easily separate from the nut. Usually the fruit falls to the ground and decays, exposing the nut. The flesh of the nut husk also smells when crushed. Black Walnut is easily distinguishable in the winter because the rough bark is deeply furrowed and the ridges are blackish. Another aid to winter identification is the large leaf scar immediately below the fuzzy dormant bud. The leaf traces appear as dark dots resembling the face of a monkey. Unlike the Butternut, Black Walnut monkey faces do not have downy caps.

Did You Know?

Querencia in Chilliwack received its name from Alan Kirkby. Mr. Kirkby read an article in his early teens of the Spanish horses that had escaped captivity and become wild when they were brought to North America. These horses, even when captured and broken to the saddle, never forgot the bit of land where they had been born, instinctively returning to it. Querencia, which means "favourite spot" or "haunt" in Spanish, was Alan Kirkby's chosen place.
• The Wark-Dumais House in Langley is a municipally designated Heritage Site. Two well-known families have been associated with the Wark-Dumais House. Robert Wark was an early warden or mayor of Langley while the second residents, the Dumais family, established and operated a large dairy farm in the area. The house was built over a period of years from 1890 – 1910. The Walnut was likely planted at the turn of the twentieth century.
• John "Jack" W. Berry, a prominent citizen of the area, built the farmstead for Belmont Dairy Farms in Langley on Old Yale Road in 1901-1902. The farmhouse was constructed of timber cleared from the land. The site contains a number of very large and mature trees including the Black Walnut. This working dairy farm is still owned by the Berry family.

Where to see the trees:
Chilliwack
Querencia, 48567 McConnell Rd, East Chilliwack.

10170 Reeves Rd, East Chilliwack, west side of the property.

Locks Pharmacy, 9181 Main St, two huge trees, one with a DBH of 125 cm.

Delta
Sacred Heart Elementary School, 3900 Arthur Dr, Ladner.

Langley
Kwantlen University College, 20901 Langley Bypass, Langley City, to the east of the Wark-Dumais Heritage House.

Belmont Dairy Farms, 21151 Old Yale Rd, Murrayville

Juglans nigra, foliage and fruit

Juglans regia

English, Persian or Common Walnut

Juglans regia, foliage

Juglans regia, Redwood Park, Surrey

English Walnut is very common in the South Fraser Region, since it grows well and the familiar edible nuts are easy to harvest. It reaches a medium mature size, growing fifteen to eighteen metres high and at least as wide. The large pinnately compound leaves of English Walnut usually have five but may have up to nine leaflets. The end leaflet is much stouter than the rest. All the leaflets are untoothed, differing English walnut from other species found locally. The lustrous leaves are medium to dark green turning yellow to brown-yellow in the fall. The glossy oblong nut husks are golf ball sized, smooth, and green speckled with yellow. The nut husks partially split open when ripe, unlike other *Juglans* species. The nut inside the husk is wrinkled and may be very thick-shelled. The bark of English Walnut is silvery grey, smooth and at maturity it is lightly fissured.

Where to see the trees:

Abbotsford

NE corner of Orchard Dr and Marshall Rd, two very large trees.

35788 Vye Rd, a beautiful open-grown farm tree.

John Mahoney Park, off Ware St, a medium-sized tree to the southeast of the bridge of the Mill Lake boardwalk.

MSA General Hospital, 2179 McCallum Rd, southeast corner of the building, a good-sized tree with a DBH of 60 cm.

Did You Know?

Hassall House in Glen Valley Regional Park in Langley, situated between the railway tracks and the Fraser River, was purchased from the Soldier's Settlement Board. Jack Hassall, born in Birmingham, England in 1886, brought his wife, Christina, to the Glen Valley in 1918. Jack Hassall was a soldier in both the Boer and Great Wars. Mr. and Mrs. Hassall were not the original owners of the house, which was built in 1917, but purchased it before it was finished. Just to the north of the house, at the foot of 272 Street, called Jackman Road originally, the riverboat *Skeena* put passengers and freight ashore.

English, Persian or Common Walnut

Where to see the trees:

Chilliwack

45726 Spadina Ave.

Gwynne Vaughan Park, Williams Rd and Hope River Rd, Fairfield Island.

7360 Prest Rd, Sardis.

No 4 Firehall, 45433 South Sumas Rd, Sardis, on the east side of the hall.

Delta

Memorial Park, 47 Ave and Delta St, Ladner, three good-sized trees approximately fourteen metres high and the largest with a DBH of 60 cm at the southeast corner of the park.

Sacred Heart Church, 3900 Arthur Dr, Ladner. The church was dedicated in June 1966.

Langley

21387- 40 Ave, Brookswood, a grove of well-grown trees.

Glen Valley Regional Park, Two-Bit Bar, 272 St and River Rd, Northeast Langley, two mature trees planted southeast of Hassall House, 9117- 272 St.

Richmond

Millennium Botanical Garden and Arboretum, N McLennan Community Park, Granville Ave and Garden City Rd.

Surrey

Provincial Courthouse, 14340- 57 Ave, Newton, south of the building.

Redwood Park, 17900- 20 Ave, South Surrey*. This fine old tree in the grass area south of the Tree House was planted by the Brown brothers in the 1890's.

Tolleson's Blue Weeping Juniper

Juniperus scopulorum 'Tolleson's Blue Weeping', Langley City

An irregular umbrella shape with strongly pendulous branches marks Tolleson's Blue Weeping Juniper. The scale-like tiny leaves are glaucous blue and are held on branchlets that drape

Where to see the trees:

Abbotsford

SW corner of Marshall Rd, two specimens in the commercial landscape.

Richmond

Fantasy Garden World, 10800 No 5 Rd.

Langley

5558- 208 St, Langley City.

Juniperus scopulorum
'Tolleson's Blue Weeping'

Tolleson's Blue Weeping Juniper

delicately from strong arching branches. A small conifer, Tolleson's Blue Weeping Juniper may reach a height of six metres. Tolleson's Blue Weeping Juniper is not commonly found in the South Fraser Region.

Juniperus squamata 'Meyeri'

Meyer Juniper, Fishback or Fish Tail Juniper

Juniperus squamata 'Meyeri', School District Offices, Surrey

Juniperus squamata 'Meyeri', foliage

Where to see the trees:

Chilliwack

Sardis Park, Sardis, several large specimens near the west entrance to the park on School Lane.

Delta

Fire Hall No 4, SW corner of Highway 99 and Ladner Trunk Rd.

Surrey

Darts Hill Garden Park, 1660- 168 St, South Surrey, Garden Bed 19.

School District No 36, Administrative Offices, 14225- 56 Ave, Newton, on the east side of Human Resources portable building.

Common in the South Fraser Region, Meyer Juniper is a gaunt and ungainly Juniper. Its multi-trunked form reaches a height and spread of six metres. The irregular stiffly held branches are clothed in sharp-pointed blue needles, which are covered in a whitish bloom. Foliage is dense and thick on young trees, but often sparse on the branches of mature trees. The dead brown needles are persistent, giving the tree an untidy look. The bark is reddish brown and peeling. The black berry ripens in October.

K

The trees were gazing up into the sky,
their bare arms stretched in prayer for the snows.

Alexander Smith, (1830–1867)

Koelreuteria paniculata, foliage

Koelreuteria paniculata, flower panicles

Koelreuteria paniculata

Golden Rain Tree

Rare in the South Fraser Region, Golden Rain Tree is a native of China and Korea. It reaches a mature height of twelve metres. Often this tree has an irregular and sparse branching pattern. It is grown for the outstanding display of small, bright yellow star-shaped flowers, which are produced on loose upright panicles 30 cm long in July. The Golden Rain Tree has large pinnately or bi-pinnately compound leaves. Each leaflet is coarsely toothed, emerges bronze, ages to dark green and turns yellow in the fall. The angular seed capsule is very showy. It is first green in late summer, then ages to reddish green and matures to brown. These seedpods, which split into three papery segments at maturity, resemble miniature Chinese lanterns as they hang in the tree in the fall.

Where to see the trees:

Delta

Police Station, 4455 Clarence Taylor Cr, Ladner, three medium-sized trees on the north side of the building.

Richmond

Millennium Botanical Garden and Arboretum, N McLennan Community Park, Granville Ave and Garden City Rd.

Surrey

Darts Hill Garden Park, 1660- 168 St, South Surrey, Garden Bed 25 and C4.

L

A man does not plant a tree for himself; he plants it for posterity.

Alexander Smith, (1830–1867)[1]

Laburnum x *watereri* 'Vossi', foliage

Laburnum x *watereri* 'Pendula'

Weeping Hybrid Goldenchain or Weeping Hybrid Laburnum

Weeping Hybrid Goldenchain is a small tree; its pendulous branchlets create a lovely umbrella form. It is a top-grafted tree and the mature height depends on the original height of the graft union. The leaves are trifoliate with three leaflets, and are bluish green in the growing season. The bright yellow flowers, which appear in May, are pea-like and borne in long hanging clusters. The fruit is a pea pod containing small, flat, black seeds.

Where to see the trees:

Rosedale
Minter Gardens, 52892 Bunker Rd.

---

[1] Alexander Smith, *Dreamthorp* (1863), ch. 11.

Hybrid Goldenchain,
Hybrid Laburnum or Voss's Laburnum

Laburnum x *watereri* 'Vossi', Municipal Hall, Langley

Laburnum x *watereri* 'Vossi', flower clusters

Hybrid Goldenchain is a small tree reaching a mature height of six to eight metres. The stiff scaffold branches enhance the strong upright vase shape. The trifoliate leaves have three leaflets and are bluish green in the growing season. The fall colour is yellow-green. The bright yellow flowers, which appear in May, are pea-like and borne in long hanging clusters, up to 45–60 cm in length. Sweetly fragrant, the flowers are profuse and very showy. The fruit, which is infrequently produced, is a pea pod containing one or two small, flat, black seeds. In winter, the remnants of the hanging flower stems and seedpods are quite messy and help identify the tree. The bark, which is olive green and smooth on young stems, is also a helpful identifier.

Where to see the trees:

Chilliwack

Canadian Forces Base, Keith Wilson Rd and Vedder Rd, Vedder Crossing, in the garden of the residence, northwest of the tennis courts.

Langley

Municipal Hall, 4914- 221 St, Murrayville.

Surrey

Darts Hill Garden Park, 1660- 168 St, South Surrey, Garden Bed 25.

The Glades, 561-172 St, South Surrey, west end of the ridge.

Larix decidua
European Larch or Common Larch

Larix decidua, Peace Arch Park, Surrey

Where to see the trees:

Abbotsford

SE corner of Primrose St and Marshall Rd, a good-sized tree.

Delta

South Delta Recreation Centre, 1720-56 St, Tsawwassen, two groups of excellent specimens.

Langley

Kwantlen University College, 20901 Langley Bypass, Langley City. There are two well-shaped trees in the lawn between the main wing and the east building on the main campus.

Surrey

City Hall, 14245- 56 Ave, Newton, a tall specimen southwest of the building to the east of the power substation.

Green Timbers Arboretum, 9800-140 St, Whalley, adjacent to the south laneway.

Peace Arch Park, King George Hwy and 0 Ave, South Surrey.

Larix decidua, foliage and cones

European Larch is a tall-growing deciduous conifer native to the Alps of Europe. It reaches a height of thirty metres and more in its native habitat. The conical form is softened by the weeping yellow branchlets while the tips of the branches sweep up. The foliage is one of two types on the same branch. Bundles of spirally arranged needles adorn the knoblike short spur branches while slightly longer needles grow singly on the current season's growth. The needles are soft to the touch, and when they emerge in the spring, are a brilliant lime green, aging to a soft light green and colouring a spectacular yellow in the fall. The cones of Larches help to distinguish them in the field. European Larch cones are upright, begin green and mature to brown and are persistent. The cones may be quite long (4.5 cm) or squat and dumpy (1.5–3 cm long). The overlapping cone scales are straight or curved toward the centre, each cone scale with a slightly wavy edge. The cone scales do not bend backwards or reflex like the cones of other larches found locally. The threadlike bract on the scale is shorter than the scale and is not as noticeable as the bracts of Western Larch. European Larch is relatively common in the South Fraser Region.

Larix kaempferi, Salmon River Uplands, Langley

Larix kaempferi, foliage and developing cones

Native to the island of Honshu in Japan, where it may reach forty-five metres in height, Japanese Larch is another very tall-growing deciduous conifer. It is similar in appearance to European Larch but there are some significant differences that aid in field identification. The needles of Japanese Larch are bluer, covered with a whitish bloom, and turn golden in the fall. The branchlets are pinkish to reddish brown and are often somewhat glaucous too. The woody cone is very distinctive; it is round, begins reddish brown and matures a dark brown. When looked at from above, the cone scales resemble the curving opening petals of a rose because each cone scale is strongly reflexed or turned back down at the tip. The cones are the size of a one-dollar coin.

Where to see the trees:

Delta
Leisure Centre, 4600 Clarence Taylor Cr, Ladner, south side of the centre, near the Rotary Park Planting.

Langley
5340- 200 St, Langley City.

D.W. Poppy Secondary School, 23752- 52 Ave, Salmon River Uplands.

24355- 48 Ave, Salmon River Uplands, the second tree on west side of the entry drive.

Richmond
Fantasy Garden World, 10800 No 5 Rd.

Surrey
Darts Hill Garden Park, 1660- 168 St, South Surrey, Garden Beds 1 and 23.

Redwood Park, 17900- 20 Ave, South Surrey, six fairly large trees near the washrooms.

Larix laricina
Tamarack or Eastern Larch

Larix laricina, foliage

Where to see the trees:
Chilliwack
47502 Swallow Cr, Little Mountain.

Surrey
Darts Hill Garden Park, 1660- 168 St, South Surrey, Garden Bed 16.

Tamarack is native to sphagnum bogs and swamps throughout Canada. In British Columbia it is more commonly found in the northeastern parts of the province. It reaches a height of ten to twenty metres. The light bluish green soft needles are similar to the larches mentioned above. The cones are entirely distinctive. Tamarack cones are very small, the size of a penny and egg-shaped, with few cone scales in comparison to other larches. The pale brown cones open in the fall and persist over the winter and into the summer of the following year. Tamarack is rarely grown in the South Fraser Region.

Larix occidentalis
Western Larch

Where to see the trees:
Rosedale
Minter Gardens, 52892 Bunker Rd, at the southern end of the Lake Garden.

Largest of the larches native to Canada, Western Larch may grow thirty or more metres high. It is very common in the Columbia Forest Region along Highway 1 into Revelstoke and beyond on the mountainsides to 1200 metres in elevation. The needles are yellowish green and turn yellow in the fall. The small oval cones are tightly closed when immature, but ripen into a prickly affair. The reddish-brown cone scales fan down and their attending bracts are long and whip-like, usually recurved, extending beyond the scales. After the seed has dropped out, the cone scales turn inward and the whip-like bract falls off. The mature bark is scaly and plated. Western Larch is rarely grown in the South Fraser Region.

Liquidambar styraciflua
Sweetgum, American Sweetgum, Starleaf Gum or Red Gum

Liquidambar styraciflua, fall colour

Native to the southern and eastern United States and parts of Central America, Sweetgum is commonly found in the South Fraser Region. It has a tidy pyramidal shape in youth, and ages to an upright oval form, with a mature height of fifteen metres. The trees in the South Fraser Region are all relatively young. The bright, shiny dark green leaves smell strongly resinous when crushed. The aromatic balsam contained in the tissues is unattractive to insects, so the leaves are usually free of insect damage. The buds also smell when crushed. The large leaves are five- to seven-lobed, and resemble the leaves of a maple but shouldn't be confused with them since Sweetgum leaves are alternately arranged while maple leaves are held opposite

Where to see the trees:

Abbotsford

Provincial Courthouse, 32202 South Fraser Way, northwest corner of building.

Median planting on Old Yale Rd from Blue Jay St to Townline Rd.

Chilliwack

Fairfield Island Park, 46000 Clare Ave, Fairfield Island. The trees at the entry to the park are twenty-five to thirty years old.

Salish Park, 45860- 1 Ave.

Townsend Park, SW corner of Ashwell Rd and Hodgins Ave, a row of trees on the south side of the baseball park.

University College of the Fraser Valley, 45600 Airport Rd.

47313 Swallow Cr, Little Mountain.

Delta

Municipal Hall, 4500 Clarence Taylor Cr, Ladner, entry drive.

North Delta Recreation Centre, 11415- 84 Ave, an entry row into the parking lot.

Langley

Kwantlen University College, 20901 Langley Bypass, Langley City, an entry row of young trees at the west entrance to campus at Glover Rd.

Williams Park, 6600 block 238 St, Salmon River Uplands.

Trinity Western University, 7600 Glover, Willoughby, a good-sized tree to the south of the Reimer Student Centre.

Liquidambar styraciflua

Sweetgum, American Sweetgum, Starleaf Gum or Red Gum

Where to see the trees:

Richmond

Williams Rd from No 5 Rd west.

Fantasy Garden World, 10800 No 5 Rd.

Rosedale

Minter Gardens, 52892 Bunker Rd, Stream Garden.

Surrey

Darts Hill Garden Park, 1660- 168 St, South Surrey, Garden Bed 19.

Provincial Courthouse, 14340- 57 Ave, Newton, east side of the building along the edge of the parking lot.

The Glades, 561-172 St, South Surrey. The tree at the east end of the west ridge was planted December 14, 1966.

one another on the stem. Sweetgum leaves are also held at right angles to the petiole, while maple leaves are held parallel to the petiole. The leaves of Sweetgum turn magnificent fall colours of orange, red and maroon. They are among the last leaves to colour in the South Fraser Region and many hang on the tree until Christmas. This characteristic makes the trees susceptible to limb breakage in the rare year when very heavy wet snow falls early in the season. The fruit is showy when ripe in late winter, looking like a brown, spiky sea anemone. The winged or corky ridges that protrude irregularly from the twigs and branches facilitate winter identification.

Liquidambar styraciflua 'Worplesdon'

Worplesdon Sweetgum

Liquidambar styraciflua 'Worplesdon', foliage

Worplesdon Sweetgum, which reaches a mature height of twelve metres, differs from the species in that its twigs are not winged or corky. The lobes of the leaves are also narrower, often divided into smaller lobes, giving it a finer texture than the parent plant. Fall colour ranges from orange to purple. Worplesdon Sweetgum is a recent introduction to the South Fraser Region.

Where to see the trees:

Chilliwack

Chilliwack Exhibition Grounds, south fence line along Hodgins Ave, Chilliwack.

Townsend Park, southwest corner of Wolfe and Ashwell Rd, five trees located in the north-south laneway separating baseball diamonds 4 and 6, Chilliwack.

On South Sumas Rd, seven trees on the north to south side from Tyson Rd to Wiltshire Rd, Sardis.

Sardis Park, Britton Av parking lot, Sardis.

Little Mountain Elementary School, 9900 Carleton St, Hope River Trail Extension, Little Mountain.

Langley

Kwantlen University College, 20901 Langley Bypass, Langley City. The tree is planted along the perimeter just to the east of the Turf Demonstration Lab.

56 Ave from 206 Ave to Glover Rd, Langley City, a street planting.

Surrey

6043- 190B St, Cloverdale, planted in 1993.

6055- 190B St, Cloverdale, planted in 1993.

2926- 139A St, South Surrey.

2940- 139A St, South Surrey.

Liriodendron chinense

Chinese Tulip Tree

Liriodendron chinense, foliage

Native to China and North Vietnam, Chinese Tulip Tree is very rare in the South Fraser Region. The leaves are similar to the more common Tulip Poplar, but are larger and the two lower lobes are separated from the two top lobes by deeper sinuses. Fall colour is golden yellow.

Where to see the trees:

Langley

Kwantlen University College, 20901 Langley Bypass, Langley City. A single tree is growing south of the west entrance along the Glover Road boulevard.

Richmond

Millennium Botanical Garden and Arboretum, N McLennan Community Park, Granville Ave and Garden City Rd.

Surrey

Darts Hill Garden Park, 1660- 168 St, South Surrey, Magnolia Walk and Pasture.

Liriodendron tulipifera

Tulip Tree, Tulip Poplar or Yellow Poplar

Liriodendron tulipifera, James Court, Langley

Liriodendron tulipifera, flower

Tulip Poplar is a tall stately tree native to the Great Lakes Region of Ontario, and across the border into Wisconsin, to Massachusetts and south to Florida and Mississippi. Mature trees in their native range may reach enormous size, up to sixty metres high. Tulip Poplar is common in the South Fraser Region with trees typically reaching a height of twenty-seven metres. The upright oval shape with short swooping branches identifies the tree in winter, particularly when the stubby cone-like fruit are found clinging upright on the branches. The leaves are unmistakable. They are lyre shaped, unlike any other deciduous tree. Each leaf has four lobes with the topmost two lobes abruptly cut off. The long petioles allow the leaves to flutter like a poplar's in the breeze. The leaves emerge sunshine yellow in the spring, mature a medium dull green and turn a rich butter yellow in November. The flower resembles a squat tulip. The petals are greenish yellow, with pumpkin orange blotches at their base. They are difficult to see since they bloom in June when the tree is in full leaf and are often found only near the tops of the tree. The smooth tan bud scales of the dormant bud fit together like a duck's bill. On mature trees, the bark is narrowly ridged, with each ridge rounded in profile.

Tulip Tree, Tulip Poplar or Yellow Poplar

Where to see the trees:

Abbotsford

2309 McCallum Rd.

2715 Mount View Ave, a lovely large tree.

33969 Hazelwood St, across from the cemetery, an excellent tree that was topped at the midpoint many years ago.

2856 Maple St.

Chilliwack

Family Place, 45845 Wellington Ave, two magnificent old trees, one with a DBH of 175 cm.

Salish Park, 45860- 1 Ave.

Sardis Park, Sardis, near the west entrance to the park on School Lane.

Stó:lo Centre, 7201 Vedder Rd, Sardis, a large tree with a DBH of 130 cm.

Townsend Park, SW corner of Ashwell Rd and Hodgins Ave, west of the baseball park.

NW corner of Hazel St and Portage Ave.

47835 Camp River Rd, East Chilliwack.

Canadian Forces Base, Keith Wilson Rd and Vedder Rd, Vedder Crossing, southeast end of the site by the Pump House.

Delta

Health Centre, 4470 Clarence Taylor Cr, Ladner, trees planted in 1974.

Fawcett House, 4532 Arthur Dr, Ladner.

11895 Woodhurst Dr, west end of Panorama Ridge, a massive mature specimen with a DBH of 104 cm.

11688- 82 Ave, North Delta, a very large tree.

Langley

20448 Park Ave, Langley City, a huge tree at the entrance to the James Court Apartments.

North side of Willowbrook Dr, between 198 St and 200 St, a row of street trees.

23203 Francis St, Ft Langley.

Richmond

City Hall, 6911 No 3 Rd, a large tree on the east side of the building.

8671 Minler Rd, a large tree with a DBH of 60 cm.

Steveston Park, 4111 Moncton St, Steveston.

Southarm Park, Garden City Rd and Williams Rd.

Rosedale

Minter Gardens, 52892 Bunker Rd, Playground area.

Surrey

City Hall, 14245- 56 Ave, Newton, perimeter of the east parking lot.

Darts Hill Garden Park, 1660- 168 St, South Surrey, Garden Bed 32.

The Glades, 561- 172 St, South Surrey*, in the Bent Tree area.

12976 Old Yale Rd, Whalley*.

124 St north of 92 Ave, Whalley.

Prince Charles Blvd, Whalley.

White Rock

859 Maple St.

Did You Know?

Prolific Ladner contractor J.B. Elliot built the Craftsman-styled home at 4532 Arthur Drive in Ladner in 1920 for the family of Arthur Thompson Fawcett. When construction began on the site, the local newspaper reported that "many fine trees were planted on this property some years ago and now it is one of the beauty spots in Delta."[2] Perhaps the huge Tulip Tree dates from that time.

[2] Szychter, G. *Beyond Ladner's Landing: Two Heritage Walks South Of the Original Village.* Delta, B.C. p 24.

Liriodendron tulipifera, branching pattern, The Glades, Surrey

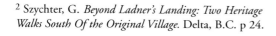

Liriodendron tulipifera 'Aureo-marginatum'
Variegated Tulip Tree

Where to see the trees:

Rosedale

Minter Gardens, 52892 Bunker Rd, west of Trillium Restaurant.

Rarely found in the South Fraser Region, the Variegated Tulip Tree has green leaves edged in gold. The variegated margin ages to greenish yellow by the end of the growing season.

Liriodendron tulipifera 'Fastigiatum'
Syn. *Liriodendron tulipifera* 'Arnold'
Syn. *Liriodendron tulipifera* 'Pyramidalis'
Arnold Tulip Tree

Where to see the trees:

Delta

North Delta Recreation Centre, 11415-84 Ave, an entry row into the parking lot.

Richmond

City Hall, 6911 No 3 Rd, a row of young trees along the north perimeter of the parking lot.

The branches of this cultivar are parallel to one another creating a stiffly upright, narrowly pyramidal shape. Arnold Tulip Tree will produce its blooms within two to three years of planting. Rare in the South Fraser Region, it has been recorded growing to fifteen to eighteen metres high with a spread of 4.5–6 metres in Europe.

It's just a thrill to find something really big. There's something charismatic about a big tree that just catches the eye of the public. It makes people aware that there's something out there worth preserving....

Robert Zahner

Magnolia acuminata, foliage and developing fruit

Magnolia acuminata
Cucumber Tree

Native to tiny pockets in southern Ontario and south into New York to Georgia and west to Illinois and Arkansas, Cucumber Tree reaches a height of twenty-five metres in its native range. It is rarely found in the South Fraser Region. The large, up to 25 cm long and half as wide, leaves are elliptical in shape and medium green, with a somewhat hairy underside. The edge of the leaf is undulating. The fall colour is a mellow yellow. The flowers, which appear after the leaves emerge, are yellowish-green and hidden by the foliage. The flower petals are large and fleshy, cupping the stamens protectively. The fruit, which resembles a contorted cucumber, is 5–8 cm long and red when ripe in October. One or two bright scarlet seeds dangle from the split husk by dainty white threads. The bark on mature trees is grey and lightly ridged.

Magnolia acuminata, Morton Arboretum, Lisle, Illinois

Where to see the trees:
Abbotsford
33865 Pine St, a magnificent tree with a DBH of 103 cm.

Surrey
Darts Hill Garden Park, 1660- 168 St, South Surrey, Garden Bed 15a.

Magnolia dawsoniana
Dawson Magnolia

Magnolia dawsoniana, flowers

Where to see the trees:

Rosedale

Minter Gardens, 52892 Bunker Rd, several specimens in the Rhododendron Garden.

Surrey

Darts Hill Garden Park, 1660- 168 St, South Surrey, Magnolia Walk and Pasture, Garden Beds C3 and 29.

Native to western China, Dawson Magnolia is not common in the South Fraser Region. It grows to eighteen metres in height with an upright oval shape. The obovate leaves are up to 13.5 cm long and about half as wide. The fragrant flowers, which are borne in March – April before the leaves, are unusual in that they flop sideways from the branchlet. Each white flower is goblet shaped, 25 cm across and lightly flushed with rose to pale purple at the base. The nine tepals relax as they age until the flower appears limp.

Magnolia denudata
Syn. *Magnolia heptapeta*
Yulan Magnolia, Chinese White Magnolia or Chandelier Magnolia

The startling white goblet-shaped blossoms of Yulan Magnolia shimmer in the rainy spring weather typical of the South Fraser Region. The 7–10 cm long flowers are borne stiffly upright on naked stems. Blooming profusely at an early age, the alabaster white blooms relax and open to 15 cm wide. They are lightly scented of lemons. Native to eastern China, Yulan Magnolia reaches a mature height of twelve to fifteen metres with a round form. The leaves,

Magnolia denudata
Syn. *Magnolia heptapeta*
Yulan Magnolia, Chinese White Magnolia or Chandelier Magnolia

Magnolia denudata, 58A Avenue, Salmon River Uplands, Langley

Magnolia denudata, flowers

Where to see the trees:

Richmond

Millennium Botanical Garden and Arboretum, N McLennan Community Park, Granville Ave and Garden City Rd.

Langley

23987- 58A Ave, Salmon River Uplands.

4681- 233 St, Salmon River Uplands.

Surrey

Darts Hill Garden Park, 1660- 168 St, South Surrey, Magnolia Walk and Pasture and Garden Bed 7 and 11.

up to 15 cm long, are a slim-waisted obovate shape. They are dark green above and somewhat hairy on the top and hairy on the veins below.

Magnolia 'Elizabeth'
Elizabeth Magnolia

An example of a hybrid Magnolia, the parents of Elizabeth Magnolia are *Magnolia acuminata* and *Magnolia denudata*. The flowers are an unusual straw yellow, which ages to a cream. The goblet-shaped flowers are large, up to 18 cm, produced in May and are held upright.

Where to see the trees:

Surrey

15300- 88 Ave, four young trees in the centre median planting.

Darts Hill Garden Park, 1660- 168 St, South Surrey, Garden Bed 32.

Magnolia 'Elizabeth', Darts Hill Garden Park, Surrey

Magnolia 'Galaxy'
Galaxy Magnolia

Where to see the trees:
Abbotsford

Median planting on McClure Rd from Gladwin east to 33300 block McClure Road.

Surrey

Darts Hill Garden Park, 1660- 168 St, South Surrey, Magnolia Walk and Pasture.

Magnolia 'Galaxy', flowers

Reaching a mature height of six to nine metres with a narrowly pyramidal form, Galaxy Magnolia is a relatively recent addition to the South Fraser Region. Unusual for a Magnolia, it maintains a strong central leader. Galaxy Magnolia is a good example of one of the many hybrid Magnolias now readily available. *Magnolia liliiflora* and *Magnolia sprenger* 'Diva' are its parents. The later and long blooming season of its *Magnolia liliiflora* parent is evident while the other parent contributed the rosy blush of the tepals (tepals are the evolutionary hybrid between sepals and petals). The scented flowers of Galaxy Magnolia appear in late April to May. Each goblet-shaped bloom is 20 cm wide; the tepals are purplish-pink at the base, then suffused rosy pink. The mid-green leaves are obovate in shape and up to 20 cm long.

Magnolia grandiflora
Evergreen Magnolia or Southern Magnolia

Evergreen Magnolia is the only Magnolia to retain its leaves over the winter. It is native to northern Carolina, south to Florida, and into Arkansas and Texas where it reaches a mature height of eighteen to twenty-four metres. It grows substantially less here, to ten to twelve metres in height. The leaves of Evergreen

Magnolia grandiflora
Evergreen Magnolia or Southern Magnolia

Magnolia are elliptical in shape; often with a lovely rusty felt covering the underside. Each leaf is up to 25 cm long, very leathery and shiny dark green on the top surface. Evergreen Magnolia prefers a warm, sunny, south-facing aspect to successfully bloom in the South Fraser Region. Borne in July through August, the luxurious flowers are creamy white and the size of dinner plates. Their musky perfume is deeply cloying. The young shoots and buds are also covered in rusty felt. Evergreen Magnolia is relatively common in our area.

Where to see the trees:

Delta
5039- 44 Ave, Ladner, a small tree.

Langley
Sendall Gardens, Langley City, south wall of the residence.

Trinity Western University, 7600 Glover Rd, Willoughby, centre of the fountain.

Richmond
Minoru Park, 7700 Minoru Gate, six young trees.

Surrey
The Glades, 561-172 St, South Surrey, south of the Bent Cedar and north of the waterfall.

Holland Park, Old Yale Road at 134 St, Whalley.

Magnolia grandiflora 'Samuel Sommer'
Samuel Sommer Evergreen Magnolia or Samuel Sommer Southern Magnolia

Magnolia grandiflora 'Samuel Sommer', Darts Hill Garden Park, Surrey

Magnolia grandiflora 'Samuel Sommer', fruit

This cultivar of Evergreen Magnolia has extra large flowers.

Where to see the trees:

Surrey
Darts Hill Garden Park, 1660- 168 St, South Surrey, Garden Bed C1.

Magnolia kobus

Kobus Magnolia or Northern Japanese Magnolia

Magnolia kobus, Salmon River Uplands, Langley

Magnolia kobus, flowers

Where to see the trees:

Chilliwack

A Bookman Store, 45939 Wellington Ave. A pair of fine trees frame the entrance to this store while hundreds of Kobus Magnolias line the streets in the Chilliwack city centre.

Langley

209 B St North of 44A Ave, Brookswood.

9134 Wright St, Fort Langley, two large trees.

Douglas Cr, Langley City, a street tree planting with *Robinia* 'Purple Robe' and *Pyrus* c. 'Chanticleer'.

5400 block 203 St, Langley City.

24057- 53 Ave, Salmon River Uplands, a large tree with a height of 7.5- 8 metres and a spread of the same.

Richmond

Millennium Botanical Garden and Arboretum, N McLennan Community Park, Granville Ave and Garden City Rd.

Surrey

The Glades, 561- 172 St, South Surrey*, Magnolia Walk.

Native to central and northern Japan, Kobus Magnolia grows fifteen to twenty metres in height with a round form. The flower buds are grey, fuzzy and shaped like a fist, which are good winter identifying characteristics. The leaves emerge after the flowers. The obovate leaves are 15 or more cm long with a pale green underside and hairy veins. The flowers are medium-sized for a Magnolia, at 10 cm in diameter. The six to nine shockingly white petals appear in March or early April; often the petals will have a flush of pink at their base. They make the tree look a bit untidy, as they tend to flop sideways. The pinkish fruit, about 5 cm long, looks like a small deformed cucumber. When ripe, the scarlet seeds hang from threads before falling. The stem when crushed has deep sweet scent. Kobus Magnolia is common in the South Fraser Region.

Magnolia kobus var. *læbneri* 'Leonard Messel'
Syn. *Magnolia* x *læbneri* 'Leonard Messel'

Leonard Messel Magnolia or Pink Star Magnolia

Magnolia kobus var. *læbneri* 'Leonard Messel',
unfolding flowers

Magnolia kobus var. *læbneri* 'Leonard Messel', foliage
and fuzzy buds

Growing six metres high with an equal spread, Leonard Messel Magnolia is a grand addition to the early spring landscape. It blooms prolifically in March to early April. The flower buds are fuzzy and greyish green. The emerging flowers are deep purplish pink, when in tight bud. As the twelve to fifteen spoon-shaped tepals unfold, they mature to a medium pink on their exterior, which is suffused at the base with a band of rose pink. The inside of the tepal is soft white. The flowers are deliciously fragrant. Bruised stems and the fleshy white roots of this plant are also aromatic. The dark green leaves are up to 15 cm long, oblong in shape and turn a pleasant yellow in the fall. Leonard Messel Magnolia is abundant in the South Fraser Region.

Where to see the trees:

Langley:

Longlea Estates, 5101- 203 St, Langley City, a lovely tree on the northwest corner of 203 St and the entrance to the complex.

6047- 237A Place, Salmon River Uplands.

Magnolia kobus var. *læbneri* 'Merrill'
Syn. *Magnolia* x *læbneri* 'Merrill'
Syn. *Magnolia* x *læbneri* 'Dr. Merrill'

Merrill Magnolia or Improved Star Magnolia

Magnolia kobus var. *læbneri* 'Merrill', flowers

Magnolia kobus var. *læbneri* 'Merrill', Darts Hill Garden Park, Surrey

Where to see the trees:

Chilliwack

Fairfield Island Park, entrance on Clare Ave, Fairfield Island, on the south side bed.

Surrey

Darts Hill Garden Park, 1660- 168 St, South Surrey, Garden Bed 14.

Growing 7.5–9 metres high with an equal spread, Merrill Magnolia blooms heavily in March to early April. The flower buds are fuzzy and greyish green. As the fifteen spoon-shaped tepals unfold, they are flushed pink at first then mature to white. The flowers are deliciously fragrant. Bruised stems of this plant are also aromatic. The dark green leaves are up to 15 cm long, oblong in shape and turn a pleasant yellow in the fall. Merrill Magnolia is often a multi-stemmed tree. It is commonly found in the South Fraser Region

Magnolia kobus var. *stellata*
Syn. *Magnolia stellata*

Star Magnolia or Starry Magnolia

Magnolia kobus var. *stellata*, Salmon River Uplands, Langley

Magnolia kobus var. *stellata*
Syn. *Magnolia stellata*

Star Magnolia or Starry Magnolia

Magnolia kobus var. *stellata*, flowers

Very common in the South Fraser Region, Star Magnolia is a welcome harbinger of spring. Densely twiggy and most often shrubby, it may eventually grow six to eight metres high with a spread of the same. The leaves are elliptical in shape and medium dull green in colour; they turn mustard yellow in the fall. It is the spectacular display of flowers in March and April that Star Magnolia is noted for. The lightly scented flowers are produced in great abundance even on the tiniest of plants. Each flower is a dizzying swirl of bright white wavy tepals (tepals are the evolutionary hybrid between sepals and petals). Nine to twenty long, thin tepals unfurl to create a star-like flower 10 cm in diameter. When the flower matures, the lax tepals arch backward. The flowers are delicately perfumed of Jasmine. The floral display is very long lasting, as the buds do not open all at the same time but over several weeks. The grey flower buds of Star Magnolia are very plump and fuzzy while the fuzzy leaf buds are more slender. The stem, when crushed, has a deep sweet smell. Star Magnolia is native to central Honshu in Japan.

Where to see the trees:

Abbotsford

35074 McKee Rd.

Trethewey House (M.S.A. Museum), 2313 Ware St, a small tree on the east side of the house.

Chilliwack

Municipal Hall, 8550 Young Rd.

Salish Park, 45860- 1 Ave.

University College of the Fraser Valley, 45600 Airport Rd.

7032 Chilliwack River Rd, Sardis.

Langley

NE corner of Eastleigh Cres and 56 Ave, Langley City, two small trees.

23736- 59 Ave, Salmon River Uplands.

Richmond

Fantasy Garden World, 10800 No 5 Rd.

Steveston Park, 4111 Moncton St, Steveston, east side of the entrance to the Martial Arts Centre.

Millennium Botanical Garden and Arboretum, N McLennan Community Park, Granville Ave and Garden City Rd.

Surrey

Darts Hill Garden Park, 1660- 168 St, South Surrey, Garden Bed 25.

City Hall, 14245- 56 Ave, Newton. There is a large specimen on the south side of the concrete retaining wall on the east side of the building.

Magnolia kobus var. *stellata* f. *rosea*
Syn. *Magnolia stellata* f. *rosea*
Syn. *Magnolia stellata* 'Rosea'

Pink Star Magnolia

Where to see the trees:

Surrey

Darts Hill Garden Park, 1660- 168 St, South Surrey, Garden Bed 8.

Magnolia kobus var. *stellata* f. *rosea*, flowers

Growing to 6–8.5 metres tall, Pink Star Magnolia differs from the species in that the flower buds are pink in bud. As the flowers emerge, the petals mature to white.

Magnolia liliiflora 'Nigra'
Purple Lily Magnolia or Lily Magnolia

Magnolia liliiflora 'Nigra', flowers

Much later to bloom than the more common Saucer Magnolia, Purple Lily Magnolia blooms well after the leaves have emerged in late May and into June. Growing four to five metres in height, with a round form, it provides spectacular late spring colour. The slim champagne flute-like flowers are deep reddish purple, paler on the inside, about 12 cm wide and held upright on the branchlets. They are somewhat hidden by the leaves but are showy nonetheless. The dark green leaves are elliptical in shape and up to 20 cm long. Purple Lily Magnolia is relatively common in the South Fraser Region.

Where to see the trees:

Rosedale

Minter Gardens, 52892 Bunker Rd, just in front of the main garden entry gate.

Surrey

Darts Hill Garden Park, 1660- 168 St, South Surrey, Garden Beds 9 and 13.

Magnolia macrophylla, looking skyward through the massive leaves

A giant among magnolias in leaf and blossom, Bigleaf Magnolia is a grand sight. It reaches a mature height of twenty metres in its native range from Ohio to Florida and west into Arkansas and Louisiana. The tropical looking leaves are generously sized at 30–80 cm long. The leaves are noted for their conspicuous fuzzy silver underside. The flowers are huge too, sometimes reaching 30 cm and more across when fully open. The creamy white flowers appear late in June and into July, and are usually high up in the tree. The three inner tepals are flushed with purple at their base. Bigleaf Magnolia is exceedingly rare in the South Fraser Region.

Where to see the trees:
Surrey

Darts Hill Garden Park, 1660- 168 St, South Surrey*, Garden Bed 13.

Magnolia macrophylla, summer, Darts Hill Garden Park, Surrey

Magnolia macrophylla, bark

Magnolia sieboldii
Oyama Magnolia

Where to see the trees:

Rosedale

Minter Gardens, 52892 Bunker Rd, Playground Area.

Surrey

Darts Hill Garden Park, 1660- 168 St, South Surrey, Magnolia Walk and Pasture.

Magnolia sieboldii, flower

Native to Japan, Manchuria and Korea where it reaches ten metres high, Oyama Magnolia has a horizontal oval form. The smallish leaves are oblong in shape and 10–15 cm long. Egg-shaped buds poke delicately amongst the new leaves. Opening in late May and June, the creamy-white flower is 7–10 cm across and deliciously fragrant. The cup-shaped flower is decorated with bright red stamens that look like a tiny wagon wheel at the centre of each flower. The small, to 7 cm, long, twisted pink cone is produced in October. When the cone is ripe, the scarlet-orange seeds inside are revealed.

Magnolia x *soulangiana*
Saucer Magnolia or Tuliptree

Very common in the South Fraser Region, Saucer Magnolia reaches a mature size of six to nine metres with an equal spread. It is often a multi-stemmed tree with branches that swoop up at the tips. The dormant bud is very large and covered in silky grey fuzz. The leaves are large, up to 15 cm long and 6–7 cm wide. They are obovate in shape. The leaves are medium green on top and softly hairy on the bottom. Fall colour is not spectacular, but can

Magnolia x *soulangiana,* MSA General Hospital, Abbotsford

Magnolia x *soulangiana,* flowers

often be a satisfying yellow. The flowers are a hallmark of springtime in our region, blooming in March to early April. Huge goblet-shaped blossoms proudly sit upright on the branches. Each one is at least 15–20 cm long. The nine tepals of the flower are pale purple to dark pink on the outside with a pale white interior. As the tepals age the flower becomes more lax until it fully opens and is almost flat in presentation. Flowers may be sporadically produced over the summer months. The fruit is a twisted greenish cucumber. When ripe, the fruit is pink in colour, splitting to reveal the bright orange fruit inside. Fruit is seldom produced in any quantity. The stems of Saucer Magnolia are fragrant when bruised.

Where to see the trees:
Abbotsford
Jubilee Park, McCallum Rd south of Essendene, a well-shaped tree on the south side of the park.

MSA General Hospital, 2179 McCallum Rd, at the Emergency entrance, a huge mature specimen.

33151 Nelson Ave, a mature tree.

Chilliwack
Gwynne Vaughan Park, Williams Rd and Hope River Rd, Fairfield Island, a very large tree overhanging the entry drive.

45691 Wellington Ave, a mature tree in the rear garden.

9640 Cook St.

9688 Young Street.

Reimer's Nursery Ltd, 4586 No 3 Rd, Yarrow.

Delta
Jubilee Farm, later the Augustinian Monastery of British Columbia, 3900 Arthur Dr, Ladner, a massive specimen, with multiple trunks.

Langley
4516 Southridge Cr, Murrayville.

Timms Community Centre, 20355 Douglas Cr, southeast corner.

Surrey
Darts Hill Garden Park, 1660- 168 St, South Surrey, Garden Bed 25.

Magnolia x *soulangiana* 'Alexandrina Alba'

White Alexandrina Saucer Magnolia

Where to see the trees:

Surrey

Darts Hill Garden Park, 1660- 168 St, South Surrey, Garden Bed 13.

Magnolia x *soulangiana* 'Alexandrina Alba', flowers

The flowers of this cultivar of Saucer Magnolia are white with a purplish pink flush at the base of the tepals. The inside of the tepals is white.

Magnolia x *soulangiana* 'Lennei'

Lenné Saucer Magnolia

Where to see the trees:

Surrey

Darts Hill Garden Park, 1660- 168 St, South Surrey, Garden Bed 15a.

Fraser Region Health Offices, 14265- 56 Ave, Newton, a tree on the northeast corner of the building in the planter.

Magnolia x *soulangiana* 'Lennei', flowers

Lenné Saucer Magnolia has large, deep purple goblet-shaped flowers with milky-white inside the tepals. Each flower has six very thick tepals. Lenné Saucer Magnolia blooms in late April to May.

Magnolia x soulangiana 'Lennei Alba'

Lenné White Saucer Magnolia

Magnolia x *soulangiana* 'Lennei Alba', flower.

Large, pure white goblet-shaped flowers, each with nine tepals mark this cultivar of the Saucer Magnolia. Lenné White Saucer Magnolia blooms in late April to May.

Where to see the trees:

Abbotsford

5880 Riverside St, Matsqui village.

Chilliwack

Reimer's Nursery Ltd, 4586 No 3 Rd, Yarrow, a lovely tree on the north side of the house.

Langley

20768 Douglas Cr, Langley City.

Surrey

Darts Hill Garden Park, 1660-168 St, South Surrey, Garden Bed 14.

Magnolia x *soulangiana* 'Lennei Alba', flowers, Riverside Street, Abbotsford

Magnolia tripetala

Umbrella Tree or Umbrella Magnolia

Magnolia tripetala, flower buds and unfurling leaves in spring

Magnolia tripetala
Umbrella Tree or Umbrella Magnolia

Magnolia tripetala, bark and stems

Magnolia tripetala, ripening cone

Where to see the trees:

Abbotsford

Jubilee Park, McCallum Rd south of Essendene, a very large tree on the south side of the MSA Centennial Library. This tree was likely planted in 1967 when the library was built, it started to bloom in 1979. When in full bloom it perfumes the entire park.

Chilliwack

45646 Storey Ave, Sardis.

Richmond

Fantasy Garden World, 10800 No 5 Rd, on the southwest edge of the pond, mislabeled as *Magnolia acuminata.*

Surrey

Darts Hill Garden Park, 1660- 168 St, South Surrey, Garden Bed 15b.

Native to southern Pennsylvania to northern Georgia and west to Kentucky and Arkansas, Umbrella Tree grows to nine to twelve metres in its native habitat. The leaves are large, up to 50 cm in length, elliptical in shape and whorled at the ends of the branches like a parasol. The leaf bases are tapered, differentiating this large-leaved species from the later-blooming Bigleaf Magnolia, which has earlobe-shaped leaf bases and silvery undersides. The bottoms of the leaves of the Umbrella Magnolia are hairy while young and light green. The flowers, produced in May and early June, are upright, creamy-white and to 25 cm across. Their heavy citrus scent is overpowering and unpleasant. The buds are 4–5 cm long, very slender and pointed, pencil-like, while the bark is pleasingly patterned in grey splotches. The cone is very showy, reaching 10 cm long. It ripens in late October to November, turning watermelon red; as the cone splits the scarlet seeds inside are revealed. Each cone scale has a sharp spine, which curls back as the seed head ripens. Umbrella Tree is rare in the South Fraser Region.

Magnolia wilsonii, flower

Where to see the trees:

Surrey

Darts Hill Garden Park, 1660- 168 St, South Surrey, Garden Bed 13.

The Glades, 561- 172 St, South Surrey*, at the beginning of Garyland Trail east, planted in February 1956.

Wilson's Magnolia is native to western China, where it grows 7.5–9 metres tall. Multi-trunked, it is usually horizontal oval in form. The leaves are lance-shaped, dull green in colour and finely hairy on the underside. The abundant flowers, which nod gracefully, are best appreciated when looking up into the branches. The flowers are 7.5–10 cm across, white, saucer-shaped and boldly punctuated at their centre by a splash of rose-purple stamens. Sweetly scented, they bloom in May. Wilson's Magnolia is exceedingly rare in the South Fraser Region.

Malus fusca
Pacific Crabapple or Western Crabapple

Malus fusca, foliage

Malus fusca, crabapple and fall colour

Malus fusca
Pacific Crabapple or Western Crabapple

Where to see the trees:

Richmond

Millennium Botanical Garden and Arboretum, N McLennan Community Park, Granville Ave and Garden City Rd.

Surrey

Surrey Big Bend Regional Park, north foot of 104 St, Guildford, a very large tree five hundred metres west of the ferry car park on the river dyke.

Native to the Pacific Northwest coast from southern Alaska to northern California, Pacific Crabapple is an unassuming small tree reaching a mature height of ten to twelve metres. It is often irregular in shape and found growing at stream or swamp edges. The lance-shaped leaves are toothed along the margins and often have one or more shallow lobes. Fall colour is yellow-orange to burgundy. Short little branches called spur shoots bear the flowers and later the fruit. The five-petalled white flower is sweetly scented, showy, and appears in May. The tiny oblong crabapple is produced in pendulous clusters. Each crabapple is yellow or red and tartly edible. The bark on mature trees is very scaly and cracked.

Malus 'Rudolph'
Rudolph Crabapple

Where to see the trees:

Chilliwack

Spruce Grove Park, off Rochester Ave, Sardis.

Surrey

6663- 142A St, Newton.

6673- 142A St, Newton.

Rudolph Crabapple is an example of one of the many crabapple cultivars that are common in the South Fraser Region. It grows 6.5–7 metres high with a spread of four metres. Ovate in shape, the leaves are up to 8 cm long. They are lustrous and bronze when they unfold in the spring, turning dark green. Five cm across, the large flowers are deep red in bud, opening to a lovely rose-red in late April to May. The thumbnail-sized fruit is a little orange-yellow crabapple and hangs on the tree well into the fall.

Malus sieversii, flowers

Malus sieversii, a lovely pruned specimen at Trinity Western University, Langley

Native to central Europe, Common Apple is familiar as the orchard apple, which bears the fruit of named apple cultivars such as Red Delicious and Macintosh. If left to its own devices, Common Apple would easily reach a mature height of seven to ten metres with an upright oval or round form. Common Apple trees are pruned hard to lower their height and encourage lateral branching, which encourages flowers and fruit development and eases the harvest. The leaves are oval in shape, medium green in colour and very hairy on the bottom surface. Pink in tight bud, the flower buds open to pale rose in late April to May and fade to white. Each flower is five-petalled, deliciously fragrant, and highly attractive to bees. The soft drone of the pollinating honeybees is a familiar spring accompaniment to the prolific display of blossoms. The plump buds are softly woolly and flower buds are borne on very short spur branches. These branches, which zigzag many times within their tiny length, may remain productive for twenty or more years and are a good winter identifying feature. The bark on mature trees is scaly, plated and shallowly ridged.

Where to see the trees:

Chilliwack
Gwynne Vaughan Park, Williams Rd and Hope River Rd, Fairfield Island, an old orchard of Transparent, Spartan and Gravensteen apples.

Langley
Northeast side of 208 St overpass, Northwest Langley.

Trinity Western University, 7600 Glover, Willoughby, a very artistically pruned tree to the south of the Reimer Student Centre.

Surrey
Darts Hill Garden Park, 1660- 168 St, South Surrey, in the orchard.

Elgin Heritage Park, a lovely grove east of the Historic Stewart Farm located at 13723 Crescent Road, South Surrey.

Did You Know?

A three-year-old apple tree, 1.5–2.1 metres tall, cost thirty-eight cents in 1879, when purchased from P.T. Johnston and Co., a nursery in Victoria. The 1896 catalogue of Layritz Nurseries Limited, another Victoria nursery grower, lists fifty-seven different summer, fall and winter bearing apple varieties, very few of which are commercially available today.

Malus 'Thunderchild'
Thunderchild Crabapple

Malus 'Thunderchild', crabapples

Where to see the trees:
Chilliwack

46415- 46507 Ferguson Pl, Promontory Heights.

Thunderchild Crabapple is an example of one of the dozens of cultivars that are commonly grown in the South Fraser Region. It grows six metres high with a tight horizontal oval to round shape. The leaves are dark copper bronze. Deep red in bud, the flowers open in late April to May to deep red, fade to pale rose, then to white. The fingernail-sized fruit of Thunderchild Crabapple is dark red-purple and persists well into the fall.

Did You Know?

Thunderchild Crabapple was introduced by P.H. Wright of Saskatoon, Saskatchewan in 1973. Rudolph Crabapple is an older cultivar, introduced in 1954 by Dr. F.L. Skinner of Dropmore, Manitoba. Rudolph Crabapple is one of the many successes of Agriculture Canada's plant breeding program to develop prairie hardy trees and shrubs.

Malus toringo
Syn. *Malus sieboldii*
Toringo Crabapple

Malus toringo, flowers

Where to see the trees:
Surrey

Darts Hill Garden Park, 1660- 168 St, South Surrey, Garden Beds 29 and 34. Mrs. Francisca Darts planted this lovely double row of six trees from apple pips.

Native to Japan, Toringo Crabapple reaches a mature height of four metres with a horizontal oval or round form. The leaves are oval in shape, dark green and downy on the top and bottom surfaces. Pink in tight bud, the flower

Malus toringo
Syn. *Malus sieboldii*
Toringo Crabapple

buds open to pale rose in late April to May and fade to white. Each flower is five-petalled, fragrant, and highly attractive to bees. The tiny yellow or red crabapples are showy in the fall. The bark of mature trees is scaly.

Malus toringo ssp. *sargentii*
Sargent's Crabapple

Malus toringo ssp. *sargentii*, flowers   *Malus toringo* ssp. *sargentii*, crabapples

Native to Japan, Sargent's Crabapple reaches a mature height of three metres with a horizontal oval shape. The leaves are three-lobed, bright green, hairy on the top and bottom surfaces. Pale pink in tight bud, the flower buds open to pale rose in late April to May and fade to white. Each flower is five-petalled, fragrant, and highly attractive to bees. The tiny red crabapples are showy in the fall. The bark of mature trees is scaly.

Where to see the trees:
Surrey
Darts Hill Garden Park, 1660- 168 St, South Surrey, Garden Beds 17 and 26.

Mespilus germanica
Syn. *Pyrus germanica*

Medlar

Mespilus germanica, flowers

Mespilus germanica, fruit

Where to see the trees:

Surrey

Darts Hill Garden Park, 1660- 168 St, South Surrey*, Garden Bed 25.

Exceedingly rare in the South Fraser Region, Medlar is native to southeastern Europe and central Asia where it is grown for its fruit. It becomes a small shrubby tree about 3.5 metres tall with a similar spread. The leaves are elliptical and colour variously in the fall, sometimes orange-gold, red and purple. The flowers are typical of the rose family with five petals, which are whitish-pink and bowl-shaped. The flowers, appearing in late May to June, are a little larger than a two-dollar coin. The brown fruit is very unusual. It is ready for picking in late October into December. It is dome-shaped and very hard until ripe. For full ripeness and for maximum flavour, the fruit must be partially rotted and mushy. A little crown of calyx lobes at the apex of the fruit gives it a distinctive appearance.

Metasequoia glyptostroboides
Dawn Redwood

Metasequoia glyptostroboides, Redwood Park, Surrey

Metasequoia glyptostroboides, foliage

Dawn Redwood is common in the South Fraser Region. It is an unusual deciduous conifer native to west-central China, where it was thought to be extinct until discovered in 1941. Since the oldest trees were mere seedlings just a few decades ago, the mature height this tree will reach in our area is as yet unknown. It has been recorded to thirty-five metres in other areas of North America. Strongly pyramidal in shape in youth, it becomes more upright oval as it ages. The branches are often twisted and spiral upwards. The leaves are needle-like, two-ranked and produced in soft flat sprays. When the leaves emerge in April, they are bright lime green, freshening the spring landscape. The leaves mature to soft green, and turn glorious shades of yellow and orange and finally burnt umber before they fall in October. The small woody cone is oval in shape, 2.5–3 cm long, medium green and matures to a dark brown. The bright yellow buds are held on the branchlets like old-fashioned upright Christmas tree lights. The bark of the tree is reddish brown and fibrous. As the tree ages the base becomes heavily buttressed, appearing very muscular and sinuous.

Where to see the trees:
Abbotsford

Clearbrook Public Library, 32320 Dahlstrom Ave, a young specimen on the northeast corner of the building.

2287 Mountain Dr, a young tree.

2564 Clearbrook Rd, several trees in the median planting.

Chilliwack

Fairfield Island Park, 46000 Clare Ave, Fairfield Island, six young trees on the west side of the pond.

University College of the Fraser Valley, 45600 Airport Rd, west of Building B, Agriculture.

Delta

Municipal Hall, 4500 Clarence Taylor Cr, Ladner, a small tree on the north side of the pond.

7226- 116 St, North Delta, a good-sized tree.

Langley

Kwantlen University College, 20901 Langley Bypass, Langley City, two specimens in the lawn between the admissions wing and the west wing on the main campus.

Sendall Gardens, 20166- 50 Ave, Langley City.

5726- 246B St, Salmon River Uplands, two good-sized trees.

7977- 229 St, Northeast Langley.

Metasequoia glyptostroboides
Dawn Redwood

Richmond

Fantasy Garden World, 10800 No 5 Rd.

Millennium Botanical Garden and Arboretum, N McLennan Community Park, Granville Ave and Garden City Rd.

Hugh Boyd Park, No 1 Rd and Francis Rd, a row of young trees on the west side of the park and also in the parking lot on Francis Rd on the south side.

Rosedale

Minter Gardens, 52892 Bunker Rd, located to the west of the Wedding Chapel.

Surrey

Darts Hill Garden Park, 1660- 168 St, South Surrey, Garden Bed 9.

Green Timbers Arboretum, 9800- 140 St, Whalley.

The Glades, 561- 172 St, South Surrey*, centre of the ridge on the south side.

Redwood Park, 17900- 20 Ave, South Surrey*, several splendid trees in the open area west of the parking lot.

Metasequoia occidentalis, fossils

Did You Know?

An ancient relative of the commonly cultivated Dawn Redwood is *Metasequoia occidentalis*, Western Dawn Redwood. *Metasequoia occidentalis* become extinct millions of years ago. It is a frequent find in fossil-bearing rocks in and around Princeton, British Columbia.

Morus alba 'Pendula'
Weeping Mulberry

Morus alba 'Pendula', foliage

Morus alba 'Pendula'

Morus alba 'Pendula', Salmon River Uplands, Langley

A somewhat common weeping tree in the South Fraser Region, Weeping Mulberry grows three to four metres in height with an umbrella shape and sharply pendulous branches. It is a top-grafted small tree. The large hand-sized emerald green leaves are lustrous, and bi- or tri-lobed. Fall colour is usually straw yellow. The flower is insignificant but Weeping Mulberry does produce an edible dark red fruit shaped somewhat like a blackberry in July and August.

Where to see the trees:

Abbotsford
Corner of Mountain Dr and Foothills Cr, a young tree.

Chilliwack
University College of the Fraser Valley, 45600 Airport Rd, a young tree planted in 2002 in the Shakespeare Garden.

Langley
5758- 244B St, Salmon River Uplands.

20520- 98 Ave, Walnut Grove.

Rosedale
Minter Gardens, 52892 Bunker Rd, a small specimen growing at the entry of the Arbor Garden on the west side.

Surrey
Green Timbers Arboretum, 9800- 140 St, Whalley, at the west entrance to the Millennium Plantation.

N

*Green is the color of primeval wealth – sappy green fields, the green air
of a woodland glen – everyone can revel in it. It is, of course,
this thin layer of green plant cells that keeps us breathing, keeps us fed, keeps us alive.
No wonder we adore it, long for it when without it.* [1]

Nori and Sandra Pope, Canadian garden designers

Nothofagus antarctica, foliage

Nothofagus antarctica
Antarctic Beech

Native to Argentina and Chile, Antarctic Beech is rarely grown in the South Fraser Region. It is a deciduous tree reaching a mature height of fifteen to seventeen metres, though usually not growing as tall locally. The leathery dark green glossy leaves are small and puckered, with tiny teeth along the edges. The leaves smell sickly sweet when crushed and perfume the air on warm days. The tiny fruit contains three nutlets. Good winter identifiers are the unusual herringbone branching pattern and the straggly twisted habit of the tree.

Nothofagus antarctica, bark

Where to see the trees:
Abbotsford
2506 Clearbrook Rd, several trees in the median planting.

Chilliwack
Portage Park, Portage Av and Woodbine St.

University College of the Fraser Valley, 45600 Airport Rd, west of Building B, Agriculture.

Richmond
Millennium Botanical Garden and Arboretum, N McLennan Community Park, Granville Ave and Garden City Rd.

Surrey
14950- 88 Ave, Fleetwood, a group of trees in the centre median.

8790- 148 St, Fleetwood.

14934- 88 Ave, Fleetwood.

Darts Hill Garden Park, 1660- 168 St, South Surrey*, Garden Bed 26.

[1] Nori and Sandra Pope, *Color by Design,* 1998, pp. 34-35

Black Gum, Sour Gum or Tupelo

Nyssa sylvatica, fall colour

Native to the Great Lakes area of southern Ontario and south to Florida and Texas, Black Gum is rarely grown in the South Fraser Region. Trees available for viewing are all small young specimens. Black Gum reaches fifteen metres in height in its native range; in youth it has a very pyramidal form, with swooping, tangled branches similar to a young Pin Oak. At maturity it grows into an upright oval. The leaves are elliptical, deep green and lustrous, with a slightly wavy edge near the tip. Fall colour is outstanding; the leaves turn vibrant shades of scarlet, orange or maroon. The colour is often held well into November. The flowers are insignificant but the fruit, produced singly, in twos or clusters of three ripens in the late fall. Edible, it resembles a thin-bodied blue cherry. The dark grey bark is often heavily ridged, each ridge broken into short knobbly pieces.

Where to see the trees:

Abbotsford

Clearbrook Public Library, 32320 Dahlstrom Ave, two groups of three young trees in the south lawn area.

Delair Park, Delair and Old Yale Rds.

Delta

Memorial Park, 47 Ave and Delta St, Ladner, five very young trees placed at the southeast corner of the park.

Langley

Kwantlen University College, 20901 Langley Bypass, Langley City, a small specimen on the east side of the Turf Demonstration Lab.

Surrey

12434- 69 Ave, Newton.

6888- 124A St, Newton.

Darts Hill Garden Park, 1660- 168 St, South Surrey, Garden Beds 21 and 33.

O

Keep a green tree in your heart and perhaps the singing bird will come.

Chinese proverb

Ostrya virginiana, foliage and fruit

Ostrya virginiana
Hop Hornbeam or Ironwood

Hop Hornbeam is very rare in the South Fraser Region. Growing twelve metres tall, it is native to southern Ontario, Quebec and the Maritimes. In leaf, the trees are almost undistinguishable from the much more common Hornbeam or *Carpinus betulus*. The grey brown bark of Hop Hornbeam flakes into thin strips, which are free at both ends, while the bark of *Carpinus betulus* is smooth and sinewy. The elliptical yellowish-green leaves of Hop Hornbeam are sharply toothed along the edge and turn a golden yellow in the fall. The stiff winter catkins, usually in threes, develop into long, flowing, flowering catkins as the new leaves emerge in the spring. The fruit is unusual, resembling the fruit of a hop plant. Pendulous, the clusters of bladder-like sharp-pointed fruit sacks are green during the summer, ripen to a tawny brown in September and fall from the tree during the winter.

Ostrya virginiana, Morton Arboretum. Lisle, Illinois

Where to see the trees:
Surrey

Darts Hill Garden Park, 1660- 168 St, South Surrey, Magnolia Walk and Pasture.

Sourwood, Sorrel Tree or Lily-of-the-Valley Tree

Oxydendrum arboreum, fall colour and developing fruit capsules

Often recommended for planting in the South Fraser Region, Sourwood is a highly ornamental small tree but it has scarcely lived up to its billing since it not reliably vigorous in our area. It is native to the eastern United States where it grows 7.5–9 metres high. The sour-tasting elliptical leaves colour very well in November, often turning yellow, orange and scarlet all on the same tree. The flowers are produced in late July into early September. They are small, white and fragrant, resembling the flowers of blueberries or heather plants. The flowers are produced in clusters of racemes up to 25 cm long, each drooping raceme gracefully upturned at its tip. Once the petals are spent, the developing small green fruits are quite noticeable. These mature into woody brown capsules, which are held upright on the long stalks that persist at the end of the slightly weeping branches well into the winter.

Where to see the trees:

Abbotsford

2435 Guilford Dr, a good-sized young tree.

Richmond

NW corner of Williams and Greenlees Rd.

Surrey

Darts Hill Garden Park, 1660- 168 St, South Surrey, Garden Beds 9 and 40.

The Glades, 561-172 St, South Surrey, tree located in the front circle of the garden.

P

We stand in awe: some of these heritage trees are more than 1000 years old....
Nowhere can we better feel the flow of life and our place in the universe
than standing beneath these ancient giants.

Bristol Foster

Parrotia persica, fall colour

Parrotia persica, bark

Parrotia persica

Parrotia or Persian Ironwood

Native to northern Iran, Parrotia reaches a height of six to twelve metres. It has an upright vase shape in youth becoming more rounded with age. Branches arise at 45-degree angles to the main trunk and some-times twist irregularly. Parrotia is often multi-stemmed and more shrub-like unless pruned to a single trunk. The strongly veined leaves are 10 cm long, leathery in texture with a wavy edge. As the leaves unfold, they are edged in carmine and age to medium green. Parrotia comes into its own in November

Where to see the trees:

Abbotsford

Clearbrook Public Library, 32320 Dahlstrom Ave, several young trees at the south entrance.

Chilliwack

University College of the Fraser Valley, 45600 Airport Rd, west of Building B, Agriculture.

Delta

Leisure Centre, 4600 Clarence Taylor Cr, Ladner, one tree one the west side of the building.

when its leaves turn a fabulous array of vibrant shades from butter yellow, orange to scarlet and purple-red. The petal-less flowers are spider-like, scarlet and appear in late winter, well before the leaves. The smooth grey bark on older trees peels and tan, beige, lime green and orange jigsaw puzzle patches of colour adorn the trunk.

Where to see the trees:

Langley

210 A St north of 44 Ave, Brookswood.

4863- 248 St, Salmon River Uplands.

5108- 246 St, Salmon River Uplands.

Richmond

Fantasy Garden World, 10800 No 5 Rd.

No 4 Rd, on the west side a street tree planting from Blundell Rd south to Granville Ave.

Surrey

Darts Hill Garden Park, 1660- 168 St, South Surrey*, Garden Bed 25.

The Glades, 561-172 St, South Surrey, east of the frog pond.

68th Ave, between 127th St and 128th St, Newton, a street tree planting.

12110- 88 Ave, Whalley.

9010- 120 St, Whalley.

Paulownia tomentosa
Empress Tree, Royal Paulownia, Foxglove Tree or Princess Tree

Paulownia tomentosa, Darts Hill Garden Park, Surrey

Paulownia tomentosa, flowers

Paulownia tomentosa

Empress Tree, Royal Paulownia, Foxglove Tree or Princess Tree

Where to see the trees:

Abbotsford

1745 Clearbrook Rd.

2873 Horn St.

31839 King Rd.

Chilliwack

Brooks Ave and Cramer Dr, north side of Brooks.

NW corner of Watson Rd and Glemore Dr, Sardis.

Yarrow Community Park, north end of Community St, Yarrow.

Delta

4416- 50 St, Ladner.

Langley

Aldergrove United Church, NW corner of 272 St and 26 Ave, a good-sized specimen.

Kwantlen University College, 20901 Langley Bypass, Langley City.

5799- 244B St, Salmon River Uplands.

25926 Fraser Hwy, Southeast Langley, the largest tree in Langley.

Richmond

Millennium Botanical Garden and Arboretum, N McLennan Community Park, Granville Ave and Garden City Rd.

Surrey,

City Hall, 14245- 56 Ave, Newton, on the south side of the pond, a young tree.

19082- 32 Ave, South Surrey.

Darts Hill Garden Park, 1660- 168 St, South Surrey*, Garden Beds C4 and 30.

Green Timbers Arboretum, 9800- 140 St, Whalley, north of the uncovered bunker.

Heron Park, Beecher St, Crescent Beech, South Surrey, two trees at the east end of the park.

White Rock

The Pier, foot of Martin St and Marine Drive, two trees on either side of the main stairway.

Paulownia tomentosa, seed capsules

Tropical in appearance, Empress Tree has the largest leaves of any tree found in the South Fraser Region. The stout upswept branches are clothed in dinner plate-sized leaves. Each heart-shaped leaf feels like an angora sweater to the touch as both top and bottom surfaces are intensely hairy. The fall colour of the leaves is soft yellow to brownish-yellow. The flowers, which spring from plump woolly brown buds, are borne on upright stalks. They appear before the leaves in late May. Shaped like foxglove flowers, they are lilac-purple and fragrant. In some years, cold temperatures severely damage the flowers buds and few flowers result. The seeds are produced in woody beaked capsules about the size of a one-dollar coin. When the seeds are ripe in the late fall, the seedpods can be rattled, just like castanets. Dark brown in colour, the seedpods persist well into the spring of the following year on the tree. Growing into an upright oval form, Empress Tree reaches a mature height of fifteen to eighteen metres. It is originally from China and Korea. Empress Tree is somewhat common in the South Fraser Region.

Picea abies, Jubilee Park, Abbotsford

Picea abies, cones

Norway Spruce is a very common conifer found in many landscape settings ranging from parks and school grounds to residential gardens. It is native to Europe where it grows fifty metres tall. Broadly pyramidal in form, Norway Spruce, with its tidy habit and very large cones is easily identified. On mature trees the branches hang limply from upswept scaffold limbs. The needles are 1–2.5 cm long and sharply pointed. As the needles die or are pulled from the stem, a peg, or remnant stalk, is left on the branchlet. This is quite different than *Abies* or true fir; when their needles fall, they leave a pitted stem. The branchlets of Norway Spruce are mustard yellow, which stands out against the dark green to yellowish-green needles. The cones are up 18 cm long, and are the largest cones of any spruce found locally. Purplish when young and ripening to a warm tan colour, the cones have thin, overlapping notched scales. They are usually produced at the tops of the trees and hang from the branches in great bunches. The cones fall intact to the ground and are greatly favoured by squirrels for their seeds. The bark of Norway Spruce is flaking and reddish-brownish.

Where to see the trees:

Abbotsford

Jubilee Park, McCallum Rd south of Essendene, a grove on the north side of the park.

Dunach Elementary School, 30357 Downes Rd, a large tree along the east fence line with a DBH of 75 cm.

Chilliwack

Hope River Corbould Park, north end of Corbould St, a row of good-sized trees.

Portage Park, Portage Ave and Woodbine St.

Canadian Forces Base, Keith Wilson Rd and Vedder Rd, Vedder Crossing, a tree on the southwest corner of Calais Cr at Caen Rd.

Townsend Park, SW corner of Ashwell Rd and Hodgins Ave, a planting south of the soccer fields.

University College of the Fraser Valley, 45600 Airport Rd, around parking lots 5 and 6.

Delta

4493 Arthur Dr, Ladner, a large specimen with a DBH of 70 cm.

Beadlestone House, 4506 Arthur Dr, Ladner.

Langley

Sendall Gardens, 20166- 50 Ave, Langley City.

Picea abies
Norway Spruce

Where to see the trees:
Richmond

Fantasy Garden World, 10800 No 5 Rd.

Millennium Botanical Garden and
Arboretum, N McLennan Community
Park, Granville Ave and Garden City Rd.

Steveston Park, 4111 Moncton St,
Steveston.

Surrey

The Glades, 561-172 St, South Surrey, on
the west ridge opposite the Cherry.

Picea breweriana
Brewer's Spruce, Siskiyou Spruce or Weeping Spruce

Picea breweriana, foliage

Where to see the trees:
Surrey

Darts Hill Garden Park, 1660- 168 St,
South Surrey, Garden Beds 1 and 8.

12731 Beckett Rd, South Surrey*

Reaching sixty metres tall in its native range in
the Siskiyou Mountains in southwestern
Oregon and northwest California, Brewer
Spruce is rare in the South Fraser Region; only
small trees are known here. Broadly pyramidal
in shape, Brewer Spruce is identified by its
swooping branches draped with pendulous
branchlets, cascading gracefully downward.
These weeping stems can reach two metres or
more in length. The flattened lax needles are
bluish-green and 2.5–3.5 cm long. The brown
cones are flecked with resin.

Picea englemannii, University College of the Fraser Valley, Chilliwack

Picea englemannii, foliage

Englemann Spruce reaches skyward in a tidy tall spire of thirty metres or more in height. It is native to the interior mountains of British Columbia, into Alberta, south into Washington and Oregon and east into Idaho and Montana. Englemann Spruce is not found on the coast. It naturally grows at the higher elevations of one to two thousand metres in a subalpine habitat. The soft needles are 2 cm long, bluish-green and curve toward the tip of the branch-let. There are lines of white dots on both the top and underside of the leaves. When crushed, the needles are pleasantly scented. The needles of Englemann Spruce will roll between your fingers, unlike Sitka Spruce, which is the common native spruce in the South Fraser Region. The cones of Englemann Spruce are yellowish brown, each scale with a notched tip. The cones are up to 7 cm long. The thin buff-coloured bark of Englemann Spruce is very scaly on mature trees.

Where to see the trees:

Chilliwack

University College of the Fraser Valley, 45600 Airport Rd, around parking lots 5 and 6.

Picea glauca
White Spruce

Where to see the trees:

Abbotsford

1930 Eagle St, a good-sized tree.

Chilliwack

Exhibition Park, 45530 Spadina Ave, a number of good-sized trees on the southern boundary of the park.

Did You Know?

White Spruce or *Picea glauca* is Manitoba's arboreal emblem, which was adopted by the province in May 1991.

Native to almost all of Canada except the coastal regions of British Columbia, White Spruce reaches twenty-five metres and more in height at maturity. It has broadly pyramidal form when grown in landscape settings in the South Fraser Region, where it is somewhat common. The needles are greyish green, stiff and pointed. They radiate around the shiny yellowish twigs. When bruised, the needles smell unpleasant. The cones are pendulous, about 3–6 cm long and tan. The seed scales of the cones have smooth margins. They are not notched like Englemann Spruce, which has notched cone scales. The cone scales of White Spruce are relatively soft or pliable when pressed.

Picea omorika
Serbian Spruce

Picea omorika, foliage and cones.

Native to Yugoslavia, Serbian Spruce is common in the South Fraser Region. It is favoured because of its compact, narrowly pyramidal form and neat drooping branching pattern. With a mature height of twenty metres and a spread of 6–7.5 metres, it is one of the few large-growing conifers that can be accommodated on smaller properties. The branch tips swoop gracefully up, while the dark bluish green needles radiate around the stem. The needles are flat and up to 2.5 cm long. The pendulous cone is produced at the tops of the tree. When young, the cone is a delightful deep purple, and ripens to shiny dark brown. The cone is often resin-flecked. The bark on mature Serbian Spruce trees is plated and cracked.

Where to see the trees:

Chilliwack

Salish Park, 45860- 1 Ave, south-east corner of the tennis courts.

University College of the Fraser Valley, 45600 Airport Rd.

Delta

Leisure Centre, 4600 Clarence Taylor Cr, Ladner, several good-sized trees on the north end of the building.

Langley

City Park, 207 St and 48 Ave, Langley City, north of the Langley Community Music School.

Richmond

7660 Minoru Gate.

Rosedale

Minter Gardens, 52892 Bunker Rd, several perfect specimens in the garden, a group growing by the English Cottage.

Surrey

Darts Hill Garden Park, 1660- 168 St, South Surrey, Garden Bed 2.

City Hall, 14245- 56 Ave, Newton, several large trees on the south-west corner of the building.

White Rock

Firehall, 15315 Pacific Ave, on the east side of the building.

Picea orientalis
Oriental Spruce

Picea orientalis, Trinity Western University, Langley

Picea orientalis, foliage and cones

Oriental Spruce is relatively uncommon in the South Fraser Region. It is native to Caucasus and Asia Minor where it grows thirty-five to forty metres and more in height. Broadly pyramidal in form, Oriental Spruce, with its dense habit and tiny, dark needles is easily identified. The needles, which are less than one cm long and blunt at the tip, are the smallest of all the spruces cultivated locally. The resin-flecked cones are 5–10 cm long. Reddish-

Where to see the trees:

Abbotsford

John Mahoney Park, off Ware St, a small tree to the east of the bridge of the Mill Lake boardwalk.

Chilliwack

Fairfield Island Park, 46000 Clare Ave, Fairfield Island. There are three trees in the northwest corner and two trees on the east side of the park by the soccer pitch.

Picea orientalis
Oriental Spruce

Where to see the trees:

Langley

Peterson Road Elementary School, 23422- 47 Ave, Salmon River Uplands, two trees on the northwest side of the gymnasium.

Trinity Western University, 7600 Glover Rd, Willoughby, two mature trees to the southwest of the Reimer Student Centre.

Surrey

Darts Hill Garden Park, 1660- 168 St, South Surrey*, Garden Bed 22, a large tree.

purplish when young and ripening to dark brown, the cones have small smooth-edged scales. The cones are sparsely produced throughout the crown of the tree. The bark of Oriental Spruce is flaking and brownish.

Picea orientalis 'Aurea'
Gold Oriental Spruce

Picea orientalis 'Aurea', foliage

Where to see the trees:

Chilliwack

Portage Park, Portage Ave and Woodbine St, five young trees.

Gold Oriental Spruce, which is rare in the South Fraser Region, maintains a yellowish appearance well into early summer. The new needles are golden yellow and become green as they age.

Colorado Blue Spruce
or Blue Spruce

Picea pungens 'Glauca Group', foliage

Colorado Blue Spruce reaches a mature height of twenty-five metres or more. It is native to the Rocky Mountains of Colorado, into Utah to New Mexico and Wyoming. The horizontal branches are stiffly and regularly whorled, giving this tree its characteristic formal appearance. The extremely sharp pointed needles are 2 cm or more long, bluish-green to silver white and radiate around the orange-brown stem. The needles are covered with a whitish bloom that is very thick on new leaves, wearing off on older leaves. There are lines of white dots on both the top and underside of the leaves. The needles of Colorado Blue Spruce will roll between your fingers. The cones of Colorado Blue Spruce are green with a purplish tinge when young, and age to tan; each wavy scaled with a notched tip. The cones, produced sparingly at the tops of the trees, are up to 5–10 cm long. The purple-grey bark of Colorado Blue Spruce breaks up into thick scales on mature trees.

Where to see the trees:

Abbotsford

32366 Peardonville Rd

2824 Laurnell Cr, a pair of trees.

Hougen Park, south off Highway 1 on Cole Rd

Jubilee Park, McCallum Rd south of Essendene, on the west side of the park.

Chilliwack

9385 Broadway St.

The Waverly, 8445 Young St.

Fairfield Island Park, 46000 Clare Ave, Fairfield Island.

Gwynne Vaughan Park, Williams Rd and Hope River Rd, Fairfield Island.

Portage Park, Portage Ave and Woodbine St.

Salish Park, 45860- 1 Ave.

Skelton Park, opposite Chilliwack Municipal Hall at 8550 Young Rd, a good-looking tree.

University College of the Fraser Valley, 45600 Airport Rd.

Stó:lo Centre, 7201 Vedder Rd, Sardis.

7084 Eden Dr, Sardis, a tree with very good form.

University College of the Fraser Valley, 45600 Airport Rd, around parking lots 5 and 6.

Yarrow Central Park, Southeast corner of Kehler St and Yarrow Central Rd.

Langley

Northwest corner of 200 St and 56 Ave, Langley City, two tall very narrow trees.

Southeast corner of 208 St and 72 Ave, Willoughby.

Richmond

Fantasy Garden World, 10800 No 5 Rd.

Surrey

Darts Hill Garden Park, 1660- 168 St, South Surrey, Garden Bed 23.

Green Timbers Arboretum, 9800- 140 St, Whalley.

Provincial Courthouse, 14340- 57 Ave, Newton, south side of the building.

Picea pungens 'Koster'
Koster's Blue Spruce

Where to see the trees:
Chilliwack
Fairfield Island Park, 46000 Clare Ave, three trees in the northwest corner of the park, Fairfield Island.

Richmond
Fantasy Garden World, 10800 No 5 Rd.

Surrey
Green Timbers Arboretum, 9800- 140 St, Whalley, between the garage and the office.

Koster's Blue Spruce reaches a mature height of fifteen metres with a neat pyramidal form. The branching pattern is whorled or layered, which is typical of spruce. The needles are glaucous blue. Koster's Blue Spruce, valued for its strongly coloured foliage, is very commonly grown in the South Fraser Region.

Picea sitchensis
Sitka Spruce

Picea sitchensis, Vine Maple Drive, Surrey

Picea sitchensis, Buttressed roots

Sitka Spruce reaches a lofty height of seventy metres or more. It is native to the coastal region of British Columbia, Alaska, south into Washington and Oregon. Long horizontal scaffold limbs create the broadly pyramidal form of Sitka Spruce. The dangerously sharp pointed needles are 1-3 cm long and bluish-green. There are lines of white dots on both the top and underside of the leaves. When crushed, the needles are pleasantly scented. The flattish needles of Sitka Spruce will not roll easily between your fingers, unlike Englemann Spruce. The cones of Sitka Spruce are pale reddish-brown, each scale with a notched tip. The cones are quite brittle and up to 7 cm long. The bark on mature trees is thin reddish-brown to grey and breaks up into chunky scales. The trunk on old trees is heavily buttressed at the base.

Picea sitchensis, Carl Lamb, Tynehead Regional Park, Surrey

Did You Know?

The second largest Sitka Spruce in Canada is named "Maxine's Tree". It resides along West Walbran Creek on Vancouver Island. This towering Sitka Spruce reaches skyward for almost eighty-one metres. It has a remarkable girth of 12.65 metres and a diameter at breast height of 402 cm..

Where to see the trees:

Abbotsford

Dunach Park, NW corner of Mt Lehman Rd and Downes Rd, a good-sized tree with a DBH of 75 cm.

South Fish Trap Creek Park, Mitchell St and De Havilland Dr, a good-sized tree with a DBH of 101 cm, 15 metres high and in very good condition.

Chilliwack

Elk Creek Rainforest, Chilliwack Forest District, a number of large trees, one with a DBH of 105 cm.

Langley

Portage Park, 52 St and 204 Ave, Langley City, several massive trees one hundred metres south of the park in the floodplain of the Nicomekl River.

9188 Church St, Ft Langley, a large tree with a DBH of 160 cm.

Ponder Park, 25199- 76 Ave, Northeast Langley, two trees known as the "Two Sisters".

27606 River Road, Northeast Langley.

Richmond

Millennium Botanical Garden and Arboretum, N McLennan Community Park, Granville Ave and Garden City Rd.

Steveston Park, 4111 Moncton St, Steveston, a very large specimen to the north of the Martial Arts Centre, along with a row of smaller Stika Spruce.

Surrey

13398 Vine Maple Dr, Surrey*, this tree has a massive trunk flare with impressive anchoring roots.

Tynehead Regional Park, Serpentine Hollow picnic area entrance at 161 St and 101 Ave, Guildford, Surrey*, two large specimens, 160 and 120 cm DBH. The first tree is growing in the forest on the south side of the trail near Hjorth Creek crossing. The second tree is open grown, with branches right to the ground just to the southwest of the second bridge crossing of the Serpentine Loop Trail.

Surrey Big Bend Regional Park, north foot of 104 St, Guildford, a number of large trees in the park.

Pinus aristata

Bristlecone Pine or
Colorado Bristlecone Pine

Picea aristata, foliage with white dots of resin

Where to see the trees:

Surrey

Darts Hill Garden Park, 1660- 168 St, South Surrey, Garden Bed 25.

Native to the high, dry mountains of western Colorado, northern New Mexico and northern Arizona, Bristlecone Pine is rare in the South Fraser Region. It reaches a mature height of eighteen to twenty metres with a broadly pyramidal form in its native range. Only very small trees are known in the South Fraser Region. Grown for its picturesque habit, the branches of Bristlecone Pine are irregular and dense with the ends of the branches upswept. The stiff sharp-pointed needles are deep green, curved and are presented in tufts. Bristlecone Pine has five very short needles (2–4 cm long) per bundle. The needles are unmistakable because they are copiously flecked with tiny bright dots of resin that superficially appear to be an insect infestation. The bark is reddish-brown to blackish, and on mature trees is fissured. The cones of Bristlecone Pine are brown and up to 7 cm long with each cone scale bristle-tipped. The cones are also flecked with resin.

Pinus contorta var. *contorta*,
Fort Langley National Historic Site, Langley

Pinus contorta var. *contorta*, dormant bud and foliage.

Native to the maritime Pacific Northwest from southern Alaska to Oregon, Shore Pine is very common in the South Fraser Region. It reaches a mature height of twenty metres with an upright oval form. The branching habit is often irregular and moderately dense with the ends of the branches upswept. On windy exposed sites, Shore Pine may become picturesque as the crown twists and contorts. The branches of Shore Pine on the rocky western coastline of Vancouver Island often are swept backwards due to the strong winter winds. Trees in the South Fraser Region are often found growing in boggy sites in dense thickets. The stiff sharp-pointed needles are dark green and slightly twisted. Shore Pine has two short needles (2–7 cm long) per bundle. The bark is dark brown to blackish, and on mature trees is lightly fissured into small squares. The cones of Shore Pine are brown and up to 7 cm long with each cone scale bristle-tipped.

Where to see the trees:
Abbotsford
Hougen Park, south off Highway 1 on Cole Rd

33083 Bevan Ave, southeast side of Mill Park.

Delta
Police Station, 4455 Clarence Taylor Cr, Ladner, tree on the north side of the building.

Delta Nature Reserve, parking lot to access trails located at 10388 Nordel Court, North Delta.

Langley
20734- 39A Ave, Brookswood, Langley City.

Fort Langley National Historic Site, 23433 Mavis St, Ft Langley, on the south side of the site.

Richmond
Richmond Nature Park, 11851Westminster Hwy.

Southarm Park, Garden City Rd and Williams Rd.

Surrey
Surrey Big Bend Regional Park, north foot of 104 St, Guildford, a grove of mature trees at the west end of the park.

Pinus coulteri
Bigcone Pine or Coulter Pine

Pinus coulteri, cones

Pinus coulteri, cone

Did You Know?

Sam Monahan planted the Bigcone Pine on 216 Street in Murrayville from seed collected on a family trip to the coast of California in the late 1960's. Sam, like his father Robert before him, was the caretaker of the Murrayville Cemetery until his retirement.

Native to the coastal mountains of southwestern California and northwest Mexico, Bigcone Pine is exceedingly rare in the South Fraser Region. It reaches a mature height of thirty metres with a broadly pyramidal form in its native range. Only very small trees are known in the South Fraser Region. The branches of Bigcone Pine are regular and dense with the ends of the branches upswept. The stiff sharp-pointed needles are blue-green. Bigcone Pine has three extremely long needles (20–32 cm long) per bundle. The bark is brown to blackish, and on mature trees is scaly. The cinnamon brown cones of Bigcone Pine are gigantic, up to 40 cm long and weighing three kg when fresh. Each cone scale is wickedly tipped with a woody claw.

Where to see the trees:

Langley
4800 block 216 St, Murrayville, a very attractive tree.

Surrey
Darts Hill Garden Park, 1660- 168 St, South Surrey, Garden Bed 1.

Pinus densiflora 'Umbraculifera'
Japanese Umbrella Pine, Tanyosho Pine, or Japanese Table Pine

Pinus densiflora 'Umbraculifera', foliage

Pinus densiflora 'Umbraculifera', Morton Arboretum, Lisle, Illinois

Japanese Umbrella Pine is rare in the South Fraser Region. It reaches a mature height of eight to nine metres with an unusual mushroom shape. The short trunk gives rise to a multi-stemmed crown, where the upright branches mature into the flat-topped form characteristic of this cultivar. The stiff needles are bright green. Japanese Umbrella Pine has two needles (7–10 cm long) per bundle. The thin bark is very attractive. It is a bright orange-brown and shreds into fine curling strips. The colourful bark is most apparent on younger stems and branches, while the bark of mature trees is rust-brown and fissured The cones of Japanese Umbrella Pine are tan and up to 6 cm long. The cones are produced in clusters of a dozen or more.

Where to see the trees:
Richmond

Steveston Park, 4111 Moncton St, Steveston, the building opposite the interior court of the Martial Arts Centre.

Fantasy Garden World, 10800 No 5 Rd.

Surrey

Darts Hill Garden Park, 1660- 168 St, South Surrey, Garden Bed 2.

Pinus flexilis 'Vanderwolf's Pyramid'
Syn. *Pinus flexilis* 'Fastigiata Glauca Vanderwolf'
Vanderwolf's Pyramid Pine

Strongly conical in youth, Vanderwolf's Pyramid Pine reaches a mature height of twenty metres. The striking bluish-green needles are five in a bundle and 5–8 cm long. The cones are 6–14 cm long. The branches of this pine are very flexible and held upright.

Where to see the trees:
Chilliwack

Chilliwack Public Library, 45860- 1 Ave, two young trees on the west side of the building.

Pinus flexilis 'Vanderwolf's Pyramid'
Syn. *Pinus flexilis* 'Fastigiata Glauca Vanderwolf'

Vanderwolf's Pyramid Pine

Pinus flexilis 'Vanderwolf's Pyramid', foliage

Pinus flexilis 'Vanderwolf's Pyramid', Public Library, Chilliwack

Pinus monticola

Western White Pine

Pinus monticola, Peace Arch Park, Surrey

Where to see the trees:

Surrey

Peace Arch Park, King George Hwy and 0 Ave, South Surrey.

Redwood Park, 17900- 20 Ave, South Surrey, east of the Tree House.

Western White Pine is native to maritime southern British Columbia, Washington and south into Oregon. It grows in the Columbia forest region of the province as well. It reaches a mature height of forty metres in its native range, with a symmetrical narrowly pyramidal form. Western White Pine is not very common in the planted landscape of the South Fraser Region. The horizontal branching habit is open with the ends of the branches slightly upswept. The soft drooping needles are blue-green. Western White Pine has five thin needles (5–10 cm long) per bundle. The dark grey to black bark of mature trees is broken into scaly plates. The curved pendulous cones of Western White Pine are medium brown and much longer and chubbier than the slender cones of the more commonly planted Eastern White Pine. Up to 30 cm long, they are held in clusters of one to three. The cone scales are resin-tipped.

Pinus nigra, Stö:lo Centre, Sardis, Chilliwack   *Pinus nigra,* foliage and cone

Native to southeast Europe, from southern Austria to Romania, central Italy and Yugoslavia, Black Pine is very common in the South Fraser Region. It reaches a mature height of forty metres with an upright oval form in youth. Black Pine becomes flat-topped with great age. The branching habit is regular and dense with the ends of the branches swooping up. The stiff sharp-pointed needles are dark green and very straight. Black Pine has two needles (8-14 cm long) per bundle. The bark on younger stems and branches is pale orange brown, while the bark of mature trees is strongly fissured. The cones of Black Pine are grey-brown and up to 8 cm long.

Did You Know?

Edward A. Forrer built the single story cottage at 4580 Arthur Drive in Ladner in 1891. Forrer was a salmon packer at the Fisherman's Cannery at Port Guichon, just west of Ladner's Landing. The house passed hands several times, but Elizabeth and Smith Wright bought it in 1943. The Wrights may have been responsible for planting the Black Pine as they created the garden on the property.

Where to see the trees:

Abbotsford

2398 Midas St, a group of three.

Chilliwack

NE corner of Second Ave and Nowell St, a large tree with sculptural limbs and trunk.

Fairfield Island Park, 46000 Clare Ave, south of baseball diamonds B and D, Fairfield Island.

University College of the Fraser Valley, 45600 Airport Rd.

Canadian Forces Base, Keith Wilson Rd and Vedder Rd, Vedder Crossing, a very large tree at the very corner.

Stö:lo Centre, 7201 Vedder Rd, Sardis, a good tree with a DBH of 80 cm.

Yarrow Central Park, Southeast corner of Kehler St and Yarrow Central Rd, two large specimens.

Salish Park, 45860- 1 Ave.

Delta

4580 Arthur Dr, Ladner, a mature tree with an artistic form and a DBH of 90 cm.

Leisure Centre, 4600 Clarence Taylor Cr, Ladner.

Langley

23667- 40 Ave.

Richmond

6091 Blundell Rd, a large tree with a DBH of 60 cm.

Steveston Park, 4111 Moncton St, Steveston.

Southarm Park, Garden City Rd and Williams Rd.

Pinus parviflora 'Glauca'
Japanese White Pine

Pinus parviflora 'Glauca', Darts Hill
Garden Park, Surrey

Pinus parviflora 'Glauca', foliage and cones

Native to mountains of south and central Japan, Japanese White Pine is not very common in the South Fraser Region. It reaches a mature height of twenty metres with a pyramidal form. The branching habit of Japanese White Pine is often irregular and artistic. The stiff stubby needles are bluish green and twisted, radiating higgledy-piggledy around the branchlet. Japanese White Pine has five needles (3–6 cm long) per bundle. The bark is grey-black, breaking into small plates on mature trees. The cones of Japanese White Pine are brown and up to 8 cm long. The cone scales are cupped and contorted, giving the cone a unique appearance.

Where to see the trees:

Chilliwack
Townsend Park, Ashwell Rd and Hodgins Ave, north of playground.

Langley
NE corner of the Fraser Hwy and 201 A St, Langley City.

City Hall, 20399 Douglas Cr.

Richmond
Fantasy Garden World, 10800 No 5 Rd.

Surrey
Darts Hill Garden Park, 1660- 168 St, South Surrey, Garden Bed 25.

Ponderosa Pine or Western Yellow Pine

Pinus ponderosa, 88 Avenue, Fort Langley   *Pinus ponderosa,* cones

Native to the southern dry interior of British Columbia, Ponderosa Pine is somewhat common in the South Fraser Region. It reaches a mature height of thirty-five metres with an upright oval form. The branching habit is regular and open with the ends of the branches slightly swooping up. The very sharp pointed needles are sage green and straight. Ponderosa Pine has three pliable needles (12–24 cm long) per bundle. Ponderosa Pine is the only three-needle pine that is native to the province and has the longest needles of any native pine as well. The cinnamon orange bark of mature trees is deeply fissured. In the South Fraser Region, the bark usually doesn't colour well, simply appearing grey-brown with orangish fissures. On very warm days on the coast, a delicate whiff of vanilla can be had by pressing your nose to the cracks of the bark. In the Okanagan Valley, the strong fragrance of Ponderosa Pine permeates the hot summer breeze. The bark breaks away into hand-sized irregular plates that litter the ground along with the large cones in the open parkland of its native range. The plump prickly cones of Ponderosa Pine are medium brown and up to 15 cm long.

Where to see the trees:

Abbotsford

2284 Hillside Dr.

NE corner of Sherwood Ave and Clearbrook Rd.

Fraser Valley Trout Hatchery, 34345 Vye Rd, a grove of good-sized trees.

Chilliwack

General Hospital, 45600 Menholm Rd.

Chilliwack Golf and Country Club, 41894 Yale Rd West, Greendale, a row of good-sized trees north of the clubhouse around the parking lot.

100 metres south of the main gate of Fairfield Island Park, 46000 Clare Ave, Fairfield Island, in a subdivision.

46443 Prairie Central Rd, Sardis.

Langley

Newlands Golf Course, 21025- 48 Ave, Murrayville, east end of the parking lot.

22843- 88 Ave, Ft Langley.

Trinity Western University, 7600 Glover Rd, Willoughby, two stands of trees, one north of the Reimer Student Centre, the second northeast of the Enoch E. Mattson Centre.

Williams Park, 6600 block 238 St, Salmon River Uplands.

Surrey

8261- 152 St, Fleetwood*.

10375- 133 St, Whalley*.

Pinus strobus
Eastern White Pine

Pinus strobus, foliage and dormant bud

Pinus strobus, Christian Life Assembly, Langley

Where to see the trees:

Chilliwack
Skelton Park, opposite Chilliwack Municipal Hall at 8550 Young Rd.

10647 McSween Rd, Fairfield Island.

4490 Boundary Rd, Yarrow, a very large tree.

Langley
20400 block 53 Ave, City of Langley, on the north side of the street.

Christian Life Assembly, 21277-56 Ave, Murrayville, several trees on the north side of the parking lot.

23556- 47 Ave, Salmon River Uplands, two trees.

Richmond
Richmond Nature Park, 11851 Westminster Hwy, at the main entry and on the south side of the parking lot.

Rosedale
Minter Gardens, 52892 Bunker Rd, several largish specimens on the east hill above the Arbor Garden.

Surrey
Green Timbers Arboretum, 9800- 140 St, Whalley, along the east driveway.

Darts Hill Garden Park, 1660- 168 St, South Surrey, Garden Bed 35.

The Glades, 561- 172 St, South Surrey* a very large tree in the Bent Tree area.

Native to southern Ontario, Quebec, the Maritimes and south into the northeastern States, Eastern White Pine is quite common in the South Fraser Region. It reaches a mature height of thirty metres in its native range, with a broadly pyramidal form. The horizontal branching habit is open with the ends of the branches slightly upswept. The soft drooping needles are blue-green. Eastern White Pine has five thin needles (5–15 cm long) per bundle. The brown bark of mature trees is deeply fissured. The narrow pendulous cones of Eastern White Pine are medium brown. Up to 20 cm long, they are held in clusters of one to three and are splotched with white resin.

Did You Know?
Eastern White Pine or *Pinus strobus* is the arboreal emblem of the province of Ontario. The official tree was adopted in May 1984.

Pinus strobus 'Fastigiata'
Upright White Pine

Pinus strobus 'Fastigiata', Langley

Pinus strobus 'Fastigiata', foliage

Aptly named, the branches of Upright White Pine are held at a 45-degree angle to the main trunk. In youth the tree has very tight spiraling fastigate branches and a columnar form. When the tree is mature the branches open and the tree becomes more pyramidal in shape.

Where to see the trees:

Langley
4481- 232 St, Salmon River Uplands.

Pinus strobus 'Pendula'
Weeping White Pine

Very free-form in habit, the branches of Weeping White Pine cascade to the ground, creating an impressive focal point in the landscape. Weeping White Pine's organic appearance is reminiscent of the flow of an octopus as it glides over the ocean floor. Always irregular in shape, some trees sprawl upright and others are low and mounding but in all cases the branchlets are arching and pendulous. Weeping White Pine reaches a mature height of eight metres. Young trees are very common in the South Fraser Region.

Where to see the trees:

Abbotsford
Corner of Munroe Ave and Marshall Rd.

Richmond
Fantasy Garden World, 10800 No 5 Rd.

Rosedale
Minter Gardens, 52892 Bunker Rd, a small plant just outside of the main entry gate.

Pinus sylvestris
Scots Pine

Pinus sylvestris, foliage

Pinus sylvestris, General Currie Elementary School, Richmond

Where to see the trees:

Abbotsford

MSA General Hospital, 2179 McCallum Rd, a grove of young trees north of the Emergency entrance.

Trethewey House (M.S.A. Museum), 2313 Ware St, two medium-sized trees on the northwest side of the property.

Provincial Courthouse, 32202 South Fraser Way, southeast corner of the building.

Chilliwack

Municipal Hall, 8550 Young Rd.

10312 McGrath Rd, Rosedale.

Sardis Park, School Lane and Manuel Rd, Sardis.

Park, SE corner of Manuel Rd and Vedder Rd, Sardis, a very large specimen.

University College of the Fraser Valley, 45600 Airport Rd.

Delta

Justice Building, 4455 Clarence Taylor Cr, Ladner, a row of good-sized trees on the south side of the building.

Peden/Rawlins Residence, 2194 Westham Island Rd, Westham Island.

Langley

23101- 40 Ave, Southeast Langley.

Bedford House, 9272 Glover Rd, Ft Langley.

Native to northern Europe, East Asia and Siberia, Scots Pine is very common in the South Fraser Region. It reaches a mature height of thirty metres with an upright oval form. The branching habit is irregular compared to other pines. Some of the branches of Scots Pine are upright ascending, others horizontally whorled and a few droop. The sharp-pointed needles are slightly twisted, bluish-green with a whitish bloom. Scots Pine has two needles (4–6 cm long) per bundle. The thin bark is very handsome. It is a bright orange-brown and shreds into fine curling strips. The colourful bark is most apparent on younger stems and branches, while the bark of mature trees is thick and fissured. The cones of Scots Pine are grey-brown and up to 7 cm long.

Richmond

Fantasy Garden World, 10800 No 5 Rd.

General Currie Elementary School, 8220 General Currie Rd, a very fine sculptural umbrella-shaped specimen on the south side of the old school.

Richmond Nature Park, 11851 Westminster Hwy, framing the entrance to the Nature House.

Southarm Park, Garden City Rd and Williams Rd.

NW corner of Wellington Cr and Douglas Cr, Burkeville.

Surrey

Darts Hill Garden Park, 1660-168 St, South Surrey, Garden Beds 1 and 16.

The Glades, 561-172 St, South Surrey, corner of Wood Duck and Meadow lanes.

Pinus sylvestris
Scots Pine

Pinus sylvestris, cones

Pinus sylvestris 'Fastigiata'
Columnar Scots Pine or Sentinel Pine

In youth, Columnar Scots Pine has very tight upright branches and a columnar form. The branches are held parallel to the main trunk. When mature the tree maintains its pencil-thin silhouette, reaching a mature height of ten metres with a scant spread of one metre.

Where to see the trees:

Surrey

Darts Hill Garden Park, 1660- 168 St, South Surrey, Garden Bed 34.

Pinus sylvestris 'Fastigiata', Darts Hill Garden Park, Surrey

Pinus sylvestris 'Glauca Nana'
Dwarf Blue Scots Pine

Small in stature, Dwarf Blue Scots Pine reaches a mature height of four metres with an equal or greater spread with a roundish shape. The needles are shorter than the species but are deeply glaucous blue in colour. The orange peeling bark is stunning on this multi-trunked small tree and older specimens benefit from thinning to reveal the upright stems.

Pinus sylvestris 'Glauca Nana'

Dwarf Blue Scots Pine

Where to see the trees:

Abbotsford

2348 Mountain Dr, a young tree.

35074 McKee Rd.

Chilliwack

Chilliwack Municipal Airport, 46244 Chilliwack Airport Rd, a grove on the southeast corner of the Terminal building.

Delta

242- 67 St, Boundary Bay.

Langley

Sendall Gardens, 20166- 50 Ave, Langley City.

Richmond

Fantasy Garden World, 10800 No 5 Rd.

White Rock

Tourist Bureau, 15150 Russell Ave.

Pinus sylvestris 'Glauca Nana', Delta

Pinus thunbergii

Japanese Black Pine

Pinus thunbergii, Kwantlen University College, Langley

Pinus thunbergii, foliage and cones

Native to maritime Japan and southern Korea, Japanese Black Pine is not very common in the South Fraser Region. It reaches a mature height of twenty metres with a pyramidal form. The stiff needles are dark green and twisted.

Japanese Black Pine

Japanese Black Pine has two needles (7–14 cm long) per bundle. The dormant bud is long and slender, like a pencil, and covered in fine silver hairs. It is very noticeable in the winter months. The bark is black-grey, and furrowed on mature trees. The cones of Japanese Black Pine are brown and up to 7 cm long.

Where to see the trees:

Chilliwack
Skelton Park, Young Rd at Southlands Dr.

Langley
Kwantlen University College, 20901 Langley Bypass, Langley City, five trees planted in 1993 in the central turn-around at the main entrance to the main campus.

Richmond
Millennium Botanical Garden and Arboretum, N McLennan Community Park, Granville Ave and Garden City Rd.

Pinus wallichiana

Himalayan White Pine, Blue Pine or Bhutan Pine

Where to see the trees:

Surrey
Darts Hill Garden Park, 1660- 168 St, South Surrey, Garden Beds 1 and 10.

The Glades, 561-172 St, South Surrey, corner of wood duck lane and meadow lane.

Pinus wallichiana, foliage

Native to the Himalayan Mountains from Afghanistan to Assam, Himalayan White Pine is rare in the South Fraser Region. It reaches a mature height of fifty metres in its native range, with a broadly pyramidal form. The horizontal branching habit is loose and open with the ends of the branches slightly upswept. The soft drooping needles are blue-green. Himalayan White Pine has five thin needles (11–17 cm long) per bundle. The grey-brown bark of mature trees is fissured. The narrow

Pinus wallichiana
Himalayan White Pine, Blue Pine or Bhutan Pine

pendulous cones of Himalayan White Pine are tan. Up to 28 cm long, they are held in clusters of two to three and are covered with resin.

Platanus x *hispanica*
London Plane

Platanus x *hispanica,* exfoliating bark

Platanus x *hispanica,* Milner Education Centre, Langley

Very commonly grown as boulevard or park tree in the South Fraser Region, London Plane reaches huge size, growing thirty metres tall by twenty to twenty-four metres wide. It has a dense roundish form. The leaves are dinner plate-sized and deeply lobed much like a maple leaf. Light to medium green, they are fuzzy on the underside. The leaves of London Plane turn butter yellow to yellow-brown in the fall. The leaves drop continuously over a long period. The large fallen leaves in combination with the ripe fruit, which breaks apart when it falls to the ground, creates a great deal of litter. The fruit, which is a brown bristly ball about the size of a one-dollar coin, hangs, two to four fruit balls per stem, in the tree until November. In the winter months the thin jigsaw-puzzle bark is very appealing. A satisfying tan, cream and pale orange-patterned underbark is revealed as the older bark flakes away.

Where to see the trees:

Abbotsford

Abbotsford City Hall, 32315 South Fraser Way. There is a very large tree on the south side of the building.

The Gardens, 34909 Old Yale Rd, several trees in the visitors parking area.

Provincial Courthouse, 32202 South Fraser Way, northwest corner of the building.

Chilliwack

Chilliwack Fairgrounds, 45530 Spadina Ave, a row of trees on the north side of the site that have received directional pruning but nonetheless are massive specimens, the largest with a DBH of 180 cm.

Chilliwack Museum, 45820 Spadina Ave. Two rows of trees to the rear of the Museum that are carefully pollarded annually frame the cenotaph.

Chilliwack Cemeteries, 10010 Hillcrest Dr, Little Mountain.

46915 Yale Rd East. This tree has an artistic form as the seven mature stems create a massive candelabra.

Farmer's and Women's Institute Hall, 49300 Elk View Rd, Ryder Lake.

Stó:lo Centre, 7201 Vedder Rd, Sardis.

Sardis Elementary School, 45775 Manuel Rd, Sardis.

Park, SE corner of Manuel Rd and Vedder Rd, Sardis, a very large specimen.

Canadian Forces Base, Keith Wilson Rd and Vedder Rd, Vedder Crossing, three large trees on the east side of the tennis courts on Sicily Rd at Normandy Dr.

Delta

Delta Secondary School, 4615- 51 St, Ladner, a medium-size specimen on the east side of the school.

Hospital, 5800 Mountain View Blvd, Ladner, a double row of trees at the Mountain View Extended Care entrance.

North Delta Recreation Centre, 11415- 84 Ave.

Langley

City Park, 207 St and 48 Ave, Langley City, a large specimen on the west side of the parking lot.

Milner Equestrian Centre, 21795- 64 Ave, Milner.

Milner Education Centre, 6656 Glover Rd, Milner.

Derby Reach Regional Park, 2200 Block Allard Cr, Northwest Langley. There is a planting of several good-sized specimens on the west side of the parking lot.

Richmond

Burkeville Park, 1031 Lancaster Cr, Burkeville. There are a number of very fine large trees in this small park.

Southarm Park, Garden City Rd and Williams Rd.

McLean Park, 2500 McLean Ave, Hamilton

Did You Know?

Previously known as the Chilliwack Prairie, the land that now houses the Chilliwack Fairgrounds was first described as "the prairie though small in comparison to the ones on the other side of the mountains is most lovely, covered with flowers and strawberries and even in this early period of the year, the grass is nearly up to the waist."[1] Isaac Kipp (1839–1921) preempted the land, which eventually became the Fairgrounds, in 1862. The London Plane trees were likely planted after 1909 when the Chilliwack Fairs and Agricultural Society and the City purchased the land for the present fair site. The 1910 exhibition at the Fairgrounds hosted "speeding" or horse racing events on the newly built half-mile track, soccer and football matches and unusual events such as the men's pillow-fighting contest. The exhibition of livestock and horticultural produce such as fruit and grain was a mainstay of early fairs.

[1] Stanley, George F.G. ed, *Mapping the Frontier: Charles Wilson's Diary of the Survey of the 49th Parallel*, 1858-1862, University of Washington Press, Seattle, 1970.

Platanus x *hispanica*
London Plane

- The pollarded London Plane trees are planted to the rear of the Chilliwack Museum, boldly surrounding the cenotaph. The Museum building was Chilliwack's original City Hall, constructed in 1911 to 1912 to a plan by Vancouver architect Thomas Hooper. It was designed in a Classical Revival style and meant to face the Five Corners intersection. The citizens of Chilliwack, imbued with youthful optimism, felt that the building of a Hall was justified due to the burgeoning growth in their city's population; 3,690 people in 1901 to 9,172 in 1911, a whopping forty percent increase. Sixty-nine years later, growth again caused a move, when the city of Chilliwack amalgamated with the Town-ship of Chilliwack to form the District of Chilliwack. A new larger City Hall was needed to accommodate a much larger municipal staff. The site of the Old City Hall, now the Chilliwack Museum, was designated a National Historic Site in 1987.

"I like these trees," he said, "because they do not look to me at all like trees. They look like the skeletons of umbrellas in the dump. They look like they have had arthritis for a long, long time. They look like spiders with tumors on their elbows. They look like what the bone structure of octopi would look like if octopi had bones. I am very, very fond of these trees."[2]

- The Farmer's and Women's Institute Hall at Ryder Lake in Chilliwack was officially opened on August 3, 1963. Five hundred citizens participated in the dedication of the building and grounds. Mrs. Edward Marshall and Mrs. A. W. Voight planted the London Plane in the Memorial garden. Completion of the Institute Hall, park and picnic area was the culmination of many volunteer hours. Work bees were held to prepare the site. Local businessmen donated a variety of things such as the use of heavy equipment, stumping powder, blasting caps, tractor oil and grass seed to aid in the construction of the Hall. The women of the Women's Institute were ever helpful, supplying food for the volunteer workers.

Platanus x *hispanica,* Cenotaph, Chilliwack

Platanus x *hispanica,* foliage

2 Urquhart J. *Storm Glass,* page 66, 1987.

Exceedingly rare in the South Fraser Region, Oriental Plane grows thirty metres tall. It has an upright oval form. The leaves are dinner plate-sized and deeply lobed much like a maple leaf. Light to medium green, they are fuzzy on the underside. The thin, slightly drooping leaves of Oriental Plane turn butter yellow in the fall. The fruit, which is a brown bristly ball about the size of a one-dollar coin, hangs, three to six fruit balls per stem, in the tree until November. In the winter months the thin jigsaw-puzzle bark is very appealing. A satisfying tan, cream and pale orange patterned underbark is revealed as the older bark flakes away. Oriental Plane is native to the Balkan Peninsula and southwest Asia.

Platanus orientalis, 152 Street, Surrey

Did You Know?

These two trees, planted as seedlings in 1977 by Peter Thompson, have impeccable lineage. Seed was originally collected from an ancient Oriental Plane tree on the Island of Cos, off the coast of Asia Minor. Hippocratic legend suggests that Hippocrates, the Father of Modern Medicine (d. 400 B.C.) taught under this Plane tree. The Oriental Plane on the Island of Cos is hollow, with major limbs supported by marble columns, lesser limbs supported with wooden props. Oscar Siklai, a forestry professor in Forest Genetics at UBC, originally from the Sopron University faculty of Forestry in Hungary and William Gibson, a professor of the History of Medicine, UBC and later Chancellor of the University of Victoria, brought the seeds of the Oriental Plane tree to Canada to grow seedlings for fund-raising purposes.

Where to see the trees:

Surrey

4117 - 152 St, South Surrey*, two good-sized trees, the larger of the two with a DBH of 40 cm. These two trees are not visible from the public road.

Populus alba
White Poplar

Populus alba, foliage

Populus alba, Steveston Park, Richmond

Where to see the trees:

Richmond

RCMP Detachment, 6900 Minoru Blvd, a row of large trees on the east side of the parking lot.

2300 Westminster Hwy, two large trees.

Steveston Park, 4111 Moncton St, Steveston, several very large trees just southwest of the Fentmen Place entrance.

Somewhat common in the South Fraser Region, White Poplar grows thirty metres tall with a round billowy form. The large leaves are coarsely toothed and dark green on the top surface and fuzzy white underneath. Varying in shape, the leaves on young vigorous growth are often lobed like a maple leaf while other leaves on the same tree are simply bumpy edged and ovate in shape. The leaves are held on stalks and waggle in the breeze, showing the bright white underside to great advantage. The fall colour is yellow. The smooth grey bark of White Poplar is very attractive in the winter landscape as it is deeply cut with triangular black slits. White Poplar is native to north Africa and west central Asia.

Populus alba 'Pyramidalis'
Bolleana Poplar or Pyramidal White Poplar

Bolleana Poplar is very similar to White Poplar but it has a bold upright oval form.

Where to see the trees:

Langley

City Park, 207 St and 48 Ave, Langley City, a stately row at the north end of the park.

Sendall Gardens, 20166- 50 Ave, Langley City.

Richmond

Fantasy Garden World, 10800 No 5 Rd.

Populus alba 'Pyramidalis', City Park, Langley

Populus balsamifera ssp. *trichocarpa*
Syn. *Populus trichocarpa*
Black Cottonwood

Black Cottonwood is the tallest Balsam Poplar native to the Canada. Its native range extends from southern Alaska south to Oregon, throughout most of British Columbia and into Alberta, Idaho and Montana. It reaches a statuesque fifty metres in height. It has an upright oval shape with short lateral branches that are upswept at the tips. The leaves are triangular, glossy dark green with a toothed edge. The fall colour is yellow or yellow-brown. The reddish-brown buds easily identify Black Cottonwood in the winter months because they are very sticky. When crushed the buds smell cloyingly sweet. When the bud scales drop in the spring as the young leaves unfold, the air is filled with their unmistakable fragrance. The flower is a catkin and the fruit produced is a tiny woolly seed. The ground is completely covered by the white fluffs of Black Cottonwood seed, particularly near the Victoria Day Weekend in May, when millions of the seeds are released. The dark grey bark of mature trees is beautifully sinuous, with heavy ridges and deep furrows.

Populus balsamifera ssp. *trichocarpa*, Derby Reach Regional Park, Langley

Populus balsamifera ssp. *trichocarpa*
Syn. *Populus trichocarpa*

Black Cottonwood

Where to see the trees:

Abbotsford

Hogan Family Nature Park, 2860 block Debruyne Rd. A very short walk into the park beside the bridge crossing the Salmon River leads to a massive tree with a DBH of 164 cm.

Chilliwack

Hope River Corbould Park, north end of Corbould St, several large trees on either shore of Hope River.

East bank of the Sumas River, south of the CNR tracks, near the confluence of the Fraser River. The world's largest Black Cottonwood, discovered in 2000, has a circumference of 11.92 metres, a DBH of 365 cm, a height of 43.3 metres and a crown spread of 29.6 metres.

Langley

Marina Park, north end of Church St, Ft Langley.

27606 River Rd, Northeast Langley.

Derby Reach Regional Park, Allard Cr, Northwest Langley. There are two grand specimens on the south side of the trail approximately one hundred metres east of the east end of the campsite and several very large tree on the south side of the handicap access trail.

Richmond

No 7 Road Pier Park, River Rd and No 7 Rd.

13060 Steveston Hwy. This is a significant grove of very large trees at the south end of the field approximately one hundred metres from the Steveston Highway. These trees are easily visible from Highway 99 as well.

The largest tree in this grove has a trunk circumference of 7.6 metres, several others are in the 5.5- 7.6 metre range.

12051 Shell Rd, south foot of Shell Road near the Horseshoe Slough Trail access point. There is a gigantic tree to the east of this address. This tree, with a trunk circumference of 8.2 metres, is growing at the west end of an industrial warehouse complex, and can be viewed by crossing the ditch overpass and the rail tracks. The little marsh around this tree and several others likely saved them from the developers axe. This is the largest Black Cottonwood west of the Sumas River trees in Chilliwack.

Surrey

Surrey Big Bend Regional Park, north foot of 104 St, Guildford, a number of very large trees in the park.

Did You Know?

To reach the world's largest Black Cottonwood in Chilliwack be prepared for a muddy hike along a fisher's path. Take the Yale West Road exit off Highway 1, proceed to the raised gravel dyke road which heads west toward the Sumas River. From the stop sign, travel 1.6 kilometres on the dyke road to a river access track. Follow the fisher's track on the east bank of the Sumas River approximately ten to eleven minutes. Look west to note the shoulder of Sumas Mountain. Do not cross the Canadian Nation Rail line (CNR) tracks. Upon reaching a bushy swale with a 40 cm diameter cottonwood log which crosses it at right angles, pass under the log, head east up the swale for approximately seven minutes. The gargantuan trunk of the world's largest cottonwood sits on a slightly raised bench above a marshy area. Access is through the wetlands to the north of the tree. Blackberries make the access from other sides of the tree almost impossible. The world's largest Black Cottonwood is hollow. You can stand with your arms completely outstretched inside the tree, with room to spare. A cone of light from a huge branch failure, its diameter the size of most ordinary Black Cottonwood trunks, illuminates the hollow core. The tree is ancient, with huge broken and angular limbs, but it grows new green leaves every year. Two other massive companions are within sight of the world's largest cottonwood. Eagles find the tops of this grove of gigantic trees excellent winter perches. This area of the Sumas River is a very rare undyked stretch of

Black Cottonwood

the Fraser River flood plain. Approximately one hundred hectares in size, it contains the third and fourth largest known Black Cottonwoods in North America and five of the top ten of this species in terms of size.

This stretch of the Fraser is one of the last deciduous old-growth flood plain forests left in Canada. The monster Black Cottonwood and the army of ancient giants that grow just half a kilometre to the east of it are growing on Crown Land. The Western Canada Wilderness Committee has proposed the "Black Cottonwood Big Tree Park" to protect this very fragile and unique riverine landscape.

• No 7 Road Pier Park was the site of the Canadian National Rail line crossing of the north arm of the Fraser River. Freight cars were barged across the river here. The rail lines are embedded into the pathway. There are many very fine good-sized cottonwoods growing from this park along the shoreline of the river east, remnants of a much larger riverine belt of trees.

The author and the world's largest Black Cottonwood, *Populus balsamifera* ssp. *trichocarpa*, Chilliwack. © Ralf Kelman

---

Populus deltoides ssp. *monilifera*

Plains Cottonwood

The native range of Plains Cottonwood extends from the southern parts of Alberta, Saskatchewan and Manitoba south to Texas. It reaches thirty metres in height. It has an upright oval shape with short lateral branches that are upswept at the tips. The leaves are triangular, bright green with a coarsely toothed margin. The teeth are rounded giving the margin a notched appearance. The fall colour is butter yellow. The plump sharp green buds easily identify Plains Cottonwood in the winter months because they are smooth with tiny hairs. The buds are very sweet smelling. The flower is a catkin. The pale grey bark of mature trees is beautifully sinuous, with heavy ridges and deep furrows.

Where to see the trees:
Abbotsford

Upper Sumas Elementary School, 36321 Vye Rd. There are four trees with massive trunks on the east side of the school playing fields. These trees were likely planted in 1919 when the original section of the present Upper Sumas Elementary School was built.

Delta

NW corner of Frew Rd and Tamboline Rd, Westham Island, a farm row of good-sized trees.

Populus nigra 'Italica'
Lombardy Poplar

Populus nigra 'Italica', Fairmeade Farm, Langley

Very common in the South Fraser Region, Lombardy Poplar is often grown as a hedgerow or found lining the rural farm roads. It reaches a height of thirty metres with a scant spread of 2.5–3 metres. The stiffly upright branches, which parallel one another and the columnar form, easily identify this tree in the winter months. The leaves are triangular, sharply toothed and medium to dark green. The fall colour is bright yellow. The grey-brown bark of Lombardy Poplar is muscular and ropy.

Where to see the trees:

Abbotsford
2500 block Cyril St, a row of four trees on the west side of the street.

Chilliwack
10806 McSween Rd, Fairfield Island.

48687 Prairie Central Rd, Sardis, a farm row.

Delta
South of Ladner Trunk Rd on 72 St, a pleasant hedgerow of twenty-metre-tall trees interspersed with Horse Chestnut.

Langley
Fairmeade Farm, 6750- 232 St, Salmon River Uplands, a stately double entry row.

Williams Park, 6600 block 238 St, Salmon River Uplands.

Richmond
Corner of Airport Rd and Hudson Ave, a row of very fine trees marking the entry to Burkeville.

Populus tremula 'Erecta'
Syn. *Populus tremula* 'Columnaris'
Swedish Columnar Poplar or Swedish Columnar Aspen

Populus tremula 'Erecta', foliage

Rare in the South Fraser Region, Swedish Columnar Poplar reaches a height of twenty metres with a slender spread of 2.5–3 metres. The upright branches, which parallel one another and the columnar form, easily identify this tree in the winter months. The thin leaves are oval, wavy edged with round teeth and green. The fall colour is bright yellow. The dark grey bark of Swedish Columnar Poplar is fissured on mature trees.

Populus tremula 'Erecta', Boundary Bay Road, Delta

Populus tremula 'Erecta'
Syn. *Populus tremula* 'Columnaris'

Swedish Columnar Poplar or Swedish Columnar Aspen

Where to see the trees:

Chilliwack

5600 block Stonehaven Rd, Promontory Heights.

Corner of McGuire Rd and Chilliwack River Rd, Sardis, two trees.

Delta

Corner of Boundary Bay Rd and 3 Ave, Boundary Bay, a row of young trees in the centre median of 3 Ave.

Langley

North end of 208 St, Langley City, a double row of young trees.

Richmond

South Arm Park, east of No 3 Rd.

Populus tremuloides
Trembling Aspen or Quaking Aspen

Common in the South Fraser Region, Trembling Aspen is often naturalized at the edges of disturbed areas. It is native to the dry interior and northern British Columbia, and is found in natural groves on Vancouver Island. Trembling Aspen has the widest natural range of any deciduous tree on the continent, growing from the Yukon south to Mexico and from coast to coast. Twenty to twenty-five metres tall with a spread of eight metres, Trembling Aspen has an upright oval form. The thin roundish leaves are finely toothed and dark green on the top surface and paler underneath. The leaves are held on long stalks and waver readily in the slightest breeze. The fall colour is rich butter yellow. The grey smooth bark of Trembling Aspen is very attractive in the winter landscape.

Populus tremuloides, fall colour

Where to see the trees:
Abbotsford

Ravine Park, Bourquin Cr East access, a very tall tree with a DBH of 60 cm, the tree is five minute walk on the west side of the trail, take the right hand track at all times.

Prunus 'Accolade'
Syn. *Prunus* x *subhirtella* 'Accolade'

Accolade Cherry

Where to see the trees:

Chilliwack
Townsend Park, southwest corner of Ashwell Rd and Hodgins Ave, a double row at the north side of the field house between baseball diamonds 3 and 5.

Richmond
Williams Rd from No 4 Rd to Shell Rd, a street tree planting on the north side of the street.

Surrey
Darts Hill Garden Park, 1660- 168 St, South Surrey, at the north end of the Magnolia Walk.

15132- 23A Ave, South Surrey.

15120- 23A Ave, South Surrey.

14994- 20A Ave, South Surrey.

An open-topped form, fine light branching pattern and a mature height of seven metres with a slightly greater spread, identify Accolade Cherry in the winter months. Blooming in mid-March to early April, the flowers are deep pink in tight bud, and then emerge pale pink in two to four pendulous flower clusters. Each large semi-double bloom has twelve to fifteen petals. Flowers precede the unfurling of the leaves. The bright green leaves are 10–14 cm long with a finely toothed edge. The tips of the twigs of older trees are often pendulous.

Prunus 'Amanogawa'
Syn. *Prunus serrulata* 'Amanogawa'

White Column Cherry or Apple Blossom Cherry

Prunus 'Amanogawa', flowers

A very short trunk that quickly breaks into stiff vertical branches, paralleling one another, easily identifies White Column Cherry. It reaches a mature height of six to eight metres with a scant spread of 1.5 metres. As the tree matures, the tight form relaxes, with branches twisting and looping out of formation. The lightly scented flowers are a delicate pink in bud and open in late April to May. The flowers are single or semi-double and are produced in dense upright clusters. The blooms age from light rose to white. The leaves, which unfold at the same time or slightly later than the bloom time unfold bronze and soon age to bright green. The leaves are 10–15 cm long with a fine fringe along the margin. The fall colour of White Column Cherry varies from yellow to purple-red.

Prunus 'Amanogawa'
Syn. *Prunus serrulata* 'Amanogawa'

White Column Cherry or Apple Blossom Cherry

Where to see the trees:

Chilliwack

Chilliwack Public Library, 45860-1 Ave, several groups in the west parking lot.

Townsend Park, southwest corner of Ashwell Rd and Hodgins Ave, at the west end of the park, a number of young trees.

Langley

W.C. Blair Recreation Centre, 22200 Fraser Hwy, Murrayville, a row of young trees on the south side of the centre.

56 Ave and 203 St, Langley City, a good-sized tree on 56 Ave at the street entrance to the mall.

5996- 237A St, Salmon River Uplands.

Richmond

Fantasy Garden World, 10800 No 5 Rd.

Rosedale

Minter Gardens, 52892 Bunker Rd, north end of the Hillside/Alpine Garden.

Surrey

City Hall, 14245- 56 Ave, Newton, two trees on the south side of the building.

2248- 136 St, South Surrey.

2340- 140A St, South Surrey.

Darts Hill Garden Park, 1660- 168 St, South Surrey, Garden Bed 29.

The Glades, 561-172 St, South Surrey, southwest corner of the house.

Prunus cerasifera 'Nigra'
Purpleleaf Plum

Prunus cerasifera 'Nigra', Spadina Avenue, Chilliwack

Purpleleaf Plum reaches a mature size of seven to eight metres with a round lollipop shape. The leaves are a deep purple and turn a rich red-purple in the fall. The single five-petalled flowers are light pink and appear in great profusion in late March to April. The air is sweetly scented by the strong perfume of this tree, which is common in the South Fraser Region.

Where to see the trees:

Chilliwack

Airport Rd across from the Airport

Spadina Ave, from Main St to Corbould St, Chilliwack, planted as two row of street trees and a third row of trees in the median.

Townsend Park, southwest corner of Ashwell Rd and Hodgins Ave, Chilliwack.

Surrey

6183- 187 St, Cloverdale, a number of trees planted on this street.

5415- 184 St, Cloverdale.

8189- 154B St, Fleetwood.

Prunus cerasifera 'Nigra'
Purpleleaf Plum

Prunus cerasifera 'Pissardii'
Syn. *Prunus cerasifera* 'Atropurpurea'
Pissard Plum, Purpleleaf Plum or Copper Plum

Prunus cerasifera 'Pissardii', flowers

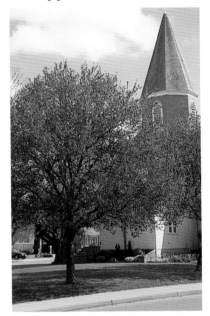

Prunus cerasifera 'Pissardii', St Thomas Anglican Church, Chilliwack

Perhaps even more ubiquitous than *Prunus cerasifera* 'Nigra' in our landscape, Pissard Plum reaches a mature size of eight to ten metres with a round winter silhouette. The single five-petalled flowers are pale pink, fading to white and appear in mid to early March and into early April just before the leaves unfurl. The air is sweetly scented by the strong perfume of this tree and the Purpleleaf Plum, both of which are very common along the streets of the communities of the South Fraser Region. Young leaves are copper coloured, age to reddish purple and turn a deeper red-purple in the fall. Occasionally dark red plums about the size of nickels are produced in August.

Prunus cerasifera 'Pissardii'
Syn. Prunus cerasifera 'Atropurpurea'

Pissard Plum, Purpleleaf Plum or Copper Plum

Did You Know?

The lovely St. Thomas Anglican Church in Chilliwack was built in 1897 in Port Douglas. It was transported down Harrison Lake and further downstream on the Fraser River on six Haida canoes to Chilliwack in 1873. It was reassembled on land at the Five Corners donated by Isaac Kipp. It was moved again, to its present location in 1909. The architectural style, designed by Architect R.P. Sharp is English Gothic. The three part lancet windows with wooden ornaments are made to look like stone.

Where to see the trees:

Chilliwack
St Thomas Anglican Church, 46040 Gore Ave, a row of trees.

Delta
295- 66 St, Boundary Bay, two exceptionally large trees.

Langley
St Andrew's Anglican Church, 20955 Old Yale Rd, Langley City, a large tree at the north end of the parking lot.

Surrey
City Hall, 14245- 56 Ave, Newton, a mature tree on the southeast corner of the building.

Prunus emarginata
Bitter Cherry

Prunus emarginata, flowers

Prunus emarginata, Murrayville Cemetery, Langley

A very common native tree, usually found at the forest edge, Bitter Cherry grows to fifteen to twenty metres tall. In its native range it is found in most of southern British Columbia and south into Washington and Oregon. The yellowish green leaves, which emerge a lovely

Prunus emarginata
Bitter Cherry

Where to see the trees:

Abbotsford

Winfield Park, a massive old tree of thirty metres and a DBH of 68 cm on the south side of the trail.

Langley

Murrayville Cemetery, 21405- 44 Ave, Murrayville.

copper colour, are oval in shape and turn yellow in the fall. The flowers, which brighten the natural landscape, are produced in April. They have five petals, are white with a tuft of bright yellow stamens at their centre. The flowers are produced in flat-topped clusters and are quite showy. The dark red fruit, which ripens in July to August, is very tart but favoured by birds. The red-brown or grey bark is marked by the orange horizontal lenticels that are typical of cherries.

Prunus 'Kwanzan'
Syn. *Prunus serrulata* 'Kwanzan'
Kwanzan Cherry

Prunus 'Kwanzan', flowers

Prunus 'Kwanzan', Jubilee Park, Abbotsford

Stiff and ungainly, with heavy branches outstretched at 45-degree angles, the unmistakable vase shape of young Kwanzan Cherry is easy to identify in the winter landscape. As it matures the tree becomes wide-spreading and flat-topped. Kwanzan Cherry reaches a mature height of eight to twelve metres with a similar width. The flowers are produced at the same time as the bronze-red fringed leaves unfold. Frothy, deep pink double flowers cling to the heavily laden branches. Kwanzan Cherry can be overwhelming in its exuberant April display.

Kwanzan Cherry

The large leaves age to a bright green and fall, golden yellow in October. Kwanzan Cherry is very common in the South Fraser Region.

Where to see the trees:

Abbotsford

2457 Sugarpine St.

Jubilee Park, McCallum Rd south of Essendene, mature trees on the west and east boundary of the park.

Old Yale Rd and South Fraser Way, several mature trees in the triangular median strip.

School District No 34 Administrative Offices, 2790 Tims St, a row of good-sized trees.

Yale Secondary School, 34620 Old Yale Rd, a large tree.

Chilliwack

Municipal Hall, 8550 Young Rd, a row of old trees to the rear of the building along the parking lot, several trees with A DBH of 60 cm.

Chilliwack Public Library, 45860- 1 Ave, at the rear of the building.

Evergreen Hall, 9291

Corbould St, a mature tree on the east side of the building.

Langley

SE corner of 208 St and 56 Ave, Langley City, a row of semi-mature trees.

Fort Langley Cemetery, 23105 St Andrews St, Fort Langley.

19909- 64 Ave, Willoughby.

Richmond

Williams Rd, from Garden City to No 4 Rd on the north side of the street, a street tree planting.

Surrey

19088- 64 Ave, Cloverdale, a number of trees on this street block.

1698- 133A St, South Surrey, a number of trees on this street block.

14271- 18A Ave, South Surrey.

The Glades, 561-172 St, South Surrey.

Did You Know?

A beautiful Kwanzan Cherry is planted in front of what was the original location of Matheson House in Langley, originally built by John Matheson in 1898. Matheson, a blacksmith, came to Langley from California. The property is under redevelopment; the house has been moved two hundred metres to the adjacent Langley Meadows Park and will be refurbished for community use.

Pink Perfection Cherry

Pink Perfection Cherry is similar to Kwanzan Cherry; the flower buds of Pink Perfection Cherry are dark red. The double pink blooms are a clear pink with no purple overtones. The leaves unfurl a delicate bronze and age to mid-green. Pink Perfection Cherry grows 6–7.5 metres in height. It has a vase shape, particularly when young.

Where to see the trees:

Chilliwack

Fairfield Island Park, 46000 Clare Ave, Fairfield Island, seven trees between ball diamonds A and C.

Surrey

17548- 63 Ave, Cloverdale, three street trees.

1274- 161A St, South Surrey.

1302- 160A St, South Surrey.

Prunus sargentii
Sargent Cherry

Prunus sargentii, flowers

Where to see the trees:
Richmond
Fantasy Garden World, 10800 No 5 Rd.

Round in form, with a mature height of six to nine metres, Sargent Cherry offers two seasons of interest, as the fall colour is as noteworthy as the floral display. Native to Japan, the leaves of Sargent Cherry are obovate in shape with sharply toothed margins. The leaves unfurl a lovely copper colour, age to dark green in the growing season and turn fiery orange and red in the fall. The flowers are borne in April and are single medium pink and held in pairs. The bark is a lovely shining reddish brown-mahogany colour. Sargent Cherry is relatively uncommon in the South Fraser Region.

Prunus serotina
Black Cherry

Where to see the trees:
Langley
27119- 36 A Crescent, Aldergrove, a very large mature tree. There are several more trees on the south side of 36 A Crescent.

Rarely found in the South Fraser Region, Black Cherry is native to southern Ontario, Quebec and the Maritimes. It is a large deciduous tree reaching a height of twenty metres with an upright oval winter silhouette. The leathery leaves are very shiny, lance shaped with a toothed edge. Each tiny tooth is hooked at its tip. The flowers, appearing in late May to early June, are single, white and produced on spikes 10–15 cm long. The pea-sized fruit, which ripens in September, is black and held in long

Prunus serotina, flowers

drooping chains. The bark on mature trees is unusual for a cherry. It is strongly plated, with the plates uplifted at the ends giving Black Cherry an untidy look.

Prunus serrula
Birchbark Cherry, Tibetan Cherry or Red-Bark Cherry

Prunus serrula, branching pattern

Prunus serrula, foliage

Rare in the South Fraser Region, Birchbark Cherry is noteworthy for its outstanding burnished reddish-brown bark. On mature trees, the colourful bark shreds in fine strips and is studded with the pencil-thick horizontal bands of lenticels; creating striking winter interest. Birchbark Cherry grows ten to twelve metres tall, with a round silhouette. The leaves are

Where to see the trees:
Surrey
The Glades, 561-172 St, South Surrey, west ridge midway, north side.

Prunus serrula
Birchbark Cherry, Tibetan Cherry or Red-Bark Cherry

narrowly lance shaped, dark green and have small sharp teeth along the edges. The white flowers appear in May and are held in clusters of two and three. Birchbark Cherry is native to China and Tibet.

Prunus 'Shirofugen'
Syn. *Prunus serrulata* 'Shirofugen'
Shirofugen Cherry

Prunus 'Shirofugen', flowers

Shirofugen Cherry is among the last of the cherries to bloom in the South Fraser Region. It reaches a mature height of ten to eleven metres with a horizontal oval form. The buds of Shirofugen Cherry are dark pink. Fragrant flowers appear in late April–May. They emerge a delicate pink-white, age to deeper pink and finally turn white. Hanging from long stalks, and fully double, the flowers of Shirofugen Cherry are easy to distinguish as the centre of each sports several tiny green leaf-like structures. Shirofugen Cherry blossoms last for four weeks, the longest blooming period of any of the cherries blooming in the spring. The oblong leaves, which unfold in shades of copper just before the flowers are borne, age to dark green. Shirofugen Cherry is abundant in the South Fraser Region.

Prunus 'Shirofugen'
Syn. *Prunus serrulata* 'Shirofugen'

Shirofugen Cherry

Prunus 'Shirofugen', Salmon River Uplands, Langley

Where to see the trees:

Abbotsford:

3075 Trethewey St, several trees at the entrance to the housing complex.

NE corner of Tims Ave and Clearbrook Rd, a row of street trees.

Chilliwack

Hodgins Ave and Corbould St, two trees on the south side of Hodgins Ave.

Fairfield Island Park, 46000 Clare Ave, Fairfield Island, twelve trees in the laneway south of Ball Diamond D.

Townsend Park, SW corner of Ashwell Rd and Hodgins Ave, a row of trees on the west side of the baseball park, planted in the laneways separating baseball diamonds 3 and 5 from diamonds 4 and 6, in the east to west lane.

Delta

Mountain View Boulevard and 44 Ave, Ladner. There are mature tees on both sides of the boulevard and on the south side of 44 Avenue.

Langley

NW corner of 204 A St and 62 Ave, Langley City, a lovely tree with many more throughout the warehouse complex.

6010- 237 A St, Salmon River Uplands, a perfect specimen.

4506 Southridge Cr, Murrayville, a mature tree.

Rosedale

Minter Gardens, 52892 Bunker Rd, entry row of trees into the rose garden.

Surrey

Kensington Prairie Elementary School, 16824- 32 Ave, South Surrey, a magnificent tree on the west side of one of the portable classrooms.

Guildford Station Pub, 10176- 154 St, a row of trees at the entrance.

15676- 93 Ave, Fleetwood.

15671- 93 Ave, Fleetwood.

12963- 19A Ave, South Surrey.

12951- 19A Ave, South Surrey.

White Rock

White Rock Elementary School, 1273 Fir St, a row of street trees on the north side of the school.

Prunus 'Shirotae'
Syn. *Prunus serrulata* 'Shirotae'
Syn. *Prunus serrulata* 'Mt. Fuji' or 'Mount Fuji'

Mount Fuji Japanese Cherry

Prunus 'Shirotae', Cenotaph, Langley City

Where to see the trees:

Abbotsford

1916 McCallum Rd, four large trees in the parking lot.

Chilliwack

Hodgins St near Corbould Ave intersection on the south side.

Mary St, west side near Patten Ave and Ontario Ave.

Salish Park, 45860- 1 Ave, there is a double row of trees at the east entrance to the park.

Yarrow Central Rd at Eckert St, Yarrow.

SW corner of Bole Ave and Fletcher St, two mature trees.

Langley

Cenotaph, northwest corner of Eastleigh Cr and 56 Ave, Langley City. A lovely grove of trees flanks the cenotaph.

Fort Langley Community Hall, 9167 Glover Rd, Ft Langley.

Kwantlen University College, 20901 Langley Bypass, Langley City. There are two small trees pond-side in the Gazebo Garden at the Field Lab.

Rosedale

Minter Gardens, 52892 Bunker Rd, bend in the zigzag path along the Stream Garden.

Surrey

City Hall, 14245- 56 Ave, Newton, a row of five trees on the west side of the path around the pond.

Surrey Pretrial Services, 14323-57 Ave, a double row of eight trees frame the entrance.

Prunus 'Shirofugen', flowers

A froth of white in the early spring marks the arrival of the blossoms of Mount Fuji Cherry. With the palest blush of pink in bud, the fragrant semi-double white flowers open earliest of all of the Sato-Sakura group of Japanese flowering cherries. In winter, the strong horizontal branching habit, almost flat like a tabletop, easily identifies Mount Fuji Cherry. The bright green leaves unfurl after the flowers and are delicately fringed along their margins. Fall leaf colour is yellow. Mount Fuji Cherry is common in the South Fraser Region. It grows 6–6.5 metres high with a spread of eight metres.

Green Cherry

Prunus 'Ukon', flowers

Growing eight to twelve metres tall with a rounded form, Green Cherry is somewhat common in the South Fraser Region. Green in bud, the large semi-double flowers are unusual because their pale yellow is tinted green and eventually the flower fades to red in the centre. The buds and later the tips of the flowers are also lightly touched with pink. The flowers are at their peak in late April. The leaves, as they unfold are bronzy-green, turning midgreen with reddish to purple fall colours.

Where to see the trees:
Chilliwack
Townsend Park, southwest corner of Ashwell Rd and Hodgins Ave.

Langley
Trinity Western University, 7600 Glover Rd, Willoughby, to the northeast of the Reimer Student Centre.

Prunus virginiana 'Schubert'

Schubert Chokecherry or Purpleleaf Chokecherry

Prunus virginiana 'Schubert', in the fall, Salmon River Uplands, Langley

Prunus virginiana 'Schubert', fall colour

Prunus virginiana 'Schubert'

Schubert Chokecherry or Purpleleaf Chokecherry

Where to see the trees:

Langley

23894- 58A Ave, Salmon River Uplands.

Chilliwack

46551- 46566 MacGregor Pl, Promontory Heights.

5650 Stonehaven St, Promontory Heights.

Corner of Rosa Villa and Monte Villa, Vedder Crossing.

Schubert Chokecherry is a small tree reaching a mature height of 7.5 metres. It has an upright branching habit and a pyramidal-upright oval form. The oval leaves unfold green, then age to a delightful deep purple. The fall colour is reddish-purple. The five-petalled flowers are small but showy. Pendulous racemes of flowers decorate the tree in May. Ripening to dark purple in September, the edible fruit hangs on the branches like clusters of grapes. The stems of Schubert Chokecherry, when crushed, smell of bitter almond. The bark is greyish-brown when young, blackish with age. The lenticels are unlike most Cherries; they run up and down the stem not across it.

Prunus x *yedoensis* 'Akebono'
Syn. *Prunus* x *yedoensis* 'Daybreak'

Akebono Cherry or Daybreak Cherry

Prunus x *yedoensis* 'Akebono', Douglas Park, Langley

Akebono Cherry is very common in the South Fraser Region. The branches arch upward at a 45-degree angle giving this cherry an uplifting look. It is quite flat-topped at maturity. The flowers are produced in late March to April and completely hide the stout branches. They are

Akebono Cherry or Daybreak Cherry

Prunus x *yedoensis* 'Akebono', flowers

five-petalled, pink in bud opening to blushed pink-white fading to white. Each petal has a wavy apex. The floral display is not long-lived, particularly if it's a blustery spring. The petals, swirling to earth like dainty snowflakes, are as attractive there as they are on the tree. The leaves are bright green and colour yellow in the fall. Yoshino Cherry grows 7.5 tall with a similar spread.

Did You Know?

The grove of trees in Kuno Garden was planted in November 2, 2000 to honour the Japanese pioneers who immigrated to B.C. and lived and worked in the Steveston area in Richmond. The trees were planted by the BC Wakayama Kenjin Kai, an association formed in 1965 to promote the legacy of those from the Wakayama Prefecture in Japan. 1988 marked the centennial year of the arrival of the first Japanese immigrants to Canada from Wakayama Prefecture. A plaque in Kuno Garden reads, "We respectfully honour the courage and spirit of the pioneers led by Mr. Gihei Kuno."

Where to see the trees:

Abbotsford

Abbotsford City Hall, 32315 South Fraser Way, a double ring of trees to the north of the hall.

Chilliwack

Happy Wilkinson Park.

Kipp St at Mary St, northwest side.

Townsend Park, SW corner of Ashwell Rd and Hodgins Ave, a double row at the north entrance to the baseball park, planted on the laneways separating baseball diamonds 3 and 4 from baseball diamonds 5 and 6, the north and south lane.

Victoria Ave at Mill St on the north side.

Wellington Ave at Mary St on the southwest side.

Langley

Trinity Western University, 7600 Glover Rd, Willoughby.

88 Ave from 204 St to 216 St, Walnut Grove, a street planting.

SW corner of Willowbrook Dr and 200 St, Willowbrook, three trees as part of a service station landscape.

W.C. Blair Recreation Centre, 22200 Fraser Hwy, Murrayville, several rows of young trees on the south and east side of the centre.

Municipal Hall, 4914- 221 St, Murrayville, a mature tree on the north side of the building.

Douglas Recreation Centre, 20550 Douglas Cr, Langley City, a splendid tree on the west side of the centre in Douglas Park.

Richmond

Garry Point Park, west end of Moncton St, Steveston, a row of trees on the north side of the Kuno Garden.

4111 Moncton St. Steveston, a row of trees to the south of the playground.

Surrey

11033- 155 St, Fleetwood.

14888- 57B Ave, Newton.

14891- 57B Ave, Newton.

Pseudotsuga menziesii

Douglas Fir

Pseudotsuga menziesii, foliage

Pseudotsuga menziesii, King Street, Fort Langley

Douglas Fir is ubiquitous in the South Fraser Region and the dominant native conifer in some areas. The majority is second growth timber and seldom approach the gigantic proportions of first growth veteran record holders found elsewhere in the province. The world champion Douglas Fir is called the "Red Creek Tree". Truly a forest giant, it soars to a breathtaking height of 74 metres with a colossal girth of 13.28 metres. The Red Creek Tree is growing near the San Juan River on Vancouver Island.

Douglas Fir is easily identified by its robust size and broadly pyramidal outline. The horizontal branches are long with the tips of each branch upswept. The soft fragrant needles of Douglas Fir are held askew as compared to the rigid radiating needles of most *Picea* or spruce. The flat needles are dark green with two conspicuous white bands on the bottom surface. The terminal bud is sharp pointed and glossy mahogany red. The pendulous red brown cones are very distinctive. The forked bract that peeps out of each cone scale resembles the hind legs and tail of a mouse. The bark of Douglas Fir is exceptionally thick, on very old trees it may be thirty cm thick. It is deeply fissured and dark brown. Douglas Fir is native to the coast of British Columbia and south to California.

Where to see the trees:

Abbotsford

Downes Bowl Park, Trethewey St pedestrian entrance (no car parking at this entrance). A ten minute walk down a ridgeline leads to an old growth grove of Western Red Cedar and Douglas Fir, the largest fir has a DBH of 120 cm and is forty-five metres high.

Trethewey House (M.S.A. Museum), 2313 Ware St, four very large trees southeast of the house almost a metre in diameter at breast height. These trees were topped some time ago but still look good.

Glen Ridge Park on McKee Rd, a large tree on the northwest side of the park adjacent to McKee Rd.

Hoon Park, 33300 Holland Drive.

Provincial Courthouse, 32202 South Fraser Way, a grove of good-sized trees to the west of the building.

Ravine Park, Bourquin Cr east access, a number of large trees in the park.

Chilliwack

Elk Creek Rainforest, Chilliwack Forest District.

10665 Standeven Rd, East Chilliwack.

Chilliwack Golf and Country Club, 41894 Yale Rd West, Greendale.

Fairfield Island Park, 46000 Clare Ave, Fairfield Island, small young trees.

Canadian Forces Base, Keith Wilson Rd and Vedder Rd, Vedder Crossing, many fine and large open-grown trees.

Stó:lo Centre, 7201 Vedder Rd, Sardis, a very wide-spreading tree.

Townsend Park, SW corner of Ashwell Rd and Hodgins Ave, at the west end of the park, a number of young trees.

University College of the Fraser Valley, 45600 Airport Rd.

North shore of Cultus Lake, Park Drive. Many exceptional trees can easily be viewed while walking the beach.

Sunnyside Campground, Cultus Lake.

Teapot Hill, Cultus Lake. A half hike up a steep hill brings you one of the largest Douglas Firs in the area.

Delta

Sunbury Park, Centre St and Dunlop Rd, North Delta, four massive trees, the largest specimen 132 cm DBH with an approximate height of forty-five metres. The trees are growing thirty metres to the north of the baseball diamond on the slope down to the historic fishing village of Annieville.

Heath Elementary School, 11364-72 Ave, North Delta, a large tree to the south of the school at the edge of the playing fields.

Langley

272 St and 8 Ave, Southeast Langley.

9040 Trattle St, Ft Langley.

9094 Church St, Ft Langley.

9136 King St, Ft Langley.

22089 Telegraph Trail, Walnut Grove, a grove of large trees.

Richmond

9400 Alexandra Rd.

9791 Alexandra Rd, 90 cm DBH.

Millennium Botanical Garden and Arboretum, N McLennan Community Park, Granville Ave and Garden City Rd.

Surrey

18558- 56 Ave, Cloverdale*.

St Oswald Anglican Church, 19016- 96 Ave, Port Kells*.

1990- 134 St, South Surrey*.

Bell Park, 136 St and 18 Ave, South Surrey*.

Mound Farm, 168 St and 50 Ave, Cloverdale*.

13600- 55A Ave and 13614- 56 Ave, Newton*.

14158 Hyland Rd, Newton*.

Hwy 1. This large stump is decorated with commemorative crosses.

15100 - 22 Ave, South Surrey* a very tall tree measured at forty-eight metres high.

Park at Kilkee Pl, Newton*.

Green Timbers Arboretum, 9800- 140 St, Whalley.

Pseudotsuga menziesii, bark and branching pattern

Pseudotsuga menziesii

Douglas Fir

Did You Know?

The last ancient rainforest in the South Fraser Region is found in the Elk Creek Rainforest in Chilliwack. To access this magnificent stand of old growth Douglas Fir take the Annis Road exit from Highway 1. Cross Annis Road and travel east on Hack Brown Road, which parallels Highway 1. Turn right on Nixon Road; turn left on Ruddock Road and travel up the switchbacks to the top of Ruddock Road. The top of Ruddock Road is approximately 450 metres above sea level.

The access to the Elk Creek Giants is, at the present time, through private property. The landowner of the access point is Mr. Clint Marvin; the giant trees are located on Crown Land just below Elk Creek Falls.

This stand of trees is unparalleled anywhere in the South Fraser Region. The Douglas Firs are colossal giants reaching eighty-eight metres and more in height. It would take fifty-nine people of average height standing on each other's shoulders to equal the height of these tall trees. They range from 210–270 cm diameter at breast height. Their circumference ranges from 7.3–8.2 metres. Many of these beautiful ancient trees rise up, unbranched for 30 metres, with great stovepipe-like trunks. In 1492, when Columbus arrived in North America, some of these firs, now 450–500 plus years old, were young trees.

This outstanding natural area, with its gigantic trees and surrounding pristine, ancient mossy forest deserves immediate protection from the logging activities that are slated to occur there in the near future. The Elk Creek Giants are, in size and age, comparable to the great forest at Green Timbers in Surrey that was completely logged in 1930.

In addition to the Elk Creek Giants, the watershed contains many huge *Thuja plicata*, Western Red Cedar trees that are easily the largest in the South Fraser Region as well.

• In Cultus Lake, thirty metres southeast of the entry kiosk to the Sunnyside Campground, there sits a massive old Douglas Fir tree, with a DBH of 240 cm. A tree of similar size was removed recently from the same area; the age of this tree, as calculated from the tree rings, was 458 years old. Some of the rings were so tiny they were examined with a hand lens.

• Massive Douglas Fir trees shade tiny St Oswald's Anglican Church, in Port Kells, Surrey, which was built in 1911. The church is a lovely example of a Late Victorian eclectic architectural style. The simple white painted façade with its pale green trim resembles spartan Early American meeting houses. The altar and cross inside the sanctuary are made of cypress from the Mount of Olives and were carved in Switzerland. St Oswald's, one of Surrey's oldest churches, celebrated its ninetieth anniversary May 5, 2001 with the opening of a new memorial garden.

Elk Creek Giants, *Pseudotsuga menziesii,* Chilliwack

Pseudotsuga menziesii, cones

- In June of 1964 Premier William Bennett opened the Port Mann Bridge, marking the official opening of the Trans Canada Highway through the Fraser Valley. The route of the freeway closely followed that of the Old Telegraph Trail. Many farmers bitterly fought the expropriation of their land for the freeway. Of these, Charlie Perkins of Port Kells had built a small park on his property to honour his fallen air force comrades from World War I. A huge ivy-clad Fir tree stood proudly in one corner of the park, over which Charlie stood guard as the construction crew advanced. The stubborn farmer aroused such a protest in the community that the highways department finally engineered a curve around the old Fir. Unfortunately, the tree was later vandalized by fire and now only a tall stump remains standing. Small crosses are visible amongst the ivy covering the stump honouring the young men of the First World War.

- One hundred and twenty-one Douglas Fir trees were planted on March 15, 1930 to mark the beginning of reforestation in British Columbia in the Green Timbers Inaugural Plantation in Surrey. Harry Baker and his brother Fred prepared a thirty metre

by thirty metre plot of land for the planting.

It was a wet spring and the rain turned the ground into a mud hole. Harry and Fred found it difficult to dig the drainage ditches needed to drain the site and to clear away the stumps and logging slash. The stumps caused special problems and Harry flagged down traffic on Pacific Highway (later named Fraser Highway) while his friend Tom Wells loosened the huge stumps by blasting them. Horses pulled off the stumps and root balls and the huge depressions were filled with soil. A large two-handled scraper called a "skip" was attached to a long cable and then to a team of horses to drag soil into the root ball holes. As the planting day loomed near, Harry laid out planks of clear cedar for the dignitaries to keep their feet clean. March 15, 1930 was dry. Harry Baker, son of Fred Baker, one of the protestors to the removal of the virgin forest at Green Timbers, helped the dignitaries plant the tiny seedlings. On March 15, 1990, during the sixtieth anniversary Commemorative Replica planting of the original Inaugural Plantation, Harry Baker was invited back again, this time as an honoured planter.

Pterocarya fraxinifolia
Caucasian Wingnut

Pterocarya fraxinifolia, foliage

Where to see the trees:
Surrey

Darts Hill Garden Park, 1660- 168 St, South Surrey, Magnolia Walk and Pasture.

Caucasian Wingnut is exceedingly rare in the South Fraser Region. It is native to southwest Asia, where it grows twenty-five metres high. Caucasian Wingnut has very large, 20–40 cm long, pinnately compound leaves. The eleven to twenty-one oval leaflets, are olive green as they unfurl, age to dark green and drop green in the fall. Showy catkins appear in June and hang in long pendulous racemes from the branches. Winged nutlets, ripening in August, hang from their long stalks and persist well into the winter. The seed wings of this tree are stubby and rounded. Caucasian Wingnut is often a multi-stemmed tree.

Pterocarya stenoptera
Chinese Wingnut

Pterocarya stenoptera, Darts Hill Garden Park, Surrey

Chinese Wingnut

Pterocarya stenoptera, foliage

Where to see the trees:

Surrey
Darts Hill Garden Park, 1660- 168 St, South Surrey, Garden Bed 28.

Chinese Wingnut is exceedingly rare in the South Fraser Region. It is native to China, where it reaches a mature height of thirty metres. Chinese Wingnut has very large, 20–40 cm long, pinnately compound leaves. The leaf stalk, which holds the eleven to twenty-three oval leaflets, is winged. This feature differentiates Chinese Wingnut from Caucasian Wingnut, which does not have a winged leaf stalk. Very long showy catkins, up to 30 cm, appear in June and hang in long pendulous racemes from the branches. Two long narrow birdlike wings attend the nutlets, which ripen in August.

Pyrus calleryana Aristocrat™

Aristocrat™ Pear

Pyrus calleryana Aristocrat™, fall colour and fruit

Pyrus calleryana Aristocrat™

Aristocrat™ Pear

Where to see the trees:

Chilliwack

5405- 5501 Alpine Cr, north of Teskey Way, Promontory Heights.

Alpine Cr south of Braeside, Promontory Heights.

46664 Braeside, Promontory Heights

University College of the Fraser Valley, 45600 Airport Rd, seven trees in a circle at the Airport Rd turnaround.

Surrey

5667- 184 St, Cloverdale.

17257- 26A Ave, South Surrey.

17260- 26A Ave, South Surrey.

An open-spreading branch with a pyramidal silhouette identifies Aristocrat™ Pear in the winter months. It reaches a mature height of 12–14 metres with a spread of 6–7.5 metres. The very shiny leaves undulate at the margins. Dark green throughout the growing season, the leaves turn outstanding fiery oranges and purple reds in the fall. The flowers are produced in April in very dense clusters. Each flower is five-petalled, white and very showy. Aristocrat™ Pear produces a small hard pear-like fruit about the size of a dime in October.

Pyrus calleryana 'Capital'

Capital Pear

Pyrus calleryana 'Capital', foliage and fruit

Where to see the trees:

Chilliwack

5469- 5489 Highroad Cr, Promontory Heights.

46427- 46443 Mullins Rd, Promontory Heights.

5541- 5595 Teskey Rd, Promontory Heights.

SE Corner of College St at Victoria Ave.

Mary St at Kipp Ave on the east side.

A columnar form identifies Capital Pear in the winter months. It reaches a mature height of ten metres with a slender spread of 3.5 metres. The lustrous dark green leaves turn reddish purple in the fall. The flowers, produced in April, are in very dense clusters. Each flower is five-petalled, white and very showy. Capital Pear produces a small hard pear-like fruit about the size of a dime in October.

Pyrus calleryana Chanticleer®,
Douglas Park, Langley

Pyrus calleryana Chanticleer®, flowers

Strongly upright branches identify Chanticleer® Pear in the winter months. It reaches a mature height of twelve metres with a spread of 4.5 metres. The glossy leaves are medium green throughout the growing season and turn purple red in the fall. The flowers are produced in April in very dense clusters. Each flower is five-petalled, white and very showy. Chanticleer® Pear produces a small hard pear-like fruit about the size of a dime in October.

Where to see the trees:

Abbotsford

City Hall, 32315 South Fraser Way, a row along the entrance road on the west side of the building.

Delair Park, Delair and Old Yale Rds.

Median planting on McClure Rd from Gladwin east to 33300 block McClure.

Chilliwack

46423- 46497 Edgemont Pl, Promontory Heights.

5722 Thornhill St, Promontory Heights.

On South Sumas Rd between Tyson Rd and Wiltshire Rd, on the north to south side, Sardis.

Langley

City Park, 207 St and 48 Ave, Langley City, several good-sized trees at the west entrance to the park.

Douglas Park, 20550 Douglas Cr, Langley City, a row of street trees on the west side of the Park.

Douglas Cr, Langley City, street tree planting with *Robinia* 'Purple Robe' and *Magnolia kobus*.

Richmond

Francis Rd from Ash St to Garden City Rd, a street tree planting.

Granville Ave from Riverdale to No 1 Rd, a street tree planting.

Surrey

11294- 159B St, Fleetwood.

11318- 159B St, Fleetwood.

Provincial Courthouse, 14340- 57 Ave, Newton, south of the building.

On 152 St from 20 Ave to 29A Ave, South Surrey.

Pyrus communis
Common Pear or Domestic Pear

Pyrus communis, flowers

Pyrus communis, Gwynne Vaughan Park, Chilliwack

Where to see the trees:

Abbotsford
University College of the Fraser Valley, Abbotsford Campus, King Rd. At the east entrance of the campus off McKenzie Rd, two mature trees stand, remnants of an early orchard.

Chilliwack
Gwynne Vaughan Park, Williams Rd and Hope River Rd, Fairfield Island, an orchard of old trees.

45652 Princess Ave.

Delta
Pioneer Library, 4683- 51 St, Ladner, an orchard of twelve mature trees on the west side of the Library.

Richmond
2460 River Rd. A very tall tree with very large fruit, fifteen metres high is visible from the dike on the east side of the house.

9411 Beckwith Rd, a huge specimen with a DBH of 110 cm and a height of twenty metres with tiny perfect pears.

Steveston Park, 4111 Moncton St, Steveston.

Surrey
Darts Hill Garden Park, 1660- 168 St, South Surrey, Orchard.

Very common in the South Fraser Region, Common Pear is originally from Europe and western Asia. Pear trees can reach great size but are usually pruned to lower heights to make harvesting of the fruit easier. The leaves are lustrous, deep green and toothed along the margins. In late October to November, the leaves color a satisfying purple-red. The flowers are borne abundantly in April to May. They are five-petalled, white and very showy. The bark of mature trees is cracked into a checkerboard pattern. Barlett Pear is one of the more common cultivated pear varieties grown locally.

Did You Know?
The orchard of Common Pear and English Holly trees at the Pioneer library in Ladner, is growing on land originally owned by William H. Ladner, the founder of the community which now bears his name. Paul Ladner, his son, planted the orchard surrounded the farmhouse which burned down in 1980, almost a century after its construction. Paul Ladner sold sprigs of bright red-berried English Holly at Christmas time locally and to Eastern Canada and beyond. His widow, Winifred continued to market cut Holly branches after his death in 1944.

Pyrus communis
Common Pear or Domestic Pear

- A two-year-old pear tree, 1.5–1.8 metres tall, cost seventy-five cents in 1879, when purchased from P.T. Johnston and Co., a nursery in Victoria. The 1896 catalogue of Layritz Nurseries Limited, another Victoria nursery grower lists twenty-nine different pear varieties, very few of which are commercially available today.

Pyrus pyrifolia
Oriental Pear Tree, Japanese or Chinese Pear or Apple Pear

Oriental Pear Trees are not common in the South Fraser Region as ornamental trees, though there are several small commercial orchards. Native to China, it flowers profusely in early April. The leaves are ovate with a finely toothed edge. Fall colour is pleasantly orange-red. The tasty fruit, ripening in November, is remarkably large, up to 8 cm across, and round in shape. Trees can grow to ten to twelve metres high with a round form.

Where to see the trees:

Delta

4691 Arthur Dr, Ladner, a small specimen.

Pyrus salicifolia 'Pendula'
Weeping Willowleaf Pear or Weeping Silver Pear

Weeping Willowleaf Pear is a small pendulous tree reaching five to six metres in height. Its strong weeping form and elegant silver foliage make it suitable for use as a specimen tree or focal point in the landscape. The branches stick out higgledy-piggledy giving the tree a ragged weeping outline as compared to the precise umbrella shape of other small trees such as Weeping Mulberry. Willow-like, the leaves are slim and silver grey. The cream flowers of Weeping Willowleaf Pear, appearing in April, are held in thick bunches. The firm greenish-yellow fruit is a tiny pear, which ripens in October. Weeping Willowleaf Pear is not common in the South Fraser Region.

Pyrus salicifolia 'Pendula', fruit

Where to see the trees:

Surrey

Darts Hill Garden Park, 1660- 168 St, South Surrey, Garden Beds 4 and 33.

The creation of a thousand forests is in one acorn.

Ralph Waldo Emerson (1803–1882),
American essayist, poet and philosopher

Quercus acutissima

Sawtooth Oak, Bristle Tipped Oak or Oriental Chestnut Oak

Native to the Himalayas, China, Korea and Japan, Sawtooth Oak reaches twenty metres in height at maturity. The trees are often pyramidal in youth with a round crown later in life. The leaves of Sawtooth Oak are very similar in shape to the American Chestnut. Each long lance-shaped leathery leaf is sharply toothed, each tooth is bristle tipped. The lustrous green leaves turn a tan brown colour very late in the fall, often hanging on young trees over the winter. The leaves emerge a showy bright yellow in the spring. The deep brown acorn is enclosed by a fringe of threadlike light brown scales, the scales cupping the nut like a miniature bird's nest. The bark of Sawtooth Oak is furrowed, corky, pale grey to black in colour. Sawtooth Oak is very rare in the South Fraser Region.

Quercus coccinea

Where to see the trees:

Richmond
Millennium Botanical Garden and Arboretum, N McLennan Community Park, Granville Ave and Garden City Rd.

Surrey
Darts Hill Garden Park, 1660- 168 St, South Surrey, Garden Bed 16 and Magnolia Walk and Pasture.

Sequoia Drive, west end of 80 Ave, Fleetwood.

Langley
Kwantlen University College, 20901 Langley Bypass, Langley City, two trees west of the flag poles.

Quercus alba, Morton Arboretum, Lisle, Illinois

Quercus alba, foliage

Very rare in the South Fraser Region, White Oak is native to southern Ontario and Quebec, into Maine to Minnesota and south to Florida and Texas. In its native range it is a stately deciduous tree reaching a height of thirty metres. The leaves are typical oak-shaped with seven to nine gently rounded lobes. As the leaves emerge in the spring they are felty and pinkish in colour. When mature, the dark green leaves are hairless on the top and bottom, while the bottom remains pale in colour. The fall colour ranges from brown to orange-red. The acorn is oval in shape with a short knobby cap that encloses 1/4 to 1/3 of the acorn. The bark is a very light ash grey and its colour is the reason the tree is named White Oak. The bark texture is very variable; it can be scaly or fissured into short vertical blocks.

Where to see the trees:

Chilliwack

Family Place Centre, 45845 Wellington Ave, a magnificent old tree, with a DBH of 150 cm.

Did You Know?

Built in 1949, the bungalow-styled building of Family Place Centre was originally the city of Chilliwack's Library.

Quercus bicolor

Swamp White Oak

Where to see the trees:

Richmond

Garry Point Park, west end of Moncton St, Steveston, a group of young trees on the south side of the parking lot.

Very rare in the South Fraser Region, Swamp White Oak is native to southern Ontario and in the area adjacent to Montreal in Quebec. Its range continues south to Georgia and west into Michigan and Arkansas. Swamp White Oak is a medium-sized deciduous tree reaching a height of fifteen to eighteen metres in its native range. The leathery leaves are widest toward the tip from the middle of the leaf and taper to a wedge shape at their base. The leaves are variable, sometimes wavy edged but usually lobed with the lobes triangular in shape and blunt at the tip. The upper surface is lustrous dark green while the underside is covered with lovely soft white fuzz, hence the species name bicolor. The midrib and leaf stalk are yellow and threadlike hairs subtend the downy buds. The fall colour of Swamp White Oak is yellowish brown. The acorn is oval in shape; hooked scales distinguish the cap that encloses 1/3 to 1/2 of the acorn. The bark is a greyish brown and furrowed when mature.

Quercus x *bimundorum* Crimson Spire™
Syn. *Quercus* 'Crimschmidt'

Crimson Spire™ Oak

Where to see the trees:

Chilliwack

Fairfield Island Park, 46000 Clare Ave, Fairfield Island, on the east property line of park.

Crimson Spire™ Oak is new to the South Fraser Region. The parents of this hybrid oak are *Quercus robur* and *Quercus alba*. Crimson Spire™ Oak has been well named; at maturity it reaches a height of fourteen metres with a slim spread of 4.5 metres. The fastigiate branches are tightly held parallel to the main trunk, which is characteristic of the English Oak parent. The dark green to bluish green mildew-resistant leaves turn deep red in the fall, a result of the White Oak parentage of this cultivar. A strong exclamation point in the landscape, Crimson Spire™ Oak is a welcome addition to the limited list of good columnar trees.

Quercus canariensis, The Glades, Surrey

Quercus canariensis, foliage

Very rare in the South Fraser Region, Mirbeck's Oak is native to North Africa and the Iberian Peninsula. In its native range, it is a tall deciduous tree reaching a height of forty metres but it is seldom more than thirty metres in cultivation. The leaves are oval in shape and shallowly lobed. As the leaves emerge in the spring they are woolly and rust brown in colour. When mature, the dark green leaves are hairless on the top surface with remnant rusty brown hairs on the lower midrib and leaf stalk. A whitish bloom clothes the bottom of the leaf. The fall colour is yellow brown and the leaves often persist well into the fall. The acorn is oval in shape with a downy-scaled cap that encloses 1/3 of the acorn. The thick bark is black.

Where to see the trees:

Surrey

The Glades, 561- 172 St, South Surrey*, east of house on the path to the frog pond.

Darts Hill Garden Park, 1660- 168 St, South Surrey, Garden Bed 37.

Quercus coccinea

Scarlet Oak

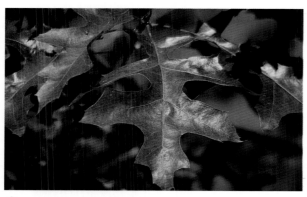

Quercus coccinea, fall colour

Quercus coccinea
Scarlet Oak

Where to see the trees:
Abbotsford
Mill Lake Park, west of the Mill Lake Rd parking lot, two young trees.

Chilliwack
46000 Acacia Dr, a huge tree.

45573 Princess Ave, a good-sized tree.

7032 Chilliwack River Rd, Sardis.

7700 block Chilliwack River Rd, Sardis, a large tree on the east side of the road.

On South Sumas Rd from Silverthorne east, Sardis.

Sardis Park, School Lane and Manuel Rd, Sardis, several young trees planted around the playground.

University College of the Fraser Valley, 45600 Airport Rd.

Langley
Kwantlen University College, 20901 Langley Bypass, Langley City, two trees adjacent to the pedestrian overpass.

Williams Park, 6600 block 238 St, Salmon River Uplands.

Richmond
Garden City from Williams Rd to Frances Rd, a boulevard planting on the west side of Garden City.

Fantasy Garden World, 10800 No 5 Rd.

Southarm Park, Garden City Rd and Williams Rd.

Surrey
10410 King George Hwy, Whalley.

10090 King George Hwy, Whalley.

White Rock
White Rock Elementary School, 1273 Fir St, one tree planted at the east end of a row of Red Oaks on the south side of the school.

Quercus coccinea, Kwantlen University College, Langley.

Commonly planted in the South Fraser Region, Scarlet Oak is native to southern Ontario and Quebec, into Maine to Minnesota and Missouri and south to Florida. In its native range it is a stately deciduous tree reaching a height of thirty metres with branches ascending upright with an oval winter silhouette. The large leaves, up to 12 cm long and wide, are the familiar oak shape; usually with seven acutely pointed bristle-tipped lobes. The sinuses between the lobes are deeply "C" shaped. The leaves emerge first in the spring densely white and silky then turn bright yellow. When mature, they are shiny green and hairless on the top surface while the axils of the veins on the bottom are tufted with hair. The fall colour is a rich scarlet or deep red. The dormant bud resembles a rugby ball in shape. About the size of a penny, the small acorn of Scarlet Oak is oval to round. A deep cup, covered in smooth scales, encloses 1/3 to 1/2 of the acorn. The bark is a very light grey-brown and formed into thin scaly plates.

Quercus garryana, Fort Rodd Hill and Fisgard Lighthouse National Historic Sites, Victoria

Quercus garryana, foliage

The only oak native to British Columbia, Garry Oak is common in Victoria and the Saanich Peninsula and Gulf Islands. It is very rare in the South Fraser Region, only appearing as natural stands on the south side of Sumas Mountain in Abbotsford and at Yale in the Fraser Canyon. Garry Oak are often picturesque when they are open grown, with their stout and twisted limbs. Trees may reach twenty-five metres in height but often much less on rocky sites. The leathery lustrous leaves have five to seven lobes. The dark green lobes are very rounded with narrow but deep sinuses. The topmost lobe is often delicately notched at its tip, suggesting one or two small teeth. The underside of the leaf is greenish-brown and often covered in a woolly brown felt. Fall colour is yellow-brown. The acorn cup is densely hairy as well. The strongly furrowed and ridged brownish-grey bark of Garry Oak is an attractive feature of this native oak.

Quercus garryana

Garry Oak or Oregon White Oak

Where to see the trees:

Abbotsford

Quadling Farm, 39897 Quadling Rd. One km west of the residence on a private farm road, there is a grove of Garry Oak, ranging from the youngest seedling to teenagers with a DBH of 10 cm to very old specimens with a DBH of 30 cm plus.

Langley

Kwantlen University College, 20901 Langley Bypass, Langley City, a small specimen growing on the west boulevard adjacent to the Highway 10 Bypass.

Richmond

Millennium Botanical Garden and Arboretum, N McLennan Community Park, Granville Ave and Garden City Rd.

Surrey

Green Timbers Park and Urban Forest, 140 St and 96 Ave, Fleetwood*.

Did You Know?

The stand of Garry Oak in Abbotsford are growing on a south-facing rock bluff at the base of Sumas Mountain in the shade of huge Douglas Fir trees. These trees are very irregular and lopsided, as they must compete for light. While Garry Oak are common in the Victoria area, it is very rare to find a naturally occurring Garry Oak stand on this side of Georgia Strait. This part of Sumas Mountain has not been logged and is likely Crown land but access to the trees is through private property. This stand of Garry Oak trees deserves protection as an Ecological Reserve.

Quercus palustris
Pin Oak or Swamp Oak

Where to see the trees:
Abbotsford
Delair Park, Delair and Old Yale Rds.

Hougen Park, south off Highway 1 on Cole Rd.

Matsqui Centennial Auditorium, 32315 South Fraser Way, a row of young trees on the east side.

Chilliwack
The Waverly, 8445 Young St.

Canadian Forces Base, Keith Wilson Rd and Vedder Rd, Vedder Crossing, a grove of young trees south of the RCMP Complex on Calais Cr.

University College of the Fraser Valley, 45600 Airport Rd, west of Building C, Health Sciences.

Delta
Municipal Hall, 4500 Clarence Taylor Cr, Ladner, three young trees.

Langley
Kwantlen University College, 20901 Langley Bypass, Langley City, an entry row planted in 1993 on both sides of Kwantlen Way.

Williams Park, 6600 block 238 St, Salmon River Uplands.

Richmond
McLean Park, 2500 McLean Ave, in the Hamilton area.

Cambie Rd, from No 4 Rd to Shell Rd, a street tree planting on the north side.

Rosedale
Minter Gardens, 52892 Bunker Rd, a grove of young trees at the north end of the Formal Garden.

Surrey
South Surrey Arena, 2199- 148 St, South Surrey.

Quercus palustris, Kwantlen University College

Ubiquitous, Pin Oak is often grown as a park or street tree in the South Fraser Region. In its native range from southern Ontario in a small area adjacent to the Great Lakes and from Massachusetts to Delaware and west into Wisconsin and Arkansas, it reaches a mature height of eighteen to twenty-one metres. The dark lustrous green leaves are pale on the underside and emerge a bright yellow in the early spring. A bristle tips each of the five to seven slender lobes and the sinuses separating the lobes are deeply "U" shaped. The fall colour is usually a deep red and the leaves in some years are held on the stems until the new growth pushes them off the following spring. The branching habit is the most distinguishing feature of this medium-sized tree. The trunk is clothed in many small flexible branches, which is very different than the stout limbs of other oaks. The lower branches swoop to the ground, the branches in midcrown are horizontal, while the branches at the top of the tree ascend upwards. Pin Oak has a very pyramidal form in youth; at maturity it becomes an upright oval. The tiny acorn is roundish with

Quercus palustris, fall colour

only its base covered by a thin-scaled cup. The smooth grey bark of young trees gives way to low narrow ridges as the tree ages.

Quercus palustris 'Crownright'

Crownright Pin Oak

The more upright habit of Crownright Pin Oak distinguishes it from the species, Pin Oak. The branches ascend at a 30–60 degree angle from the main trunk, avoiding the low-slung branches which swoop to ground that are typical of the common Pin Oak.

Where to see the trees:

Abbotsford

Median planting on Old Yale Rd to McClure Rd from Townline Rd to Clearbrook Rd, in front of Ellwood Park.

Chilliwack

Fairfield Island Park, 46000 Clare Ave, Fairfield Island, southwest corner of park.

Townsend Park, southwest corner of Ashwell Rd and Hodgins Ave, at the west end of the park, in the outfield of the baseball park, behind baseball diamonds 3, 4, 5 and 6.

Surrey

7488- 122A St, Newton.

14476- 18A Ave, South Surrey.

2050- 129B St, South Surrey.

2065- 129B St, South Surrey.

Quercus petræa
Durmast Oak or Sessile Oak

Where to see the trees:
Surrey

Green Timbers Arboretum, 9800- 140 St, Whalley, in the southeast portion of the arboretum.

Very rare in the South Fraser Region, Durmast Oak is native to Europe and western Asia. It is a stately tree in its native range reaching a height of thirty-five metres. Similar in appearance to the common English Oak, Durmast Oak differs in several very important ways. The lustrous dark green leaves of Durmast Oak have four to six pairs of rounded lobes and but do not have the earlobe-like leaf base that is typical of English Oak. In addition the acorns of English Oak are held on long stalks while the acorns of Durmast oak are stalkless. The leaves of Durmast Oak have long yellow stalks or petioles while the leaves of English Oak are very short stalked or stalkless. Garry Oak, our native Oak with its rounded leaf lobes usually has a brown fuzzy leaf underside while the underside of Durmast Oak is whitish or somewhat hairy.

Quercus phellos
Willow Oak

Where to see the trees:
Langley

24355- 48 Ave, Salmon River Uplands, on the east side of the entry driveway

Kwantlen University College, 20901 Langley Bypass, Langley City, a small specimen growing on the boulevard to the west of the main entrance adjacent to the Highway 10 Bypass.

Surrey

12625- 68 Ave, Newton.

12713- 68 Ave, Newton.

Quercus phellos, foliage

Native from New York to Florida and west to Missouri and Texas, Willow Oak is not commonly grown in the South Fraser Region. In its native range it reaches a mature height of twelve to eighteen metres. The dull green leaves of Willow Oak are long and narrow, quite willow-like in appearance with a wavy margin.

The fall colour ranges from yellow to burnt orange. Willow Oak colours late and holds its leaves well into the late fall. The branching pattern is similar to Pin Oak, the lower branches sweep to the ground, while the branches mid-crown are more horizontal or ascending. At maturity it has an upright oval to round shape and a distinct fine texture, which is unusual among the oaks grown locally. The roundish acorn is very small, to one cm, the cup just covering the top of the acorn.

Quercus robur
English Oak, Pedunculate Oak or Truffle Oak

Quercus robur, very unusual form, Chilliwack River Road, Chilliwack

Quercus robur, 88 Avenue, Fort Langley

English Oak is the most common Oak found in the South Fraser Region. In some areas it has become naturalized and its acorns are an important source of food for wildlife. It is native to Europe, North Africa and the Caucasus, where it reaches massive size. The largest trees in the South Fraser Region are about one hundred years old and of reasonable size. In Great Britain one-thousand-year-old trees, such as the Major Oak in Sherwood Forest are uncommon but speak to the toughness and longevity of the

Where to see the trees:

Abbotsford

2699 McMillan Rd, east side.

Hougen Park, south off Highway 1 on Cole Rd.

Fishtrap Park North, Old Yale Rd and McClure Rd, three trees at the north end of the parking lot by the Judo Club.

Quercus robur
English Oak, Pedunculate Oak or Truffle Oak

Where to see the trees:

Chilliwack

42045 Yale Rd West, Greendale.

Stó:lo Centre, 7201 Vedder Rd, Sardis.

7032 Chilliwack River Rd, Sardis.

7045 Eden Dr, Sardis, a tree with very good form well framed by a concrete curb.

47813 McGuire Rd, Sardis, a magnificent old farm row of several different species of trees on the south side of the road with two large English Oak.

Yarrow Central Park, southeast corner of Kehler St and Yarrow Central Rd, a large specimen with a DBH of 85 cm on the southwest side of the park.

Delta

North side of Memorial Park, 47 Ave and Delta St, Ladner.

Southeast corner of Delta St and 47 Ave, Ladner, a row of medium-sized trees of 50 cm DBH.

Delta Secondary School, 4615- 51 St, Ladner, southeast corner. This is a large specimen with a DBH of 75 cm.

Delta Secondary School, 4615- 51 St, Ladner, southeast corner, several large specimens of 75 DBH.

John Oliver Municipal Park, 11600 block Ladner Trunk Rd, a huge tree with a DBH of 104 cm.

1100- 56 St, Tsawwassen. The eleven English Oak trees on the street easement were designated by Delta Council as Heritage Trees on August 13, 1990*.

10785 Ladner Trunk Rd.

Langley

22843- 88 Ave, Ft Langley.

Fort Langley National Historic Site, 23433 Mavis St, Ft Langley.

John Nash residence, 8985 Nash St, Ft Langley.

Glen Valley Regional Park, Two-Bit Bar, 272 St and River Rd, Northeast Langley, a large specimen planted to the northeast of the Hassall House.

species. English Oak grows to a wide-spreading roundish form with huge scaffold branches. The Major Oak has a gigantic crown spread of ninety-two metres. The leaves emerge a lovely chartreuse and age to medium to dark green. They are short stalked, with three to six pairs of blunt lobes. The best identifying feature is the earlobe-like base of the leaf, which easily separates this oak from most others. The yellow-brown fall colour is unremarkable in the South Fraser Region in comparison to the colourful autumn display of Red, Pin and Scarlet Oak. The large oval acorns, which are often produced in clusters of two and threes, are held on a long stalk, hence the name Pedunculate Oak, peduncle meaning stalk. The acorns fall in October. The acorn cup encloses 1/4 to 1/3 of the acorn. Deeply fissured and grey-brown, the bark is useful for winter identification along with the tightly clustered arrangement of the branches and yellow-brown buds.

Did You Know?

• The English Oak trees on the north side of Memorial Park in Ladner, Delta were planted on Coronation Day, May 12, 1937 to mark the coronation of King George VI.

• The English Oak planted at the southeast corner of Delta Secondary School has a plaque at its base that is dedicated as follows, "This oak of Windsor Forest in memory of Mrs. E.A. Sauerberg First President Delta's Women's Institute 1933–1949." Ernest and Elsa Sauerberg were among the first to buy property in the Delta Manor area of Ladner. In 1930 Ernest began a wholesale egg business including an egg grading station. In addition to her volunteer work with the Women's Institute, Elsa Henrietta Sauerberg was known in the community an art teacher and painter of fine china.

English Oak, Pedunculate Oak or Truffle Oak

On May 12, 1937, when King George VI was crowned King of England, Canadian communities celebrated the occasion in many different ways. Commemorative tree planting, particularly the planting of English Oaks, was common. This English Oak tree on the school grounds in Delta was one of many planted as seedlings or acorns to mark the coronation. It was actually planted the week previous to the Coronation Day by Irene Kirkland, Delta's May Queen for 1936-37. The Delta's Farmers Institute organized the event. The Oak tree was just a tiny seedling. The hope was that it would "grow into a lordly oak." The Oak grew undisturbed until the Women's Institute decided to place a plaque at the base of the tree on April 26, 1954, honouring their first president, Mrs. Sauerberg. The minutes of the Women's Institute in 1953 reported that the sixteen-year-old tree was "25 ft high (and) 10 inches thick".[1]

• The Women's Institutes of Canada was founded in 1897. The motto of the Women's Institutes was "For Home and Country." During their active years, the Institutes might be described as the voice of women in Canada. Often they were formed to benefit farmwomen. Members welcomed newcomers into their communities. They helped with fund raising and the establishment of hospitals, libraries, parks, youth training work projects, dental clinics, and scholarship and bursary funds. They were very active during World Wars One and Two. Women's Institutes in all locales comforted and cared for the sick, and the homeless.

• In 1953, there were thirty branches in the South Fraser division of the Women's Institutes of Canada. At a spring conference in Cloverdale in Surrey at that time, two hundred and fifty women gathered to send a resolution to Ottawa supporting the implementation of a National Heath Plan. In addition to such weighty national matters, the group also criticized the dangers inherent in gangster radio shows and crime comics. Today the good works originally sponsored by the Women's Institutes of Canada have largely been taken over by other service groups.

Where to see the trees:

Langley

21799- 49 Ave, Murrayville.

24520 Fraser Hwy, Southeast Langley, two large trees.

Richmond

6380 Blundell Rd, south of the playground.

Blundell Elementary School, 6480 Blundell Rd, a large tree with a DBH of 90 cm on the west side of the school on the lawn.

6900- 7700 River Rd, a very fine street planting adjacent to the dike of mostly English Oak, but interplanted with some Elm, Horse Chestnut and Black Cottonwood and European Mountain Ash.

6911 Camsell Cr, a huge tree with as DBH of 105 cm.

Surrey

1987- 2986 King George Hwy, South Surrey, forty-eight trees.

13997- 90 Ave at 140 St*.

Surrey Centre Cemetery, 16671 Old Mclennan Rd, Cloverdale*.

9381- 160 Ave, Fleetwood*.

Morgan Creek Golf Course, 3500 Morgan Creek Way, South Surrey. This English Oak is not clearly visible from the street but is located on the third tee of the golf course. It is notable because it was planted as an acorn from a tree in Sherwood Forest in Great Britain.

White Rock

White Rock Elementary School, 1273 Fir St. The English Oak tree is not on the school grounds but is on the north side of Roper Avenue directly across from the old school buildings.

[1] Scycher, G. *B.C. Historical News*- Fall 1995, page 5.

Quercus robur

English Oak, Pedunculate Oak or Truffle Oak

• Twenty-one -year-old John Oliver arrived penniless in British Columbia in May of 1877 from Ontario. He worked hard as an axe man on a survey party blazing trail to the coast for the Canadian Pacific Railway that summer. With money in his pocket, he lived in a cabin and homesteaded 65 hectares of land near Sullivan in Surrey. He quickly became involved in municipal politics, becoming Clerk of the Municipal Council. In 1882, he sold his Surrey homestead and preempted a quarter section of land in East Delta, Mud Bay Flats, for $2.50 per hectare. John Oliver was one of the first settlers in this area of Delta. This parcel of land would later become known as the Oliver Farm and eventually become John Oliver Municipal Park.

Farming in Delta at that time was very difficult when the soil was wet particularly after heavy rains. The horses were shod in wooden shoes to prevent them from sinking into the gumbo-like mud. Some of the early settlers used three or four teams of oxen to pull their ploughs but even these beasts would sink to their knees in mud. John Oliver was the first farmer to drain his fields using a subsurface drainage system. His design was used successfully throughout Delta. Cedar planking 15 cm wide was joined to create a triangular pipe. The drainage pipe was buried approximately one metre below the fields with the apex of the triangle pointing up. The drainage pipes were placed every ten or twenty metres across the width of the field, with ditch outlets to the dykes.

"Honest" John Oliver carried on his political career, first as school trustee, then on Delta municipal council and becoming Reeve of Delta. Provincial politics beckoned and Oliver was elected the Minister of the Legislative Assembly (MLA) for the community of Delta. Straight from his farm in Mud Bay Flats, he would appear in his Sunday suit at the Provincial Legislature in Victoria. At first provincial politics were a struggle, but Oliver became an adept politician, becoming Minister of Agriculture in 1916. He finished his career in public service as the Liberal Premier of the Province of British Columbia. John Oliver died after a long battle with cancer while still in office August 17, 1927. As premier of the province, one of his final acts was to pass his Old Age Pension Bill, making British Columbia the first province to adopt this pivotal piece of legislation.

• The English Oak tree at the Fort Langley National Historic Site was planted by the Langley Women's Institute to mark the coronation of Queen Elizabeth II in 1953.

• The large English Oak at 8985 Nash Street, Fort Langley, with a DBH of 85 cm is part of the original landscaping of the front garden of the house built for John A. Nash, circa 1914. Mr. Nash was also the namesake for Nash Street. The small house is a typical example of the Craftsman Bungalow style of architecture prevalent at that time.

• Hassall House, situated between the railway tracks and the Fraser River in Glen Valley Regional Park, was purchased from the Soldier's Settlement Board. Jack Hassall, born in Birmingham, England in 1886, brought his wife, Christina, to the Glen Valley in 1918. Jack Hassall was a soldier in both the Boer and Great Wars. Mr. and Mrs. Hassall were not the original owners of the house, which was built in 1917, but purchased it before it was finished. Just to the north of the house, at the foot of 272 Street, called Jackman Road originally, the riverboat *Skeena* put passengers and freight ashore.

• Archie Payne, Langley's first municipal administrator (this term was later known

English Oak, Pedunculate Oak or Truffle Oak

as Reeve, then Mayor), returned from World War I with English Oak acorns in his kit. He planted the two trees at 21799- 49 Avenue as saplings at the site of the township of Langley's first municipal hall about 1925. The municipality eventually sold the property and the building was torn down but the two trees, which originally framed the municipal hall, remain.

• Coach drivers tied their teams of horses to the two English Oak trees in the yard at 24520 Fraser Highway, Langley, while stopping overnight en route to points east. This portion of Fraser Highway was originally Old Yale Road. Old Yale Road connected New Westminster to the Cariboo Road at Yale. It was the wagon road from New Westminster into the interior of British Columbia.

• The King George VI Highway, from the Patullo Bridge south to the American border in Surrey was officially opened on October 16, 1940 with a dedication ceremony at

'Royal Oak', *Quercus robur*, planted on King George VI Highway, Surrey

Peace Arch Park. At that time, Surrey was a rural community with a population of five thousand. The Highway's name was changed from Peace Arch to King George VI, during Their Majesties, King George VI and Queen Elizabeth's Royal Tour of Canada in 1939. The English Oaks were planted at that time along the length of the Highway, in honour of the new name. The English Oaks were planted at a spacing of 30 metres apart on both sides of the road from the Patullo Bridge to the Peace Arch. Today forty-eight of the possible nineteen hundred trees remain of that original 1939 installation. New trees planted south of 14 Avenue to replace the missing "Royal Oaks" ensure a continuing legacy.

The original "Royal Oaks" were likely sent as acorns and saplings to the British Columbia government from the Saville Gardens at the Royal Forest in Windsor, England, to mark the coronation of King George VI on May 12, 1937. A large number of Royal acorns were sent to Canada, as at least eight hundred saplings had been planted by October of 1939, as recorded in *British Columbia Pubic Works Magazine*.

New young Oaks have been propagated from acorns taken from the 1939 planting of the "Royal Oaks" that line the southern portion of the King George VI Highway. These saplings, which will be of plantable size in a few years, are part of the Surrey School Oak Tree Program. Children at three Cloverdale Elementary Schools have a young seedling registered in their name. When the trees are large enough, each child's tree will be planted along the King George VI Highway.

• The English Oak at Surrey Centre Cemetery was planted to commemorate the coronation of King George VI and Queen Elizabeth on May 12, 1937. One hundred citizens watched as Chas. Raine, with

Quercus robur

English Oak, Pedunculate Oak or Truffle Oak

Surrey Reeve J.T. Brown, planted the tree after speaking a few words about the history and role of the English Oak tree in the building of the British Empire. A bronze plaque is set at the tree's base on the boulevard of Old Mclennan Road.

• An English Oak was planted to commemorate the coronation of King George VI and Queen Elizabeth on May 12, 1937 on or near the school grounds of White Rock Elementary in White Rock. H.T. Thrift assisted in the planting of the young oak tree from Windsor Forest. Thrift dressed that day in his regimentals; the bright scarlet tunic given to him when he accepted the Queen's shilling and joined the Hampshire regiment in 1877. The White Rock Coronation Celebration Committee was able to get two hundred acorns and a score of young saplings from Windsor forest. As reported in the *Surrey Leader* "some of the acorns looked as though they had been too thoroughly fumigated upon entering Canada; some will surely survive and though not indigenous to this part of the country, will be lasting mementos of a great occasion." [2] Surrey Reeve J.T. Brown also attended the planting ceremony held in White Rock at 2:00 PM that Coronation Wednesday. Reeve Brown first proclaimed the King and Queen of the Coronation Day Carnival and presented to the children at the celebration Coronation mugs and medals. After the planting of the tree, there were sports for the children and a luncheon on the school grounds.

Quercus robur f. *fastigiata*

Columnar English Oak or Fastigiate English Oak

Reaching fifteen to eighteen metres high with a spread of 4.5 metres, Columnar English Oak is narrowly upright or columnar in form but the fastigiate branches undulate and twist as they ascend upward. The foliage and acorns are similar to the species. Columnar English Oak is uncommon in the South Fraser Region.

Where to see the trees:

Chilliwack
The Waverly, 8445 Young St, on the corner of the building near the main entrance.

Langley
Aldergrove Park, 271 St and 32 Ave, Aldergrove, a row of trees on the west side of the parking lot at the entrance to the park.

23253 Francis Ave, Fort Langley.

Richmond
Steveston Park, 4111 Moncton St, Steveston, north side of the Martial Arts Centre.

Surrey
17058 Hereford Place, Cloverdale.

17055 Hereford Place, Cloverdale, the entire street was planted in 1985.

50 metres east of the ferry slip, Barnston Island.

1869- 168 Ave, South Surrey.

2 *Surrey Leader* 1937 05 26.page 3

Quercus robur 'Pendula'
Moccas Weeping Oak

Very rare in the South Fraser Region, Moccas Weeping Oak has pendulous arching branches; mature trees are medium-sized and irregularly weeping in form.

Where to see the trees:

Langley

Traas Nursery, 24350- 248 Ave, Salmon River Uplands, on the north side of the road to the east of the Quonset storage building.

24355- 48 Ave, Salmon River Uplands, on the west side of the entry driveway.

4870- 236 St, Salmon River Uplands.

Quercus robur 'Pendula', Salmon River Uplands, Langley

Quercus rubra
Syn. *Quercus maxima*
Syn. *Quercus borealis*
Red Oak or Northern Red Oak

Quercus rubra, foliage

Quercus rubra and *Acer pseudoplatanus* Atropurureum Group, Fort Langley Elementary School, Langley

Common in the South Fraser Region, Red Oak is native to southern Ontario, Quebec and the Maritimes and south into Pennsylvania and west to Minnesota and Iowa. It grows to great size, thirty metres under optimum conditions. The large dull leaves have three to five pairs of

Quercus rubra
Syn. *Quercus maxima*
Syn. *Quercus borealis*

Red Oak or Northern Red Oak

lobes; the lobes are triangular in shape, sharply pointed and bristle tipped. While the body or leaf blade of Pin Oak, another common local species, is narrow, the leaf blade of Red Oak is sturdy and wide, hand-sized in width on vigorous trees. New leaves emerge bronze-red in the spring while the fall colour is a dull red turning brown, then the leaves fall from the tree. The cup of the large acorn encloses the nut by 1/3. The sharp pointed buds are bright shiny red-brown. The round winter silhouette of Red Oak and the branching pattern are good winter identifiers as the lowest scaffold branches become thick and ponderous with age. The grey bark is initially smooth, becoming ribbed at maturity.

Quercus rubra, Murrayville Cemetery, Langley

Did You Know?

Red Oak or *Quercus rubra* is the arboreal emblem of the province of Prince Edward Island. This provincial tree was adopted in May of 1987.

• The massive Red Oak with a DBH of 110 cm at 23137– 96 Ave, Ft Langley, is likely a remnant of the elaborately landscaped grounds of the estate home constructed by architect Charles Edward Hope in 1909 and called "Illahie" or in Salish "My Home." The main house burned down in 1929 but the carriage house of the two-hectare estate where the Red Oak is found is just a stone's throw away at 23155– 96 Ave.

• The first two-room school, Belmont School, now Murrayville Elementary School, was built in 1911 on this site in Langley. The mature Red Oaks that line 48 Avenue were likely planted at the same time that the school was built in 1911.

• Murrayville Cemetery opened in 1891 but the Red Oaks were likely planted in the early 1920's.

• The Craftsman-style bungalow, at 27090– 88 Avenue, Northeast Langley, owned by Mrs. D.E. McKenzie, was built circa 1910. It is typical of the Craftsman style of architecture. The four Red Oaks that line 88 Avenue are mature.

Where to see the trees:

Red Oak or Northern Red Oak

Abbotsford

34912 Hamon Dr.

Corner of Midas St and Merlin Dr.

Dunach Elementary School, 30357 Downes Rd. This tree along the east fence line has a massive trunk with a DBH of 135 cm and is one of the largest Red Oaks in the South Fraser Region.

Simpson Traditional Middle School, 30691 Simpson Rd.

Chilliwack

Evergreen Hall, 9291 Corbould St, a large tree to the southeast of the building.

45910 Hocking Ave.

Delta

Justice Building, 4455 Clarence Taylor Cr, Ladner, five young trees.

Langley

23137- 96 Ave, Ft Langley.

Fort Langley National Historic Site, 23433 Mavis St, Ft Langley.

8956 Nash St, Ft Langley.

9093 Wright St, Ft Langley.

Fort Langley Elementary School, 8877 Bartlett St, Ft Langley, a mature row of tall Red Oak trees on the west side of the school ground adjacent to Glover Road. The largest tree has a DBH of 110 cm.

Belmont School, now Murrayville Elementary School, 21812- 48 Ave, Murrayville.

Murrayville Cemetery, 21405- 44 Ave, Murrayville, Langley. The very fine trees in the cemetery are among the largest Red Oaks in the South Fraser Region.

D.E. McKenzie residence, 27090- 88 Ave, Northeast Langley.

Richmond

8100- 8300 Minler Rd, a row of large trees with a superb specimen on the northwest corner of Lucas Rd and Minler Rd.

Burkeville Park, 1031 Lancaster Cr, Burkeville, a number of very fine trees in this small park.

Fantasy Garden World, 10800 No 5 Rd.

Steveston Park, 4111 Moncton St, Steveston, two large trees on the east side of the parking lot.

Southarm Park, Garden City Rd and Williams Rd.

Surrey

13722- 56 Ave, Newton*.

City Hall, 14245- 56 Ave, Newton, on the south side of the east parking lot.

Redwood Park, 17900- 20 Ave, South Surrey*.

White Rock

White Rock Elementary School, 1273 Fir St. The four trees were planted in a row on the south side of the school approximately fifty-five years ago.

R

*A woodland in full color
is awesome as a forest fire,
in magnitude at least;
but a single tree is like
a dancing tongue of flame
to warm the heart.*

Hal Borland

Rhamnus purshiana, foliage

Rhamnus purshiana

Cascara

Native to the southwestern coast and Columbia Valley of British Columbia and common in woodland areas in the South Fraser Region, Cascara is a small deciduous tree to ten metres tall. The leathery leaves are slightly wavy at the edge and furrowed at the veins. Ten to fifteen pairs of parallel veins, which bend toward the leaf tip, are prominently displayed. The dark lustrous green leaves turn yellow when growing in the shade and reddish-purple on exposed sites in the fall. The star-shaped greenish-yellow flowers are inconspicuous but the black berry-like fruit are the size of a penny and ripen in late August to October. The hairy dormant buds are unprotected by bud scales so a pair of leaves perch at the branch tips looking like tiny folded butterfly wings. The smooth silver-grey bark is dimpled with triangular pits and very bitter to the taste, as are the twigs.

Rhamnus purshiana, Kwantlen University College

Where to see the trees:

Langley

23095- 88 Ave, Fort Langley, a large open-grown tree.

Kwantlen University College, 20901 Langley Bypass, Langley City, on the east side of the Turf Demonstration Lab in the natural area.

Richmond

Millennium Botanical Garden and Arboretum, N McLennan Community Park, Granville Ave and Garden City Rd.

Surrey

Bear Creek Park, south east corner of King George Highway and 88th Ave, Fleetwood.

The Glades, 561- 172 St, South Surrey, east of holding area.

Staghorn Sumac or Velvet Sumac

Rhus typhina, fall colour

Staghorn Sumac is very common in the South Fraser Region. It is usually a shrubby small tree with a thicketing habit, reaching a mature height and spread of seven to eight metres. It is native to southern Ontario, Quebec and the Maritimes. All parts of Staghorn Sumac are profusely hairy. The glossy green leaves are huge and pinnately compound, each with eleven to thirty-one toothed leaflets. Fall colour is spectacular, ranging from flame orange to iridescent scarlet. The coarse-textured reddish-brown branches are very noticeable in the winter landscape. With their stiffly upright habit and dense hair, they resemble the horns of a deer during the velvet stage of antler development. The tiny greenish flowers of both male and female trees appear in cone-shaped clusters in July. Later the crimson fruit is held in stiffly upright furry cone-shaped clubs that persist all winter long.

Where to see the trees:
Abbotsford

City Police Department, 2838 Justice Way, a lovely tree on the west side of the building.

Langley

NE corner of 203 St and 32 Ave, Brookswood, a row of five trees.

5744- 246 St, Salmon River Uplands.

Rhus typhina 'Dissecta'

Cutleaf Staghorn Sumac or Fernleaf Sumac

Where to see the trees:

Rosedale

Minter Gardens, 52892 Bunker Rd, northwest end of the Arbor Garden.

Langley

Fort Langley National Historic Site, 23433 Mavis St., Ft Langley, east end of the parking lot.

Rhus typhina 'Disseccta', foliage

Not as commonly grown in the South Fraser Region, nor as large as the species, Cutleaf Staghorn Sumac also differs because its foliage is finely divided, giving this small deciduous tree a delicate fernlike look. The fall colour is a brilliant orange-red.

Robinia pseudoacacia

Black Locust or False Acacia

Robinia pseudoacacia, flowers

Robinia pseudoacacia, 16 Avenue, Langley

Black Locust or False Acacia

An open-arching deciduous tree reaching twenty-five metres in height, Black Locust is very common in the South Fraser Region. It often forms naturalized thickets at woodland and road edges. Iron-clad in constitution, it grows in the driest and poorest of soils. The long compound leaves, with nine to nineteen blue-green leaflets, turn a dull yellow in the fall. Each leaflet has a tiny spine at its tip. The pea-like flowers bloom in late May and are very fragrant. Each cluster of flowers is up to 20 cm long and showy for several weeks. The flattened dark brown irregularly shaped seedpods persist over winter. Another excellent winter identifying feature is the sinuous ropy blackish-brown bark. The branches, which often zigzag, are wickedly spined. Black Locust is native to Pennsylvania to Iowa, south to Georgia and Oklahoma.

Robinia pseudoacacia, 56 Avenue, Langley City

Where to see the trees:

Abbotsford

Abbotsford Elementary School, 33886 Pine St, a row of good-sized trees.

Aberdeen Cemetery, 29200 Fraser Highway, two large open-grown trees.

Belmont Ridge, 1973 Winfield Dr, a huge landmark tree on the southwest corner of the property.

Chilliwack

Hope River Corbould Park, north end of Corbould St, a number of large trees.

Langley

Douglas Park, 20550 Douglas Cr, Langley City, a row of street trees on the east side of the park.

1600 block 200 St, Southwest Langley, a very large open-grown specimen.

SE corner of Highway 10 Bypass and 56 Ave, Langley City, a row with *Prunus* x *yedoensis* 'Akebono'.

Richmond

5200 Hollybridge Way, a long avenue of a mixed planting of large Black Locust and Siberian Elm.

6340 Francis Rd, a very large single tree.

10171 Finlayson Dr, a grand tree.

4440 Smith Cr, three large trees.

3971 Garry St, Steveston, a massive tree just recently part of a redevelopment on the site.

Robinia pseudoacacia 'Frisia'

Golden Locust

Robinia pseudoacacia 'Frisia', Melrose Street, Surrey

Robinia pseudoacacia 'Frisia', foliage

A delightfully colourful addition to the land-scape, Golden Locust is relatively common in the South Fraser Region. Its rich golden leaves remain brightly coloured all summer long and turn a shimmering yellow in the fall. The branches of Golden Locust are upright, irregular and arching, creating an oval crown twelve metres high at maturity. The white pea-like blooms, hanging in wisteria-like clusters, are fragrant. Red thorns decorate the youngest stems of Golden Locust.

Where to see the trees:

Abbotsford

Bevan Ave and Cannon Ave, a young tree in the road median.

Chilliwack

Townsend Park, Ashwell Rd and Hodgins Ave, three trees on the west side of the concessions building.

9238 Broadway St.

Corner of Charles St and Angela Ave.

Fairfield Island Park, 46000 Clare Ave, Fairfield Island.

Promontory Park West, Teskey Rd, Promontory Heights.

41395 Yarrow Central Rd, Yarrow.

Richmond

McNair Secondary School, 9500 No 4 Rd, a row on the west side of the school on Number 4 Road.

Rosedale

Minter Gardens, 52892 Bunker Rd, two specimens, one adjacent to the Floral Peacock and one to the west of the Formal Garden.

Surrey

City Hall, 14245- 56 Ave, Newton, south of the east parking lot.

Peace Portal Par Three, 17065- 4 Ave, South Surrey, a double entry row of young trees.

The Glades, 561- 172 St, South Surrey, west ridge up from the tool shed.

14239 Melrose, Whalley*.

Holland Park, Old Yale Road at 134 St, Whalley, several lovely trees in the park.

Robinia pseudoacacia 'Lace Lady'
Twisty Baby™ Black Locust

Rare in the South Fraser Region, Twisty Baby™ Black Locust is a diminutive cultivar reaching no more than three metres high and the same wide. It may be a multi-stemmed shrub or more tree-like in form. It is noted for its corkscrew zigzagging branches that show well in winter silhouette. The tightly curled leaves, which unfold lime-green in the spring and age to dark green, add to the unusual appearance of this landscape focal point. Twisty Baby™ Black Locust does not produce blooms.

Where to see the trees:
Langley

23862- 58A Avenue, Salmon River Uplands.

Chilliwack

45700 block Lewis Ave, on the north side of the street.

Delta

Leisure Centre, 4600 Clarence Taylor Cr, Ladner, six small trees on the west and south side of the building.

Robinia pseudoacacia 'Lace Lady', Leisure Centre, Delta

Robinia pseudoacacia 'Umbraculifera'
Syn. *Robinia pseudoacacia inermis globosa*
Syn. *Robinia pseudoacacia* 'Globosum'
Mop-Head Acacia, Mushroom Locust or Globe Locust

Justly named the Mop-Head Acacia, this top-grafted cultivar grows into a very dense globe shape. At maturity, Mop-Head Acacia is six to seven metres high. It usually lacks flowers and the spines, which are typical of *Robinia pseudoacacia* along its stem.

Where to see the trees:
Langley

20644 Eastleigh Cr, Langley City, a grouping of two and three on either side of the building stairway.

Northeast corner of 56 Ave and Eastleigh Cr., a tree in the pocket park.

23847- 58A Ave, Salmon River Uplands, Langley.

Surrey

Holland Park, Old Yale Road at 134 St, Whalley, several lovely trees in the park.

Robinia pseudoacacia 'Umbraculifera', Salmon River Uplands, Langley

Robinia 'Purple Robe'
Syn. *Robinia slavinii* Purple Robe™

Purple Robe™ Locust

Robinia 'Purple Robe', flowers

Robinia 'Purple Robe', Fraser Highway, Langley

With its pea-shaped flowers of violet-purple, Purple Robe™ Locust is the very first Black Locust to bloom in the South Fraser Region. The compound leaves, with seventeen to twenty-one leaflets, emerge bronze-red and age to purplish-green, turning yellow in the fall. The branches of Purple Robe™ Locust arch up and out creating an upright oval crown to fifteen metres high.

Where to see the trees:

Chilliwack

47350 Swallow Cr, Little Mountain.

No 4 Firehall, 45433 South Sumas Rd, Sardis.

Langley

Median planting south of Fraser Highway on 206 St.

Street tree planting on Douglas Cr, Langley City.

Surrey

Darts Hill Garden Park, 1660- 168 St, South Surrey, Garden Beds C1 and 17.

S

*...trees, well, they are my obsession, there's just no other way of putting it.
We are talking about the biggest, the oldest, the tallest things on earth.* [1]

Robert Van Pelt, *Big Tree Expert*

Salix caprea 'Kilmarnock', McBurney Lane, Langley City.

Salix caprea 'Kilmarnock'
Syn. *Salix caprea* 'Pendula'

Weeping Pussy Willow,
Kilmarnock Willow

Salix caprea 'Kilmarnock', foliage

Weeping Pussy Willow is a top-grafted weeping tree usually growing less than six metres high with a spread of the same. It has a very distinct umbrella form with the branches cascading to the ground. It is very effective pond-side where it grows well in moist soils. Weeping Pussy Willow is primarily grown for its outstanding display of grey male catkins, which appear in March and April. They are exceedingly fuzzy and as they age, bright yellow anthers pop out, the tree becoming a bright beacon in the landscape. The elliptical leaves are wrinkled along the edges, medium green above and grey-green on the bottom. The branches are yellowish brown and stout. Weeping Pussy Willow is not common in the South Fraser Region.

Where to see the trees:

Chilliwack
University College of the Fraser Valley, 45600 Airport Rd, a young tree planted in 2002 in the Shakespeare Garden.

Langley
Kwantlen University College, 20901 Langley Bypass, Langley City, a small specimen pond-side in the Gazebo Garden at the Field Lab.

McBurney Lane, 20505 Fraser Hwy, Langley City, several small trees in the concrete planters.

Rosedale
Minter Gardens, 52892 Bunker Rd, Rosedale, directly north of the Maze.

[1] *The Vancouver Sun*, October 20, 2001, p D 5.

Salix lucida ssp. *lasiandra*
Syn. *Salix lasiandra*

Pacific Willow, Pacific Black Willow, Lanceleaf Willow or Yellow Willow

Salix lucida ssp. *lasiandra,* foliage and catkins

Salix lucida ssp. *lasiandra,* Yale Road West, Chilliwack

Where to see the trees:

Chilliwack

Yale Road West.

Langley

Kwantlen University College, 20901 Langley Bypass, Langley City, a small specimen to the east of the Gazebo Garden at the Field Lab on the south side of the Turf Demonstration Lab.

Nicomekl River floodplain, west of the Senior Resource Centre at 51B Ave and 206 St, Langley City.

Surrey

Surrey Big Bend Regional Park, north foot of 104 St, Guildford

Native to the provinces of British Columbia and Alberta, Pacific Willow is a very common deciduous tree along streams, river courses and marshy areas particularly on the Pacific Coast. Growing twelve metres in height, Pacific Willow is one of the largest native willows in British Columbia. The lance-shaped leaves are 5–15 cm long by 2.5 cm wide with long slender pointed tips. They are lustrous dark green on the top surface and whitish below. Dainty yellow catkins appear as the leaves are unfolding. The bright yellow stems and yellow buds are good winter identifiers; the buds resemble duckbills. The bark is blackish and shaggy on old trees.

Did You Know?

To reach this stand of exceptionally tall Pacific Willow in Chilliwack, take the Yale West Road exit off Highway 1, proceed to the raised gravel dyke road which heads west toward the Sumas River. From the stop sign, go west 1.4 kilometres on the dyke road. The marshy area on the north side of the dyke road contains a lovely grove of these trees.

This area of the Sumas River is a very rare undyked stretch of the Fraser River flood plain. Approximately one hundred hectares in size, it contains the third- and fourth-largest known Black Cottonwoods in North America and five of the top ten of this species in terms of size. This stretch of the Fraser River is one of the last deciduous old growth flood plain forests left in Canada. The Western Canada Wilderness Committee has proposed the "Black Cottonwood Big Tree Park" to protect this very fragile and unique riverine landscape.

Salix babylonica var. *pekinensis* 'Tortuosa'
Syn. *Salix contorta* or *Salix matsudana* 'Tortuosa'

Corkscrew Willow, Curly Willow or Contorted Willow

Salix babylonica var. *pekinensis* 'Tortuosa'

Salix babylonica var. *pekinensis* 'Tortuosa', contorted foliage

Somewhat common in the South Fraser Region, Corkscrew Willow is noted for its fantastic curling and twisted appearance. All parts of the tree, from large heavy limbs, to branches, the yellow twigs and leaves are contorted. It grows to a moderate size, reaching ten to twelve metres when mature with an upright oval to round shape. Unfortunately large branches breakout under the weight of the heavy wet snow, which occasionally falls in the South Fraser Region. The narrow leaves are medium green, paler beneath and curling to the point of deformity. An attractive yellow catkin is produced in April.

Where to see the trees:

Abbotsford

34662 Mila St.

2271 Mountain Dr, a young tree.

SE corner Vye Rd and Kenny Rd, two large trees.

Chilliwack

6000 Promontory Rd, Promontory Heights.

Did You Know?

Edna Horstead planted the Corkscrew Willow in the front garden of 101 Clovermeadow Crescent in Langley in 1983. Edna owned a little flower shop on Fraser Highway and often used Corkscrew Willow stems in her floral design. The stems sold for a dollar and sometimes more at that time. When a bunch of fifteen had sprouted roots, the wholesaler gave then to Edna, and announced that it was unlikely that she could get them to grow. Edna stuck them in a bucket outside the back door, in anticipation of later planting them in her garden. Temperatures plunged below zero and when she went to plant the stems they were thickly encased in ice. Edna thought the branches would surely die, but two weeks later they had broken dormancy and sprouted leaves. She promptly planted them and they have thrived.

Salix babylonica var. *pekinensis* 'Tortuosa'
Syn. *Salix contorta* or *Salix matsudana* 'Tortuosa'

Corkscrew Willow, Curly Willow or Contorted Willow

Where to see the trees:

Langley

8935 Glover Rd, Ft Langley.

21520 Old Yale Rd, Murrayville.

101 Clovermeadow Cr, Salmon River Uplands.

Richmond

Fantasy Garden World, 10800 No 5 Rd.

Rosedale

Minter Gardens, 52892 Bunker Rd, north side of the pond in the Lake Garden.

Surrey

Darts Hill Garden Park, 1660- 168 St, South Surrey, Garden Bed 11.

Fraser Health Region office, 14265- 56 Ave, Newton, on the northwest side of the building in the lawn.

The Glades, 561- 172 St, South Surrey, in the meadow garden.

Salix pentandra
Bay Willow or Laurel Willow

Salix pentandra, Portage Park, Langley City

Salix pentandra, Portage Park, foliage

Native to Europe, Bay Willow is not common in the South Fraser Region. It grows twelve to fifteen metres high with an upright oval form. The leaves are its most notable feature. They are up to15 cm long and 5 cm wide, very leathery, glossy and dark green above, a paler green underneath. The margins of the leaves are serrated. The leaves are aromatic when crushed. Little if any fall colour is normal, as the leaves drop green from the tree. The midrib of the leaves and the dormant buds are golden yellow; as are the catkins that appear in May or June after the leaves have unfolded.

Where to see the trees:

Langley

Portage Park, 20300 block 51A Ave, Langley City.

Salix x *sepulchralis* var. *chrysocoma*, foliage

Salix x *sepulchralis* var. *chrysocoma*
Syn. *Salix alba* 'Tristis'
Syn. *Salix babylonica* 'Aurea'
Golden Weeping Willow

Salix x *sepulchralis* var. *chrysocoma*, summer, 164 Street, Surrey

Grown in parks, golf courses and larger properties adjacent to watercourses, Golden Weeping Willow is the most common cultivated willow found in the South Fraser Region. Generous and wide spreading, it easily reaches twenty metres high with a spread of thirty metres. The mounding lumpy form and golden branches, which cascade gracefully to the ground, make this tree easily identifiable. The long narrow, medium green leaves hang limply from the branchlets. Thin textured, they delicately rustle in the merest breeze. The fall colour is yellow. The catkins are up to 5 cm long and appear in late April to May.

Did You Know?

The Dennison's were a significant family in the development of Tsawwassen in Delta in the 1930's. The house on Dennison Place was built in 1932. Eventually the Dennison's had a substantial farm here and became well known for growing flowers. The family grew bulbs such as tulips and daffodils commercially. Mrs. Zoe Dennison, a true green thumb, founded the Evergreen Garden Club.

Where to see the trees:

Abbotsford

Hougen Park, south off Highway 1 on Cole Rd, a number of very large trees, one of the larger trees has a DBH of 84 cm.

29295 Huntingdon Rd.

5743 Bell Street. This tree is a massive specimen of great girth with a DBH of 107 cm, a crown spread of 21 metres and an estimated height of 20 metres.

Chilliwack

Ballyduff Farms, 49169 Castleman Rd, East Chilliwack.

Parkholm Lodge, 9090 Newman Rd, a large tree on the west side of the garden.

Hope River Corbould Park, north end of Corbould St.

47597 Yale Rd East, a very tall tree.

48580 Prairie Central Rd, Sardis.

Sardis Park, School Lane and Manuel Rd, Sardis, many pleasing trees well sited around the pond.

Leghorn Ranch, 6530 Chilliwack River Rd, Vedder Crossing.

42181 Keith Wilson Rd, Vedder Crossing.

Salix x *sepulchralis* var. *chrysocoma*
Syn. *Salix alba* 'Tristis'
Syn. *Salix babylonica* 'Aurea'

Golden Weeping Willow

Where to see the trees:

Delta

Dennison House, 5139 Dennison Pl, Tsawwassen.

John Oliver Municipal Park, 11600 block Ladner Trunk Rd, three huge trees.

Langley

Belmont Golf Course, 22555 Telegraph Trail, Fort Langley.

St. Andrew's Anglican Church, 20955 Old Yale Rd, Langley City.

Richmond

NE corner of Garden City Rd and Francis Rd.

3600 Steveston Hwy.

Surrey

2977 King George Hwy, South Surrey, a large tree on the north side of the entrance.

2865- 164 St, South Surrey*.

Salix udensis 'Sekka'

Japanese Fantail Willow or Fantail Willow

Where to see the trees:

Chilliwack

Gwynne Vaughan Park, Williams Rd and Hope River Rd, Fairfield Island.

Langley

Kwantlen University College, 20901 Langley Bypass, Langley City, on the north side of the Turf Demonstration Lab in the natural area.

Surrey

Darts Hill Garden Park, 1660- 168 St, South Surrey, Garden Bed 6.

Salix udensis 'Sekka', foliage and branch fasciation

Exceptionally rare in the South Fraser Region, Japanese Fantail Willow is deserving of greater attention. Native to Japan, it is a small tree or large shrub, growing to 3–4.5 metres high with the same width. It has a thicketing habit. Like the Corkscrew Willow, Japanese Fantail Willow is grown for its extraordinary branches. The reddish branches are curling and thickened, looking as if several have been fused together. This condition is called branch fasciation. The lance-shaped dark green leaves are 10–15 cm long and fan out at the branch tips like the tail feathers of a bird. Fuzzy silver-grey catkins appear in March. The fasciated branches and emerging catkins are extremely showy and highly valued for floral arrangements.

Sciadopitys verticilliata, Sendall Gardens, Langley City

Sciadopitys verticilliata, foliage

Rare in the South Fraser Region, Umbrella Pine is an attractive conifer deserving of a place in the landscape. When mature it has a stately, narrowly pyramidal shape. A native of Japan, it grows fifteen to twenty metres tall. The strap-like waxy leaves are up to 15 cm long, glossy deep green. Umbrella pine is easily identified because these distinctive leaves are clustered and radiate from a central point on the twig like the spokes of an umbrella. Both top and bottom of the leaf are grooved while the bottom has two startling white bands. The reddish brown buds are plump and round. The branches are upright ascending and usually dense and thickly clothed with foliage, particularly when the tree is young. The egg-shaped cones are rarely produced here.

Where to see the trees:

Langley

Kwantlen University College, 20901 Langley Bypass, Langley City, several small specimen at the Field Lab on the berm adjacent to Highway 10.

Sendall Gardens, 20166- 50 Ave, Langley City.

Richmond

Millennium Botanical Garden and Arboretum, N McLennan Community Park, Granville Ave and Garden City Rd.

Surrey

The Glades, 561- 172 St, South Surrey, Bent Cedar area.

Sequoia sempervirens

Coast Redwood or California Redwood

Sequoia sempervirens, foliage and cones

Where to see the trees:

Chilliwack

Park, southeast corner of Manuel Rd and Vedder Rd, Sardis, a good-sized specimen.

Delta

4578- 53 St, Ladner, two small six-metre tall specimens in good condition.

8508 Terrace Dr, North Delta, a good-sized tree with a DBH of 35 cm and a height of 10.5- 12 metres tall on the south side of the property.

Langley

Sendall Gardens, 20166- 50 Ave, Langley City, on the east side of the parking lot.

Compost Demonstration Garden, 4885- 221 St, Murrayville, Langley.

Surrey

Darts Hill Garden Park, 1660- 168 St, South Surrey, Garden Bed 1.

Green Timbers Arboretum, 9800- 140 St, Whalley.

Redwood Park, 17900- 20 Ave, South Surrey, east of the Tree House.

The Glades, 561- 172 St, South Surrey, along the east fence line.

Coast Redwood in its native range grows over 110 metres in height; it is the tallest growing tree in the world. It is native to the fog-drenched coastal regions of southwest Oregon and northern California and is at its northern-most limits in our area. Rare in the South Fraser Region, it does not grow to gargantuan size here. The evergreen leaves are yew-like. The short stiff bluish-green needles lie flat in two rows on the branchlet. The woody dark brown cone is very tiny for a tree of such grand stature; they are a mere thumbnail width in size. The spongy reddish bark is a luxurious 30 cm thick and easily poked into with a finger. Strongly furrowed on mature trees, the bark readily shreds and peels. Mature tree trunks are heavily buttressed, while the tree is broadly pyramidal in shape. Long-lived, Coast Redwood has been recorded to 2200 years old in northern California.

Giant Sequoia, Sierra Redwood or Big Tree

Far more common in the South Fraser Region because it grows very well here, Giant Sequoia is a forest behemoth at maturity. It reaches ninety metres in height and has a bulky stout trunk that would rest heavily in a giant's hand. Giant Sequoia is native to the 900–2200-metre elevations of the western foothills of the Sierra Nevada Mountains in California. In youth, the tree is a compact and tidy symmetrical pyramid. As the tree matures it becomes broadly pyramidal, with short swooping branches and a massive trunk. The bluish-green, tiny sharp-pointed awl-shaped leaves are tightly held to the branchlet. When crushed, the leaves have a spicy sour smell. The branches with their leaves look somewhat like a thin braided rope. The brown cone, with its stubby egg shape, is significantly larger than the Coast Redwood cone, growing to 8 cm long. The bark is also very thick to 50 cm on mature trees. It is reddish dark brown, fibrous and very soft, almost punky to the touch. Giant Sequoia is a very long-lived tree in its native range, with several specimens recorded to over 3200 years old.

Sequiadendron giganteum, 96 Avenue, Langley

Where to see the trees:

Abbotsford

30639 Burgess Rd, four young trees.

33249 Nelson Ave, several trees in a small pocket park.

34195 Hazel St, two trees.

Chilliwack

9708 Corbould Ave.

Municipal Hall, 8550 Young Rd.

Fairfield Island Park, 46000 Clare Ave, Fairfield Island.

Salish Park, 45860- 1 Ave.

Townsend Park, Ashwell Rd and Hodgins Ave, several groups of trees on the north side of the park.

Delta

Municipal Hall, 4500 Clarence Taylor Cr, Ladner, young trees.

5776 Ladner Trunk Rd, Ladner, three well-formed younger specimens.

Did You Know?

In 1909 Charles Edward Hope bought two hectares of land in Fort Langley. He built a beautiful home on 96 Avenue, called "Illahie," which in Chinook means "My Home." Hope also bought a 219-hectare farm west of the Salmon River called Deep Creek Farm where he raised registered Aberdeen Angus cattle. He planted this magnificent row of Giant Sequoia trees from seed obtained from France, along the border of his farm. Charles Hope was ahead of the times; he planted the Giant Sequoia to increase the appreciation of large trees in an era when stately forest giants were cut to make way for development. This row of beautiful Giant Sequoia is a municipally designated Heritage Site.

Sequoiadendron giganteum

Giant Sequoia, Sierra Redwood or Big Tree

• Mr. Molachi, a lumberman from Vancouver, planted the six lovely Giant Sequoias at the west end of Worrell Crescent in Langley in the late 1940's.

• The small grove of five Giant Sequoias, planted in 1976 on the grounds of Langley Community Music School is a Memorial Grove dedicated to the memory of John O. Conder, Fred Dirks, Tommy Gleig, Kenneth G. Norman and William Stevenson. These five gentlemen were prominent citizens of Langley City in their day, John Conder a former mayor and Tommy Glieg, the Chairman of the School Board.

• The Draney House, circa 1888 or earlier, is believed to be one of the oldest houses in Richmond. The Draney family, who were cannery builders, along with Thomas Kidd, who may have built the farmhouse, are among Richmond's key early pioneers. The farmhouse is located in the "Slough District," which was one of the earliest farming areas on Lulu Island. Draney House was home to many of the original pioneers who signed Richmond's petition to incorporate as a municipality. Thomas Kidd planted the Giant Sequoia on the north side of the house soon after he settled on Lulu Island in February 1874. Thomas Kidd was a versatile individual. He was one of Richmond's founding fathers, an early settler, a councillor, reeve, poet, historian, and Richmond's first member of the Provincial Legislative Assembly. Kidd was in California just prior to his arrival in Richmond in early 1874, and likely brought the seeds of the Giant Sequoia with him.

Delta

NW corner of 120 St and 64 Ave, North Delta, a number of young trees on the Safeway store boulevard.

South Delta Recreation Centre, 1720- 56 St, Tsawwassen.

Langley

21836- 96 Ave, Northwest Langley. This tree, the most easterly of a row of thirty-eight individuals, is a magnificent specimen. The row of trees ends at 9584- 216 St.

West end of Worrell Cr, a row in a field planted on the north side of Worrell Crescent, Milner.

26251 Fraser Hwy, Aldergrove.

2883- 272 St, Aldergrove.

Langley Community Music School, 4899- 207 St, Southwest Langley, five trees to the east of the school.

Richmond

Draney House, 12011- No 4 Rd, a tree with a broken top but a massive trunk flare.

NE corner of Cambie Rd and No 4 Rd, two very large trees, one topped due to the power lines but the easternmost tree appears intact.

Fantasy Garden World, 10800 No 5 Rd.

McLean Park, 2500 McLean Ave, Hamilton area.

Millennium Botanical Garden and Arboretum, N McLennan Community Park, Granville Ave and Garden City Rd.

Southarm Park, Garden City Rd and Williams Rd, a row of four good-sized trees on the north side of the Community Centre.

4055 Regent St, Steveston, an excellent tree in the rear garden of a unit of a housing complex.

Surrey

10375- 133 St, Whalley*.

Darts Hill Garden Park, 1660- 168 St, South Surrey, Garden Bed 8.

Green Timbers Arboretum, 9800- 140 St, Whalley.

Redwood Park, 17900- 20 Ave, South Surrey*.

The Glades, 561- 172 St, South Surrey, on the west ridge, to the centre of the south side.

Sequoiadendron giganteum 'Pendulum'
Weeping Giant Sequoia

Sequiadendron giganteum 'Pendulum',
Sendall Gardens, Langley City

Sequiadendron giganteum 'Pendulum', foliage and cones.

Sought after for its curious shape, Weeping Giant Sequoia is relatively abundant in the South Fraser Region. Its slender form reaches a mature height of fifteen or more metres with a scant spread of one metre. Arching, twisting, and swirling its delicate blue-green foliage and drooping branchlets about a sturdy erect stem, Weeping Giant Sequoia oscillates through the landscape like Ogopogo, the mythical serpent monster of Okanagan Lake.

Where to see the trees:

Abbotsford

34324 Mendham St. This is one of the tallest Weeping Giant Sequoias in the South Fraser Region. It is approximately twelve metres high.

Chilliwack

Salish Park, 45860- 1 Ave.

SW corner of Riverside Dr and Inglewood Cr.

Cannor Nurseries Ltd, 48291 Chilliwack Central Rd, a large specimen in the parking lot.

Delta

Police Station, 4455 Clarence Taylor Cr, Ladner.

Langley

Sendall Gardens, 20166- 50 Ave, Langley City.

Richmond

Fantasy Garden World, 10800 No 5 Rd. There is a gorgeous specimen at the entry to the garden. It was transplanted by John Massot, the creator of the garden, from his home landscape.

Surrey

Darts Hill Garden Park, 1660- 168 St, South Surrey*, Garden Bed 11.

South Surrey Arena, 2199- 148 St, South Surrey, a young tree on the west side of the building.

Green Timbers Arboretum, 9800- 140 St, Whalley, a lovely tree 100 metres to the northwest of the arboretum.

Sophora japonica

Japanese Pagoda Tree
or Chinese Scholar Tree

Sophora japonica, South Delta Recreation Centre, Tsawwassen

Sophora japonica, foliage

Where to see the trees:

Delta

South Delta Recreation Centre, 1720- 56 St, Tsawwassen. Three elegant trees are well sited on a grassy knoll to the north of the centre. The largest tree has a DBH of 70 cm.

Richmond

Steveston Park, 4111 Moncton St, Steveston, on the east side of the entrance to the Martial Arts Centre.

A beautiful round-headed deciduous tree native to China, Korea and Vietnam, Japanese Pagoda Tree is deserving of greater attention. It grows to fifteen to twenty metres high with an equal spread. The medium green leaves are pinnately compound, with seven to seventeen leaflets, which turn yellow-green in the fall. It may be confused with Black Locust, which is far more common in the South Fraser Region than the rarer Japanese Pagoda Tree. The leaflets of Japanese Pagoda Tree are sharply pointed and have a tiny stalk. In addition, the swollen base of the leaf tightly embraces the bud of the following year's growth, easily differentiating the two trees. The fragrant flowers of Japanese Pagoda Tree are produced in lax cone-shaped clusters. Each yellowish-white floret is pea-shaped; and the blooming time is late July, August and into early September. The fruit resembles a string of plastic toy pearls, with each seed discreetly separated from the next. Immature seeds are green, turn yellow and ripen to brown. The bark of Japanese Pagoda Tree is lightly ribbed and greyish.

Sorbus aria, Jubilee Park, Abbotsford

Sorbus aria, fruit

Native to Europe and Northern Africa, Whitebeam is uncommon in the South Fraser Region. It grows to twelve to fifteen metres high with an upright oval shape. Whitebeam, with its alder-shaped leaves and shocking fuzzy white undersides is easy to recognize, as few trees resemble it. The leaves, which are 8–12 cm long, are thickly hairy and grey-green on top as they unfurl, aging to smooth green on the top and felty on the underside. The white flowers are produced in flat clusters. Appearing in May, they are five-petalled and resemble tiny apple flowers. The large round fruits are spectacular orange-red and hang from the tree in bountiful sprays. Birds highly favour the fruit.

Where to see the trees:
Abbotsford
Jubilee Park, McCallum Rd south of Essendene, two fabulous trees in the centre of the park.

Surrey
Darts Hill Garden Park, 1660- 168 St, South Surrey, Garden Bed C3.

Sorbus aucuparia
European Mountain Ash

Sorbus aucuparia, fruit

Where to see the trees:

Abbotsford

Hougen Park, south off Highway 1 on Cole Rd.

Jubilee Park, McCallum Rd south of Essendene on the north side of the tennis court.

Trethewey House (M.S.A. Museum), 2313 Ware St, on the northwest side of the house.

Chilliwack

Canadian Forces Base, Keith Wilson Rd and Vedder Rd, Vedder Crossing, on the southwest of the RCMP Complex, behind the building.

Stö:lo Centre, 7201 Vedder Rd, Sardis.

46017- 2 Ave, two trees.

Delta

Justice Building, 4455 Clarence Taylor Cr, Ladner, one large specimen to the west of the building.

Leisure Centre, 4600 Clarence Taylor Cr, Ladner, a row on the west side of the building.

Langley

Christian Life Assembly, 21277- 56 Ave, Milner, a row of trees along the street.

Murrayville Cemetery, 21405- 44 Ave, Murrayville.

Richmond

Fire Department No 4, 780 Lancaster Cr, Burkeville, a huge specimen.

Surrey

The Glades, 561- 172 St, South Surrey.

Sorbus aucuparia, Trethewey House, Abbotsford

Native to Europe, North Africa, west Asia and Siberia, European Mountain Ash has naturalized in many parts of the South Fraser Region since birds readily disperse the fruit. Growing ten to twelve metres high, European Mountain Ash has an upright oval shape in youth and matures to round. The dull bluish-green leaves are pinnately compound with nine to fifteen saw-toothed leaflets. Fall colour is variable ranging from yellow and orange to yellow-brown. The five-petalled white flowers are produced in May in flat clusters. The blossoms smell foul. Birds eagerly consume the orange fruits which hang in pendulous clusters in the early fall. The fruit, when ripe, turns red-orange and drops, staining concrete and marring paint finishes. Its very fuzzy greyish buds identify European Mountain Ash in the winter. The bark is grey-brown and has horizontal lenticels much like cherry bark.

Sorbus hupehensis 'Pink Pagoda'
Pink Pagoda Mountain Ash

Sorbus hupehensis 'Pink Pagoda',
Bateman Park, Abbotsford

Sorbus hupehensis 'Pink Pagoda', fruit

Selected at the University of British Columbia from seedlings from central and western China, Pink Pagoda Mountain Ash grows eight to ten metres high. It has an upright oval form with an open habit. The green leaves, which light purplish-green, are pinnately compound with eleven to thirteen leaflets. The fall colour is purplish red. Produced in May, the five-petalled white flowers are held in dense clusters. The round fruits ripen dark pink in the early fall, turn nearly white, then darken to a rose pink and hang in clusters on the tree well into the winter. Smooth buds help identify Pink Pagoda Mountain Ash in the winter. In the future this tree is likely to be reclassified as *Sorbus oligodonta*.

Where to see the trees:
Abbotsford
Bateman Park, Bateman Rd, two trees at the north entrance to the park in the parking lot.

Langley
Kwantlen University College, 20901 Langley Bypass, Langley City, a small tree planted in 1999 in the Gazebo Garden at the Field Lab.

6086- 237A St, Salmon River Uplands, Langley.

Rosedale
Minter Gardens, 52892 Bunker Rd, at the east end of the parking lot.

Surrey
Darts Hill Garden Park, 1660- 168 St, South Surrey, Magnolia Walk and Pasture.

Sorbus x *thuringiaca* 'Fastigiata'
Oakleaf Mountain Ash

Sorbus x *thuringiaca* 'Fastigiata', Steveston Park, Richmond

Sorbus x *thuringiaca* 'Fastigiata', foliage and flowers

Where to see the trees:

Chilliwack
South Sumas Rd on the north to south side from Tyson Rd to Wiltshire Rd, Sardis.

Richmond
Steveston Park, 4111 Moncton St, Steveston, a row on the north side of the Martial Arts Centre.

Oakleaf Mountain Ash grows six to twelve metres high. It has a neat symmetrical upright oval form that looks as if it has been sheared. The leathery dark green leaves are pinnately compound with eleven to thirteen leaflets. The bottom surface of the leaflet is covered with white hair. The leaves are atypical in that the leaflets are free from the stem near the base of the leaf. Closer to the tip, the leaflet shape widens and they are attached and lobed like an oak leaf. The fall colour is yellow. Produced in May, the five-petalled white flowers are held in dense clusters. The round dark red berries ripen in the early fall. Dark red brown buds help identify Oakleaf Mountain Ash in the winter.

Stewartia monodelpha, foliage

Native to southern Japan, Orangebark Stewartia is exceedingly rare in the South Fraser Region. It reaches a height of ten to twelve metres with a round to upright oval form. The trunk is usually multi-stemmed and the branches are horizontal in habit and zigzag from bud to bud. The oval-shaped green leaves turn purple-red and rich maroon in the late fall. The white flowers have prominent stamens and are borne singly at the branch tips. Cup-shaped, the flowers are about the size of a two-dollar coin. A green leafy bract subtends each flower. When in bloom in late June into July, the tree is highly appealing. Orangebark Stewartia is usually grown for its delicately flaking, smooth reddish-orange bark. A distinctive five-parted beak makes the woody brown seed capsule very noticeable when it ripens in October.

Stewartia monodelpha, bark

Where to see the trees:
Surrey
Darts Hill Garden Park, 1660- 168 St, South Surrey, Garden Bed 15 a.

Stewartia pseudocamellia

Japanese Stewartia or Common Stewartia

Stewartia pseudocamellia, Darts Hill Garden Park, Surrey

Stewartia pseudocamellia, flower

Where to see the trees:

Richmond

Millennium Botanical Garden and Arboretum, N McLennan Community Park, Granville Ave and Garden City Rd.

On the north side of Chatham Ave at No 1 Rd, Steveston, five young trees in front of a commercial row of businesses.

Langley

Sendall Gardens, 20166- 50 Ave, Langley City, a small tree.

Rosedale

Minter Gardens, 52892 Bunker Rd, a small tree found along just outside of the northwest side of the Rose Garden.

Surrey

Darts Hill Garden Park, 1660- 168 St, South Surrey, Garden Bed 2.

12328- 73A Ave, Newton.

12352- 73A Ave, Newton.

Native to Japan, Japanese Stewartia is relatively common in the South Fraser Region. It reaches a height of ten to fourteen metres with a pyramidal oval silhouette. The elliptical-shaped leaves emerge bronze in the spring, turn green and then colour in the late fall, displaying fiery shades of yellow, orange-red, scarlet and maroon. The developing flower buds are plump promises of coming grandeur. Blooming in July, the tree is very showy and remnant flowers may appear into September. Rose-like, the white flowers are 6–7.5 cm wide, each petal with a delicately frilled edge. A green leafy bract and prominent orange-yellow stamens adorn each fragrant flower. Japanese Stewartia is noted for its outstanding reddish-orange bark which, even on young trees, peels away leaving a smooth stem with attractive tan, orangish or rusty-brown patterns. The woody brown seed capsule with its distinctive five-parted beak is interesting when it ripens in October. The seedpod persists over the winter months.

Native to central and eastern China, Chinese Stewartia is extremely rare in the South Fraser Region. Round at maturity, it grows seven to nine metres tall. The oval-shaped green leaves turn red in the fall. The scented white flowers, which bloom in July, have prominent yellow stamens. Rose, blossom-shaped, the flowers are up to 5 cm across, and a green leafy bract subtends each flower. Chinese Stewartia is usually grown for its peeling reddish bark. When peeled away, the under bark is very smooth and many-hued, often burnished copper, light grey, olive, cream or tan. The woody brown seed capsule with its distinctive five-parted beak is very noticeable when it ripens in October.

Where to see the trees:
Surrey
Darts Hill Garden Park, 1660- 168 St, South Surrey, Garden Bed 7.

Stewartia sinensis, branching pattern

Styrax japonicus
Japanese Snowbell or Japanese Snowdrop Tree

Styrax japonicus, flowers

A small elegant tree, Japanese Snowball is quite common in the South Fraser Region, though few trees are of any size. Native to Japan, Korea and China, it reaches a mature height of seven

Styrax japonicus

Japanese Snowbell or Japanese Snowdrop Tree

Where to see the trees:

Chilliwack

Fairfield Island Park, entrance on Clare Ave, Fairfield Island, in the south side bed.

University College of the Fraser Valley, 45600 Airport Rd, west of Building B, Agriculture.

Delta

Municipal Hall, 4500 Clarence Taylor Cr, Ladner, in the parking lot between the Municipal Hall and the Justice Building.

4455 Clarence Taylor Cr, Ladner.

Pioneer Library, 4683- 51 St, Ladner, a street planting on the east side of the library.

North Delta Recreation Centre, 11415-84 Ave, at the front entry to the centre.

Langley

20200- 56 Ave, Langley City, a row of five young trees and an additional row on the northeast side of 56 Ave at 203 St.

Kwantlen University College, 20901 Langley Bypass, Langley City, a small tree at the northwest foot of the highway overpass.

Trinity Western University, 7600 Glover Rd, Willoughby, a fine young tree to the west of Robson Hall.

Richmond

Fantasy Garden World, 10800 No 5 Rd.

Surrey

City Hall, 14245- 56 Ave, Newton, on the south side of the pond.

68th Ave, between 127th St and 128th St, Newton, a street tree planting.

14567- 82 Ave, Fleetwood.

14584- 82 Ave, Fleetwood.

Darts Hill Garden Park, 1660- 168 St, South Surrey, Garden Beds 1,13, 14, 15 b, 22, 25 and 30.

Morgan Creek Golf Course, 3500 Morgan Creek Way, South Surrey, a number of very good small specimens in the clubhouse garden.

to nine metres with a rounded twiggy silhouette. The elliptical leaves emerge a lovely chartreuse, age to lustrous medium green, with fall colour usually a soft yellow. The leaves are sharp pointed and with a slightly wavy edge. Blooming in June, the small flowers are produced in clusters of three to six, each flower held on a long pendulous stem, which cascades freely below the leafy branches. The white star-shaped blossoms, with their dainty yellow stamens, are best viewed from below. Japanese Snowbell is a prolific bloomer producing, even on small trees, hundreds of small scented flowers. The fruit is equally attractive. It is a hard greenish oval, less than the size of a dime. When it matures in the late fall, it is greyish and fuzzy with a small sharp point at the tip. The fruit persists until Christmas and is a good identifying feature. Young branches of Japanese Snowbell are reddish with shredding tan-coloured overlays. Older stems are tan with fine purplish-brown veining.

Did You Know?

The young Japanese Snowbell planted to the west of Robson Hall on the Trinity Western Campus in Langley was planted in memory of Jake Thiessen (1932–1998). The plaque at the base of the tree reads, "The path of the righteous is like the first gleam of dawn," Proverbs 4:16. Trinity is Western Canada's largest Christian University.

Pink Chimes Japanese Snowbell

Styrax japonicus 'Pink Chimes', flowers

A delightful addition to the list of desirable small trees for the residential landscape, the leaves of Pink Chimes Japanese Snowbell are similar to the species. It differs in that the star-shaped blossoms, which are produced in abundance, are soft pastel pink. The tips of the branches are somewhat droopy. The habit of Pink Chimes Japanese Snowbell is definitely shrub-like; the tree resents the pruning needed to direct growth into a more arboreal form. The fruit is the same as the species.

Where to see the trees:
Surrey
Darts Hill Garden Park, 1660- 168 St, South Surrey, Garden Beds 26 and 28.

Styrax obassia

Fragrant Snowbell or Bigleaf Snowbell Tree

In contrast to the dainty Japanese Snowbell, Fragrant Snowbell is robust and bold in appearance. Native to northern China, Manchuria, Korea and Japan, it grows twelve to fifteen metres tall. The almost round leaves are large, dinner plate-sized with a soft velvety texture due to their densely hairy underside. The flowers are star-shaped and white like the more common Japanese Snowbell, but are produced on long arched stalks which droop from the branchlets. The flowers are borne in late May

Where to see the trees:
Surrey
Darts Hill Garden Park, 1660- 168 St, South Surrey, Garden Beds 2, 18 and the Magnolia Walk and Pasture.

Styrax obassia
Fragrant Snowbell or Bigleaf Snowbell Tree

Styrax obassia, foliage

to June and are sweet-smelling as the common name suggests. The fall colour of Fragrant Snowbell is usually a soft yellow. The large fuzzy buds are the colour of Dijon mustard. The fruit is hard, round and green, about the size of a five-cent piece. When it matures in the fall, it is brownish-grey and fuzzy with a small sharp point at the tip. The fruit is persistent and is a good identifying feature. The bark is remarkably colourful, on young stems it peels away in long burgundy and mahogany-coloured curls. Older stems are tan-coloured with white veining like snakeskin. Mature bark is smooth and grey.

Syringa reticulata 'Ivory Silk'
Ivory Silk Tree Lilac, Japanese Tree Lilac or Giant Tree Lilac

Syringa reticulata 'Ivory Silk', flowers

Ivory Silk Tree Lilac, Japanese Tree Lilac or Giant Tree Lilac

Growing 6–7.5 metres tall, Ivory Silk Tree Lilac is a recent addition to the communities of the South Fraser Region. It has an upright arching habit, maturing to a round form. Elliptical in shape, the dark green leaves are up to 20 cm long. They are fuzzy on the underside when first emerging in the spring. Fall colour is insignificant. The overly sweet-scented cream flowers bloom in late June to July. The flowers are very showy as they are produced on large upright cone-shaped plumes in great profusion. Horizontal lenticels, typical of cherry bark, decorate the reddish-brown bark of the Japanese Tree Lilac.

Where to see the trees:

Chilliwack

5431- 5497 and 46774- 46669 Dellview St, Promontory Heights.

5552 Alpine Cr, Promontory Heights.

Surrey

14345- 78A Ave, Newton.

14351- 78A Ave, Newton.

Syringa reticulata 'Ivory Silk', seed pods

T

It's like an obsession. I know there are countless giant trees hidden out there in gullies and valleys and nobody has ever seen them. Well, I'm going to be the one to find those trees. I feel like a gold prospector, and when the trees are close, it's like I can smell them. [1]

Ralf Kelman, Tree Searcher and Artist

Taxodium distichum, knees

Taxodium distichum
Bald Cypress or Swamp Cypress

Taxodium distichum, Darts Hill Garden Park, Surrey

Where to see the trees:

Chilliwack

Townsend Park, Ashwell Rd and Hodgins Ave, three trees on the east side of the concessions building.

Richmond

Fantasy Garden World, 10800 No 5 Rd.

Rosedale

Minter Gardens, 52892 Bunker Rd, in the duck pond on the east side.

Surrey

Darts Hill Garden Park, 1660- 168 St, South Surrey, Garden Bed 20. This tree is beginning to develop knobby "knees."

Native to the swamps and wetlands of Delaware to Illinois and south into Florida and Texas, Bald Cypress reaches a mature height of fifteen to twenty-one metres. This unusual deciduous conifer is not common in the South Fraser Region, but when grown it has a conical form. The branching habit is usually alternate which distinguishes Bald Cypress from the common and also deciduous conifer, Dawn Redwood, *Metasequoia glyptostroboides*. The foliage of Bald Cypress resembles the leaves of a yew; the soft needles are flat and two-ranked. Emerging yellow and aging to a lovely soft green, the needles turn again to yellow in the autumn and finally a russet brown before the entire branchlet falls from the tree. The bark is reddish and stringy while the bole of older trees is fluted and muscular. Cypress "knees" poke up from the roots around the base of the tree and are an outstanding feature of Bald Cypress. These volcano-shaped protuberances are quite comical and may grow as high as a metre. The knees appear when the tree is growing in very moist soils or at the edge of ponds or lakes. The tidy woody cone is round or egg-shaped, green in the summer and ripens to brown. On old picturesque trees in its native range, the trunk is often bare of limbs for many metres giving rise to its common name of Bald Cypress.

Taxus baccata f. *aurea*

Golden Yew

The leaves of Golden Yew are bright yellow in spring, mellowing to yellowish green as the season advances. The tips and the edges of the needles are more intensely coloured than the rest of the leaf. Golden Yew is often shrubby in habit.

Where to see the trees:

Langley

Sendall Gardens, 20166- 50 Ave, Langley City.

Surrey

Darts Hill Garden Park, 1660- 168 St, South Surrey, Garden Bed 19.

School District No 36, Administrative Offices, 14225- 56 Ave, Newton, on the east side of the building, likely planted in 1965 when the building was constructed.

Taxus baccata f. *aurea*, foliage

Taxus baccata 'Fastigiata'
Irish Yew

Four Churchyard Yews, *Taxus baccata* 'Fastigiata', Fort Langley Cemetery, Langley

Taxus baccata 'Fastigiata', foliage and scarlet arils

Stiffly upright branches and a strong columnar form distinguish the very common Irish Yew in the South Fraser landscape. With its tight formal shape and sombre dark green needles, it is easy to identify. The leathery sharp-pointed needles, which spiral around the branchlets, are lustrous on the top and pale green on the underside. The fruit, which is produced by this female cultivar in the fall, is a bright red fleshy and berry-like aril. The green-brown seed is visible but tucked inside the colourful aril. Superficially the fruit resembles an olive and like an olive, the outer blood-red flesh is edible but the seed of Irish Yew is highly poisonous as are its leaves and bark. The bark of mature trees is reddish, scaly and peels away in thin strips.

Where to see the trees:
Abbotsford
Aberdeen Cemetery, 29200 Fraser Highway, two mature trees.

Chilliwack
Hope River Corbould Park, north end of Corbould St, two trees on the west side of the parking area.

Delta
Augustinian Monastery, 3900 Arthur Dr, Ladner.

Boundary Bay Cemetery, 56 St and 8 Ave, Tsawwassen, several very fine specimens that mark the family plot of the Burr Family.

Where to see the trees:

Langley

City Park, 207 St and 48 Ave, Langley City, located at the southwest edge of the playing fields.

Fort Langley Cemetery, 23105 St Andrews St, Fort Langley, four plump trees, examples of Churchyard Yews, mark the burial plots of the descendants of Henry and Mary Wilkie (Henry Wilkie, 1820- 1905). The first burials in Fort Langley Cemetery occurred in 1882.

Murrayville Cemetery, 21405- 44 Ave, Murrayville.

Rosedale

Minter Gardens, 52892 Bunker Rd, Rosedale, northwest of the Formal Garden.

Surrey

Darts Hill Garden Park, 1660- 168 St, South Surrey, Garden Bed 11.

Green Timbers Arboretum, 9800- 140 St, Whalley, immediately south of the Heritage Buildings.

Thuja occidentalis 'Fastigiata'
Syn. *Thuja occidentalis* 'Pyramidalis'
Syn. *Thuja occidentalis* 'Columnaris'
Pyramid Cedar or Hedging Cedar

Thuja occidentalis 'Fastigiata', Trinity Western University

Thuja occidentalis 'Fastigiata', foliage and cones

Pyramid Cedar is commonly used as a hedging material in the South Fraser Region. Its columnar form and dense upright branching habit make it a reasonable choice for this purpose, but newer cultivars, which retain their bright green foliage colour, are more desirable. Pyramid Cedar turns a dull brown-green over the winter months. The leaves are tiny, scale-like and yellow-green in the growing season. The foliage sprays are flat but usually slightly twisted and cupped at the tips. They have a

Thuja occidentalis 'Fastigiata'
Syn. *Thuja occidentalis* 'Pyramidalis'
Syn. *Thuja occidentalis* 'Columnaris'
Pyramid Cedar or Hedging Cedar

Where to see the trees:
Abbotsford
Aberdeen Cemetery, 29200 Fraser Highway.

Chilliwack
Kirkby House, 48567 McConnell Rd, East Chilliwack, a huge tree.

Langley
Trinity Western University, 7600 Glover Rd, Willoughby, two very large trees west of McMillan Hall.

sharp, slightly sweet, fusty smell. The branch-lets and stringy bark are reddish brown. The tiny brown cones are fingernail-sized, upright and yellowish. They mature to woody brown cones that open much like a tulip flower. Reaching a height of ten to twelve metres with a slim spread of 1.4 metres, the long fastigiate stems of Pyramid Cedar are damaged by the heavy wet snowfalls typical of the South Fraser Region. The branches fall open, spoiling the tree's tight appearance.

Thuja occidentalis 'Smaragd'
Emerald Cedar

Where to see the trees:
Chilliwack
10665 Standeven Rd, East Chilliwack.

Langley
23949- 58 A Place, Salmon River Uplands, a double row of tall trees.

Richmond
Fantasy Garden World, 10800 No 5 Rd.

Rosedale
Minter Gardens, 52892 Bunker Rd, two impressive groups, one growing on the east slope above the Formal Garden and a second group on the east side of the Arbor Garden.

Surrey
Darts Hill Garden Park, 1660- 168 St, South Surrey, Garden Bed 31.

Thuja occidentalis 'Smaragd', Salmon River Uplands, Langley

A very popular cultivar introduced to the South Fraser Region from Denmark, Emerald Cedar is preferred as a hedging cedar since it maintains its bright emerald green colour throughout the year. The foliage is held in upright circular sprays giving this conifer a neat, refined look. It is similar in size and habit to Pyramid Cedar, but the compact lateral branches of Emerald Cedar are less susceptible to snow damage.

Siberian Cedar is chunky in all its parts. It has a squat or broadly pyramidal form and is a slow grower, reaching a mature height of eight metres. The yellow-green foliage is dense, thick to the touch and leathery. The flat sprays are held on sturdy upright branchlets.

Where to see the trees:
Abbotsford

Matsqui Village Park, 6200 block Riverside St, Matsqui Prairie, four trees at the east end of the parking lot.

Rosedale

Minter Gardens, 52892 Bunker Rd, a group of fine specimens, at the north-west end of the Meadow Garden at a pathway intersection.

Thuja plicata
Western Red Cedar

Thuja plicata, foliage

Western Red Cedar is native to the Pacific Northwest coast from Alaska to northern California. It is also found in the Columbia Forest Region of the province. It is one of the South Fraser Region's most impressive conifers. In times gone by, it grew to massive size reaching a towering height of fifty-eight metres and gigantic girth. The "Cheewhat Lake Cedar," Canada's largest tree, growing in Pacific Rim National Park east of Cheewhat Lake has a trunk circumference of 18.34 metres, a DBH of 584 cm, is 55.5 m high, and has a crown spread of 15.6 metres. Few, if any, examples of Western Red Cedar trees of such colossal size remain in the South Fraser Region.

Where to see the trees:
Abbotsford

Downes Bowl Park, Trethewey St pedestrian entrance (no car parking at this entrance), a ten-minute walk down a ridgeline to an old growth grove of Western Red Cedar and Douglas Fir, the largest Western Red Cedar has a DBH of 140 cm.

Hogan Family Nature Park, 2860 block Debruyne Rd. There are several very big trees in the park, one of the larger trees with a DBH of 133 cm.

Hoon Park, 33300 Holland Ave.

MSA General Hospital, 2179 McCallum Rd, west of the building, a grove of good-sized trees.

Musselwhite Cemetery, southeast corner of Old Yale Rd and Marshall Rd, several good-sized specimens.

Ravine Park, Bourquin Cr, east access, a number of large trees in the park.

Chilliwack

Elk Creek Rainforest, Chilliwack Forest District.

North end of Gillanders Rd, East Chilliwack, three good-sized trees that are part of a row planting south to McConnell Rd.

Chilliwack Cemeteries, 10010 Hillcrest Dr, Little Mountain, good-sized trees.

Corner of Castleman Rd and Chapman Rd, Rosedale. This tree is locally known as the "Bus Stop Tree". It has been directionally pruned for the power lines.

Thuja plicata
Western Red Cedar

10665 Standeven Rd, Rosedale, Chilliwack.

Delta

Delta Nature Reserve, parking lot to access trails located at 10388 Nordel Court, North Delta.

Langley

Fort Langley Cemetery, 23105 St Andrews St, Fort Langley.

Walking Trail on the north side of Yorkson Creek, west of 208 Ave to the pedestrian bridge. The grove of large trees is immediately south of 207 Street and 89 A Ave in Walnut Grove.

Grey Pit, 260 St and 84 Ave, Northeast Langley, a stand of second growth trees that are nearly a century old.

Lindell Beach

2014 Lindell Ave, the road detours around this huge Western Red Cedar.

Richmond

Fantasy Garden World, 10800 No 5 Rd.

9400 Odlin Rd, a good-sized tree with a DBH of over a metre.

Millennium Botanical Garden and Arboretum, N McLennan Community Park, Granville Ave andGarden City Rd.

Rosedale

Minter Gardens, 52892 Bunker Rd. There are many good-sized individuals throughout the garden. There is a lovely walk in a grove of Western Red Cedars to the south of the Wedding Chapel.

Surrey

10648-127 St*.

The Glades, 561- 172 St, South Surrey*.

Mound Farm, 168 St. and 50 Ave, Cloverdale*.

Hazelmere United Church, northeast corner 184 St and 16 Ave, South Surrey*.

260 St and 84 Ave*.

12247- 91A Ave, Whalley.

The glossy yellowish-green scale leaves of Western Red Cedar are held in flat sprays. The scale leaves are in pairs; the side pair folded and the alternate pair tucked flat, like a braid, hence the species name plicata. The foliage when crushed has a sharp sweet fragrance. In the fall the older leaves "flag", turning orange brown and dropping from the tree. The small upright egg-shaped cones are yellowish-green in the summer and ripen to brown. When the cone scales open to release the seeds, the open cone resembles a tiny tulip flower. The reddish bark is fibrous, shredding and peeling into vertical strips. Branches swoop upward at the tips while the small branchlets droop limply. Western Red Cedar is often densely branched with foliage to the ground. On old trees the trunk is fluted and very heavily buttressed.

Did You Know?

• Western Red Cedar or *Thuja plicata* is the arboreal emblem of the province of British Columbia. The provincial tree was adopted in June of 1985. Western Red Cedar was called the "Tree of Life" by indigenous peoples as its wood, bark and roots provided building materials, clothing, medicines, implements, fuel and even transport in the form of dug-out canoes.

• The last ancient rainforest in the South Fraser Region is found in the Elk Creek Rainforest in the Chilliwack Forest District. To access this magnificent stand of Western Red Cedar trees, take the Annis Road exit from Hwy 1. Cross Annis Road and travel east on Hack Brown Road, which parallels Hwy 1 on the south side. Turn right on Nixon Road, turn left on Ruddock Road and travel up the switchbacks to the top of Ruddock Road, which lies approximately 450 metres above sea level. The access is, at the present time, through private property. The landowner of the access point is Mr. Clint Marvin. The trees are located on Crown Land just below Elk Creek Falls. This ancient rain forest is unparalleled anywhere in the South Fraser Region. The Western Red Cedar trees are huge. They range from 110 cm to 160 cm in diameter at breast height with circumferences of 3.5–5 metres. Hundreds of years old, the trunks of these beautiful trees are heavily buttressed and fluted at the base.

• The five Western Red Cedars standing to the west of the cenotaph in Fort Langley were planted by Dr. Benjamin Butler Marr shortly after the installation of the cenotaph in the early 1920's to commemorate the fallen soldiers of World War I. These trees, with their straight trunks, appear to be standing at attention in honour of Langley's war dead. Rhododendrons were planted on either side, of which only one remains today. A field gun and one or two machine guns originally stood in front of the cenotaph.

• The "Bent Cedar", a large Western Red Cedar with its unique form, is a noteworthy landmark in The Glades Garden, South Surrey. The tree is bent into a reverse "S" curve shape.

• Hazelmere United Church in South Surrey was built in 1905 on land donated by Henry T. Thrift, a former Reeve of Surrey. Thrift was an early settler of Hazelmere Valley, homesteading there from 1886–1910. The church is built in the Carpenter Gothic architectural style.

• The "Rock-tree" on 91A Avenue in Whalley is very unusual. A large Western Red Cedar tree, it is twenty metres high and with a DBH of 90 cm. It is growing out of a glacial erratic boulder that measures 1.7 metres high by 4 metres wide. The tree is perched on top of the boulder with long muscular roots reaching down into the cleft at the centre of the rock. The City of Surrey realigned the road and services and created a six-metre no disturbance zone around this tree when the subdivision was designed in 2002.

Remembrance Day wreaths decorate the Cenotaph in the Fort Langley Cemetery. Five lovely Western Red Cedar trees, *Thuja plicata*, frame the scene

Thuja plicata, Hazelmere United Church, Surrey

Thuja plicata 'Zebrina'
Syn. *Thuja plicata* 'Aurea'

Zebra Cedar

Where to see the trees:

Abbotsford

2236 Marshall Rd, a vigorous hedge.

Hougen Park, south off Highway 1 on Cole Rd.

Chilliwack

Salish Park, 45860- 1 Ave.

Townsend Park, Ashwell Rd and Hodgins Ave, several groups of trees on the west end of the park, on the west side of the property line of the sewer treatment facility.

Yarrow Community Park, north end of Community St, Yarrow.

Langley

Sendall Gardens, Langley City.

5994- 216 Ave, Milner, a row of good-sized trees.

Richmond

Fantasy Garden World, 10800 No 5 Rd.

Surrey

Darts Hill Garden Park, 1660- 168 St, South Surrey, Garden Bed 11.

Thuja plicata 'Zebrina', foliage

Reaching a mature height of twenty metres, Zebra Cedar is very common in the South Fraser Region as a solitary specimen and as hedging. It has a broadly pyramidal shape and is densely branched to the ground. The foliage is similar to the species but banded green and creamy-gold, hence the name Zebra Cedar. Significant confusion exists in the literature as there are over a dozen synonyms for this tree. One tree that often causes confusion is the less common *Thuja plicata* 'Aurea', which has antique gold-coloured foliage. The banded foliage of the Zebra Cedar is a good year-round identifying characteristic.

Hiba Arborvitæ or Hiba Cedar

Thujopsis dolobrata, Darts Hill Garden Park, Surrey

Thujopsis dolobrata, foliage

Native to Japan, Hiba Arborvitæ is rarely grown in the South Fraser Region. In its native range it reaches a mature height of thirty metres with a conical form. The foliage resembles the scale-like leaves of our native Western Red Cedar but is very glossy dark green, thick and leathery to the touch. The scale leaves of Hiba Arborvitæ are slightly hooked and catch when stroked rather than lying smoothly along the branchlets like Western Red Cedar. The underside is marked with a shocking white band, edged with green. The foliage sprays are held upright, like fans on the branchlets. The roundish woody cones are thumbnail-sized, glaucous green ripening to bluish brown. The bark of Hiba Arborvitæ is reddish brown and stringy.

Where to see the trees:

Chilliwack
Gwynne Vaughan Park, Williams Rd and Hope River Rd, Fairfield Island, a very large tree for the South Fraser Region.

Langley
4900 block 208 Ave, City of Langley.

4758- 240 St, Salmon River Uplands, on the south side of the driveway.

Richmond
Fantasy Garden World, 10800 No 5 Rd.

Surrey
Darts Hill Garden Park, 1660- 168 St, South Surrey, Garden Bed 21.

Redwood Park, 17900- 20 Ave, South Surrey* east of the Tree House.

The Glades, 561- 172 St, South Surrey, beside Semiahmoo's Tribute.

Thujopsis dolobrata 'Variegata'
Variegated Hiba Arborvitæ

Thujopsis dolobrata 'Variegata', foliage

Thujopsis dolobrata 'Variegata', Darts Hill Garden Park, Surrey

Where to see the trees:
Surrey
Darts Hill Garden Park, 1660- 168 St, South Surrey*, Garden beds 11 and 26.

Variegated Hiba Arborvitæ is exceedingly rare in the South Fraser Region and may reach a mature height of fifteen metres. The foliage of this unusual conifer is variegated creamy white in irregular splotches and blotches. Some of the foliage on some trees is well-coloured green and cream and other trees look lightly splattered with colour. Variegated Hiba Arborvitæ matures into a broadly pyramidal shape.

Tilia americana 'Redmond'
Redmond American Linden

Tilia americana 'Redmond', prominent veins on the underside of the leaves

Redmond Linden is densely pyramidal in form, reaching fifteen to twenty metres in height at maturity with a maximum spread of fourteen metres. The large hand-sized leaves are lopsided and heart-shaped with strongly toothed margins. They are dark green on the top and pale green beneath. The leaves have a firm texture and are smooth above and below, with small tufts of hairs in the axils of the prominent veins on the bottom surface. The leaves turn pale yellow in the fall. The pale yellow flowers are fragrant and bloom in loose clusters in June and July. The fruit are woody, round, about the size of peas, and produced in small loose clusters at the end of a stalk, which is attached to a strap-like leafy bract as are the flower clusters. The large flame-shaped buds are deep red in colour while the branches are crimson on the top and greenish brown on the underside. The large bud scales make the buds look lopsided. The coarse texture, including the strong branching structure of Redmond American Linden, contributes to its bold appearance in the landscape.

Where to see the trees:
Chilliwack

University College of the Fraser Valley, 45600 Airport Rd, a double row of good-looking trees on the west side of Building D, Multi-purpose Complex.

Native to England, Wales, and northeast Spain, north into Sweden and east to western Russia, Littleleaf Linden reaches thirty metres in height with an upright oval form. The leaves are heart-shaped and variable in size with a toothed margin. Thin textured and dull medium to dark green, they are smooth on top and the bottom except for tufts of tan-coloured hairs in the axils of the veins. In the South Fraser Region, where Littleleaf Linden, especially its cultivars, is commonly grown as a street or park tree, the fall colour is mellow yellow. The small yellowish star-shaped flowers are produced in pendulous clusters in late June and July. The flowers are highly attractive to honey bees; a soft drone

Tilia cordata, Jubilee Park, Abbotsford

Tilia cordata
Littleleaf Linden or Small-leaved Lime

Tilia cordata, foliage

as the bees collect the sweet nectar thrums the air. The fruit is a tiny, round thin-shelled nutlet subtended by a narrow bract, which is shaped like a fishing lure or spoon. Each nutlet is covered in fine grey hair that wears away as the nutlets ripen in the fall.

Where to see the trees:

Abbotsford

Northeast corner of Lynn Cr and Eagle St, a small tree in-between three Silver Lime trees.

Hougen Park, south off Highway 1 on Cole Rd.

ICBC Claim Centre, 2885 Trethewey St, a row on the north side along Dahlstrom Ave.

Jubilee Park, McCallum Rd south of Essendene, one tree on the west side of the park.

Chilliwack

Parkholm Lodge, 9090 Newman Rd, a large tree on the south side of the garden.

Fairfield Island Park, 46000 Clare Ave, Fairfield Island.

Promontory Park West, Teskey Rd, Promontory Heights.

Canadian Forces Base, Keith Wilson Rd and Vedder Rd, Vedder Crossing. There are many fine trees on the base. There is a large Littleleaf Linden on the southeast corner of Calais Cr and Caen Rd and another large tree on Sicily Rd at Normandy Dr.

Delta

Sacred Heart Elementary School, 3900 Arthur Dr, Ladner.

Langley

City Park, 207 St and 48 Ave, Langley City, Langley City, a grove of trees to the south of Al Anderson Memorial Pool.

Derby Reach Regional Park, Allard Cr, Northwest Langley, a planting of fairly good-sized trees on the west side of the parking lot.

Williams Park, 6600 block 238 St, Salmon River Uplands.

Surrey

Green Timbers Arboretum, 9800-140 St, Whalley.

Chancellor® Littleleaf Linden has a fastigiate branching pattern in youth but as the tree ages it becomes more pyramidal in form. Chancellor® Littleleaf Linden is commonly planted as a street tree in the South Fraser Region.

Where to see the trees:

Abbotsford

Median planting on Old Yale Rd to McClure Rd from Townline Rd to Clearbrook Rd, in front of Ellwood Park.

Chilliwack

5577- 5718 Stonehaven St, Promontory Heights.

Surrey

11056- 163 A St, Guildford.

11090- 163 A St, Guildford.

Tilia cordata 'PNI 6025'
Greenspire® Littleleaf Linden

Tilia cordata 'Greenspire', Morton Arboetum, Lisle, Illinois

Tilia cordata 'Greenspire', nutlets and attending bracts

The small, dark green leathery leaves differentiate this cultivar from the species. Reaching a mature height of twelve to fifteen metres and a spread of nine metres, Greenspire® Littleleaf Linden resembles a candle flame because of its tight pyramidal silhouette. The branches are very uniformly spaced around the tree with the youngest branches drooping at their very tips. The fall colour is an unremarkable yellowish green.

Tilia cordata 'PNI 6025'
Greenspire® Littleleaf Linden

Where to see the trees:
Chilliwack,
University College of the Fraser Valley, 45600 Airport Rd, a row of trees on the east side of the roadway south of Building C, Health Sciences.

Delta
Memorial Park, 47 Ave and Delta St, Ladner.

Langley
Kwantlen University College, 20901 Langley Bypass, Langley City. This young tree was planted in 2000 as a memorial to Mogens Koch a well-known greenhouse grower in Langley. A small plaque is placed at the base of the tree.

Surrey
1540- 133B St, South Surrey, the entire street is planted with Greenspire® Littleleaf Linden.

6569- 133A St, South Surrey.

Tilia x *euchlora*
Syn. *Tilia* x *europæa* 'Euchlora'
Crimean Linden or Caucasian Lime

Where to see the trees:
Abbotsford
Provincial Courthouse, 32202 South Fraser Way, on the southeast corner of the parking lot.

Matsqui Elementary School, 5730 Riverside Rd, Matsqui Prairie village, a tree on the north side of the school.

Chilliwack
Promontory Park West, on Teskey Rd, Promontory Heights, east side of the baseball field lawn.

Sardis Park, Sardis, several large specimens near the west entrance to the park on School Lane.

Townsend Park, southwest corner of Ashwell Rd and Hodgins Ave, playground area.

University College of the Fraser Valley, 45600 Airport Rd, several trees south of Building D, near Building C, Health Sciences.

Langley
24355- 48 Ave, Salmon River Uplands, in the middle of the west side of the entry drive.

A hybrid lime from the Caucasus-Crimea area, Crimean Linden grows into a large round tree twenty metres high. The leaves are similar to Littleleaf Linden but have a spiny serrated leaf margin. They are shiny dark green on top and pale beneath with tufts of tan-coloured hairs dotting the axils of the veins. The flowers are deep yellow and produced later, at the end of July and are usually in clusters of three to seven. Bees find this tree a powerful narcotic. The fruit, which is football-shaped and covered in down, is usually conspicuously ribbed. A thin leaf-like bract subtends both the flowers and fruit, which is typical of all the lindens. In comparison with Littleleaf Linden, which produces fruit by the bucketful, Crimean Linden is a parsimonious producer of fruit.

Richmond
City Hall, 6911 No. 3 Rd, east side of the building.

Surrey
15958- 19A Ave, South Surrey.

15955- 19A Ave, South Surrey.

13858- 23 Ave, South Surrey, an entire street planted with this tree.

European Linden or Common Lime

Tilia x *europæa*, Abbotsford

Tilia x *europæa*, foliage

European Linden is not commonly grown in the South Fraser Region. It is a hybrid between *Tilia cordata* and *Tilia platyphyllos*. European Linden is the tallest linden, one with a recorded height of forty-six metres but more typically it reaches to thirty-nine metres with an upright oval form. The leaves are dark green and lack hairs except for the pale tufts on the vein axils on the bottom of the leaf. Appearing in early June, the flowers are the earliest of the lindens. They are yellow, star-shaped and in clusters of four to ten. Buds and stems are often red-maroon in colour. The hard-shelled nutlets are velvet covered and slightly ribbed. The trunk of European Linden is often marred by the production of epicormic shoots, which thicken and form burls.

Where to see the trees:

Abbotsford

33631 St. Olaf St, Matsqui Prairie village.

Surrey

Green Timbers Arboretum, 9800- 140 St, Whalley.

Tilia 'Petiolaris'

Silver Pendent Lime, Pendent White Lime or Weeping Linden

Tilia 'Petiolaris', foliage and developing nutlets with bracts

Tilia 'Petiolaris', Jubilee Park, Abbotsford

Where to see the trees:

Abbotsford

Jubilee Park, McCallum Rd south of Essendene, two lovely trees on the west side of the park.

Langley

Traas Nursery, 24120- 48 Ave, Salmon River Uplands, a magnificent tree.

Very rare in the South Fraser Region, Silver Pendent Lime is well-deserving of greater attention. It grows into a dense upright oval, twenty-one to twenty seven metres high with a substantial spread of ten metres. Its strongly weeping habit, where the drooping laterals arise from the undersides of the large scaffold branches, is remarkable. The petiole, which is one of the longest of all the lindens, allows the palm-sized dark green leaves to pirouette in the wind, revealing the starkly white fuzzy underside. The fall leaf colour is clear yellow. The cream flowers, held in pendulous clusters, are sweetly scented. Appearing in July, the flowers are highly narcotic to bees and may be fatal to them. The fruit is typical of the lindens with a long bract attending each cluster of nutlets. Silver Pendent Lime fruit are pea-sized and very fuzzy.

Did You Know?

John C. Traas planted this beautiful Silver Pendent Lime in 1955. He obtained, from a Fraser Valley nursery grower, a four- to five-year-old grafted specimen and planted it to one side of the gravel lane. Later when the lane was widened to become 48 Avenue, the tree was moved to its present location. John C. Traas is a nursery grower too. He emigrated from

Silver Pendent Lime, Pendent White Lime or Weeping Linden

Zeeland, in the Netherlands in 1954, where he was a fruit grower. In 1953 the dyke broke adjacent to his farm, and salt water inundated the fruit orchard, killing his fruit trees. He came to Canada to begin again. Traas Nursery has maintained a reputation as propagators of fruit tree rootstocks and other unusual trees. John Traas, also a nursery grower, and son of John C. Traas carries on the family tradition. Just to the east on 24355- 48 Avenue, John has planted an exceptional entry row to his home. The trees on the east side of the entry drive were originally the last trees in a nursery production row, while the trees on the west side were planted in 1975 to create the elegant entry feature. The trees are planted at six metres on centre and alternate first one with purple, then green and then yellow foliage. A number of the trees planted are very rare including a second Silver Pendent Lime.

Tilia platyphyllos

Bigleaf Linden

Tilia platyphyllos, in the fall, Aldergrove, Langley

Tilia platyphyllos, fall colour, nutlets with attending bracts

Rare in the South Fraser Region, Bigleaf Linden is native to Europe, the Caucasus and Asia Minor. It is a coarse-textured tree, both in leaf and winter-branching silhouette, with an oval shape overall. The leaves are much

Tilia platyphyllos
Bigleaf Linden

Where to see the trees:
Langley
3100 block Station Rd, Aldergrove.

Richmond
9260 Alexandra Rd.

larger than Littleleaf Linden, growing 12–18 cm long but they are not as large as the leaves of American Linden. Bigleaf Linden leaves are hairy on both surfaces and are very velvety to the touch. They remain green late in the fall, and then turn a green yellow. The clusters of three, sometimes six, flowers are pale yellow and appear very early for a linden, in late May to early June. They are exceptionally fragrant. The buds and hairy stems are reddish green-brown. The large ribbed nutlet is round, velvety and hard shelled.

Tilia tomentosa
Silver Lime

Where to see the trees:
Abbotsford
Northeast corner of Lynn Cr and Eagle St, a row of three small trees.

Chilliwack
Park, southeast corner of Manuel Rd and Vedder Rd, Sardis, a very large and imposing tree overhanging the east bank of the creek.

Langley
24439- 56 Ave, Salmon River Uplands, a good-sized tree in the front garden.

24355- 48 Ave, Salmon River Uplands, north end of the east side of the entry drive.

Silver Lime is deserving of greater attention since it is far less attractive to aphids than some of the other lindens. Silver Lime grows thirty metres tall with a pyramidal shape in youth, aging gracefully to a rounded outline. It is native to southeastern Europe and southwest Asia. All parts of Silver Lime are clothed in soft hairs. Young leaves are softly hairy as they first emerge, as are the branchlets. The leaves are sharply pointed and become dark green on the top surface. In beautiful contrast, the bottom is velvety to the touch and bright white. The long petioles allow the leaves to twirl in the wind. Fall colour is yellow-green. Blooming in July, the yellowish white flowers of Silver Linden are the last to flower. Bees find the nectar of this tree stupefying. After supping, they fly erratically and may even die. The egg-shaped white fuzzy nutlet is five-ribbed and sports a short point at its apex. Silver Lime bark is silver-grey and smooth. It is a rare tree in the South Fraser Region.

Tilia tomentosa 'PNI 6051'
Green Mountain® Silver Linden

Green Mountain® Silver Linden reaches fifteen to twenty-one metres high at maturity with a spread of twelve metres. It develops a dense upright oval crown. The furry silver undersides of the dark green leaves are handsome as the leaf stalks allow the leaves to flutter in the breeze. Green Mountain® Silver Linden is a relatively new cultivar to the South Fraser Region.

Where to see the trees:

Surrey
68th Ave, between 127th St and 128th St, Newton, a street tree planting.

Tsuga canadensis
Eastern Hemlock or Canadian Hemlock

Where to see the trees:

Langley
Sendall Gardens, 20166- 50 Ave, Langley City, a small tree on the east side of the fountain.

Surrey
The Glades, 561- 172 St, South Surrey.

Tsuga canadensis, foliage

Native to southern Ontario, Quebec and into the Maritimes, Eastern Hemlock may reach a height of twenty or more metres. It is rarely grown as a large tree in the South Fraser Region. Dozens of cultivars of this conifer have been developed for horticultural commerce; several are popular locally while many are used in landscaping in Eastern Canada. Typical of hemlock, the evergreen needles are of different sizes on the same branchlet. The lustrous dark green leaves are blunt, with two white stripes on the underside. Eastern Hemlock has a weeping central leader and a pyramidal form. The grey-brown cones hang from the tips of the branches and are tiny, the smallest of all the hemlocks. On mature trees the bark is deeply furrowed.

Tsuga heterophylla
Western Hemlock

Tsuga heterophylla, developing cones

Where to see the trees:

Abbotsford

Hogan Family Nature Park, 2860 block Debruyne Rd, several big trees in the park, one of the larger trees with a DBH of 83 cm.

34195 Hazel St.

Chilliwack

Ryder Lake Park, 49285 Elk View Rd, Ryder Lake, many well-grown trees.

Richmond

Richmond Nature Park, 11851Westminster Hwy.

Millennium Botanical Garden and Arboretum, N McLennan Community Park, Granville Ave and Garden City Rd.

7131 Bridge St, several good-sized trees.

Steveston Park, 4111 Moncton St, Steveston.

Surrey

City Hall, 14245- 56 Ave, Newton, west side of the building.

The Glades, 561- 172 St, South Surrey, throughout the garden.

Did You Know?

"Norvan's Castle" is a colossal Western Hemlock growing in Lynn Headwaters Regional Park in North Vancouver. It is 9.12 metres in circumference, has a diameter at breast height (DBH) of 290 cm and a crown spread of 20.12 metres.

Western Hemlock is native to the Pacific Northwest coast from Alaska to northern California. It is also found in the Columbia Forest Region of the province. Graceful and airy, it is one of the South Fraser Region's most common conifers. It may grow to towering heights, reaching sixty to seventy-five metres. In the forest, it is easily recognized by its drooping leader. The branches of Western Hemlock droop at the tips as well. Two conspicuous white stripes on the underside of the short blunt needles help with identification. The needles are unequal in length, arranged higgledy-piggledy on the branchlet, some needles stand upright, and some point forward. Old leafless twigs are rough to the touch because the leaf stalks remain behind after the needles have fallen. The foliage has a fresh woodsy smell when bruised but is not as aromatic as Western Red Cedar, another native conifer that it may be found growing with. The light brown cones are very small for a tree of its stature. They are thumbnail-sized, woody and often produced in great quantity at the tips of the branches. The greyish brown bark of Western Hemlock is scaly, becoming furrowed on mature trees.

Mountain Hemlock or Alpine Hemlock

A subalpine species most comfortable at elevations of 760–1800 metres, Mountain Hemlock is native to the Pacific coast of North America. It grows at sea level in southern Alaska, and then it is found in mountainous habitats south into central California. Slender and spire-like, it reaches a mature height of forty metres, but much less at very high elevations and in cultivation. At sea level it grows slowly, and is often shrubby with branches to the ground. Compact in habit, the branches are densely clothed in bluish-green needles. The needles are radially arranged around the branchlets, which differentiates this hemlock from the preceding two, which have needles that are more or less two-ranked. In end view, the foliage of Mountain Hemlock resembles an asterisk (*). The cones, which are up to 7. 5 cm long are the largest of the hemlocks. First purplish, they mature to a soft tan colour.

Where to see the trees:

Richmond
Fantasy Garden World, 10800 No 5 Rd.

Did You Know?

The largest Mountain Hemlock in British Columbia is on Hollyburn Mountain. It is 5. 99 metres in circumference, has a DBH of 190 cm and is 44.5 metres tall. A number of very large trees are growing in Cypress Provincial Park in North Vancouver on Hollyburn.

U

Of all man's works of art, a cathedral is greatest.
A vast and majestic tree is greater than that.

Henry Ward Beecher, (1813–1887), American clergyman

Ulmus americana, foliage and samara

Ulmus americana, Matsqui Elementary School, Abbotsford

Ulmus americana
American Elm or White Elm

Native to central and eastern Canada and into the United States, American Elm, at maturity is one of the stateliest deciduous trees. It was commonly planted in the South Fraser Region approximately sixty to eighty years ago and now the trees, where left to grow undisturbed, are of grand size. Many are thirty-five metres and more in height with the typical fan or umbrella-shaped crown, with the youngest branchlets gracefully weeping at their tips. The leaves of American Elm are somewhat variable. Typically, they are dark green, 7.5 to 15 cm long, with a doubly toothed margin. Like most elms, the veins of the leaf are clearly evident and the sides of the leaves meet unequally at the base of the each leaf. Usually the upper surface of the leaves is slightly rough to the touch but this is not always so. Fall colour is a glorious rich yellow. The flowers are inconspicuous but the fruit is a flat oval-shaped, single-winged samara about the size of a dime. It ripens just as the leaves are maturing in May. The delicately fringed edge and the deeply notched tip that dips to the tiny seed at its papery centre, differentiate the seed of American Elm from all others. The dark greyish-brown bark is deeply furrowed.

Did You Know?

• The American Elm trees on the north and east sides of the school grounds of Matsqui Elementary School were planted in 1929. They were donated by the Colony Farm at Essondale in Coquitlam and were planted according to a Department of Education plan. The original school was constructed in 1903 and the adjacent high school was added in 1908.

A break in the dyke at Gifford on May 31, 1948 flooded the muddy waters of the Fraser River over Matsqui Village and the surrounding farmland. Within in a few hours the landscape at Matsqui Prairie became a 27-kilometre-long lake. Homes were submerged up to their eaves. Outhouses, chicken coops, and other small buildings floated alongside fence posts, lumber and flotsam of all types. Three hundred and fifty families were left homeless. Luckily no one died in the flooding which continued well into June. An archival photo of the Great Flood of the Fraser River shows that the American Elms were large and well established on the Matsqui Prairie school grounds at the time of the flood.

• The massive American Elm at the Ladner Community Centre resides on the site of the King George V High School, the first high school in Delta, built in 1912. The building burned down after an explosion in 1960 but it is possible the tree dates from the early part of the ninteenth century.

• The residence on Ladner Trunk Road in Delta was the manager's house for the 2,428-hectare farm of Dominic Burns, a prominent Vancouver businessman, and for whom Burns Bog is named. The house was built in 1909 in the Foursquare architectural style. The site features a mature landscape with other large trees such as *Fagus sylvatica*, European Beech, *Æsculus hippocastanum*, Horse Chestnut, and a *Catalpa speciosa*, Western Catalpa.

• The magnificent thirty-metre-tall American Elm in Memorial Park Delta, has a DBH of 120 cm; unfortunately a large branch has broken out on the west side of the tree. Delta Council designated the tree as a Heritage Tree on March 3, 1997*. The property the tree resides on was part of the original farmstead of Ladner's namesake, William H. Ladner. Later the land became Paul Ladner's

Ulmus americana

American Elm or White Elm

farm; 1.6 hectares of his land was bought in 1919, to build a park and athletic field. It was named Memorial Park to honour the fallen soldiers of World War One. A cenotaph, dedicated May 22, 1921, is placed at the south end of Delta Street in the park.

• The row of mature American Elms in front of the new Lord Byng Elementary School building were likely planted in 1930 or earlier when a fourteen-room school was built there with financial contribution from the Japanese community. A photo, circa 1935, shows trees almost the diameter of a telephone pole growing on the school grounds at that time. Steveston's first one-room school was built in 1897 on the site and a succession of schools has been built there subsequently. Steveston Public School was renamed Lord Byng School in honour of the Governor General of Canada in 1922.

Where to see the trees:

Abbotsford
Matsqui Elementary School, 5730 Riverside Rd, Matsqui Prairie village, a row of seven spectacular trees with a DBH of 120 cm on the east fence line of the school.

Chilliwack
45910 Hocking Ave.

Minter Country Garden, 10015 Young Rd North, a very large tree on the north side of the slough adjacent to the residence.

Rosedale Elementary School, 10125 McGrath Rd, Rosedale.

Stö:lo Centre, 7201 Vedder Rd, Sardis.

Sardis Elementary School, 45775 Manuel Rd, Sardis.

Delta
Ladner Community Centre, 4734-51 St, Ladner, a lofty open-grown specimen with a DBH of 170 cm.

Manager's Residence/ Burns Ranch, 7225- 7269 Ladner Trunk Rd, four mature trees.

Memorial Park, southwest side, 47 Ave and Delta St, Ladner.

8640 Ladner Trunk Rd, a large tree used by bald eagles as a winter perch.

Richmond
RCMP Detachment, 6900 Minoru Blvd. This magnificent tree is located on the north side of the parking lot. It has been designated as a Heritage Tree in Richmond and stamped with No 002*.

Minoru Park, 7660 Minoru Gate, a lovely large tree.

6080 River Rd, a large open-grown tree.

Lord Byng Elementary School, 3711 Georgia St, Steveston, a row on the south side of the school.

Handley Ave, from Douglas to Wellington Cr, Burkeville, a double row of street trees.

Rosedale
Minter Gardens, 52892 Bunker Rd, a medium-sized tree along the southeast edge of the duck pond.

Surrey
4100- 152 St, South Surrey*. These thirteen mature trees formed the entry to a long since demolished farmhouse.

Ulmus americana 'Patmore'
Syn. *Ulmus americana* 'Brandon'

Patmore Elm

Ulmus americana, Matsqui Elementary School, Abbotsford

Patmore Elm has a narrow vase shape as compared to the species. The glossy dark green leaves are held on closely spaced branchlets. The seeds for Patmore Elm were originally collected near Brandon, Manitoba.

Where to see the trees:

Chilliwack

Fairfield Island Park, 46000 Clare Ave, Fairfield Island, a row on the north side of the soccer fields.

Portage Park, southeast corner of Portage Ave and Woodbine St.

Promontory Park West, Teskey Rd, Promontory Heights.

Townsend Park, southwest corner of Ashwell Rd and Hodgins Ave, backstop of baseball diamond 1.

South Sumas Rd on the north to south side from Tyson Rd to Wiltshire Rd, Sardis.

Ulmus glabra

Scotch Elm or Wych Elm

Commonly planted in the early part of the 20th Century in the South Fraser Region, Scotch Elm, at forty metres in height is a statuesque deciduous tree. It is native to northern and central Europe and western Asia. Scotch Elm is much more wide-spreading and open than American Elm. The dull green leaves are coarsely toothed, often three-lobed at the tip, and turn yellow in the fall. The upper leaf surface is very rough to the touch, like sandpaper. The base of the leaf of this elm is decidedly lopsided, with one curving leaf half almost hiding the short leaf stalk. The single-winged samara is about the size of a one-dollar coin. Ripening in July, the tiny seed sits in the centre of the papery tan-coloured wing, differentiating Scotch Elm from many others. The twigs and buds are hairy. The bark is deeply fissured but irregularly so, in comparison to the regular fissures of American Elm.

Ulmus glabra, 184 Street, Surrey

Ulmus glabra
Scotch Elm or Wych Elm

Ulmus glabra, trunk

Where to see the trees:

Abbotsford

Dunach Park, NW corner of Mt Lehman Rd and Downes Rd, a large tree with a DBH of 120 cm.

Chilliwack

10755 Kitchen Rd, East Chilliwack.

Stó:lo Centre, 7201 Vedder Rd, Sardis, two large trees.

7032 Chilliwack River Rd, Sardis.

Langley

Hazelgrove Farm, 8651 Glover Rd, Ft Langley.

7092 Glover Rd, Milner.

Surrey

Robert Dougal MacKenzie House, 5418- 184 St, Cloverdale*.

White Rock

1164 Elm St, three street trees.

Did You Know?

Robert Dougal MacKenzie built the house at 5418–184 St, Cloverdale, in the Craftsman architectural style in 1911. At that time, the street was known as Hall's Prairie Road. The residence was one of the first homes in Surrey to have running water. The property was originally part of 28.3-hectare farm. The large barn of the farm could stable four teams of horses. Robert MacKenzie worked in construction, became a road superintendent and eventually served as the Reeve of Surrey from 1921 to 1923.

• The very large Scotch Elm at Hazelgrove Farm, Fort Langley is beautifully sited on the front lawn of the E.A. Magel residence, built circa 1939. Mr. E.A. Magel, a haberdasher by trade, established the Hazelnut farm on the banks of the Salmon River and built the half-timbered Tudor Revival style home.

• The Scotch Elms on Elm Street in White Rock are the namesakes for this tiny north to south street, which ends at Marine Drive.

Ulmus glabra 'Camperdown'
Syn. *Ulmus* x *vegeta* 'Camperdownii'

Camperdown Elm, Upside Down Elm or Umbrella Elm

Ulmus glabra 'Camperdown',
contorted branching pattern, Green Timbers
Arboretum, Surrey

Ulmus glabra 'Camperdown', Avondale, Delta

The Camperdown Elm is one of the most magnificent weeping trees found in the South Fraser Region. It is not common, but nonetheless breathtaking when mature at eight to nine metres in height. Camperdown Elm has a tight umbrella shape with curtains of thick branches, which cascade to the ground. The contorted scaffold branches, which support the crown underneath the pendulous sheath, zig zag like a corkscrew and are best viewed in the winter. The leaves, which are larger than the species, are very rough to the touch, like sandpaper, on the upper surface. The tree produces very little if any fruit. Camperdown Elm, which is usually top-grafted at two metres in height, creates a bold focal point in the landscape.

Where to see the trees:

Abbotsford

Musselwhite Cemetery, southeast corner of Old Yale Rd and Marshall Rd, a excellent tree in the centre of the cemetery.

Delta

Avondale, Rawlins Residence/Imperial Farm, 2349- 52 St, West Delta.

Langley

Dr. Marr residence, 9090 Glover Rd, Ft Langley.

Surrey

Green Timbers Arboretum, 9800- 140 St, Whalley, a perfect open-grown tree east of the cooling and sorting shed.

Did You Know?

Musselwhite Cemetery, which opened in 1892, has a number of Abbotsford area pioneers buried in its quiet grounds. The Camperdown Elm has been planted next to the headstone marking the resting place of Isabella Jackson, born on June 18, 1848. Isabella died in September 23, 1917. The umbrella canopy gracefully encloses several graves, including Isabella's.

Ulmus glabra 'Camperdown'
Syn. *Ulmus* x *vegeta* 'Camperdownii'

Camperdown Elm, Upside Down Elm or Umbrella Elm

• The impressive Camperdown Elm at Avondale in West Delta, is the largest in the South Fraser Region. With its massive size it could well be one of the largest Camperdown Elms in the Pacific Northwest. It was planted in 1915, at the same time as the existing symmetrical Foursquare farmhouse was constructed by Ed Churchill. The Rawlins family farmed the land earlier than the construction of the present house as Mrs. Louise Rawlins arrived as a bride from Ontario in 1905. The Rawlins named their farm "Avondale".

Ulmus glabra 'Lutescens'
Golden Scotch Elm or Golden Wych Elm

Ulmus glabra 'Lutescens', Redwood Park, Surrey

Ulmus glabra 'Lutescens', Redwood Park, Surrey

Where to see the trees:

Langley

Mainland Floral, 25355- 56 Ave, Salmon River Uplands, growing on the south property line under the power lines.

24355- 48 Ave, Salmon River Uplands, northern end of the west side of the entry drive.

Surrey

Redwood Park, 17900- 20 Ave, South Surrey*

Very rare in the South Fraser Region, Golden Scotch Elm is graced with foliage that emerges bright golden yellow then ages to a deep yellow-green in the summer months. The fall colour is vibrant yellow. The leaves do not sunburn, which is unusual for a golden-leafed tree. A short trunk, and a wide-spreading crown that is less than one-half the mature height of the species is typical for Golden Scotch Elm.

Pioneer Elm is a hybrid of *Ulmus glabra* and *Ulmus carpinifolia*. It was developed for its superior resistance to Dutch Elm disease. Dutch Elm disease has ravaged the American Elm population over large parts of North America. Unfortunately, the disease has been recorded recently in Seattle, Washington, and is likely to be found in the South Fraser Region in the near future. Pioneer Elm reaches a mature height of fifteen to eighteen metres, with a round crown and dense spreading branches. The large dark green leaves turn yellow in the fall.

Where to see the trees:
Chilliwack

Promontory Park West, on Teskey Rd, Promontory Heights, east side of the baseball field lawn.

Townsend Park, southwest corner of Ashwell Rd and Hodgins Ave, slope between the soccer and baseball fields.

Ulmus 'Homestead'
Homestead Elm

Reaching a mature height of fifteen to eighteen metres, Homestead Elm is a hybrid elm developed for its superior resistance to Dutch Elm disease. Homestead Elm is narrowly oval or pyramidal in youth, maturing to the more open-arching crown typical of the American Elm. The dark green leaves, which turn straw yellow in the fall are densely hairy on the underside.

Where to see the trees:
Chilliwack

Little Mountain Elementary School, 9900 Carleton St, Hope River Trail Extension between the soccer and baseball fields.

Ulmus pumila
Siberian Elm

Native to northern China, Manchuria and Korea, Siberian Elm grows fifteen to twenty metres high. The leaves are slender, short for an elm, about 5 cm long, with the leaf bases appearing equal. The smooth dark green leaves turn yellow in the fall. The dormant flower buds are pudgy, dark brown; each bud scale is edged in fine silky hairs. Siberian Elm is quite common in the South Fraser Region.

Ulmus pumila
Siberian Elm

Ulmus pumila, Douglas Park, Langley City

Ulmus pumila, bark

Where to see the trees:

Chilliwack

Canadian Forces Base, Keith Wilson Rd and Vedder Rd, Vedder Crossing, Dundern Ave and the fire lane.

North of 49520 Prairie Central Rd, Sardis.

Delta

Augustinian Monastery, 3900 Arthur Dr, Ladner, a massive specimen at the northwestern edge of the property.

Langley

Douglas Park, 20550 Douglas Cr, Langley City, immediately south of the Recreation Centre.

SW corner of 46 Ave and 217 St, Murrayville.

Richmond

5200 Hollybridge Way, a long avenue planting of Black Locust and Siberian Elm.

3171- 3291 Catalina Cr, Burkeville, a beautiful row of street trees.

Surrey

Redwood Park, 17900- 20 Ave, South Surrey, in the open area west of the parking lot.

Umbellularia californica
California Bay Tree, California Laurel, or Oregon Myrtle

Where to see the trees:

Surrey

Darts Hill Garden Park, 1660- 168 St, South Surrey*, Garden Bed 12.

The Glades, 561- 172 St, South Surrey*, Mitzie's Way.

Rarely grown in the South Fraser Region, California Bay Tree is native to southwest Oregon and California. It is a large broadleaf evergreen tree, often multi-trunked, reaching a height of twenty-five metres in its native range, but substantially less here as it is at the limit of its hardiness. The glossy dark green leathery leaves are lance-shaped and highly odoriferous when crushed. Some individuals find the smell causes a headache. On warm days the air around the tree is imbued with scent. The tiny yellowish flowers are produced in late winter to May, followed by greenish olive-like fruits, which ripen to purple-green in September.

Z

And every time I find a new, wonderful giant and it's sitting there all alone,
I think, Where is your brother? Where is the next one? What about the next mountainside?
I have no idea where it is all going; I just know they want me to find them. [1]

Ralf Kelman, tree searcher and artist.

Zelkova serrata, fall colour

Zelkova serrata
Japanese Zelkova or Sawleaf Zelkova

Native to Korea, Japan and Taiwan, Japanese Zelkova is a lofty tree; at maturity it may reach fifteen to twenty-four metres in height. The branches ascend upwards at a 45-degree angle, creating the bold vase form. The dark green elliptical leaves are slightly roughened on the top surface and have strongly toothed edges. They turn yellow and orange in the fall. The flowers and fruit are inconspicuous. Poking out of the stems at a 45-degree angle, the shiny dark brown dormant buds aid in winter identification. When young, Japanese Zelkova bark is covered in lenticels, much like the bark of cherry trees. As the bark matures it flakes, leaving smooth orange, pink and red blotches.

Zelkova serrata, Clearbrook Public Library, Abbotsford

Where to see the trees:
Abbotsford
Clearbrook Public Library, 32320 Dahlstrom Ave, a row on the west side of the building.

Chilliwack
Sardis Park, southwest corner in the Rhododendron bed.

Townsend Park, Ashwell Rd and Hodgins Ave, on the west side of the concessions building.

Yarrow Community Park, north end of Community St, Yarrow.

Richmond
Millennium Botanical Garden and Arboretum, N McLennan Community Park, Granville Ave and Garden City Rd.

[1] *The Vancouver Sun*, October 20, 2001. p D 6

Zelkova serrata Green Vase®'

Green Vase® Zelkova

Reaching a mature height of eighteen to twenty-one metres and a crown spread of twelve to fifteen metres, the strong vase shape of this cultivar differentiates it from Village Green Zelkova. The branches of Green Vase® Zelkova are stiffly upright held at a 45-degree angle. The fall colour is rusty yellow or orange-yellow.

Where to see the trees:

Chilliwack

5288, 5291, 5300, 5303 Rockwood Place, Promontory Heights.

4985, 5285 and 5309 Teskey Rd, Promontory Heights.

5286, 5289, 5302, 5305 Westwood Drive, Promontory Heights.

Fairfield Island Park, 46000 Clare Ave, Fairfield Island, southwest and southeast corners of the soccer fields and two trees south of baseball diamond D.

Sardis Park, Sardis, several young trees near the west entrance to the park on School Lane.

Langley

20500 block 53 Ave, City of Langley, five trees planted in the median.

Kwantlen University College, 20901 Langley Bypass, Langley City, two trees on the east boulevard adjacent to the Highway 10 Bypass.

Surrey

6368- 189 St, Cloverdale.

6382- 189 St, Cloverdale.

Zelkova serrata Village Green™

Village Green™ Zelkova

Village Green™ Zelkova develops a broad dense crown at maturity, growing twelve metres high and the same wide. The small, textured dark green foliage turns a rusty red in the fall.

Where to see the trees:

Chilliwack

On Sherwood Dr from Teskey Rd east, Promontory Heights.

Surrey

7419- 152 St, Newton.

6361- 189 St, Cloverdale.

6268- 189 St, Cloverdale.

List of Genera Arranged by Family

This book contains 43 tree families, 87 genera and hybrid genera (x *Chitalpa*).

ACERACEÆ: Maple Family
Acer

ANACARDIACEÆ; Cashew Family
Rhus

AQUIFOLIACEÆ; Holly Family
Ilex

ARAUCARIACEÆ; Araucaria Family
Araucaria

BETULACEÆ; Birch Family
Betula

BIGNONIACEÆ; Bignonia Family
Catalpa
x *Chitalpa*

CARPINACEÆ; Hornbeam Family
Carpinus
Ostrya

CELASTRACEÆ; Bittersweet Family
Euonymus

CERCIDIPHYLLACEÆ; Katsura Family
Cercidiphyllum

CORNACEÆ; Dogwood Family
Cornus

CORYLACEÆ; Hazel Family
Corylus

CUPRESSACEÆ; Cypress Family
Calocedrus
Chamæcyparis
Cryptomeria
Cunninghamia
Cupressus
Metasequoia
Juniperus
Sequoia
Sequoiadendron
Thuja
Thujopsis
Taxodium

DAVIDIACEÆ; Dove Tree Family
Davidia

EBENACEÆ; Ebony Family
Diospyros

ELÆAGNACEÆ; Elæagnus Family
Elæagnus

ERICACEÆ; Heath Family
Arbutus
Oxydendrum

EUCRYPHIACEÆ; Eucryphia
Family
Eucryphia

FAGACEÆ; Beech Family
Castanea
Fagus
Nothofagus
Quercus

GINKGOACEÆ; Ginkgo Family
Ginkgo

HAMAMELIDACEÆ; Witchhazel
Family
Hamamelis
Liquidambar
Parrotia

HIPPOCASTANACEÆ; Horse
Chestnut Family
Æsculus

JUGLANDACEÆ; Walnut Family
Carya
Juglans
Pterocarya

LAURACEÆ; Laurel Family
Umbellularia

LEGUMINOSÆ; Pea Family
Albizia
Cercis

Cladrastis
Gleditsia
Gymnocladus
Laburnum
Robinia
Sophora

MAGNOLIACEÆ; Magnolia
Family
Liriodendron
Magnolia

MORACEÆ; Mulberry Family
Morus

NYSSACEÆ; Tupelo Family
Nyssa

OLEACEÆ; Olive Family
Fraxinus
Syringa

PINACEÆ; Pine Family
Abies
Cedrus
Larix
Picea
Pinus
Pseudotsuga
Tsuga

PLATANACEÆ; Planetree Family
Platanus

PROTEACEÆ; Protea Family
Embothrium

RHAMNACEÆ; Buckthorn Family
Rhamnus

ROSACEÆ; Rose Family
Cratægus
Malus
Mespilus
Prunus
Pyrus
Sorbus

SALICACEÆ; Willow Family
Populus
Salix

SAPINDACEÆ; Soapberry Family
Koelreuteria

SCIADOPITYACEÆ; Sciadopitys
Family
Sciadopitys

SCROPHULARIACEÆ; Figwort
Family
Paulownia

SIMAROUBACEÆ; Quassia Family
Ailanthus

STYRACACEÆ; Styrax Family
Halesia
Styrax

TAXACEÆ; Yew Family
Taxus

THEACEÆ; Tea Family
Stewartia

TILACEÆ; Linden Family
Tilia

ULMACEÆ; Elm Family
Ulmus
Zelkova

Garden Map 1

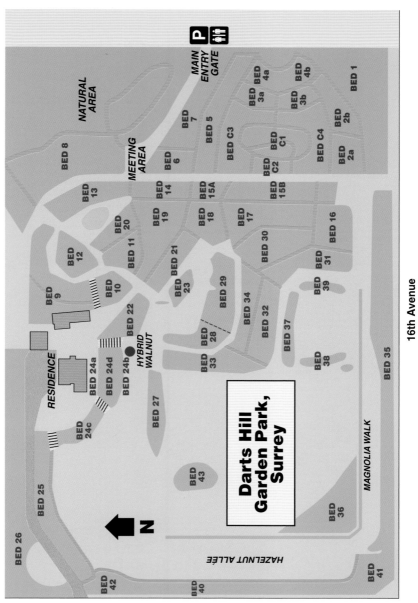

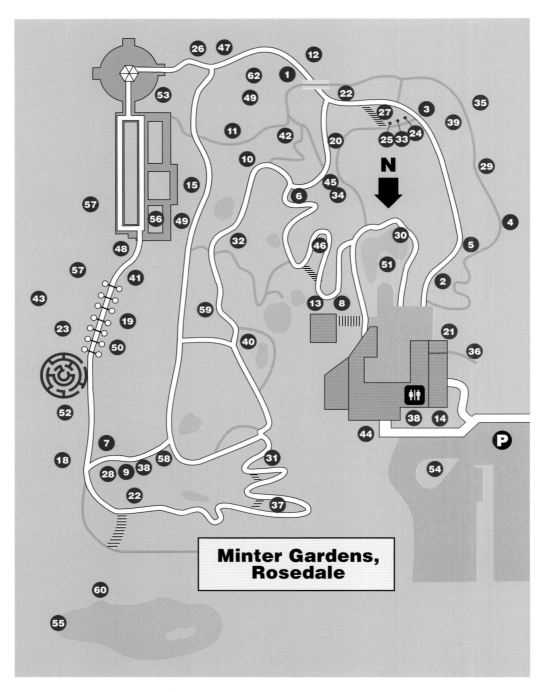

Minter Gardens, Rosedale

Map Key for Garden Map 2 – Minter Gardens, 52892 Bunker Road, Rosedale

1. *Acer cappadocicum*, Cappadocicum Maple
2. *Acer circinatum*, Vine Maple
3. *Acer davidii* 'Serpentine', Serpentine Maple
4. *Acer griseum*, Paperbark Maple
5. *Acer japonicum* 'Aconitifolium', Fernleaf (Full Moon) Maple
6. *Acer negundo* 'Variegatum', Variegated Box Elder
7. *Acer palmatum*, Japanese Maple
8. *Acer palmatum*, 'Butterfly', Butterfly Japanese Maple
9. *Acer palmatum* 'Linearilobum', Strapleaf Maple
10. *Acer palmatum* 'Shishigashira', Crested Maple
11. *Acer rubrum* Red Sunset®, Red Sunset® Maple
12. *Acer saccharinum*, Silver Maple
13. *Aralia elata* 'Variegata', Variegated Japanese Aralia
14. *Araucaria araucana*, Monkey Puzzle
15. *Betula papyrifera*, Paper Birch
16. *Betula pendula*, European White Birch
17. *Betula pendula* 'Youngii', Young's Weeping European White Birch
18. *Calocedrus decurrens*, Incense Cedar
19. *Cercidiphyllum japonicum*, Katsura Tree
20. *Cercidiphyllum japonicum* 'Morioka Weeping', Weeping Katsura
21. *Cornus florida* 'Rainbow', Rainbow Flowering Dogwood
22. *Cornus kousa*, Kousa Dogwood
23. *Cornus mas*, Cornelian Cherry
24. *Chamæcyparis nootkatensis* Pendula Group, Weeping Nootka Cypress
25. *Davidia involucrata*, Dove Tree
26. *Fagus sylvatica*, European Beech
27. *Fagus sylvatica* 'Asplenifolia', Fern-Leaf Beech
28. *Fagus sylvatica* 'Pendula', Weeping Beech
29. *Fagus sylvatica* 'Tricolor', Tricolor Beech
30. *Ginkgo biloba*, Maidenhair Tree
31. *Gleditsia triacanthos* f. *inermis*, Thornless Honeylocust
32. *Laburnum* x *watereri* 'Pendula', Weeping Hybrid Goldenchain
33. *Larix occidentalis*, Western Larch
34. *Liquidambar styraciflua*, Sweetgum, American Sweetgum
35. *Liriodendron tulipfera*, Tulip Tree
36. *Liriodendron tulipifera* 'Aureo-marginatum', Variegated Tulip Tree
37. *Magnolia dawsoniana*, Dawson Magnolia
38. *Magnolia liliiflora* 'Nigra', Purple Lily Magnolia
39. *Magnolia sieboldii*, Oyama Magnolia
40. *Metasequoia glyptostroboides*, Dawn Redwood
41. *Morus alba* 'Pendula', Weeping Mulberry
42. *Picea omorika*, Serbian Spruce
43. *Pinus strobus*, Eastern White Pine
44. *Pinus strobus* 'Pendula', Weeping White Pine
45. *Prunus* 'Amanogawa', White Column Cherry
46. *Prunus* 'Shirotae', Mount Fuji Japanese Cherry
47. *Prunus* 'Shirofugen', Shirofugen Cherry
48. *Quercus palustris*, Pin Oak
49. *Robinia pseudoacacia* 'Frisia', Golden Locust
50. *Rhus typhina* 'Dissecta', Cutleaf Staghorn Sumac
51. *Salix babylonica* var. *pekinensis* 'Tortuosa', Corkscrew Willow
52. *Salix caprea* 'Kilmarnock', Weeping Pussy Willow
53. *Stewartia pseudocamellia*, Japanese Stewartia
54. *Sorbus hupehensis* 'Pink Pagoda', Pink Pagoda Mountain Ash
55. *Taxodium distichum*, Bald Cypress
56. *Taxus baccata* 'Fastigiata', Irish Yew
57. *Thuja occidentalis* 'Smaragd', Emerald Cedar
58. *Thuja occidentalis* 'Wareana', Siberian Cedar
59. *Thuja plicata*, Western Red Cedar
60. *Ulmus americana*, American Elm

Garden Map 3

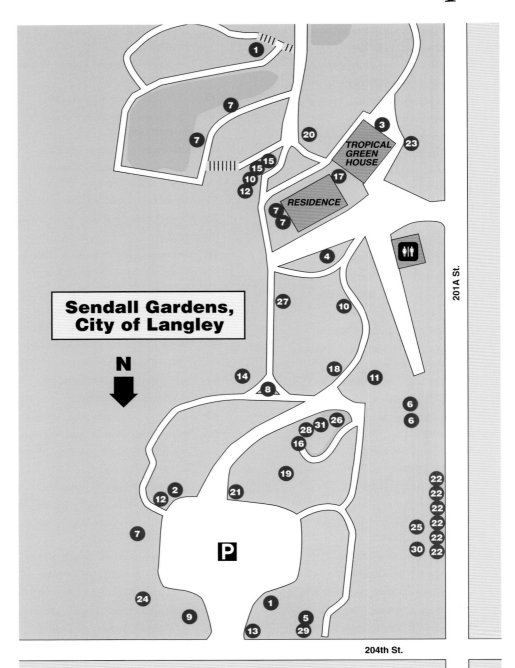

TROPICAL GREEN HOUSE

RESIDENCE

Sendall Gardens,
City of Langley

N

201A St.

P

204th St.

Map Key for Garden Map 3 – Sendall Gardens, City of Langley

1. *Acer palmatum*, Japanese Maple
2. *Acer palmatum* Atropurpureum Group, Red Japanese Maple
3. *Acer platanoides* 'Crimson King', Crimson King Maple
4. *Acer pseudoplatanus* Atropurpureum Group, Purple Sycamore Maple
5. *Æsculus* x *carnea* 'Briotii', Ruby Horse Chestnut
6. *Calocedrus decurrens*, Incense Cedar
7. *Carpinus betulus* 'Fastigata', Columnar European Hornbeam
8. *Cercidiphyllum japonicum*, Katsura Tree
9. *Chamæcyparis pisifera* f. *plumosa* 'Boulevard', Boulevard Plume Cypress
10. *Corylus avellana*, Hazelnut
11. *Corylus maxima* 'Purpurea', Purple Filbert
12. *Cornus* x 'Eddie's White Wonder', Eddie's White Wonder Dogwood
13. *Cryptomeria japonica* 'Cristata', Cockscomb Japanese Cedar
14. *Fraxinus ornus*, Flowering Ash
15. *Ginkgo biloba*, Maidenhair Tree
16. *Gleditisia triacanthos*, Honeylocust
17. *Magnolia grandiflora*, Evergreen Magnolia
18. *Magnolia kobus* var. *stellata*, Star Magnolia
19. *Metasequoia glyptostroboides*, Dawn Redwood
20. *Picea abies*, Norway Spruce
21. *Pinus sylvestris* 'Nana', Dwarf Scots Pine
22. *Populus alba* 'Pyramidalis', Bolleana Poplar
23. *Sciadopitys verticillata*, Umbrella Pine
24. *Sequoia sempervirens*, Coast Redwood
25. *Sequoiadendron giganteum*, Giant Sequoia
26. *Sequoiadendron giganteum* 'Pendulum', Weeping Giant Sequoia
27. *Stewartia pseudocamellia*, Japanese Stewartia
28. *Taxus baccata* 'Aurea', Golden Irish Yew
29. *Taxus baccata* 'Fastigiata', Irish Yew
30. *Thuja plicata* 'Zebrina', Variegated Western Red Cedar
31. *Tsuga canadensis*, Eastern Hemlock

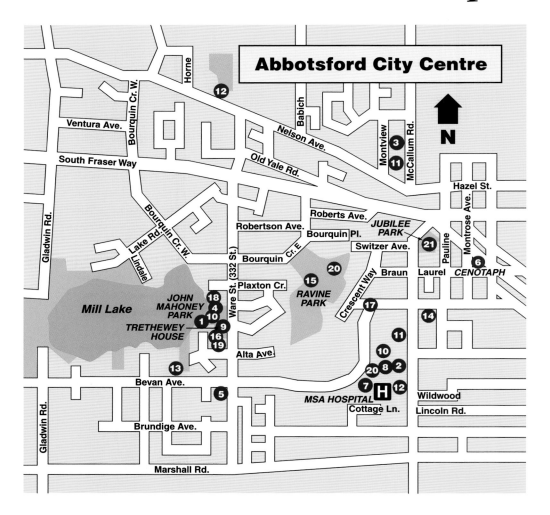

Abbotsford City Centre

N

Mill Lake

JOHN MAHONEY PARK

TRETHEWEY HOUSE

RAVINE PARK

JUBILEE PARK

CENOTAPH

MSA HOSPITAL

Gladwin Rd.
Ventura Ave.
South Fraser Way
Bourquin Cr. W.
Horne
Babich
Nelson Ave.
Old Yale Rd.
Montview
McCallum Rd.
Hazel St.
Roberts Ave.
Robertson Ave.
Bourquin Pl.
Switzer Ave.
Montrose Ave.
Pauline
Bourquin Cr. E
Braun
Laurel
Bourquin Cr. W.
Lake Rd.
Lindale
Ware St. (332 St.)
Plaxton Cr.
Alta Ave.
Crescent Way
Bevan Ave.
Brundige Ave.
Gladwin Rd.
Marshall Rd.
Cottage Ln.
Wildwood
Lincoln Rd.

Map Key for Tree Locator Map 1 – Abbotsford City Centre

1. *Acer macrophyllum*, Bigleaf Maple
2. *Acer palmatum* Atropurpureum Group, Red Japanese Maple
3. *Æsculus turbinata*, Japanese Horsechestnut
4. *Araucaria araucana*, Monkey Puzzle
5. *Betula lenta*, Sweet Birch
6. *Cedrus deodara*, Himalayan Cedar
7. *Cornus nuttallii*, Pacific Dogwood
8. *Fagus sylvatica* Atropurpurea Group, Copper Beech
9. *Juglans cinerea*, Butternut
10. *Juglans regia*, English Walnut
11. *Liriodendron tulipifera*, Tulip Poplar
12. *Magnolia x soulangiana*, Saucer Magnolia
13. *Pinus contorta* var. *contorta*, Shore Pine
14. *Pinus ponderosa*, Ponderosa Pine
15. *Populus tremuloides*, Trembling Aspen
16. *Pseudotsuga menziesii*, Douglas Fir
17. *Robinia pseudoacacia*, 'Frisia' Frisia Black Locust
18. *Salix x sepulchralis* var. *chrysocoma*, Golden Weeping Willow
19. *Sorbus aucuparia*, European Mountain Ash
20. *Thuja plicata*, Western Red Cedar

21. Jubilee Park:
   Araucaria araucana, Monkey Puzzle
   Betula pendula 'Purpurea', Purple Birch
   Betula pendula 'Youngii', Young's European Weeping Birch
   Catalpa speciosa, Western Catalpa
   Cedrus deodara, Deodar Cedar
   Chamæcyparis pisifera f. *plumosa*, Plume Sawara Cypress
   Cratægus monogyna, Common Hawthorn
   Fagus sylvatica Atropurpurea Group, Copper Beech
   Fraxinus excelsior, European Ash
   Fraxinus excelsior f. *diversifolia*, Singleleaf Ash
   Magnolia x soulangiana, Saucer Magnolia
   Magnolia tripetala, Umbrella Magnolia
   Picea abies, Norway Spruce
   Picea pungens Glauca Group, Colorado Blue Spruce
   Prunus 'Kwanzan', Kwanzan Cherry
   Tilia cordata, Littleleaf Linden
   Tilia 'Petiolaris', Silver Pendent Lime
   Sorbus aria, Whitebeam
   Sorbus aucuparia, European Mountain Ash

Tree Locator Map 2

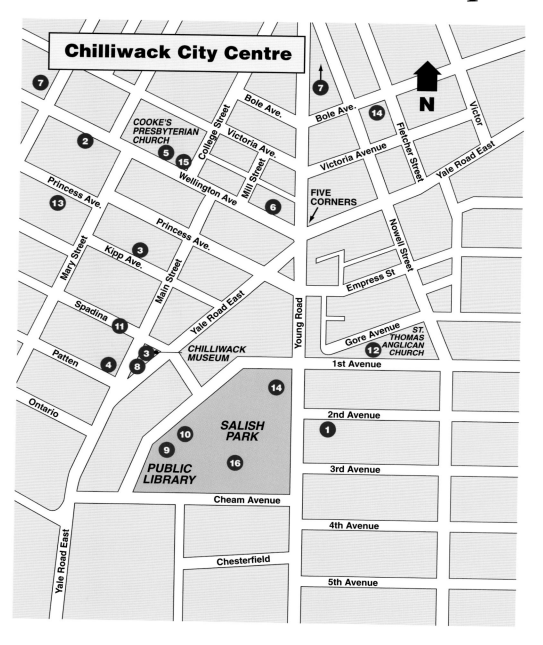

Chilliwack City Centre

COOKE'S PRESBYTERIAN CHURCH

Bole Ave.

College Street

Victoria Ave.

Mill Street

Wellington Ave

Bole Ave.

Victoria Avenue

Fletcher Street

Yale Road East

Victor

N

FIVE CORNERS

Princess Ave.

Princess Ave.

Mary Street

Kipp Ave.

Main Street

Yale Road East

Spadina

Patten

Ontario

Young Road

Empress St

Nowell Street

Gore Avenue

ST. THOMAS ANGLICAN CHURCH

1st Avenue

CHILLIWACK MUSEUM

SALISH PARK

2nd Avenue

PUBLIC LIBRARY

3rd Avenue

Cheam Avenue

Yale Road East

Chesterfield

4th Avenue

5th Avenue

Map Key for Tree Locator Map 2 – Chilliwack City Centre

1. *Betula pendula* 'Youngii', Young's European Weeping Birch
2. *Chamæcyparis lawsoniana* 'Wisselii', Wissel's Lawson Cypress
3. *Fagus sylvatica* Atropurpurea Group, Copper Beech
4. *Juglans nigra*, Black Walnut
5. *Liriodendron tulipifera*, Tulip Poplar
6. *Magnolia kobus*, Kobus Magnolia
7. *Magnolia* x *soulangiana*, Saucer Magnolia
8. *Platanus* x *hispanica*, London Plane
9. *Pinus flexilis* 'Vanderwolf's Pyramid, Vanderwolf's Pyramid Limber Pine
10. *Prunus* 'Amanogawa', White Column Cherry
11. *Prunus cerasifera* 'Nigra', Purpleleaf Plum
12. *Prunus cerasifera* 'Pissardii', Purpleleaf Plum
13. *Pyrus communis*, Common Pear
14. *Prunus* 'Shirotae', Shirotae Cherry
15. *Quercus alba*, White Oak
16. Salish Park: Salish Park is a good place to view young trees adjacent to the pond.

Tree Locator Map 3

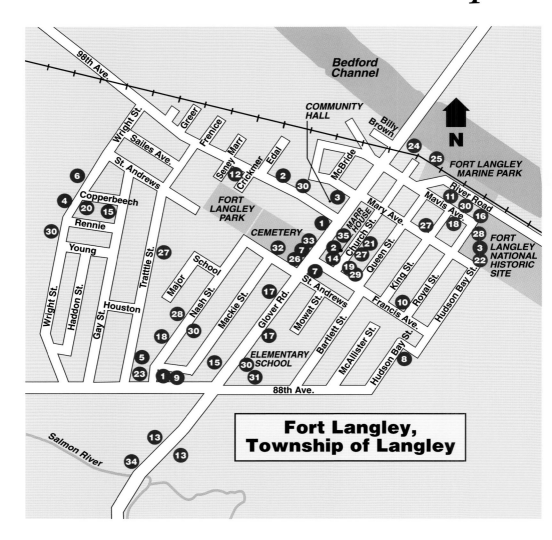

Bedford
Channel

98th Ave.

COMMUNITY
HALL

Billy
Brown

N

Wright St.

Greer

Frenice

Sailes Ave.

Seney Marr

Crickmer

Edal

McBride

24

25

FORT LANGLEY
MARINE PARK

St. Andrews

6

12

2

30

River Road

11

30

16

Copperbeech

4

20

15

FORT
LANGLEY
PARK

3

Mary Ave.

Mavis Ave.

28

FORT
LANGLEY
NATIONAL
HISTORIC
SITE

Rennie

30

CEMETERY

MARR
HOUSE

27

18

Young

Trattle St.

27

32

33

7

26

1

35

2

14

27

21

Church St.

Queen St.

3

22

Wright St.

Haddon St.

Gay St.

Houston

Major

School

Nash St.

Mackie St.

17

Glover Rd.

St. Andrews

Mowat St.

7

Bartlett St.

19

29

King St.

Francis Ave.

Royal St.

Hudson Bay St.

28

30

18

30

17

McAllister St.

10

5

15

ELEMENTARY
SCHOOL

30

Hudson Bay St.

8

23

1

9

31

88th Ave.

13

Salmon River

13

34

**Fort Langley,
Township of Langley**

Map Key for Tree Locator Map 3 – Fort Langley, Langley

1. *Acer macrophyllum*, Bigleaf Maple
2. *Acer palmatum* Atropurpureum Group, Red Japanese Maple
3. *Acer platanoides*, Norway Maple
4. *Acer pseudoplatanus* Atropurpureum Group, Purple Sycamore Maple
5. *Acer pseudoplatanus* Variegatum Group, Variegated Sycamore Maple
6. *Acer rubrum*, Red Maple
7. *Æsculus hippocastanum*, Common Horse Chestnut
8. *Ailanthus altissima*, Tree of Heaven
9. *Araucaria araucana*, Monkey Puzzle
10. *Betula papyrifera*, Paper Birch
11. *Chamæcyparis lawsoniana* 'Stewartii', Stewart's Lawson Cypress
12. *Cornus nuttallii*, Pacific Dogwood
13. *Corylus avellana*, Hazelnut
14. *Fagus sylvatica* var. *heterophylla* f. *laciniata*, Fern-Leaf Beech
15. *Fagus sylvatica* Atropurpureum Group, Copper Beech
16. *Fraxinus ornus* 'Victoria', Victoria Flowering Ash
17. *Gleditsia triacanthos* f. *inermis*, Thornless Honeylocust
18. *Juglans cinerea*, Butternut
19. *Liriodendron tulipifera*, Tulip Poplar
20. *Magnolia kobus*, Kobus Magnolia
21. *Picea sitchensis*, Sitka Spruce
22. *Pinus contorta* var. *contorta*, Shore Pine
23. *Pinus ponderosa*, Ponderosa Pine
24. *Pinus sylvestris*, Scots Pine
25. *Populus balsamifera* ssp. *trichocarpa*, Black Cottonwood
26. *Prunus* 'Kwanzan', Kwanzan Cherry
27. *Pseudotsuga menziesii*, Douglas Fir
28. *Quercus robur*, English Oak
29. *Quercus robur* 'Fastigiata', Columnar English Oak
30. *Quercus rubra*, Red Oak
31. *Rhamnus purshiana*, Cascara
32. *Taxus baccata* 'Fastigiata', Columnar Irish Yew
33. *Thuja plicata*, Western Red Cedar
34. *Ulmus glabra*, Scotch Elm
35. *Ulmus glabra* 'Camperdown', Camperdown Elm

Tree Locator Map 4

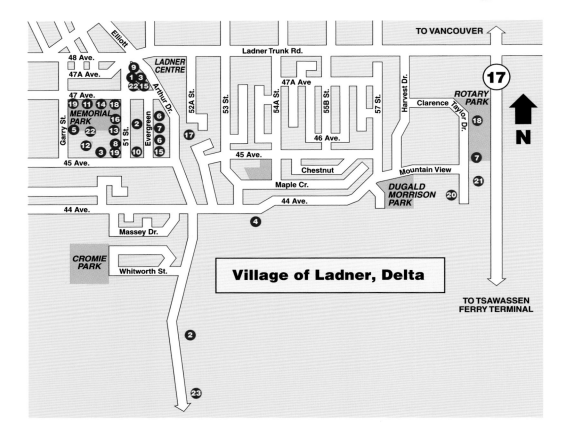

Village of Ladner, Delta

Map Key for Tree Locator Map 4 – Village of Ladner, Delta

1. *Acer palmatum*, Japanese Maple
2. *Acer pseudoplatanus*, Sycamore Maple
3. *Acer pseudoplatanus* Atropurpureum Group, Purple Sycamore Maple
4. *Æsculus* x *carnea* 'Briotii', Ruby Horse Chestnut
5. *Æsculus hippocastanum*, Common Horse Chestnut
6. *Araucaria araucana*, Monkey Puzzle
7. *Calocedrus decurrens*, Incense Cedar
8. *Catalpa speciosa*, Western Catalpa
9. *Cornus* x 'Eddie's White Wonder', Eddie's White Wonder Dogwood
10. *Cornus florida* f. *rubra*, Pink Flowering Dogwood
11. *Cratægus monogyna*, Common Hawthorn
12. *Fraxinus pennsylvanica*, Green Ash
13. *Juglans regia*, English Walnut
14. *Ilex aquifolium*, English Holly
15. *Liriodendron tulipifera*, Tulip Poplar
16. *Nyssa sylvatica*, Black Gum
17. *Pinus nigra*, Black Pine
18. *Pyrus communis*, Common Pear
19. *Quercus robur*, English Oak
20. *Quercus rubra*, Red Oak
21. *Styrax japonicus*, Japanese Snowbell Tree
22. *Ulmus americana*, American Elm
23. Jubilee Farm, later the Augustinian Monastery of British Columbia, 3900 Arthur Drive:

    Acer campestre, Hedge Maple or Field Maple

    Acer platanoides 'Schwedleri', Schwedler Norway Maple

    Acer pseudoplatanus Variegatum Group, Variegated Sycamore Maple

    Castanea dentata, American Chestnut, American Sweet Chestnut or Chestnut

    Chamæcyparis pisifera 'Squarrosa', Moss Sawara Cypress, Moss Cypress or Brown Junk Tree

    Magnolia x *soulangiana*, Saucer Magnolia

    Ulmus pumila, Siberian Elm

Tree Locator Map 5

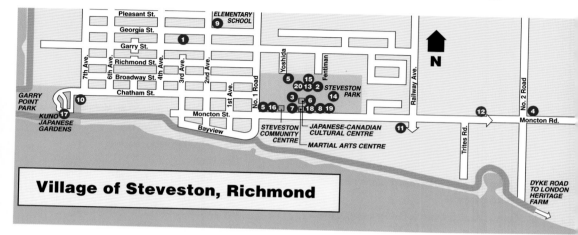

Village of Steveston, Richmond

Map Key for Tree Locator Map 5 – Village of Steveston, Richmond

1. *Abies grandis*, Grand Fir
2. *Acer circinatum*, Vine Maple
3. *Acer palmatum* Atropurpureum Group, Red Japanese Maple
4. *Acer pseudoplatanus*, Sycamore Maple
5. *Acer pseudoplatanus* Variegatum Group, Variegated Sycamore Maple
6. *Ailanthus altissima*, Tree of Heaven
7. *Aralia elata*, Japanese Aralia
8. *Cedrus deodara*, Deodar Cedar and *Cedrus deodara* 'Aurea', Golden Deodar Cedar
9. *Cedrus atlantica* 'Glauca', Blue Atlas Cedar
10. *Cratægus* x *lavalleei*, Lavalle Hawthorn

11. *Cryptomeria japonica*, Japanese Cedar
12. *Fagus sylvatica* Atropurpureum Group, Copper Beech
13. *Picea sitchensis*, Sitka Spruce
14. *Pinus nigra*, Black Pine
15. *Populus alba*, White Poplar
16. *Prunus* x *yedoensis* 'Akebono', Yoshino Cherry
17. *Quercus bicolor*, Swamp White Oak
18. *Quercus rubra*, Red Oak
19. *Sophora japonica*, Japanese Sophora
20. *Sorbus* x *thuringiaca* 'Fastigiata', Oakleaf Mountain Ash

The Wow Factor
The Author's Favourite Trees by Community

Abbotsford

Æsculus turbinata
Japanese Horse Chestnut
2770 Mount View Ave, a wonderful old tree with a
DBH of 133 cm.

Magnolia acuminata
Cucumber Tree
33865 Pine St, a magnificent tree with a DBH of 103 cm.

Magnolia tripetala
Umbrella Magnolia
Jubilee Park, McCallum Rd south of Essendene, a very large tree
on the south side of the MSA Centennial Library; this tree was
likely planted in 1967 when the library was built; it started to
bloom in 1979.When in full bloom it perfumes the entire park.

Fagus sylvatica Atropurpureum Group
Copper Beech or Purple Beech
MSA General Hospital, 2179 McCallum Rd, on the north side
of the Emergency entrance, a huge tree with a DBH of 110 cm.

Populus balsamifera ssp. trichocarpa
Black Cottonwood
Hogan Family Nature Park, 2860 block Debruyne Rd, a very
short walk into the park beside the bridge crossing the Salmon
River, a massive tree with a DBH of 164 cm.

Pseudotsuga menziesii
Douglas Fir
Downes Bowl Park, Trethewey St pedestrian entrance (no car parking at this entrance), a ten minute walk down a ridgeline to an old growth grove of cedar and Douglas fir, the largest fir has a DBH of 120 cm and is 45 metres high.

Quercus rubra
Red Oak
Dunach Elementary School, 30357 Downes Rd, a tree along the east fence line with a massive trunk with a DBH of 135 cm.

Sorbus aria
Whitebeam
Jubilee Park, McCallum Rd south of Essendene, two fabulous trees in the centre of the park.

Tilia 'Petiolaris'
Silver Pendent Lime or Weeping Linden
Jubilee Park, McCallum Rd south of Essendene, two lovely trees on the west side of the park.

Ulmus americana
American Elm
Matsqui Elementary School, 5730 Riverside Rd, Matsqui Prairie village, a row of seven magnificent trees with a DBH of 120 cm on the east fence-line of the school.

Chilliwack, including Rosedale

Acer macrophyllum
Bigleaf Maple
48685 McConnell Rd, East Chilliwack, the fifth largest Bigleaf Maple in BC with a circumference of 8.99 m and a height of 26.8 metres and a DBH of 200 cm. A second tree on the property is almost as large.

Acer pseudoplatanus Variegatum Group
Variegated Sycamore Maple
Yarrow Central Park, Southeast corner of Kehler St and Yarrow Central Rd, four large specimens, several beautifully open grown.

Betula pendula 'Youngii'
Young's Weeping European White Birch
46010 Second Ave, a splendid tree of great size.

Carya ovata
Shagbark Hickory
47835 Camp River Rd, East Chilliwack, a huge tree.

Fagus sylvatica var. *heterophylla* f. *laciniata*
Cutleaf Beech
Higginson Farm, 46050 Higginson Rd, Sardis, two immense trees with their branches sweeping to the ground. A lovely wetland in behind offers a spectacular setting for these magnificent trees.

Fagus sylvatica Atropurpureum Group
Copper Beech or Purple Beech
45723 Kipp Ave, two huge trees, the largest in Chilliwack.

Fraxinus excelsior
European Ash
47813 McGuire Rd, Sardis, a magnificent old farm row of several different species of trees on the south side of the road including three European Ash, the easternmost one with a massive girth of 190 cm.

Liriodendron tulipfera
Tulip Tree
Family Place, 45845 Wellington Ave, two magnificent old trees, one with a DBH of 175 cm.

Populus balsamifera ssp. *trichocarpa*
Black Cottonwood
East bank of the Sumas River, south of the CNR tracks, near the confluence of the Fraser River. The world's largest Black Cottonwood, discovered in 2000, has a circumference of 11.92 metres, a DBH of 365 cm, a height of 43.3 metres and a crown spread of 29.6 metres.

Pseudotsuga menziesii
Douglas Fir
Elk Creek Giants, Elk Creek Rainforest, East Chilliwack.

Quercus alba
White Oak
Family Place, 45845 Wellington Ave, a magnificent old tree, with a DBH of 150 cm.

Tilia tomentosa
Silver Lime
Park, SE corner of Manuel Rd and Vedder Rd, Sardis, a very large and magnificent tree overhanging the east bank of the creek.

Delta

Acer cappadocicum
Cappadocicum Maple or Coliseum Maple
Augustinian Monastery, 3900 Arthur Dr, Ladner, a massive specimen with a DBH of 120 cm.

Acer pseudoplatanus Variegatum Group
Variegated Sycamore Maple
Augustinian Monastery, 3900 Arthur Dr, Ladner, a massive specimen with a DBH of 150 cm.

Araucaria araucana
Monkey Puzzle
4501 Arthur Dr, Ladner, a a female tree and perfect mature specimen with a DBH of 60 cm and a height of 20 metres.

Arbutus menziesii
Madrona
White Birch Manor, 11905- 80 Ave, North Delta, a lovely symmetrical crown and perfect foliage, a very large tree.

Fagus sylvatica Atropurpureum Group
Copper Beech or Purple Beech
4618 Arthur Dr, Ladner, a fine open-grown tree with a large diameter at breast height of 115 cm DBH.

Pseudotsuga menziesii
Douglas Fir
Sunbury Park, Centre St and Dunlop Rd, North Delta, four massive trees, the largest 30 metres to the north of the ball diamond on the slope down to the historic fishing village of Annieville.

Sophora japonica
Japanese Pagoda Tree or Chinese Scholar Tree
South Delta Recreation Centre, 1720- 56 St, Tsawwassen, three magnificent trees to the north of the centre, the largest tree with a DBH of 70 cm.

Ulmus americana
American Elm
Ladner Community Centre, 4734- 51 St, Ladner, a magnificent open-grown specimen with a DBH of 170 cm.

Ulmus americana
American Elm
Memorial Park, southwest side, a magnificent 30 metres tall specimen with a DBH of 120 cm, Unfortunately a large branch has broken out on the west side of the tree. Designated by Council as a Heritage Tree(*) on March 3, 1997.

Ulmus glabra 'Camperdown'
Camperdown Elm
2349- 52 St, a magnificent specimen, the largest of its species south of the Fraser, planted in 1916 at the same time as the existing farmhouse was constructed.

Langley

Acer saccharum
Sugar Maple
5404- 216 St, Milner.

Calocedrus decurrens
Incense Cedar
Sendall Gardens, 20166- 50 Ave, Langley City.

Fagus sylvatica Atropurpureum Group
Copper Beech or Purple Beech
9147 Gay St, but growing on Copperbeech Ave, east of Wright St, Ft Langley, this is a magnificent tree; the branches sweep down to the ground.

Juglans nigra
Black Walnut
Belmont Dairy Farms, 21151 Old Yale Rd, Murrayville.

Picea sitchensis
Sitka Spruce
9188 Church St, Ft Langley.

Pinus coulteri
Big-Cone Pine
4800 block 216 St, Murrayville, planted by Sam Monahan from seed collected on family trip to the coast of California in the late 1960's.

Pseudotsuga menziesii
Douglas Fir
9040 Trattle St, Ft Langley.

Sequoiadendron giganteum
Giant Sequoia or Sierra Redwood
21836- 96 Ave, Northwest Langley, this tree, the most easterly of a row of thirty-eight individuals, is a magnificent specimen.

Tilia 'Petiolaris'
Silver Pendent Lime or Weeping Linden
Traas Nursery, 24120- 48 Ave, Salmon River Uplands.

Ulmus glabra
Scotch Elm or Wych Elm
Hazelgrove Farm, 8651 Glover Rd, Ft Langley.

Richmond

Acer macrophyllum
Bigleaf Maple
18960 River Rd, East Richmond, a large tree with a DBH of 160 cm.

Acer saccharinum
Silver Maple
10291 Gilmore Cr, a magnificent large tree.

Æsculus hippocastanum
Common Horse Chestnut
Goldie Harris House, 11620 No. 4 Rd, a mature specimen growing along the edge of the ditch.

Catalpa speciosa
Western Catalpa
151, 191 and 231 Catalina Cr, Burkeville, a row of great trees.

Fraxinus excelsior
European Ash
Pumphouse Pub and Grill, 6031 Blundell Rd, several very large trees, the one on the east margin of the parking lot is splendid.

Populus balsamifera ssp. *trichocarpa*
Black Cottonwood
12051 Shell Rd, south foot of Shell Road near the Horseshoe Slough Trail access point. There is a gigantic tree to the east of this address. This tree, with a trunk circumference of 8.2 metres, is growing at the west end of an industrial warehouse complex.

Quercus robur
English Oak
6911 Camsell Cr, a huge tree with as DBH of 105 cm.

Salix x *sepulchralis* var. *chrysocoma*
Golden Weeping Willow
NE corner of Garden City Rd and Francis Rd.

Sequoiadendron giganteum
Giant Sequoia or Sierra Redwood
Draney House, 12011- No 4 Rd, a tree with a broken top but a massive trunk flare.

Surrey

Fagus sylvatica Atropurpureum Group
Copper Beech or Purple Beech
Peace Arch Park, King George Hwy and 0 Ave, South Surrey, six trees.

Juglans cinerea
Butternut
Sullivan Park, 15300- 62A Ave, Newton,* a majestic mature tree.

Juglans cinerea x *Juglans ailanthifolia* var. *cordiformis*
Canadian/ Japanese Walnut hybrid
Darts Hill Garden Park, 1660- 168 St, South Surrey*.

Juglans regia
English Walnut
Redwood Park, 17900- 20 Ave, South Surrey*, a magnificent tree in the grass area south of the Tree House.

Picea sitchensis
Sitka Spruce
13398 Vine Maple Dr, Surrey*.
This tree has a massive trunk flare with impressive anchoring roots.

Pseudotsuga menziesii
Douglas Fir
Park at Kilkee Pl, Newton*.

Sequoiadendron giganteum
Giant Sequoia or Sierra Redwood
Redwood Park, 17900- 20 Ave, South Surrey*.

Thuja plicata
Western Red Cedar
The Glades, 561- 172 St, South Surrey*. This large tree has a very unusual form, as it is bent into a reverse curve shape, thus its name, the "Bent Cedar". It is growing in the cedar grove.

White Rock

Quercus rubra
Red Oak
White Rock Elementary School, 1273 Fir St, a row planted on the south side of the school approximately fifty-five years ago.

Best Boulevard Trees
Scenic Streetscapes by Community

Abbotsford

1. East of Clayburn village, Straitton Rd, winds beautifully along Clayburn Creek amidst the natural splendour of overhanging Bigleaf Maples and Black Cottonwood.

2. The *Fraxinus americana* Autumn Applause®, Autumn Applause® Ash is very colourful in the fall in the median planting on Old Yale Rd to McClure Rd from Crossley Drive to Clearbrook Rd, in front of Ellwood Park.

3. The median planting on McClure Rd from Gladwin east to 33300 block McClure of *Magnolia* 'Galaxy', Galaxy Magnolia is in full bloom in April.

4. The *Quercus palustris* 'Crownright', Crownright Pin Oak in front of Ellwood Park in the median planting on Old Yale Rd to McClure Rd from Townline Rd to Clearbrook Rd is colourful in the fall.

Chilliwack

1. Chilliwack River Rd, Sardis, from Promontory Rd north to Luckakuck Way is graced with many mature deciduous trees and pastoral views of the farmlands with glimpses of the gentle slough meandering beside the road.

2. Along the entire length of Camp River Rd, East Chilliwack, mature trees are beautifully sited along the banks of the slough and in adjacent farmlands.

3. Hope River Rd combines the best of the farmlands and the mature well-treed landscapes of older homes such as the one

located in Gwynne Vaughn Park as Hope River enters the centre of Chilliwack.

4. McConnell Rd to Gillanders Rd follows along a delightful slough with large trees overhanging these two rural roadways.

5. The delicate white to pink blooms in March to early April of the two row of *Prunus cerasifera* 'Nigra', Purpleleaf Plum trees and a third row of the same trees in the median on Spadina Ave, from Main St to Corbould St are beautiful.

Delta

1. Arthur Drive from Ladner Trunk Rd south to the 3900 block is graced with many heritage homes built in the 1920's with excellent trees well placed in the mature landscapes.

2. Highway 10 west from the Highway 99 interchange to 64 St is lined with *Æsculus hippocastanum*, Common Horse Chestnut and native *Crataegus douglasii*, Douglas Hawthorn. This stretch of Highway 10 is a blaze of white when these trees are blooming in May.

3. South of Ladner Trunk Rd on 72 St, a pleasant hedgerow of 20-metre tall Lombardy Poplar trees, *Populus nigra* 'Italica' are interspersed with Horse Chestnut.

4. A lovely route with farms and field unfolds east of Arthur Drive on 32B Avenue.

Langley

1. The two rows of mature Common Horse Chestnut, *Æsculus hippocastanum* in the 9000 block of Glover Rd in Ft Langley shade the route of the annual Fort Langley May Day parade.

2. A street planting of *Prunus* x *yedoensis* 'Akebono', Daybreak Cherry on 88 Ave from 204 St to 216 St, Walnut Grove, provides a frothy display of white blossoms in late March to April.

3. On 212 St, north from 88 Ave to Walnut Grove Dr, Walnut Grove, this lovely street planting of *Acer rubrum* Red Sunset®, Red Sunset® Maple is brilliant red in the fall.

4. A row of magnificent *Sequioadendron giganteum*, Giant Sequoia from 21836- 96 Ave on 96 Ave to 9584- 216 St, Northwest Langley, towers above the road on the south side.

5. From 88 Ave to St Andrews St on Glover Rd in Fort Langley, a double row of young *Gleditsia triacanthos* f. *inermis*, Thornless Honeylocust trees provide a graceful entrance to this Heritage village.

6. Both sides of 240 Street from 48 Ave to 56 Ave, are lined with mature conifers, primarily *Pseudotsuga menziesii*, Douglas Fir, and *Thuja plicata*, Western Red Cedar, creating a stately rural roadway.

7. A row of young *Quercus palustris*, Pin Oaks on 216 Ave from 56 Ave to Glover Rd, offers superb shades of scarlet fall colour while the mature trees towards Glover Road offer cool summer shade.

8. There are several old homesteads with mature trees and a row of *Acer pseudoplatanus*, Sycamore Maple, from 216 St on Old Yale Rd to Fraser Highway on the north side of the road at the Berry Farm.

9. The shocking pink blosssoms of *Prunus* 'Kwanzan' brighten the month of May on Walnut Grove Drive from 88 Ave to 212 St.

Richmond

1. There is a very fine street planting on 6900- 7700 River Rd next to the dike of mostly *Quercus robur*, English Oak. It is interplanted with some Elm, Horse Chestnut, Black Cottonwood and European Mountain Ash.

2. The planted boulevard of Garden City Rd from Granville Ave to Cambie Road is a haven of green separating two busy lanes of traffic with large deciduous and coniferous species.

3. A street planting of *Liquidambar styraciflua*, American Sweetgum on Williams Road from No 5 Rd west is especially colourful in the fall.

4. The long avenue planting of *Ulmus pumila*, Siberian Elm and Black Locust at 5200 Hollybridge Way offers cool summer shade.

5. A beautiful row of *Ulmus pumila*, Siberian Elm lines the street from 3171 to 3291 Catalina Crescent in Burkeville.

6. A double row of *Ulmus americana*, American Elm trees arch gracefully over Handley Ave from Douglas to Wellington Cr in Burkeville.

7. Number 4 Rd from Westminster Highway to Finn Rd, is a rural road with mature *Æsculus hippocastanum*, Horse Chestnut, *Acer pseudoplatanus*, Sycamore Maple and the oldest *Sequioadendron giganteum*, Giant Sequoia in Richmond, all planted by Richmond's pioneer settlers.

Surrey

1. *Pseudotsuga menziesii*, Douglas Fir towers over Crescent Rd from 144 St into Crescent Beach, framing pleasant views of the Nicomekl River.

2. A boulevard row of forty-eight *Quercus robur*, English Oak trees from 1987- 2986 King George Hwy in South Surrey were planted to honour the coronation of King George VI.

3. A row of fifteen Common Horse Chestnut, *Æsculus hippocastanum* planted adjacent to Cloverdale Elementary School, Highway 10 and 178 St in Cloverdale frames the school building very well.

4. The frothy pink blossoms of *Prunus* 'Kwanzan', Kwanzan Cherry bursts along 156A Street at 101 Avenue in Fleetwood in late April to May.

5. Queen Mary Boulevard off 132 St and 90 Av is lined with splendid *Platanus* x *hispanica*, London Plane and *Gleditsia triacanthos*, Honeylocust.

6. Ocean Park Rd from 16 Ave to 20 Ave in South Surrey offers large well-landscaped estates with mature trees.

7. The median planting on 88 Ave from Fraser Highway to King George Highway is an ever-changing delight of colour and texture.

White Rock

1. A lovely planting of *Acer rubrum* Red Sunset®, Red Sunset® Maple in the centre median on 152 St from 16 Av south to Russell Ave offers splendid fall colour.

2. A shapely row of young Thornless Honeylocust trees, *Gleditsia triacanthos* f. *inermis* shade the seaside strollers on the Promenade parallel to Marine Drive

Heritage Tree Evaluation
Formula and Form

To begin the project a Heritage Tree Evaluation format was developed by the author, and revised in consultation with City of Surrey Parks and Recreation staff and management. It is based on qualitative and quantitative tree analysis. The format was based on research of Heritage Tree programs across Canada and the USA. With the exception of the city of Victoria, which has had a Heritage Tree program in place for close to 30 years, the development of a Heritage Tree assessment tool was unique to Western Canada.

After a review of the Heritage Evaluation models available, a combined approach was chosen to develop the Heritage Tree Evaluation Form for the City of Surrey, which has subsequently been used by the Fraser Valley Heritage Tree Society in the tree hunt in Langley and forwarded on to communities throughout British Columbia.

The Evaluation Formula is as follows:

Location + Condition + Heritage Value/ 3 and multiplied by 100 to give a percentage.

Tree Location, Condition, and Heritage are equally weighted. The Location value, in the Heritage Tree formula is determined by using the International Society of Arboriculture evaluation method for location. This includes Site, Contribution and Placement Values. The Condition Value, in the Heritage Tree Formula is determined using the ISA evaluation method for condition.

The Heritage Value is determined by evaluating the tree's relative historical significance. Historical significance is determined by the tree's association with historical or famous events, the broad cultural history of the country, province, city or community, or a person or persons who have significantly added to the history of the country, province, city or community. Definitions of what is very significant, significant, somewhat significant, and so on should be determined with the assistance of the Heritage Advisory Council as was done in the City of Surrey. Tree characteristics such as age, size and type of specimen plus rarity and uniqueness of form also contribute to the Heritage value.

The five factors the Heritage Value or rating is derived from are:

1. Outstanding tree characteristics such as age, size and type of specimen.

2. Rarity, which means one of a very few of a kind.

    Very rare trees are trees that are very uncommon. These trees are seldom found in public places, and may not be represented in local botanical collections.

    Rare means trees that are uncommon but do exist in local botanical collections and a few examples may be found in private gardens.

    Fairly common means trees that are fairly common in public and private spaces.

    Occurs frequently, are trees that are indigenous or exotic species that occur frequently and are not considered rare.

3. Uniqueness, means unusual in growth or habit.
    Very Unusual
    Unusual
    Somewhat unusual
    Marginally unusual in form
    Typical form of species

4. Historical factor, as determined by the tree's relative significance.
    Very Significant
    Significant
    Somewhat Significant
    Marginally Significant
    Not Significant

5. Landmark Heritage, trees that over time have become landmarks to the community at large.

    The six-page Heritage Tree Evaluation Form lists each of

these factors. Each factor has a set of weighted criteria. For example a tree that is very rare would score five, while a tree that occurs frequently would score 1. The total points a Heritage Tree may score is twenty-five. The Heritage value is the actual score divided by twenty-five. The Location and Condition Values are usually calculated as percentages. Converting the percentages into decimals and inserting the three values into the overall formula achieves a numerical score. A minimum of sixty-two percent is needed before a tree qualifies as a Heritage Tree.

In addition to these five factors and their weighted criteria, several other types of data are recorded on the Heritage Tree evaluation form. These additional categories are: file number, maximum width of the crown, tree height, the date the tree was planted and by whom if known.

For example: a one metre diameter at breast height Douglas fir tree that is in good condition in a prominent location may be declared a heritage tree, but if is in poor heath and has poor structure with a topping cut and in a location which is difficult to access, it would not receive heritage designation.

GLOSSARY OF
Architectural Styles

Arts and Crafts Style

Roofs that slope from all sides from the peak toward the walls, a construction technique known as a hipped roof, characterize the Arts and Crafts style house. Dormers have hipped roofs as well. The second story of the houses often is half-timbered. Typical features include wide eaves, exposed rafters emphasizing the use of wood and natural building materials. The feel of this architectural style is of an English cottage.

California Bungalow Style

California Bungalow style houses are usually small boxy affairs with gently sloping roofs, solid porch posts, wide front porches and an open interior plan layout. This style of house, which is an extension of the Craftsman Style, was fashionable from 1910-1925.

Carpenter Gothic Style

The Carpenter Gothic style is characterized by gingerbread or decorated wood fretwork, sharply pointed windows similar to Gothic Church Architecture and an asymmetrical floor plan, which arises from a centre point. This style of architecture was popular in the last half of the nineteenth century.

Craftsman Style

Characteristics that typify a Craftsman style house are two-three stories, a wide gabled roofline, and a full-width, often wrap-around verandah. Wooden posts on the porch, wide eaves, wooden shingle siding, exposed brackets and exposed rafter ends, rough brick or stone chimneys, foundations and porch piers are also important characteristics. Variations of this theme were common in the ten-year period, 1910–1925, that the Craftsman architectural style was popular.

Georgian Revival Style

Built mainly in the 1920's and 1930's, a very symmetrical and formal architectural style. Typically showing a hipped roofline, stucco walls and a formal balance between the window and walls of the house.

Queen Anne Style

A very picturesque house style, which incorporates various others such as Gothic Revival, and Carpenter Gothic. Look for steeply sloping rooflines, half-timbered walls, decorative woodwork; sometimes turrets were part of the roofline.

Spanish Colonial Revival Style

This style began appearing in the late 1920's and is characterized by white stucco walls, round-topped windows, arches, tile roofs and wrought-iron balconies.

Tudor Revival Style

Decorative half timbering on the outside walls typifies this architectural style, popular in the 1920's and 1930's. Look for steeply sloped gable roofs, diamond-mullioned leaded-glass windows, black timbers interspersed with white plaster.

GLOSSARY OF
Horticultural Terms

Allée: A walk or ride through a natural woodland or one made by the close planting of trees.

Aril: A fleshy covering around a seed as in the fruit of *Taxus*, yew.

Bi-pinnately Compound Leaves: The leaf blade is divided into leaflets and each leaflet is divided once again into smaller leaflets as in *Gleditsia triacanthos* f. *inermis*, Thornless Honeylocust.

Bigeneric Hybrid: A hybrid plant resulting from crossing two different genera such as the crossing of *Catapla bignonioides* and *Chilopsis linearis* which resulted in x *Chitalpa tashkentensis*. Bigeneric hybrids are indicated by an x in front of the name.

Bract: A leaf that has been modified to protect the developing flower or leaf buds.

Bud Sport: A mutation in the genetic characteristics of a tree arising as a bud which then develops, for example, into a branch of different coloured foliage as in *Acer platanoides* 'Deborah'.

Calyx Lobe: The top portion of a free sepal: the sepals are outside of the petals of a flower as in the prominent calyx lobes on the fruit of *Mespilus germanica*, Medlar.

Catkin: Slender pencil-shaped cluster of tiny flowers typical of *Betula* or birches.

Central Leader: The dominant stem of a tree, often noticeable in trees with strong pyramidal form as in *Quercus palustris*, Pin Oak.

Crown: The above-ground parts of a tree including the trunk, branches and leaves.

Cultivar: A cultivated variety.

DBH: Diameter of a tree at breast height measured at 1.4 metres from the base of the tree.

Dioecious: Male and female reproductive organs are borne on separate plants as in *Ilex aquifolium*, English Holly.

Espalier: Technique of training a fruit tree or ornamental plant against a wall with the branches trained flat in a fan, candelabra, diamond or informal pattern.

Form: The silhouette or shape of a tree such as round or upright oval.

Fastigiate: A growth habit where the branches grow stiffly upright, often parallel to one another. It usually creates a columnar tree form.

Glaucous: Whitish bloom on the surface of a leaf or fruit like the whitish waxy appearance of the skin of a blueberry.

Group: This describes a group of unnamed tree seedlings, for example *Picea pungens* Glauca Group describes all the un-named seedlings with blue foliage that are available in the nursery trade.

Grafting: The technique of inserting a part of one plant into or on another so that the two parts become one.

Habit: The branching arrangement of a tree such as pendulous, fastigiate or horizontal.

Heartwood: Age-altered wood that may be a different colour than the sapwood of the tree. Heartwood is located at the centre of the trunk as in *Juglans nigra*, Black Walnut.

Inflorescence: A collection of flowers or florets arranged in specific way on an axis such as in a catkin, raceme or panicle.

Obovate: An ovate leaf or petal shape, which is wider at its tip and narrows at its base.

Ovate: An egg-shaped leaf or petal shape, which is wider at its base.

Palmately Compound Leaf: Leaflets arise from one central point somewhat like the fingers in a hand as in *Æsculus hippocastanum*, Common Horse Chestnut.

Panicle: Cone-shaped cluster of flowers.

Pinnately Compound Leaf: A featherlike arrangement of more than three leaflets along a stalk as in *Fraxinus pennsylvanica*, Green Ash.

Raceme: A long stalk with florets produced along its length.

Samara: A one-seeded winged fruit as in *Fraxinus* or ash or a double-winged fruit as in *Acer* or maple.

Scaffold Branch: Main branch that arises from the trunk or parent stem of the tree.

Serrate: Margin of a leaf or petal that is toothed like the edge of a steak knife.

Stomata: Gas exchange organs located on the surfaces of the leaf.

Tepal: A floral part, which cannot be differentiated as either a sepal or a petal, as in the tepals of *Magnolia* species.

Top Grafting: The attachment to a straight trunk at a specific height, usually1.5 metres or higher, of weeping branches to form an umbrella-shaped tree as in *Betula pendula* 'Youngii'.

TM : The TM designation indicates that the originator of the new plant, for example, *Pyrus calleryana* Aristocrat™, has applied for a trademarked name. The ® indicates that the plant name is a registered trademark, such as in *Pyrus calleryana* Chanticleer®. The trademark name is often the "selling name" of the plant.

References

Published Sources

Abbotsford Sumas Matsqui News (A.S.M. News). "Tree Planting Day at Matsqui Elementary," April 10, 1929.

Aldergrove Heritage Society. 1993. *The Place Between.* Cloverdale, B.C.: Friesen.

Anderson, C. 1998. "10 Best Places to Find Treasured Trees." *The Province.* Sunday, January 25, 1998. pp. A 17- 20.

Baker, H. 1997. "The Green Timbers Inaugural Plantation." *Community Heritage Information Newletter.* Heritage Services, Surrey Parks and Recreation Department. Vol. 2 Issue 2, Spring.

Bellett, G. 2001. "RCMP E Division Headquarters Eyes Move to Fraser Valley," *The Vancouver Sun*, Wednesday, December 26, 2001, Page B3.

Brickell, C., Trevor Cole, Judith D. Zuk. ed. 1997. *Reader's Digest A-Z Encyclopedia* of *Garden Plants.* Montreal, Que.: Reader's Digest Association (Canada) Ltd.

Brough, S.G. 1990. *Wild Trees of British Columbia.* Vancouver, B.C.: Pacific Educational Press.

Canada's Arboreal Emblems: An Overview of Canada's Official Trees and Their Wood. 2000. Canadian Region of the International Wood Collector's Society.

Cherrington, J.A. 1992. *The Fraser Valley: A History.* Madeira Park, B.C.: Harbour Publishing.

Chaster, G.H., D.W Ross & W.H. Warren (J. W. Neill, ed.). 1988. *Trees of Greater Victoria: A Heritage.* Victoria, B.C.: Heritage Tree Book Society.

Denman, R.W. R. 1992. *50 Years of Military Presence in the*

Fraser Valley Camp Chilliwack 1942–1992. Chilliwack, B.C.: Chilliwack Museum and Historical Society.

Dirr, M.A. 1998. *Manual of Woody Landscape Plants*. 5th ed. Champaign, Il: Stipes Publishing Co.

Dirr, M.A. 1997. *Dirr's Hardy Trees and Shrubs*. Portland, Or: Timber Press.

Eberts, T. 1995. "Surrey's 'Stanley Park' on the Fraser River." *Western Canada Wilderness Committee Educational Report* Vol. 14-No. 1 Spring.

Farrar, J.L. 1995. *Trees in Canada*. Markham, On: Fitzhenry & Whiteside Ltd, and the Canadian Forest Service, Natural Resources Canada, Ottawa in cooperation with the Canada Communication Group–Publishing Supply and Services Canada.

F.G. Architectural & Planning Consultants. 1995. *Langley's Heritage: A Listing of Heritage Resources in Langley*. Langley, B.C.: Corporation of the Township of Langley.

Feinberg J. "A Measure of Concern." *The Chilliwack Progress*. Tuesday, November 27, 2001, p. 3 and 10.

Flather, A. ed. *Surrey's Heritage: A Selection of Surrey's Historically Significant Buildings*. Surrey, B.C.: Corporation of the District of Surrey.

Gerhold, H.D., W.N. Wandell & N.L. La Casse. *Street Tree Fact Sheets*. 1993. University Park, PA: Pennsylvania State University.

Green Timbers Heritage Society. 1996. *Community Heritage Information Newsletter*. Heritage Services, Surrey Parks and Recreation Department. Summer.

Green Timbers Heritage Society. 1996. *Community Heritage Information Newsletter*. Heritage Services, Surrey Parks and Recreation Department. Autumn.

Hastings, M.L. 1981. *Along the Way*. 2nd Edition. Cloverdale, B.C.: D.W. Friesen & Sons Ltd.

Hildahl, H.& M. Benum. 1987. *Heritage Trees of Manitoba*. Winnipeg, Man: Manitoba Forestry Association Inc.

Hosie, R.C. *Native Trees of Canada.* 1990. 8th ed. Markham, On: Fitzhenry and Whiteside Ltd.

Huxley, A. Editor in Chief. 1992. *The New Royal Horticultural Society Dictionary of Gardening,* 4 vol. London: Macmillan Press Ltd.

Huxtable, B. 1995. "Take a guided walk through Sunnyside Acres." *Peace Arch News,* Visitor's Guide.

Jacobson, A.L. *Trees of Seattle. The Complete Tree Finder's Guide to the City's 740 Varieties.* 1989. Seattle, Wa: Sasquatch Books.

Jacobson, A.L. 1996. *North American Landscape Trees.* Berkeley, Ca: Ten Speed Press.

Janzen, A.J. "History of Schools: Dunach Elementary." *MSA News,* Feb 4, 1976.

Jones, Natasha. "103- year-old Home Will Be Preserved." *Langley Times,* Friday, May 4, 2001. pp. 1, 3

Kidd, T. 1927. *History of Lulu Island, and Occasional Poems.* Wrigley Printing Company, Reprinted in 1973 by Richmond Printers Ltd.

Krussmann G. 1983. *Manual of Cultivated Conifers.* Portland, Or: Timber Press.

Lauriault, J. 1992. *Identification Guide to the Trees of Canada.* Richmond Hill, On: Fitzhenry and Whiteside.

Lehmann, W. 2000. "Leader Profile: The Green Timbers Heritage Society." *The Leader B.C.'s Silviculture Digest,* March, Page 10.

Lehmann, W. 2001. *Urban Park Partnership. Surrey's Stories.* Heritage Services, Surrey Parks & Recreation and Culture Department. Summer-Fall, Page 4.

Montgomery, C. 2001. "The Man Who Shrinks Trees." *The Vancouver Sun,* Saturday, October 20, 2001. pp D 5-6.

Murray S. M. 1986. *The Nursery Industry in British Columbia.* Burnaby, B.C.: British Columbia Institute of Technology.

Orchard, I. 1983. *Growing Up in the Valley: Pioneer Childhood in the Lower Fraser Valley.* Sound Heritage Series # 40. Victoria, B.C. Provincial Archives of B.C.

Pepin, M.L. 1998. *Roads and Other Place Names in Langley, B.C.* Fort Langley, B.C.: Langley Centennial Museum and National Exhibition Centre.

Phillips, R. 1989. *Trees of North America and Europe.* London, England: Pan Books.

Portwood, J. 1996. "The Twins Who Grew Giants: David and Peter Brown were strange recluses who shut out their disapproving neighbours by inhabiting a forest of their own design." *Canadian Geographic.* V. 116 (3) May/June. pp. 80-84.

Portwood, J. 1987. "Tree Twins; plunged into a soundless void they created a forest." *Beautiful British Columbia.* V. 28(4) Spring, pp. 32-35.

Pojar, J. & A. MacKinnon, ed. 1994. *Plants of Coastal British Columbia including Washington, Oregon and Alaska.* Vancouver, B.C.: Lone Pine Pub.

Poor, J.M., ed. 1984. *Plants That Merit Attention.* Vol. 1 Trees. Portland, Or: Timber Press.

Province of British Columbia. 1995. "Heritage Conservation: A Community Guide for Local Government." 1995. Victoria, B.C.: Province of B.C.

Pynn, L. 2001. "Chilliwack's Secret Forest Goes Public in Bid to Save It." *The Vancouver Sun,* Monday December 24, 2001, p. B11.

Read, N. 2002. " Restoring a 'Knackered' Sherwood Forest." *The Vancouver Sun.* Saturday, January 26, 2002, p. A9.

Riggins, L.R. and L. Walker. 1991. *The Heart of the Fraser Valley. Memories of an Era Past.* Abbotsford, B.C.: Matsqui/Abbotsford Community Services and Matsqui Centennial Society.

Ross. L.J. 1979. *Richmond Child of the Fraser.* Richmond, B.C.: Richmond '79 Centennial Society.

Sommer, Warren. 1999. *From Prairie to City: A History of the City of Langley. Langley, B.C.* City of Langley.

Stoltmann, R. 1991. *Hiking Guide to the Big Trees of Southwestern British Columbia.* 2nd ed. Vancouver, B.C.: Western Canada Wilderness Committee.

Straley, G.B. 1992. *Trees of Vancouver.* Vancouver, B.C.: U.B.C. Press.

Surrey Leader. "White Rock Coronation Plans are Taking Shape." March 17, 1937.

Surrey Leader. "White Rock Programme for Coronation Day." May 12, 1937.

Surrey Leader. "Photograph King George VI and Queen Elizabeth." March 17, 1937.

Surrey Leader. "Oak Tree Ceremony at Surrey Centre." May 19, 1937.

Surrey Leader. "Coronation Brevities." May 26, 1937.

Surrey Leader. "Pattullo Bridge was opened on Monday." December 17, 1939.

Szychter, G. 1995. "Ladner's Windsor Oak," *B.C. Historical News*, p. 5.

Szychter, G. 1996. *Ladner's Landing of Yesteryear: Two Historic Walks in the Historic Village.* Delta. B.C.: Gwen Szychter.

Szychter, G. 1997. *Beyond Ladner's Landing: Two Heritage Walks South of the Original Village.* Delta. B.C.: Gwen Szychter.

Szychter, G. 1998. *Across the Bridge from Ladner's Landing: Delta Manor and Its Chickens.* Delta. B.C.: Gwen Szychter.

Szychter, G. 1999. *Port Guichon: Forgotten Neighbour of Ladner's Landing.* Delta. B.C.: Gwen Szychter.

Tamminga, M. 2002. "Uprooting History." *The Langley Times,* Sunday January 6, 2002, page 11.

Taylor, G. 1958. *Delta's Century of Progress.* Cloverdale, B.C.: Kerfoot-Holmes Printing Ltd.

Treleaven, G.F. 1978. *The Surrey Story*. Surrey, B.C.: Surrey Museum and Historical Society.

Vancouver Province. March 15, 1930. "First Forest Plantation in Province Established Along Highway MLA as Gardeners."

Van Pelt, Robert. 2001. *Forest Giants of the Pacific Coast*. Vancouver, B.C.: Global Forest Society.

Vertrees, J.D. 1978. *Japanese Maples*. Forest Grove, Or.: Timber Press.

Waite, D.E. 1977. *The Langley Story Illustrated*. Maple Ridge, B.C.: Don Waite Publishing.

Western Canada Wilderness Committee. *2002 Save Western Canada's Endangered Wilderness Calendar*. Vancouver, B.C.: Western Canada Wilderness Committee.

Whiteside, R.V. 1974. *The Surrey Pioneers*. Vancouver, B.C.: Evergreen Press.

Whitner, J.K. 1993. *Garden Touring in the Pacific Northwest*. Seattle, Wa: Alaska Northwest Books.

Whysell, S. "The Healing Garden," *The Vancouver Sun*, Friday May, 10, 2002, pp.E1 and 2.

Yesaki, M. and H. Steves, & K. Steves.1998. *Steveston Cannery Row: An Illustrated History*. Richmond, B.C.: Lulu Island Printing Ltd.

Yiesla, S. and F. A. Giles. 1992. *Shade Trees for the Central and Northern States and Canada*. Champaign, Ill: Stipes Publishing Company.

Zytaruk, T. 2000. *Millennium Milestones*. Richmond, B.C.: Thunderbird Press.

Brochures

Arboretum Area Field Plan. Undated. Agassiz Research Station. Agriculture Canada.

Burns Bog. Undated. Burns Bog Conservation Society

Darts Hill Garden Park. 2001. Surrey Parks, Recreation and Culture

Downtown Chilliwack Heritage Walking Tour. Undated. Chilliwack Museum and Archives.

Green Timbers Park: Explore the Salal Trail. 1992. Green Timbers Heritage Society. Surrey, B.C.

Museum Circle Tour of the Upper Fraser Valley. Undated. Mission Museum and Mission Historical Society.

Nature Trails of Surrey. Undated. Surrey Parks and Recreation.

Robert Point Rest Area Surrey Bend Regional Park. Undated. Greater Vancouver Regional District, Parks Department.

Welcome to Sunnyside Acres Urban Forest Park. Undated. Sunnyside Acres Heritage Society and Surrey Parks and Recreation Commission.

Unpublished Sources

Cannor Nurseries Ltd. Fall 1999–Spring 2000. Nursery Catalogue. Chilliwack, B.C.

Denman R. 2001. "New Ryder Lake Farmers & Women's Institute Hall Opened August 1963." Chilliwack Museum and Archives. November 20.

Denman R. undated. "The Chilliwack Fairgrounds." Chilliwack Museum and Archives.

Ibid. undated. "CFB Chilliwack Lands." Chilliwack Museum and Archives.

Ibid. undated. "Chilliwack Museum City Hall." Chilliwack Museum and Archives.

Ibid. undated. "Coqualeetza." Chilliwack Museum and Archives.

Ibid. undated. "Gwynne-Vaughan Park." Chilliwack Museum and Archives.

Ibid. undated. "Kinkora." Chilliwack Museum and Archives.

Ibid. undated. "Paisley House." Chilliwack Museum and Archives.

Ibid. undated. "Querencia." Chilliwack Museum and Archives.

Ibid. undated. "Ryder Lake." Chilliwack Museum and Archives.

Ibid. undated. "The Chilliwack Fairgrounds." Chilliwack Museum and Archives.

Ibid. undated. "St. Thomas Anglican Church." Chilliwack Museum and Archives.

Ibid. undated. "Spadina Avenue Short Version." Chilliwack Museum and Archives.

Ibid. undated. "Spadina Avenue." Chilliwack Museum and Archives.

Ibid. undated. "Webb House." Chilliwack Museum and Archives.

DMG Landscape Architects. November 1999. City of Langley Street Tree Program. Guide to the use and care of Street Trees in the City of Langley. Report submitted to the City of Langley.

Gorsuch, C. 1990. A History of Williams Park. September.

Enos, L. and Herman Schutze. 1988. Resumes of Planters. The Green Timbers Inaugural Plantation.

Green Timbers 1930 Inaugural Plantation. 2000. Description of Trees. April 28.

Legacy Heritage Consultants. 2000. Langley: First World Memorial Trees. Report submitted to the Corporation of the Township of Langley.

Lyster, T. 1995. "Royal Oaks, King George Highway, Surrey, B.C., Canada." Letter to Saville Gardens, The Great Park, Windsor, England, October 18.

Lyster, T. undated. "Royal Oaks," Addendum to a Press release.

Maarsman, P. and Wady Lehmann. January 2, 2001. Proposal for the B.C. Forest Nursery Land Presently Owned by the Provincial Government.

McKinnon, S. 1995. "Oak Trees along King George Highway." Letter to the Advisory Heritage Commission, City of Surrey, October 19.

Murray, S. M. 1996. "Development of a Heritage Tree Evaluation Form." Report submitted to the Corporation of the City of Surrey.

Murray, S.M. 1998. "Heritage Tree Identification and Commemoration Project Summary Report." Report submitted to the Community Heritage Development Program British Columbia Trust.

Murray, S.M. 2001. Plant Collections: Inventory. Kwantlen University College, Langley Campus

Murray, S.M. and R.M. Strang. 1999. Identification and Marking of Exotic Trees in Redwood Park. August.

Parks and Recreation Department, City of Chilliwack. Tree Planting Inventories 1996–2000.

Parks, Recreation and Culture, City of Surrey, Darts Hill Garden Park, Collection Inventory.

Parks, Recreation and Culture. City of Surrey. 1998. Mound Farm Park Tree Assessment, 5202- 168 Street, Surrey. Drawing No1, pp1-4, August 24.

Parks, Recreation and Culture, City of Surrey, Selected Tree Planting Inventory Entries.

Schmidt, J. Frank & Son Co. undated. Wholesale Tree Catalogue. Boring: Or.

Surrey Archives Research. Undated. The History of Green Timbers.

Surrey Archives Research. Undated. Redwood Park- Unique to Canada.

Maps and Drawings

British Columbia Forest Service. 1999. Inaugural Plantation Green Timbers Forestry Station, Pacific Highway, Surrey, B.C. March 15, 1930.

British Columbia Ministry of Forests, Victoria B.C. 1999. Green Timbers Reforestation Centre Area.

British Columbia Ministry of Forests, Silviculture Branch, Victoria B.C. 1999. Green Timbers Arboretum. 1:100 scale.

City of Abbotsford, Parks and Recreation, Trails of Abbotsford.

City of Chilliwack, Recreation Guide and Map.

The Langleys, Detail Maps of the City of Langley and the Township of Langley.

City of Surrey, 2002, Updated Site Plan, Darts Hill Garden Park, originally drawn by Marshall Surveys Ltd., October 17, 1996.

City of Surrey, Surrey Pathway + Bikeway Map.

Corporation of the Township of Langley. 1991. Williams Park.

On-Line Sources

B.C. Conservation Data Centre, Ministry of Sustainable Resources Management. British Columbia Register of Big Trees.

Burns Bog Conservation Society.

City of Abbotsford.

City of Chilliwack.

City of Langley. http://www.langley.b.c.ca

City of Richmond. Heritage Inventory. http://www.city.richmond.b.c.ca/planning/heritage/heritageinventory

City of Richmond. London Heritage Farm.

City of Richmond. Millennium Botanical Garden & Arboretum. http://www.city.richmond.b.c.ca/parks/botanical/community_park.html

City of Surrey.

Corporation of Delta.

Greater Vancouver Regional District.

MSA Museum Society Trethewey House Heritage Site.

Oldlist, http://www.rmtrr.org/oldlist.htm

Township of Langley.

Western Canada Wilderness Committee.

http://www.nyu.edu/edu/projects/julian/Oscar.html

Personal Communication

Bruce Broughton, John Dinicola, Reg Easingwood, Louise Hart, Douglas Justice, Randy Greenizian, Roy Hayes, Edna Horstead, Sandy Mathies, John Massot, Fred and Maureen Pepin, Norman Sherritt, Peter Thompson, John C. Traas, John Trass, Warren Sommer, Roy Strang, Gwen Szychter, Donald Williams, Paul Williams, Marv Woolley, Ellen Worrell

Index

A number in italics indicates a page where there is a photograph of the tree.
A number in bold indicates a page where the tree is given a full entry.
Roman type indicates a text reference.

Curly Willow *see Salix babylonica* var. *pekinensis* 'Tortuosa'
Syn. *Salix contorta* or *S alix matsudana* 'Tortuosa'
Currie, General Sir Arthur, 72
Cutleaf Beech *see Fagus sylvatica* var. *heterophylla* f. *laciniata*
Cutleaf (Full Moon) Maple *see Acer japonicum* 'Aconitifolium'
Cutleaf Staghorn Sumac *see Rhus typhina* 'Dissecta'
Cutleaf Weeping Birch *see Betula pendula* 'Laciniata'
Cypress Family *see Calocedrus, Chamæcyparis, Cryptomeria, Cunninghamia, Cupressus, Juniperus, Metasequoia, Sequoia, Sequoiadendron, Taxodium, Thuja, Thujopsis*
Cyprian Cedar *see Cedrus brevifolia*
Cyprus Cedar *see Cedrus brevifolia*

D
Darts, Edwin & Francisca, 21-22
Darts Hill Garden Park, 21-23
Davidia involucrata, 18, 29, 30, *139*, **139-140**
Dawn Redwood *see Metasequoia glyptostroboides*
Dawson Magnolia *see Magnolia dawsoniana*
Dawyck Beech *see Fagus sylvatica* 'Dawyck'
Daybreak Cherry *see Prunus* x *yedoensis* 'Akebono'
Syn. *Prunus* x *yedoensis* 'Daybreak'
De Wolf, Jim & Elfriede, 30

Deborah Maple *see Acer platanoides* 'Deborah'
Delta
    Augustinian Monastery of B.C., 9-10
    Avondale, 357
    Delta Nature Reserve, 10-11
    Jubilee Farm, 9-10
    Memorial Park, 352
    Memorial Park and Arthur Drive, 11
Delta Nature Reserve, 10-11
Dennison, Zoe, 310
Deodar Cedar *see Cedrus deodara*
dioecious, 80
Diospyros virginiana, *140*, **140**
Dogwood Cherry *see Cornus mas*
Dogwood Family *see Cornus*
Domestic Pear *see Pyrus communis*
Douglas Fir *see Pseudotsuga menziesii*
Douglas Maple *see Acer glabrum*
Dove Tree *see Davidia involucrata*
Dove Tree Family *see Davidia*
Downy Japanese Maple *see Acer japonicum*
Draney House, 315
Duchess Apple Tree *see Malus* 'Duchess'
Dunach Elementary School, 2
Dunach Park, 2
Durmast Oak *see Quercus petræa*
Dutch Elm disease, 358
Dwarf Blue Scots Pine *see Pinus sylvestris* 'Glauca Nana'
Dwarf Hinoki Cypress *see Chamæcyparis obtusa* 'Gracilis'

E
Eastern Catalpa *see Catalpa bignonioides*
Eastern Flowering Dogwood *see Cornus florida*
Eastern Hemlock *see Tsuga canadensis*
Eastern Larch *see Larix laricina*
Eastern Redbud *see Cercis canadensis*
Eastern White Pine *see Pinus strobus*
Ebony Family *see Diospyros*
Eddie, Henry M., 122
Eddie's White Wonder Dogwood *see Cornus* 'Eddie's White Wonder'
Elæagnus angustifolia, *141*, **141**
Elæagnus Family *see Elæagnus*
Elizabeth Magnolia *see Magnolia* 'Elizabeth'
Elk Creek Rainforest, 335-336
Elm Family *see Ulmus, Zelkova*
Embothrium coccineum, *142*, **142**
Emerald Cedar *see Thuja occidentalis* 'Smaragd'
Emerald Queen Maple *see Acer platanoides* 'Emerald Queen'
Empress Tree *see Paulownia tomentosa*
Englemann Blue Spruce *see Picea englemannii*
Englemann Spruce *see Picea englemannii*
English Ash *see Fraxinus excelsior*
English Hawthorn *see Cratægus lævigata* Syn. *Cratægus oxyacantha; Cratægus monogyna*
English Holly *see*